For Dianne
with admiration and thanks
for your own many fine
Contributions to International
Education

Gordan and Jean

Gaskerkide 2006

King's College Budo
A Centenary History
1906-2006

Gordon P. McGregor
Emeritus Professor of Education, University of Leeds
Hon. Visiting Professor, Oxford Brookes University

FOUNTAIN PUBLISHERS
Kampala

Fountain Publishers Ltd
P. O. Box 488 Kampala
E-mail:fountain@starcom.co.ug
Website:www.fountainpublishers.co.ug

Distributed in Europe, North America and Australia by African Books
Collective Ltd. (ABC), Unit 13, Kings Meadow Oxford OX2 0DP,
United Kingdom. Tel: 44-(0) 1865-726686, Fax:44-(0)1865-793298
E-mail: orders@africanbookscollective.com
Website: www.africanbookscollective.com

ISBN (10) 9970-02-544-9
ISBN (13) 978-9970-02-544-2

Dedication

For the students, staff and governors of Budo
past, present and future
with admiration, thanks – and high expectations.

All royalties from the sale of this book
will go to the
BUDO CENTENARY FUND
to assist girls and boys who have won places at Budo
but whose families are not able to pay the full fees.

Contents

Preface and Acknowledgements		*vii*
Foreword		*xi*
Historical Background		*xv*
1.	Spadework and Foundation: 1898-1906	1
2.	Building up and Spreading out: 1906-1912	16
3.	War, Problems and Possibilities: 1912-1926	30
4.	Vision and Disappointments: 1925-1934	52
5.	Consolidating: 1935-1939	87
6.	Crisis and Convalescence: 1939-1947	99
7.	Towards Maturity: 1948-1957	123
8.	Through Independence Towards the Gathering Storm: 1958-1970	149
9.	School Democracy under National Tyranny: 1971-1975	196
10.	Keeping the Budo Train on the Rails: 1975-1979	241
11.	False Dawns — Then Uphill all the Way: 1979-1989	275
12.	Peaceful Expansion: The Challenges of Success: 1989-1999	322
13.	Twenty-First Century: Progressive Conservatism? 2000-2005	364
14.	Afterword	380
Bibliography		388
Order of Merit		391
Index		395

Preface and
Acknowledgements

I did not at first want to write this Centenary History but am glad to have done so. In the final paragraph of my 1965 University of East Africa thesis - published by Oxford University Press in 1967 as *King's College Budo: The First Sixty Years* — I wrote:

> In the end it must be Africans who decide what their countries want and need. It will, no doubt, be such an African who will chronicle the next sixty years of King's College Budo...

I had left Uganda in 1966 to help to launch the University of Zambia, Lusaka, and in 1970 returned to England, for family reasons. For the next twenty-five years, I was a fortunate but disgruntled principal successively of two Church of England teachers' colleges which both developed into large university colleges, in spite of niggardly "support" from the UK government, which never approached the enthusiasm and generosity I had known, as a young teacher and lecturer, from the governments of Uganda and Zambia. My wife, Jean, and I kept in touch with many former Budo colleagues and students - lasting friendship has been one of the school's greatest gifts to its members - but I was both flattered and disappointed to be pressed by many Old Budonians to "write us some more history", for the muted celebrations of the 80th anniversary and the more exuberant ones of the 90th. My response was to remind them of my 1965 valedictory paragraph and to urge that only those who had lived the later years ought to write about them.

I had long nourished the hope of returning to Budo and Makerere to try to pay back a little for the teaching and research opportunities they had given me as a young man. Retirement and continuing good health made that possible. After a stimulating visiting professorship at Fort Hare, South Africa, in 1997, I was invited back to Makerere in

1998 for the first of many happy returns. My main commitment was to student and in-service teachers of English but, after many welcoming courtesies, Budonians were soon at me. Indeed, before this first visit, at the AGM of the UK Old Budonians, Dr Tom Boto had asked me to find time for more Budo research. With characteristic Ugandan guile, he laughingly subverted my disclaimer: "But Tom, I've been away for thirty-two years" - to which he replied, "Exactly! And you can therefore bring an objectivity to the story which we could not. We have been too close."

My friend and former student, Professor Apolo Nsibambi - then Minister of Education and shortly to become Prime Minister - added the ultimate persuasion: "We all understand your reservation and you are right to want a Ugandan author. You know so much about Uganda and Budo and you served the school so diligently that you are uniquely qualified to write the Centenary History of Budo." Further resistance seemed ungracious. But I set one firm condition: Budonians, past and present, must give me the Ugandan voices to speak through. They assured me that they would and their promises have been most generously kept. So I have many obligations.

The first eight chapters of the present book closely follow those of *The First Sixty Years*, with some revisions and additions. I have not indulged in hindsight, but have corrected a few factual errors and added only important incidents of which I had found no record in 1965 but would certainly have included if I had known of them. A notable example was the Budo experience, in the 1920s, of Prince Badru Kakungulu, the leader of Uganda's Muslim community. So, to all the colleagues and friends who so generously helped an ignorant enthusiast with his first book I repeat my thanks:

> Dr Roy Bridges, Professor Edgar Castle, Barbara Collins, Dr Trevor Coombe, Rev Dick Drown, Canon Myers Grace, Michael Grace, Aloysius Kaddu, Professor Senteza Kajubi, Professor Eric Lucas, Eridadi Mulira, Eapen Oommen, David Ponting, Professor Merrick Posnansky, Ian Robinson (who first suggested, in 1962, that I should write about Budo), Ernest Sempebwa, Douglas Tomblings and Stephen Wright.

For generous help and hospitality during my five stays as Visiting Professor at Makerere since 1998 I am most grateful to Professor Senteza Kajubi, Dr Suleiman Kiggundu, Dr David and Rita Matovu, John Nagenda, Professor Apolo and the late Rhoda Nsibambi, Ernest Sempebwa, Professor Kate Parry and Professor Abdul Kasozi, George and Helen Semivule, the staffs of the Makerere University and Namirembe Guest Houses, and the Old Budonians UK Branch.

For the chapters covering the years 1966 to 2005 I am greatly indebted to four key "readers" who have saved me from many errors and false impressions, been consistently encouraging, meticulous in their critical analyses, and prompt in their written responses. All this made heavy demands on their time and my warm thanks and admiration go to Dr Robina Mirembe, Stephen Kamuhanda, Colin Davis and Ian Robinson. Colin also gave me generous access to one of two unexpected and invaluable sources. This was the detailed personal journal he maintained of his years at Budo, including extracts from many letters from students and colleagues. The second remarkable written source was the carefully preserved series of weekly letters written from 1972 to 1974 from Budo, by Alan and Eleanor Rayden to their parents in England, giving vivid impressions of Budo during the early years of the Amin terror.

For information and guidance offered in individual interviews, group discusssions and informal conversations I owe much to Dr Martin Aliker, Christine Bawuuba, Sam Busulwa, Patrick Bakka Male, Tim Godding, Professor Senteza Kajubi, Ernest Kalanzi, Stephen Makaya Kalanzi, Rhoda Kalema, Professor Abdul Kasozi, Dr Edward Kayondo, Dr Suleiman Kiggundu, Dan Kyanda, Chris Luswata, Dr David Matovu, Dr Ham Mukasa Mulira, John Nagenda, Marjorie Nsereko, Professor Apolo Nsibambi, Veronica Nyakana (Kiddu), George and Helen Semivule, Ernest Sempebwa, Alan Shonubi, Peter and Ida Songa, Ishmael Uyirwoth, Henry Wamala, Susannah Whitty (McCrae) and Bryan Wilson. My obligations to written sources are, I hope, fully recorded in the notes, references and bibliography, but I must record special thanks to Professor Abdul Kasozi for his friendly guidance and for his outstanding research study *The Social Origins of Violence in Uganda 1964-1985*.

All these friends - my "Ugandan voices" - have helped me to write in the spirit of that elegant historian GM Young, who believed that "The real, central theme of history is not what happened but what people felt about it when it was happening."

No chronicler could have had more willing and careful advisers. Remaining errors, shortcomings, or faulty judgements are entirely mine.

Gordon P. McGregor

September 2005

Foreword

Professor P. McGregor, who was my teacher at King's College Budo, was invited by Budonians to write a Centenary History of the school. He had already written a good book entitled *Budo: The First Sixty Years*. The Centenary book is a history based largely on the work of the twelve headmasters who have served the school diligently with their Staff and Board of Governors. The headmasters are: H.W. Weatherhead, his brother Thomas Candy Weatherhead, Canon Grace, Gaster, Lord Hemingford, Timothy Cobb, Ian Robinson, Daniel Kyanda, I. Uyirworth, F. Bawuba, Sam Busu and G. Semivule, the current headmaster. He summarised the contribution of each one of them to Budo succinctly.

One of the aims of the school was to train leaders by, *inter-alia*, creating an environment in which students would identify their talents and put them to use. No wonder King's College Budo has produced three heads of state, a vice-president, a Speaker of Parliament , a Chief Justice, four prime ministers, a Lady Deputy Chief Justice, kings (or traditional leaders); ministers, vice chancellors of universities, Hon. Members of Parliament, permanent secretaries; ambassadors, high commissioners, prominent businessmen, professors, physicians, surgeons, engineers, bishops, head-teachers and other leaders. Most of these leaders, as demonstrated by Professor McGregor, have invariably shaped the destiny of Uganda with distinction.

Professor McGregor has ably shown that although Budo was initially designed to admit sons and daughters of chiefs from the Kingdom of Buganda, it broadened its policy by admitting students based on merit from all areas of Uganda. It also admitted non-Ugandans such as Professor Rubadiri, a former Vice-Chancellor of the University of Malawi, and Charles Njonjo, a former Attorney General of Kenya. Dr Martin Aliker, an Acholi who attended King's College Budo, observed that Budo was the first institution to try to bring Ugandans together. Budo also admitted people of different religions. In so doing, the school enhanced national integration.

Professor McGregor has established that although co-education was initially resisted at Budo, it was later fully accepted. Budo has produced diligent and independent-minded women who are capable of holding their own in a world where men have dominated women. The women include Justice Leticia Kikonyogo, the Deputy Chief Justice; Julia Sebutinde, a Judge who has chaired Commissions of Inquiry in sensitive areas; the late Mrs Gladys Wambuzi, a leading educationist; Mrs Joy Male, an effective head-teacher of Gayaza High School; the late Hon. Betty Okwir, a former Deputy Speaker of Parliament; and Mrs Sarah Ntiro, an enterprising administrator who was the first Ugandan woman to study at Oxford University.

Budo was founded by the Church Missionary Society, which was broadbased in its membership. Although the school inculcated Christian values into the students by, for example, making regular attendance of chapel compulsory, it provided space for other religious groups. Muslims like Prince Kakungulu, Hon. Adoko Nekyon and the late Abu Mayanja were welcome to Budo. Indeed, Abu Mayanja, a prominent Muslim, came top in the Scripture Paper of the Cambridge School Certificate.

The challenges of King's College Budo include the following:

- First, Budo must continue performing in an excellent manner in the academic and other fields.

- Second, it must continue developing the whole person, i.e. the body, mind and spirit.

- Third, the school must continue the important role of nurturing leadership qualities among the students.

- Fourth, Budo must preserve our progressive cultural values and reject immoral values, some of which are foreign.

- Fifth, Budo must continue giving co-curricular activities such as football, swimming, athletics, music, rugby, drama, cricket and others the weight they deserve. I enjoyed and benefited from being a member of the Nightingales Club, playing the organ, the piano and being a goalkeeper at King's College Budo. These activities must be part and parcel of the education system of all schools in Uganda.

- Sixth, in order to accelerate innovation, invention and harnessing of Uganda's scarce resources, Budo and other schools must design strategies for giving more weight to science and technology.
- Lastly, the alumni of the school must continue making financial, academic and other contributions to the school.

Professor McGregor has raised pertinent and critical issues which are relevant to other schools. They include the following:

- First, the problem of financing quality boarding schools. On one hand, many parents cannot afford to pay for expensive boarding schools. On the other hand, maintaining quality boarding schools is expensive. This problem must be addressed.
- Second, what should be a proper relationship between a Board of Governors and a head-teacher?
- Third, what should be a healthy relationship between a head-teacher, staff and students?
- Fourth, how should students' strikes and arson be avoided?
- Fifth, how should students relate to their neighbouring environment? I have greatly appreciated noting that Grace, a headmaster of Budo, encouraged Budo boys to go out of school to build, repair, whitewash, dig and teach reading and writing in schools which Grace said were dying for someone to take an interest in them.
- Sixth, some founding bodies, such as the Catholic Church, the Church of Uganda and the Muslim Education Association, wish to play a dominant role in the selection of head-teachers as opposed to Government wishes. This matter must be resolved between Government and the founding bodies.
- Seventh, the size of the students' population has become so large in most secondary schools that the schools have lost a sense of

commitment and friendliness. Furthermore, the staff: student ratio is so high that students hardly get personal attention from the staff. Consequently, identifying students with bad behaviour is difficult. Some of the students may resort to arson and other malpractices. It is essential for schools to identify the optimum levels of intake.

I am delighted to have been one of the people who persuaded McGregor to write Budo's Centenary History. This book is an analytical, detailed and refreshing memoir which contains a lot of useful references and has raised issues which are useful to Budo and other schools. I strongly commend it.

Professor Apolo R. Nsibambi

THE RT. HON. PRIME MINISTER OF UGANDA

February 2006

Historical Background

This is the story of a school in Uganda, a country in East Africa, 236,000 square kilometres in area - a little larger than the United Kingdom. Bounded by the Sudan, Kenya, Tanzania, Rwanda and Democratic Republic of Congo, it lies astride the Equator, at heights of 900 to 5100 metres, 800 kilometres west of the Indian Ocean and largely within the basin of the Upper Nile. In 2006 it has about 27 million inhabitants, mainly of the Bantu, Hamitic and Nilotic peoples. A hundred years ago, when Budo was founded, the total population was probably about two million.

In 1862 Speke and Grant brought the region its first known contact with Europe when they reached the capital of Buganda, the largest and most influential kingdom of what was to become Uganda, and were welcomed by the Kabaka (King) Mutesa I. In 1875 Stanley visited Buganda and, in a letter to the *Daily Telegraph*, made his famous appeal for missionaries to come to Mutesa's court. The first Protestant missionaries, sent by the Anglican Church Missionary Society (CMS), arrived in 1877 and were followed within a week by Roman Catholic White Fathers. Mutesa became confused and unsure of what decision to take. When he died in 1884, his son, Mwanga, became hostile and killed many of the Baganda Christians and their first appointed bishop, James Hannington, who had not quite reached Buganda.

In 1888 Mwanga was deposed and there followed two years of sporadic fighting between Christians and Muslims. Meanwhile, British influence in East Africa had been assigned, by Royal Charter, to the Imperial British East Africa company and in 1890 Lugard led a Company expedition to Buganda, which he found impoverished and divided. He made a treaty of protection with Mwanga, who had been restored to the Kabakaship, but the Company's activities in the country were proving too costly and it announced that it must withdraw. The news raised a public outcry in England and, following Portal's 1893 expedition to assess the potential of the region, Uganda was declared a British Protectorate in 1894.

There were more disturbances in 1897, when Mwanga was again deposed in favour of a regency under his infant son Daudi Chwa, and a mutiny of Sudanese troops threatened the whole Protectorate. The administration was reorganised by Sir Harry Johnston, who was appointed special commissioner in 1899 and negotiated the Buganda Agreement of 1900, the basis of the security and development which followed.

This was the political background to the first twenty years of missionary work in Uganda. The missionaries did not at first attempt to provide formal education but they taught their converts to read the gospels before baptising them. The Anglican Bishop Tucker reckoned that by 1898 there might have been as many as 100,000 CMS "readers", as the missionaries began to organise a system of schools throughout the country. Within seven years came the foundation of King's College Budo.

Spadework and Foundation
1898-1906

> Our aim is not only to bridge the gap between primary and
> university education, but by the discipline of work and games in
> a boarding school so to build up character as to enable the Baganda
> to take their proper place in the administrative, commercial and
> industrial life of their own country (A.R. Tucker, *Eighteen Years
> in Uganda and East Africa*, 1908).

> Nothing like the Budo influence is to be found elsewhere in modern
> Africa (Elspeth Huxley, Forks and Hope, 1964).

Between these two observations on King's College, Budo, lie more than
fifty years of turbulent change and idealistic hard work. Bishop Tucker
was one of the leading enthusiasts for the idea of a boarding secondary
school for Ugandan boys and as soon as he found the right man to start
it he gave him strong support. But he realised that a lot of educational
spadework had to be done before the missionaries could realistically
think in terms of a "Budo".

From 1877, all the early Western-style education, in what was to
become Uganda, was missionary. The pioneer surgeon Sir Albert Cook
wrote of the first permanent schools:

> It must be remembered that all these educational efforts were
> being made nearly twenty years before the government took up
> the question of education.[1]

The missionaries knew they could have done much more with more
money, but Tucker described how real progress was made from the
start, almost inadvertently. The young Anglican Church in Uganda
insisted that no one, unless blind or infirm, could be baptised without
having learned to read.

> Education was not our first object in making this rule. It was made rather as a test of sincerity. Large numbers were coming forward and asking for baptism. Of their lives we knew nothing. They said, "We believe and wish to be baptised." "Very well," was our answer. "We don't know you; we must test you. We must see that you have an intelligent knowledge of the way of salvation. Here are the gospels. We will teach you to read them and when you have read them we shall expect you to give an intelligent answer to the questions we shall ask you." ... And so it came to pass that many thousands acquired the art of reading. Many of these taught their fellows and so the thing spread.[2]

Tucker had come to Africa in 1890, with the title Bishop of Equatorial Africa. When he became Bishop of Uganda in 1897 he began organising formal education. He invited a CMS missionary, C.W. Hattersley, to set up a system of primary schools and to train teachers for them. Hattersley's later work at Mengo was of most importance to the foundation of Budo, but any account which tries to set the school in the context of national educational development must take note of his work all over Uganda. It is easy, a hundred years later, to see its weaknesses; one of his outstanding missionary successors, J.V. Taylor summarised them:

> He was in some ways a strange choice, though it is certainly no discredit to him that his own education had never proceeded beyond that of an elementary board school in England and training as a Pupil Teacher. With immense energy he at once set about providing for Ugandan children in their thousands the same kind of education he had received himself, and if that was educationally hide-bound Hattersley himself was not to blame. The curriculum was entirely academic and there was no attempt to relate school to life by any inclusion of agricultural, industrial or health training.[3]

When Hattersley himself had been a schoolboy, the British parliament had only recently passed its famous 1870 Education Act and begun to take seriously the possibility of universal primary education in Britain, so he could hardly be expected to produce imaginative plans for Uganda. The founders of Budo recognised that he had often been wide of the mark and they tried to make their curriculum more relevant. But it was to his work, whatever its shortcomings, that they owed their opportunity. It was the "immense energy" that mattered most.

Working outwards from Mengo, the capital of Buganda, where the CMS had its headquarters on Namirembe Hill close to the Kabaka's palace, Hattersley urged parents, especially chiefs, to send their sons and daughters to the new schools. He organised the training of teachers as fast as he could and Tucker recorded that whereas in 1898 there had been only a few hundred children being taught, by 1903 the school registers showed 22,000 pupils.[4] He started a day school in the bush, wherever he found a group of parents willing to send their children. He then tried to build up groups of such bush schools around centres of population, in which he set up larger central schools, also for day pupils. The system was completed, as he had planned, by the opening of large high schools, of which his own at Mengo was the first. The titles were deceptive; all three types of school were what in Britain were called "Elementary". The central schools followed a curriculum similar to that of the bush schools, but soon began to supply teachers for them. The high schools eventually produced teachers for both bush and central schools.

Hattersley borrowed some of the features of Dr Andrew Bell's "monitorial system" - which had been adopted in Britain in the 1820s by the National Society of the Church of England - and of the pupil teacher system which developed from it. He also followed the National Society principle of requiring a contribution from the local community to supplement the church grant. But his method of launching a school was even more specific and austere. He began with a teacher. Boys could then come along to be taught but only if they were clean and neat. If they wanted to be taken seriously they had to bring their own pens, ink and paper. At first there were no desks; these were made as soon as there was an established class and money to pay for them. Hattersley recorded that in one school a boy was refused a desk because he had brought no pen or paper. He went off and earned some money by carrying baggage up-country for a European traveller and returned in triumph, suitably equipped, to claim his desk.

At first Hattersley himself ran the largest of the central schools, at Mengo. It opened in 1898 and only two years later, by which time he had opened schools all over the country, it had 240 students and was becoming well known.[5] By 1902 it had over 500 pupils, from Buganda, Busoga, Bunyoro, Toro and Ankole. The Katikkiro (prime minister) of Buganda, Apolo Kagwa, who was to do great things for education in Uganda, did perhaps the most important thing when he sent his son to Hattersley's school.

So there was no doubt that at Mengo parents were keen. Hattersley had no doubt, either, that their sons were intelligent. He set them problems such as:

> If 40 canoes go to Usukume to fetch loads, each canoe carrying 12 bales, the rate of pay for which is 5 rupees and 200 cowrie shells each; the Katikkiro takes $1/_5$ of this, the chief of the canoe $1/_7$, another under-chief $1/_{12}$ and the headman $1/_{20}$; each canoe has 12 paddlers. How much does each paddler get when the balance is divided?[6]

– which makes Taylor's "no attempt to relate school to life" seem rather severe.

While Hattersley was on leave in 1902 the Mengo school was run by A.G. Fraser, later headmaster of Trinity College, Kandy in Ceylon (now Sri Lanka) and then first principal of Achimota College in the Gold Coast (now Ghana). They reckoned that by 1903 about 3000 boys had learned to read and write fairly well at Mengo. But Hattersley could already see a serious weakness in the system. He wrote ruefully that no boy had yet become really well educated because as soon as any of them made good progress they were sent up-country to open new schools.[7] By the end of 1904 there were 21 central schools all over the country, each with a "Mengo-trained" teacher. With the number of regional schools increasing, numbers at Mengo had declined to 320.

Meanwhile, the Roman Catholic missions had also been hard at work. The 1903 report of the commissioners for Uganda summarised the growth of education in terms of numbers of schools and teachers.[8] The White Fathers had established 38 "native schools" and had 797 teachers; the Mill Hill Fathers had 12 "established schools" but teacher numbers were not recorded. The Anglican CMS was credited with 16 "permanent schools" (Hattersley's central schools) and 1930 teachers. The Commissioners seem to have discovered more about the apparent quantity of school education than the quality and levels of it, but it was clear that the Catholic missions, too, had made good progress.

In March 1902 the Mill Hill Fathers founded Namilyango College, about twelve miles from Kampala, to provide a higher level of education than their ordinary schools. The main aim, as with the CMS schools, was still to train boys to teach and to preach Christianity, but the Namilyango school log-book noted:

> Boys on whose education time and money have been spent but who are incapable of becoming catechists, will either be sent away or, if their characters are good, will receive additional education to fit them for government clerkships.[9]

This is the first recorded statement of a secular aim for education in Uganda and in 1906 the Catechist School was actually separated from the college at Namilyango. In 1902 two CMS missionaries, Madox and Phillips, had visited the college[10] and would certainly have reported back to Hattersley and Fraser who were consdering the next stage of CMS provision. They were convinced that at least one good boarding school was needed to solve the most urgent problem. Tucker summarised emphatically:

> So far little or nothing had been done for the children of the upper classes, who in many respects were worse off than the children of the peasants. They were rarely brought up by their parents. They were in consequence neglected, out of hand and allowed to run almost wild. We felt strongly that if the ruling classes in the country were to exercise in the days to come, an influence for good upon their people and have a sense of responsibility towards them, it was absolutely essential that something should be done and that speedily, for the education of these neglected children on the soundest possible lines.[11]

He encouraged Hattersley to go ahead with his plan for a boarding school at Mengo for the sons of chiefs. Mengo High School was officially opened by the Acting Commisioner, George Wilson, on 25 January

1905. He said he hoped that the education given in this new school would be of a practical kind and not merely such as to make people dissatisfied with their surroundings. It had been difficult in the past to get agreement among chiefs of different nations, but he thought that the united instruction of these young lads could do much to solve the problem in the future. Hattersley, as headmaster, said that he had been sure for some time that the only answer to the way the leading natives neglected their sons was to remove the boys from their old surroundings. He knew he might be accused of introducing caste into the country, but he had no intention of making any distinction between chiefs and peasants. It was simply that the sons of chiefs had been the most difficult to keep in regular attendance at the ordinary day schools. His object in having the sons of the chiefs in the school was that they seemed most likely to influence the future of the country. The report of the ceremony in CMS *Uganda Notes* recorded a striking feature.[12] This was the attendance of Prince Mbogo, brother of the late Kabaka Mutesa I, leader of Uganda's Muslims. He publicly thanked God for the united effort which had created the school and the spread of education throughout the country.

Mengo High School began with forty boys, all chiefs or sons of chiefs, divided into four Houses, each with its own dormitory. Sir Albert Cook recorded that the money for the first was given by friends of the CMS in England; for the second by the Katikkiro and two great chiefs; for the third by the British "authorities" and for the fourth by sixteen lesser chiefs. So the school had been half-built by the chiefs themselves and was to be entirely maintained by them.[13]

The High School was more popular than had been expected and with 100 pupils by 1906 had already outgrown its new buildings. The CMS had also established Uganda's first school for girls, at Gayaza, twelve miles from Kampala. Some informal teaching had been given there for six years but after opening in 1905 with four pupils, Miss Allen who was the only European teacher until 1909, had recruited 43 by July. The school buildings were formally opened by Bishop Tucker in March 1906.

The first aim of Gayaza was to train Christian wives and mothers and to bridge the intellectual gap between husbands and wives. The curriculum included cultivation, handwork, child-care and needlework as well as scripture, reading and writing, arithmetic and geography.[14]

Gayaza flourished as a primary school for more than thirty years, moving to junior secondary level in 1940 and eventually becoming one of Uganda's most successful senior secondary schools.

Meanwhile, there was visionary enthusiasm for a higher level school yet. Again Bishop Tucker led the way:

It was ... with the conviction that university education must sooner or later find a place in any well-devised scheme of education for the Baganda, that early in 1903 we planned a school for intermediate education. AG Fraser who was the prime mover in the scheme, was obliged, on account of his wife's health, to return home. So it was taken up by HW Weatherhead, who worked at it with unbounded enthusiasm.[15]

Confident of Tucker's support, Weatherhead seized his chance at a CMS conference at Mengo in June 1904.[16] During a sublimely optimistic debate on the possible introduction of compulsory education, he successfully proposed the speedy founding of an intermediate school, astutely linking it to a proposal for a separate theological college, thereby firmly establishing the distinction between the two. Both were accepted and he outlined a three-year curriculum for the school, to be taught in the vernacular, but with intensive teaching of English, to enable the boys to read and enjoy English literature. The conference report seemed to imply that he was thinking along traditional academic lines and that the school would produce well educated men mainly destined to be clergymen.

Henry Walter Weatherhead had other ideas. He was a graduate of Trinity College, Cambridge and after ordination left England as one of seven CMS missionaries to Uganda. The party included Albert Cook who graphically described their walk up from the coast. He and Weatherhead climbed Mount Longonot on the way.[17] Weatherhead was posted to Busoga and was involved in the Nubian mutiny of 1897.

He then got a bad dose of blackwater fever, which was often fatal, and was ordered home to England in 1900. He recovered and on his return was sent to the Sesse Islands, where he was joined a year later by his wife and brother, Herbert Thomas Candy Weatherhead. In 1904 he was recalled to Mengo to teach ordinands. Forty years later he wrote to the headmaster of Budo:

> What a chance came my way when Bishop Tucker gave me almost carte blanche to draw up a scheme, choose and secure a site, plan, build and start a senior school.[18]

Weatherhead was headmaster of Budo for the first six years. Long after he left he wrote a fine letter to the third headmaster, H.M. Grace, who had asked for an account of the founding of the school. It is an invaluable primary source:

> The first task was the choosing of the site. Any site by the Lake was barred by sleeping sickness. I don't know who first told me about Budo Hill, but it did not take me long to decide upon it as the most desirable place for the purpose - the unusually broad, level top, the good water spring close by and, I will admit, the fine view of the Lake. But having chosen the site of Budo we found we were up against the whole of Uganda. I may say that our mainstay throughout the whole business was the Prime Minister, Apolo Kagwa, who was genuinely keen on Christian education and on starting a more advanced school for the sons of chiefs and others.
>
> Without him we should never have succeeded. On telling Apolo that I wanted Budo, he said that it was flatly impossible. It was the King's Hill and not only Royal property but also of peculiar sanctity as being the Coronation Hill. It was unthinkable. The people of Uganda would never consent. So I had to begin to think again.
>
> I visited fourteen sites within a radius of about a dozen miles of Namirembe. None of them had anywhere near the suitability of Budo... I had never given up in my own mind the original choice of Budo and now I saw my opportunity and indulged in the regular British bluff. I remember well the interview with Apolo Kagwa in his house.

Bishop Tucker kindly came down with me and pressed the matter.

I bluntly told Apolo that I would now take Budo or nothing; that if he really wanted a school let him build it himself - or else let him get Budo for us. I washed my hands of it if I could not have Budo. This attitude clinched the matter, for Apolo was genuinely keen. We owe the splendid site of Budo to Apolo Kagwa who as First Regent agreed to the transfer of Budo Hill, under certain conditions for the use of a school. He did this in the teeth of tremendous opposition throughout Uganda. It needed great pluck for even a big chief to take such a stand and push the thing through.[19]

The site for which Apolo Kagwa fought lies about ten miles west of Namirembe and twelve from the centre of modern Kampala. Fraser had visited it with Ham Mukasa in 1903 and thought it an ideal spot for a school or college.

According to Kiganda legend[20] the old name of the hill was Nagalabi. It had been famous as the headquarters of Bemba, a tyrannical ruler, believed to be King of the Snakes. Kintu, who was then living on the Sesse Islands, determined to attack Bemba and free his people. He gathered an army, camped at Bukesa, attacked Bemba and killed him. [Another version of the legend is that a tortoise offered to kill Bemba for him, went to Nagalabi and told Bemba that if he would cut off his hands and feet - as the tortoise did every time he went to sleep - he would live for ever, as the tortoise was going to. The tortoise then demonstrated by withdrawing into his shell. Bemba did as the tortoise had suggested - and bled to death.]

The legends agree that Kintu ordered that Bemba's head be buried at the spot where he had died, which is now known as Nakibuuka. Kintu was now undisputed ruler of the land and settled in Bemba's house, called "Buganda", from which the kingdom took its name. He called the clans that he had united "Baganda": "The people who have been gathered together".

The name of the hill, Nagalabi, was changed to Budo shortly before Namugala became Kabaka of Buganda, towards the end of the seventeenth century.   A man called Budo had come from the Sesse Islands to live at Nagalabi. He was a "doctor" and had a charm which was much sought after. When Namugala inherited the kingdom, he went to Budo to receive the power of the charm. When Budo died he was buried on the hill, perhaps near Nakibuuka. For at least four hundred years Kabakas of Buganda have been crowned there. So all three coronations in the twentieth century took place beside King's College.

A few weeks after the opening of Mengo High School, Weatherhead and H.G. Dillistone, who was to be in charge of the building work, went up the hill to survey the site. Among the first challenges was the removal of the many huge termite mounds, within a quarter-mile radius, and of the large number of snakes. These included some horned puff-adders, which were thought sacred by some of the villagers, who fed them with milk. Weatherhead calculated that it would be possible to lay out a central quadrangle slightly bigger than the largest college court he knew of - the main court of his own Trinity College, Cambridge. So they did and had it grassed and planted with trees and shrubs which have kept it beautiful ever since. It soon had its effect:

> I am glad that I started with what seemed a really ambitious scheme
> of a large quad. That quad, with its stretches of green lawn, well
> kept, had a considerable influence on European visitors, when they
> came - often with ill-disguised condescension - to have a look at
> the missionary effort.[21]

The original buildings were a schoolroom, fifty feet by thirty, with classrooms on either side, and one dormitory divided into cubicles. Weatherhead had particularly asked for these. Many of his "boys" were grown men and he believed that having an individual cubicle would foster self-respect and independence. He also thought that a great deal of instruction in hygiene was needed in Uganda. If each boy was responsible for the cleanness and neatness of his own space, there was a chance that he might take good habits back with him to his home. Each cubicle measured seven feet by six and contained a bed with a storage box underneath, a small table and chair, and some hooks for hanging clothes. The dormitory had two bathrooms and a central lobby with two fireplaces at which the boys could boil water for baths and for tea. There were to be twenty-three boys in the dormitory, for reasons which, Weatherhead wrote, "will be obvious to anyone who knows anything about football." [22]

This sumptuous accommodation was much admired by visitors at the opening ceremony, but there were mutterings at the degree of freedom it offered:

> The leading native clergyman at the time, Revd Henry Kitakule, urged me strongly to put bars on all the windows and to bolt and lock all the doors. I told him that I should do nothing of the kind, but plainly tell the boys that there were no bars or locks, that it was easy for them to break the rules and go out, but that I expected something better of them.[23]

He knew what kind of education he wanted his boys to have and what kind of work he wanted it to prepare them for. The 1904 conference had preferred to think of the new school mainly as an advanced seminary. Weatherhead did not - and Bishop Tucker was with him:

> The Bishop was one of the few in the mission who thoroughly understood and appreciated our aims in founding the school. I made no secret of being out for an institution that was to help provide the country with well-educated Christian laymen, who would in time take the lead in the development of their own country. Too many missionaries expected a kind of seminary to turn out native clergy or church workers. But the Bishop was I think as keen as I was on the adaptation of our English public school method to the African race.[24]

Tucker showed how keen he was by financing the whole project - which Weatherhead reckoned had cost about £ 2000 - from Diocesan funds. The purpose of Budo was often to be questioned in the early years, notably at the CMS conference of 1915. Weatherhead's manifesto is the more significant because surprise is still sometimes voiced that a secondary school should have had a strong influence on the political and social development of the country. Budo was founded to do that.

The faith of Tucker and Weatherhead in "the adaptation of our English public school method to the African race" may raise wry smiles in the twenty-first century, but two points are worth noting: First, they, like Hattersley, paid Uganda the compliment of trying to bring it the best education they knew - however unsuitable it may now seem. Secondly, in at least one respect the boarding school turned out to be an appropriate institution to transplant. Tucker had generalised bluntly that chiefs tended to neglect their sons, but Roscoe, in his perceptive early study of the Baganda, recorded a strong tradition that, wherever possible, boys should be sent away from their immediate family to be educated:

> When children were weaned it was customary to send them to a member of the father's clan to be trained... If the relative saw that the boy was bright and quick he would possibly get him into the household of some chief; there the boy, if he was attentive, might soon make his way, become a trusted servant and be sent on important business. He might even become a page to the King and in this position, if he gained favour by his alertness, promotion would be certain.[25]

The CMS choice of the boarding school was not as capricious as has sometimes been assumed.

Towards the end of 1905 the dormitory on Budo Hill was almost ready for occupation and sites had been marked out for two more, and for a chapel - when there was money to build them. Weatherhead was eager to start. The question is still sometimes put, "Exactly when was Budo founded?" Some institutions date their foundation from the first recorded activity and others from the occasion of a ceremonial opening, if there was one. Weatherhead had actually begun teaching a class of six boys in October 1905 and had continued, with twenty-one, in January 1906, three months before the school was formally opened on March 29th. The nearest convenient day to that date has ever since been celebrated as Founders' Day.

The opening was an occasion. In the schoolroom lunch was served for 140 guests including, at a high table, the young Kabaka, Daudi Chwa, the three regents, Acting Commissioner George Wilson and Bishop

Tucker. Wilson and other officials had come 20 miles by rickshaw from Entebbe and had to be pushed up the last steep slope of the hill by a crowd of enthusiastic bystanders, to join the 16 county chiefs and more than 100 other chiefs in the schoolroom. While they lunched, a crowd of more than 10,000 feasted - according to the report of CMS Uganda - on 1053 baskets of food, 4 roasted bullocks, 3 goats and 36 gourds of banana juice. Fifty years later Harold Ingrams reflected:

> There must have been something in the idea of the school which very much fitted into the Buganda mystique, for Sir Apolo Kagwa to have been so insistent, not only on its foundation but on its siting. There was of course opposition, quite strong opposition, for it was a revolutionary idea. But the multitude at the opening ceremony indicated that it had the inner sympathy of the Baganda.[26]

After lunch the visitors were given a tour of the school, the schoolroom was cleared, and all assembled for the formal opening. Bishop Tucker stressed that although one object of the school was to build up the Church in Uganda, every boy would be free to choose his own calling and he had no doubt that many would take their share in the administration of the country. The first aim was to produce men who were trustworthy. He thanked the administration for the interest it had shown in the school, but reminded all present that two more dormitories were needed quickly if the school was to build up to the 80 pupils hoped for. Another £ 6000 was needed to build a school that would be second to none in East Africa.

Weatherhead said that he had chosen the lion as the school crest to remind the boys that they were sent to learn to be brave in heart and brave for the truth. One of the things he feared was that they might become conceited and he asked all the chiefs to help to stop this. Now was the time to do so, while the boys were few in number.

Sir Apolo Kagwa said he believed that the Baganda were not yet worthy of trust in administrative positions, but he hoped they would become so. The government would be willing to help the school if the boys learned well there. Christianity had spread into other parts of Uganda from Buganda, and if the Baganda became wiser and cleverer then the other countries would again follow their lead. The chiefs might be too old to learn but their children could redeem the country.

The speech of the day came however from the Sekibobo (saza chief of Kyaggwe) Ham Mukasa. He had recently visited England with Sir Apolo and must have warmed the hearts of all Oxonians present when he pronounced that teaching was the root of all that was good and that the English believed that so strongly that they had a whole town given over to the purpose of teaching young people. It was called Cambridge. All the wisdom of the English came from there and all the cleverest people went there to be taught. A few also went to London. He believed that Budo would become in time the Cambridge of Uganda. The fancy seemed innocent enough on this happy afternoon in 1906, but it was to give a good deal of trouble to the Budo of future decades.

The proceedings ended with a short service at which Bishop Tucker dedicated the school as "The King's School" because it was built on royal land given by the regents on behalf of the Kabaka. Weatherhead noted a quiet incident during the ceremony. The young Kabaka Daudi Chwa told Sir Apolo Kagwa that he would like to visit the sacred places on Budo Hill as he was now so close to them. But the regents persuaded him that this would be unwise; the vast crowd might think that he was assuming the full powers of the Kabakaship and that the regency was ended. Such was the power of the tradition of the Royal Hill.[27]

So the school was launched, but Bishop Tucker cautioned that there was still much to be done:

> To complete the scheme we have still to build a technical school, a gynmnasium, a chapel and a sanatorium.[28]

Weatherhead saw a technical school and a chapel completed. The sanatorium was opened in 1963. Budo is still waiting for the gymnasium.

Notes

[1] Cook, Sir Albert, *Uganda Memories*, Kampala Uganda Society 1945. p. 208

[2] Tucker A.R. *Eighteen Years in Uganda and East Africa.* London; Arnold 1908, Vol. 2 p. 151

[3] Taylor J.V. *The Growth of the Church in Buganda.* London: SCM, 1958, p.93

[4] Tucker *op. cit.* p.327

[5] CMS Proceedings 1899-1900, London, 1900, p.122

[6] *Ibid* 1901-2, p.127

[7] *Ibid* 1903-4, p.107

[8] *Uganda Notes.* CMS Mengo April 1905, p.53 and March 1905, p.35.

[9] Gale H.P. *Uganda and the Mill Hill Fathers.* London: MacMillan, 1959, p.246.

[10] *Ibid* p.247.

[11] Tucker *op.cit.* p.237

[12] *Uganda Notes,* March 1905, pp. 42-46

[13] Cook *op. cit.* p. 207

[14] Cox J. Richards B., and Warren S., *Gayaza High School 1905 – 1995,* Kampala 1995 p.3

[15] Tucker *op.cit* p. 329

[16] *Uganda Notes* July 1904, p. 99

[17] Cook *op. cit.* p.35

[18] Weatherhead H.W. to Herbert D.G., 15 february 1945. KCB archives.

[19] Weatherhead H.W. to Grace H.M. Undated, but presumably 1930s. Copy in KCB archives. Original believed to be in possession of Old Budonian F.D.R. Gureme. See 'The Budonian -90 Years,' 1996. p. 7.

[20] *Uganda Church Review,* no. 41, October 1936. Oxford, Broome, p. 69.

[21] Weatherhead H.W. to Herbert D.G. 24 February 1946. KCB archives.

[22] Weatherhead H.W. to Grace H.M. *op.cit.*

[23] *Ibid*

[24] *Ibid*

[25] Roscoe J. *The Baganda.* London: MacMillan 1911, pp. 74-76

[26] Ingrams H. *Uganda.* London HMSO 1960 p. 123

[27] *Uganda Notes,* October 1910 p. 156

[28] Tucker *op. cit* p. 330

2

Building up and Spreading out 1906-1912

The new Budo way of life must have seemed very strange to the first pupils. Fortunately, fifty years before Budo achieved a telephone line, the writing of long personal letters was popular in Uganda and Y.L. Zerubaberi who had joined the school in January 1906 described his impressions for Revd E.S. Daniell, a CMS missionary. Daniell was a staunch supporter of the school and was later appointed warden of Bishop Tucker College at Mukono - the theological college which Weatherhead had proposed, along with Budo, in his 1904 CMS conference motion.

King's School, Budo.

February 1st 1906.

To Revd E.S. Daniell.

How are you Sir? Are you still in good health? I am in good health. We have begun our work, but English is difficult, too much for me. I was reading in the First class, but the other day he gave us a Bible and chose a passage - whatever he liked - and we turned it from Luganda into English, but I found it very difficult. There were four of us who could not translate it well and at last, when I saw that I had no meaning that I could get out of those words, I went back into the class of the beginners. Our work which we do every day is as follows:

First in the morning when we have got up, we arrange properly our beds. If you do not arrange it properly there is judgement or rebuke when the Europeans make a visit, and if the mistress [Mrs Weatherhead] on her round finds it untidy, then there is rebuke. And everyone sweeps out his own cubicle. And then we read, everyone silently, in his own cubicle. And at 7 o'clock we meet in the large room and have prayers and afterwards everyone goes and does as he likes. And at 7.45 the headmaster orders us to put on our clothes for going into school and at 50 minutes we go into school. On the front of our caps there is sewn the likeness of a lion. That it is by which the scholars of Budo may be known. And no one may eat anything in the cubicle, nor coffee which they chew, but only in the verandah where food is eaten.

We sing one hymn and then we pray and then we learn English in a book called the "Infant Reader". At 10.30 we come out and go to our room and rest till 12 o'clock, when we have our midday meal. At 1 o'clock any who like to sleep, sleep. When there remain 15 minutes they wake us all up, if you are on your bed and everyone only sits. When it is nearly 2 o'clock he gives us a Luganda Bible to translate into English - and that is what beats me. At 3 o'clock on that day he talks in English. We who are in the class of the fools sit and listen. We have not anything to answer.

When we come out at 4 o'clock we go and play football, on one side eleven and on the other side eleven and we arrange every man in his place - goalkeeper and back men and ba-halfback and ba-forward. We stop at six and everyone puts on his efalunu [sweater] to prevent cold and we return and wash. At 7 o'clock in the evening we go and have prayers and return and have our evening meal, and then go back and learn what we have been taught during the day, until 8.30 when they refuse to let us read saying "stop reading" and we begin to simply talk together until 9.30 when we return to our cubicles and light every man his lamp and sit in our cubicles till 10 o'clock when they order us all to put out our lamps and to go to sleep and not to remain talking nor to leave your cubicle, to do that is forbidden. If they hear of one doing that they take away his lamp and do not return it for as many days as the headmaster likes.

When we are at our school we do not pay visits, but if we want to go visiting [in English "go for a walk" which means in Luganda "gossiping at any house"] he tells us to walk only in the high road; and no one may go for a walk by himself, but two or more together. Well Sir, Goodbye.

I am your affectionate child

Y L Zerubaberi[1]

For the privilege of conforming to this exotic routine, the boys, or their parents, paid annual fees of 100 rupees - about £ 7 in English money - which was considered a lot to pay for schooling in Uganda in 1906. The government, through the personal interest of George Wilson, established five scholarships for boys whose parents could not raise the fees. The rest of the school's income came from mission funds and gifts from friends.

It is surprising that Zerubaberi did not mention the manual work that he was required to do. All the work of maintaining the school, except the cooking of food and carrying of water, was done by the boys. In addition to cleaning their own cubicles and the main schoolroom, they did all their own washing and maintained all the school grounds - a rather severe "adaptation of our English public school method".

But Weatherhead was not content to leave it at that. A few weeks after the opening, he took all the boys across Lake Victoria to Kisumu. He conducted them all over the steamer, including the engine room, and at Kisumu they went for short runs, in small groups, on the footplate of a railway engine. Then they went off in the train to see the only tunnel on the Uganda Railway and the highest viaduct. Weatherhead himself went on the footplate for this trip to make sure that the train stopped at all the right places. They all got out and walked through the tunnel. As he had hoped, the whole trip was an eye-opener for the boys and what seemed to impress them most was not only the knowledge of the Europeans, but the way they set to and made things with their hands.

On the Sunday after they returned, Weatherhead reminded them of all that they had seen and then said that he wanted volunteers to begin some hard work for the school - making a swimming pool. All but one of the boys responded at once and they did not give the one much time to change his mind. So the swimming pool was started

and by the following term some form of manual labour - digging
foundations, levelling football pitches and some actual building
- had become a regular part of the timetable. Weatherhead knew
that he had crossed a big bridge:

> I have often wondered that there was not more open
> opposition, for using a hoe and digging were very derogatory
> to any man. Was it not entirely women's work? Curiously
> enough, the most definite protests came from two senior
> missionaries. They wrote and said that I was breaking the
> boys hearts by this revolutionary action. My answer was
> to ask them to come out to Budo and pick up the pieces
> of broken hearts, for the boys themselves had taken up the
> matter with zest.

> In this connection I remember well a prince from Ankole
> coming to see the school. After showing him round we
> returned to my house. He was pleasantly polite, but a trifle
> nervous.

> "I like what I have seen," he said "and I should like to come
> to the school. But ..." I knew what was coming. "It is the
> digging," he said. "My prestige in my own country would
> be gone if they knew I was doing work of that kind." "I'm
> sorry," I replied, "but that's the rule of the school. If you
> come here you will certainly do some digging with the others.
> There is no difference here between prince and peasant." So
> he went away and for a week I heard nothing and naturally I
> thought his prestige had been too much for him. But it hadn't.
> He came to the school and played the game wonderfully. He
> was among the boys who built the porters' lodge near the
> entrance gate.[2]

In October 1906 Weatherhead (HW) was joined at Budo by his
brother Herbert Thomas Candy Weatherhead (HTC) who was
as keen as he was on practical work as an antidote to the kind
of snobbery which an entirely academic curriculum might have
fostered in Uganda. Weatherhead was another Cambridge man,
from Emmanuel College. After ordination he had come out to
join the CMS mission in 1900. He spent his first year in Bukoba
and then joined his brother on the Sesse Islands where he trained

teachers and visited them at work in the most populated islands. In 1905, on his way to England for leave, he went to South Africa to visit schools and technical training centres. On leave he took a London County Council certificate course for teachers of handwork, quickly adapting what he had learned to the needs of Budo. The brothers hoped that the school could run a full technical course as well as the practical work of the ordinary curriculum and in 1907 they launched an appeal for £ 500 to provide a well-equipped workshop. It was to be a memorial to Alexander Mackay, who had been the kind of missionary Stanley had thought right for Uganda - "A man who can turn his hand to anything".

H.W. Weatherhead begged much of the money during his own home leave in 1907 and by the end of 1908 the workshop was complete and in use. It still stands today, one of Budo's most handsome buildings, greatly enlarged by the students themselves in 1930-31 to serve for the past 75 years as the school dining hall - "Mess". But for more than 20 years it served as the Weatherheads had planned:

> Teaching Budo boys to be competent amateurs who would respect and enjoy manual skills.[3]

Practical work took a useful step forward - in the tradition of the great Mackay - a few years later in 1910, as Weatherhead was proud to inform Grace:

> The existence of a printing press at Budo, with its subsequent starting of "Ebifa" [a popular Church journal] was due to a happy chance quickly seized. AB Lloyd had been appointed to open out the work among the Nilotic tribes of Bukedi. He brought out the printing press but was prevented - by doctors or some other reason - from taking up the work. I at once applied for the press and he let us have it at a very reasonable price. Of course one of the chief reasons for having the press was its value for teaching accuracy. It is so easy to make mistakes and so easy for everyone else to see them when printed.[4]

According to tradition the press was transported to the school from Kampala by a porter who walked all the way with it balanced on his head. [I thought this a tall tale until I saw a sturdy young man in Kigezi perform a similar feet for half a mile - with a huge meatsafe crammed with food and groceries.] However it got there, its output was soon large and influential. A great deal of the Anglican Church's literature was printed on it, including some of the CMS reports quoted in this book. In 1911 it published a revised Luganda Grammar and the first of the Weatherhead's popular' Letters to Old Budonians', which included a comment on the activity which had produced it:

> This year saw the beginning of printing here at Budo. Fifteen boys were selected to help Mr Kiyingi. Several of them bound books, especially those of English Grammar, others arranged letters and quite a few had by the end of the year learned enough to do the actual printing.[5]

The same circular letter described another typical Weatherhead excursion which in those days must have been quite a feat of organisation:

> Perhaps the most spectacular event of the year was our trip to Nairobi. There were forty-five students and two Europeans. Baganda do not much like travelling on the Lake but on this trip we were lucky ...We saw lots of things in Nairobi which pleased the students, especially the train shed, where metal was being cut just as you cut paper.[6]

The practical side of this early Budo curriculum merits emphasis because in 1924 the visiting Phelps-Stokes Commission had justly criticised many mission schools for being slavishly academic, and unrelated to the life of the people. The Weatherheads knew the balance they wanted between book learning and practical skills and they worked hard to achieve it. There was soon more going on in the classroom than the English of the "Infant Reader" and the Bible that so daunted Zerubaberi. History, geography and mathematics were prominent on the timetable. Some lessons were taught in Luganda but the Weatherheads thought it inevitable that English would become the lingua franca of this linguistically rich and varied country, so they gradually increased the amount of teaching in and of English. Some examination papers have survived from the first "Finals" of 1908. The problems in arithmetic were as taxing as any of Hattersley's Mengo gems and in English boys were asked:

> What do you understand by a Possessive Adjective, an Interrogative Pronoun and an Auxiliary Verb?[7]

The geography paper which was set in Luganda invited them to 'Say what you know about the continent of Africa and the peoples who live in it.'[8]

A friend in England regularly sent HW copies of *The Sphere* and he used its articles as a basis for discussion in what he called his "General Ignorance Class" held every week with the senior boys. There was urgent need for a library and while H.W. was on leave in 1907, his brother made a start with 50 useful books which had been given by a Mr Cyril Davies. H.T.C. wrote to the editor of CMS *Uganda Notes* explaining that the intention was to build up a library which would be useful not just to the school but to people all over the country, on the lines of one he had seen at Lovedale in South Africa. He added caustically that this was worth trying even though the Bishop's library at Namirembe had been so badly treated by borrowers.[9]

In 1906 only one dormitory had been ready for occupation and had at once been called "England". The second one, ready by the end of the year was, mysteriously, christened "Turkey". The English public school house spirit soon began to catch on and at the end of 1907 the boys who were to live in the third dormitory called it "Australia". This apparently made the boys of "Turkey" feel distinctly unimperial. In a letter of 1945, H.W. Weatherhead described what followed. He had become known to the school and to the Baganda as *Sabaganzi* - "The much-loved One" and was writing to thank Budo for naming the new girls' dormitory Sabaganzi in his honour:

> I don't remember for certain how the houses came to be named. I think it was the boys' own fancies. I do remember that one was at first called "Turkey" and that after a time a deputation waited on me to ask for this name to be changed. I said "Certainly. You may call it anything you like" - that answer shows that there was no

formal naming. They then said "But it is impossible to change a name without the agreement and authority of a chief."[10]

"Turkey" became "Canada" and has been ever since. In his six years as headmaster Sabaganzi saw numbers at Budo rise steadily and education developing all over the country. He had begun in 1905 with 6 boys, had 21 in 1906, 32 in 1907 and 37 in 1908. At the end of that year the first 19 boys completed the planned three-year course and became the first full "Old Budonians" - a few others having left earlier and gone on to useful work without completing the entire course. 1910 began with 53 boys and of 1911 Weatherhead wrote in his second letter to Old Budonians:

> We started off with 68 students. I am pleased to say that our school is becoming popular and many people in Buganda are getting to like it. It used to be said that boys feared to come to Budo because here students were made to work much too hard, and were too hedged in by school rules. I am glad to say that this attitude is changing and in fact many scramble for places.[11]

In 1912 there were 76 boys and the fourth house was almost full. Meanwhile, by 1907 there were 53 girls at Gayaza and at Mengo High School Winston Churchill, visiting Uganda as Under-Secretary of State for the Colonies, opened new buildings to accommodate the 130 boys.[12] By 1910 Gayaza had 75 girls and there were high schools for boys in Bunyoro and Busoga. In 1912 the demand for places at Budo was three times the supply, but it was considered that the fees were too high for all but wealthy chiefs and the five scholarship winners. So the CMS founded Bishop's School at Mukono, 15 miles from Kampala, to make day school education of a high standard available to the sons of less wealthy parents.[13] Hattersley's system had worked so well that in Mukono district alone there were by this time fifty bush schools with a total of about 6000 pupils, creating a demand for the next stage of education.[14]

The first Old Budonians could claim credit for some of this expansion. Of the 19 who left at the end of 1908, four went to teach in the new high schools and five took up their chieftainships and did much to arouse enthusiasm for education among their clans. Five others went into government service as clerks, one became a government surveyor and two became clerks in commercial firms.[15] By the end of 1910 there were 39 Old Budonians. Two were now teachers at Budo; the senior posts in all the CMS high schools were held by Budonians and several more had entered government service, two as interpreters. The success of the Old Budonian teachers was soon to have important repercussions when the mission tried to formulate a teacher-training policy. There were periodic rumblings in Church circles about the true purpose of Budo; because of sickness and leave among missionaries it had proved hard to find enough teachers for classes of ordinands. CMS *Uganda Notes* commented:

> In some quarters the belief is entertained that the King's School, Budo is a Normal School [ie a teacher-training college]. But the Revds HW and HTC Weatherhead point out that this is a misconception and that its object, as clearly stated at the outset, is to prepare boys to occupy positions in government offices, or as rulers of counties, while at the same time it is hoped that some will become teachers and preachers.[16]

H.W. insisted that the school was to produce laymen but he wanted "good Christian laymen" and believed that he could not run a Christian school, as he understood it, without a chapel. He had already reserved a site and when a chance came to raise the money he took it with characteristic opportunism.

Bishop Wilkinson, Anglican Bishop, in Northern Europe had read the story of the Uganda boy martyrs and wrote to Bishop Tucker, offering to pay for a church in Uganda as a memorial to them. H.W. at once suggested that the most suitable place for such a memorial chapel would be a school at which boys of much the same ages as the martyrs were now receiving Christian education. Tucker, never needing much persuasion to help Budo, put the proposal to Bishop Wilkinson, who accepted it. But H.W. could no longer call on the services of his architect, Dillistone, who had left Uganda. He had to do his best with the plan of a small parish church in England, sent out to him by CMS, and with such skilled labour as he could muster:

I found a good Indian carpenter to undertake the roof business and I managed, without saying much, to modify the original plan. The bricklayers were all unskilled and I remember having to rush out from a classroom, seeing a disastrously crooked layer of bricks just laid, and promptly knocking it down. But before that stage we had to make and burn the bricks. I got plans for a kiln from HR Madox, an architect in Toro, but as we had no lime we had to use only firewood for burning the bricks. This meant careful organisation, for we had to keep the fire going hard for three days and nights.

So headmen were appointed to keep the workmen awake - and I had to keep the head-men awake. But the result was very gratifying, a very decent red brick being turned out.

Then I determined that black pointing would look better than white, but I hadn't the ghost of a notion how to make the mortar black. My native headman came to the rescue and suggested mixing charcoal with the cement. This acted very well in making a fine blue-black pointing. I ordered special pointing trowels from England and the Baganda at once began by breaking off the points. Finally they were allowed to follow their own way and point with large French nails.[17]

H.W. saw the building completed but not furnished, before he left in 1912. It still stands sturdily beside the main quadrangle, having been outgrown as a chapel but housing the main library for 40 years and probably convertible for other use when the large new library building is finished.

The loyalty of Old Budonians was soon a source of strength to the school. The annual letters kept them informed of events, of where every OB was and what he was doing - changes of address and job being carefully updated. The first Speech Day was held on Easter Monday 1908 and, with the Kabaka and Governor Sir Hesketh Bell present, the boys must have felt that being a Budonian was really going to matter. But in his first "annual report" Weatherhead tempered praise with criticism and was "more plain than polite" with some of the less diligent scholars.[18] The Governor assured the boys that he would be watching their progress carefully after they left Budo and would be ready to help them. But he urged them to watch out for "swelled-headedness" and to maintain the courtesy and grace of manner for which the Baganda had become famous. He also took the opportunity - as several later governors have done at Budo Founders' Days - to make a formal statement of government policy. On this occasion the topics were agriculture and taxation. Weatherhead translated into Luganda for him and the speech was "warmly applauded". He ended by presenting two personal prizes to the boys who had been judged "best all-round in tone and influence on the school". The head prefect, Samson Bazongere, proposed a vote of thanks - in English.

Old Budonians have been welcomed in large numbers to Founders' Days ever since. For many years, until numbers became too large, they were also invited to the end of year supper in honour of leavers. H.W. wrote to his wife, who had returned to England, describing the third of these events in 1910. It was a double celebration because that afternoon Budo had for the first time won the Kabaka's Athletics Challenge Cup, competing against the Kabaka's athletes.

> Soon after seven, Millar and I went to the classroom where the feast was to be, and found a very long table set out, with a fine vase of flowers on it and the Athletics Challenge Cup in the centre. A good number of Old Boys turned up and we sat down 28 in all... they evidently thoroughly enjoy it, meeting their old school fellows and it was very nice to see all these men, as they are, neatly, cleanly but not loudly dressed, sitting and chatting together. Millar was greatly struck by it all and was taken back vividly to England and his visits to his own old school, Clifton College. I doubt if we ever get so close to the atmosphere of an English public school as upon these occasions.

> ...Later I went to prayers and congratulated everyone afterwards and said how pleased I was with the keenness and enthusiasm they had shown at the athletics meeting. Then I suggested chairing Blasio, as the hero of the sports, round the quad, which we did with a great deal of shouting and noise. As I left I saw them gathered round Blasio, and Gwani began an English song. What do you think it was? - "Poor Old Joe"!![19]

[Revd Ernest Millar had come out at his own expense to work with CMS and was to prove a strong supporter of Budo - see chapter 3.]

The first 'Letter to Old Budonians' described this event in great detail and praised the much improved keenness for football and athletics, the successful re-digging of the swimming pool and the fine support H.W. had received, while his brother was on leave, from the school's first Old Budonian teachers, Gideon Nsalambwa and Erasito Bakaluba.

The second Letter, for 1911, was to be H.W. Weatherhead's last, though he did not know it at the time. He wrote that he was very pleased to have had so many letters from Old Boys, asking for help and advice and he hoped that they would go on writing and visiting the school when they could - "even when you grow old and wear grey beards. Remember all the time that you are Old Budo students." He reported that the school had retained the Kabaka's cup for football and that the boys had cleared and levelled a second football pitch. There was also fresh enthusiasm for tennis and he suspected that this was because he had accused the boys of being unwilling to play anything on their own, unless they had been told to do so. They were now playing tennis at weekends, from morning till evening - to prove him wrong.

He thought that the academic progress had been fairly good, so the Board of Governors [20] had been willing to introduce a half-term holiday - a week's rest in the middle of the second and third terms. During the first of these breaks the boys had rested and amused themselves at the school, but for the second, Weatherhead arranged an expedition. He took them to the forestry reserves in Kyaggwe, where they also visited plantations and studied the processes of growing coffee and cocoa. One other activity at Budo may have been unique. In 1908 the first branch, in Uganda, of the Mothers' Union was opened - at Budo, for the wives of the "boys". [21]

H.W. must have felt that the school had come a long way in a short time. But he knew that there was much more to be done and chose a school motto accordingly. In 1908 he invited the Director of the Uganda Company, Mr Barbour, to talk to the boys. He told them about the progress of South Africa and the work of Cecil Rhodes, quoting Rhodes's famous phrase "So little done - so much to do." The boys were so taken with this notion that they set themselves to find a Luganda equivalent. After a while one of them brought to Weatherhead the proverb *Gakyali Mabaga.* "This is the reply made to passers-by who congratulate a man on having started to build his house, when he is only just tying up the first ring, which is the apex of the roof. The words mean literally "We are still at the tying" ie "We have only just begun". Surmounted by the red lion they have formed the Budo crest ever since.[22] Weatherhead liked to translate them "Still at the scaffolding stage" and used to quote, by way of explanation, Browning's "Ah, but a man's reach must exceed his grasp - or what's a heaven for?"

H.W. Weatherhead arrived in England for leave in January 1912, expecting to be back at Budo later in the year. Within a month he had been ordered by doctors not to return to Africa. He never saw his school again. He himself best described what he wanted to make at Budo and how he felt about it. In 1946, D.G. Herbert, then headmaster, visited Weatherhead and his wife in England. H.W. wrote:

> You know the thing that sticks out in the memory of our talks with you is what you told us of the reality of the Budo spirit, which struck you so much on your arrival from Achimota, and seems as strong in influence today, "forty years on" - as the Harrow song puts it. That delights us more than anything else and I feel inclined to chant a "Nunc Dimittis", feeling that I have accomplished a share in the start of something really worthwhile.[23]

His letter to Grace, quoted at length, ends as follows:

> Well, I am sure that by now you have discovered I have reached the age of garrulity.

> But I think you will find some day, when you are perhaps in some quiet English country parsonage, that the best part of your life - sometimes you will be tempted to say the only part of your life that really counts - was the years spent at Budo. [24]

Notes

[1] Daniel E.S., typed copy in KCB archives

[2] Weatherhead H.W. to HM Grace, KCB archives

[3] *Ibid*

[4] *Ibid*

[5] *Ebaluwa eri banabudo abe* King's School 1911, in KCB archives

[6] *Ibid*

[7] KCB archives

[8] *Ibid*

[9] *Uganda Notes,* November 1907, Kampala, Uganda Company p. 190

[10] Weatherhead H.W. to D.G. Herbert, 10 February 1945, KCB archives

[11] *Ebaluwa eri banabudo abe* King's School, 1912, KCB archives

[12] *Uganda Notes* December 1907, Kampala, Uganda Company

[13] Proceedings of the CMS 1912-13, London 1913, p. 63

[14] *Ibid,* 1913-14, p.70

[15] *Ibid,* 1908-9, p. 67

[16] *Ibid,* p.66

[17] Weatherland H.W. to H.M. Grace, *op. cit*

[18] *Uganda Notes,* May 1908, p. 68

[19] Weatherhead H.W. to Mrs A. Weatherhead, 18 December 1910, KCB archives

[20] Bishop Tucker was chairman but I could find no record of the membership. Weatherhead always stressed that he was given a free hand. An influential board was set up only in 1927, cf. chapter 4.

[21] *Uganda Notes,* January 1909, p. 15

[22] *Uganda Church Review,* No 39, July – September 1935, p.56

[23] Weatherhead H.W. to D.G. Herbert, 10 February 1946, KCB archives.

[24] Weatherhead H.W. to H.M. Grace *op.cit*

3

War, Problems and Possibilities: 1912-1926

When the school re-opened for the new year 1912, H.T.C. Weatherhead the new headmaster, was the only European teacher and he remained headmaster for the next 12 years. There were 76 students and, in the annual 'Letter to Old Budonians', he paid tribute to the conscientious and effective work of his three African assistant masters, who were all Old Budonians. But he also entered a plea for more European help:

> The European, if alone here, has the following duties all upon him, in addition to teaching and wanting leisure to get to know the boys individually. Building: We are not yet free of it. This year a dormitory is being completed which was half built last year. Two underground tanks have been roofed with corrugated iron. The Chapel interior has been completed. Upkeep: Not only are there, in each holiday, repairs to see to, but frequently one is called out in term time to repair a mowing machine, see to some breakage or look after the grounds.
>
> School Plantations: We have 60 acres in one direction a mile and a half distant, lent us by the Kabaka, and ten acres close by, leased from the Queen Mother. On the near plantation we grow food for the school, and have planted two acres of cocoa under the shade of the bananas. On the far plantation we planted six or seven acres of food and some sixteen of coffee and rubber. We hope in time to secure an income for the school from these plantations, but meanwhile they mean much work of oversight for the European.
>
> Another office which has taken time and thought has been that of Secretary to the Board of Education of the Church of Uganda. In connection with this I have under-taken two tours of inspection of schools in two of my school holidays. We have this year begun the arrangement of three holidays in the year instead of two, so that half of two of those holidays, or a month a year, may be devoted to such tours of inspection.[1]

Weatherhead had also to keep an eye on the printing department which was of growing importance to the Mission and he was editor of the monthly journal, referred to by H.W. in his letter to Grace, *Ebifa mu Buganda* - roughly "What's going on in Buganda"- which by 1915 had a circulation of 1300. He was also expected in his "spare time", to help and advise village pastors in the neighbourhood of Budo.

In the same annual Letter he suggested that the school routine continued much the same, but in fact he soon introduced an incentive to foster more enthusiasm for practical education. In 1913 six boys were granted special entry to concentrate on carpentry or printing. They were not required to sit the English paper in their entrance examination and when admitted were taught English in a separate class. But they were to be taught all other subjects in the normal classes and "to join in all school activities on an absolutely equal footing".[2] They were required to pay only three-quarters of the normal annual fee. It was an enterprising idea, but in his Letter for 1914, Weatherhead conceded:

> Our scheme for entering some boys on a technical side at lower fees has not caught on. The people do not regard this school as intended for such training and they will manage to find the full fees to enable their boys to attend the ordinary course.[3]

It was a well-intentioned initiative, but the school might have done more to encourage a high value for practical skills by maintaining the standard fee; the human conviction that what costs less must be inferior, seems to run deep in most civilisations.

The students were responding well, however, to a range of opportunties intended to "supplement the ordinary bookwork". Handicrafts, gymnastics, games, debates, lantern-slide shows - given on a lantern presented by a Dublin parish - and lectures by visitors on topics of general interest, were all well supported. The students also helped to complete the furnishing of the chapel, making the original font and lectern in the Mackay workshop.[4] At the service in July 1912, at which Bishop Willis dedicated the chapel to the memory of the Martyrs, Yusufu Lugalama, Maliko Kakumba and Nuwa Serwanga, the choir sang a hymn composed by some of the members and a senior student was at the organ. Many of the "boys" had been church Sunday school teachers before coming to Budo, and in their spare time they helped in the nearby village parishes. Weatherhead wrote:

> I have paid surprise visits to some of the churches during the year and on the last occasion heard the service reverently led by one boy and a really thoughtful sermon preached by another. On one occasion the sermon began by emphasising the honour that the village folk were enjoying by having a visit from the European in charge of the King's School! Another of our boys has been teaching four of our cooks and the school porter the gospel, preparatory to baptism.[5]

For many years there had been a great demand for overseas scholarships for Ugandan students. Budo received its first in 1912. Ernest Millar had been ordered by the mission doctors to return to England for rest and offered to take two young Baganda, who had received some education, on a tour of Britain. He chose his own secretary and Yacobo Sajabi, one of the masters at Budo, who taught printing and was sub-editor of *Ebifa.* "They were both asked to keep diaries of their tour and to write articles for *Ebifa*, to share their experiences with their countrymen. They visited Cambridge - and Oxford - and Clifton College, where their visit coincided with one from King George V and Queen Mary. They were also received by the Archbishop of Canterbury. One of the things that interested them most was the education of young children in a Council elementary school."[6]

The year 1913 saw the first rise in school fees, after seven years. The costs of food and wages had been rising steadily and Weatherhead announced that fees must be increased from 100 to 120 rupees a year. He hoped that, as students had little trouble in earning 15 rupees a month as soon as they left, the parents would be willing to pay the higher fees.

The blow may have been softened by the arrival of a second European teacher, Revd George Garrett who, with his wife, had worked in Sierra Leone for several years, and had just arrived in Uganda. He was to be associated with Budo for the next thirteen years, but spent only five of them as a member of staff. He taught with Weatherhead for six months in 1913 before being appointed headmaster of Mengo High School.

In his prize giving address in 1913, HTC Weatherhead announced that numbers had risen as fast as he had hoped. There was accommodation for 92 students and at present there were 80. He doubted whether a healthy demand would be much more than this for a few years. He denied any risk that the school might be "educating the native too much". Great stress was being laid on the school spirit, which he was convinced was the strength of the English public school; boys were being developed by this spirit, while remaining "as African as ever."[7] His work for other schools, inspecting and advising as far afield as Bunyoro, was highly valued and he himself was presented with a "prize". It was a motor-cycle, subscribed for by the Kabaka, the Katikkiro, the regents, chiefs and Old Budonians.

Though 1914 ended bleakly, it was a good year for the school. Until Garrett left for Mengo the staffing position was comfortable. A new development was the regular teaching of Hygiene by doctors from Mengo Hospital, who set terminal examinations along with all other subjects.[8] In June H.T.C. Weatherhead took 40 boys to Nairobi, on an expedition similar to HW's in 1910. But the great event of the year was not a school activity. On 7 November, Kabaka Daudi Chwa II, now of age, was invested as Kabaka of Buganda in the school chapel. He had been a frequent visitor and, after he had made an educational tour of Britain in 1912, had intimated that he wished to be regarded as an Old Budonian.[9]

Daudi Chwa II was the first Christian Kabaka and though some of the traditional ceremonies were observed at the investiture the service also followed many features of the British coronation service. First, Daudi strode up the last rise of the road to the top of Budo Hill and was challenged, according to custom, by *Semanobe*, though there was no mock fight. Then he walked in procession to the chapel, where Anglicans, Catholics and Muslims joined in the service, with the singing led by the school choir. The procession then moved to a pavilion, specially built near the chapel, where the new Kabaka took an oath to be faithful to the law and custom of the country, to which all previous Kabakas had been declared superior. He was then presented, by selected chiefs, with:

A shield - for he must be a defence to his people.

A rod - for he must rule his people righteously and in judgement remember mercy.

A short sword - with which he shall cut a just judgement.

A handful of twigs - of which baskets are made-to betoken a long life, for however often a basket falls to the ground, yet it is not broken, as a vessel of clay.[11]

This impressive occasion with its blend of Kiganda and British traditional ceremony may have encouraged Budo students and teachers in their own efforts to take what was good from an alien culture while keeping what was best in their own.

As the number of students and the pressure for places continued to grow, Weatherhead insisted that it was quality not numbers that mattered:

Our only honours list can be the esteem in which our Old Boys are held. The reports we hear of them are good on the whole and it is certainly the case that a Budo boy finds no difficulty in obtaining the higher kinds of employment in the country. Amongst the Old Boys themselves there is a healthy esprit de corps and several times we have had some of them, who live close enough, spending Sunday at Budo.[12]

At the farewell supper in December 1912, however, he read out a letter he had received from some Old Boys who said that after he had retired they would no longer attend the suppers because the European who would replace him would not know them. He told the Old Boys and "leavers" present that this must not be so. They did not come for the sake of the headmaster but for the school which they had passed through. They must continue coming, whoever was headmaster.[13] His plea seems to have been heeded and the Old Boys began to think beyond the "Weatherhead Era". In March 1914 the Old Budonian Association was formed, with the Kabaka as its patron; the president was to be "the headmaster of Budo, whoever he will be".[14] The first secretary of the Association was S.W. Kulubya, at that time deputy speaker of the National Assembly, later Mayor of Kampala and for many years *Omuwanika* (Treasurer) of the government of Buganda.

One of the first of his many services to the Association was to arrange the production of a Budonian blazer. But he endorsed the frequent warnings that Budo students received against snobbery and bad example:

> Please note that the blazer is only to be worn when coming to the functions of the school, or for sports. It is not to be worn when going to work or to try to impress other people, because this will only cause ill-feeling among non-Budonians, and we shall be despised by the Europeans and the older Baganda.[15]

The association soon became well known in East Africa, not only for its interest in the school but also for social and sporting activities. Many members have served on the Board of Governors and it has usually been a strength - and always a stimulus - to headmasters. After the Second World War it was also to become influential in Ugandan party politics.

Budo now became involved in the 1914-1918 War. Soon after it began in August 1914, several students volunteered for the army. Among them Ashe Mukasa was quickly promoted sergeant and later commissioned lieutenant; Nasanaeri Mayanja commanded a detachment which manned part of the Buganda border. Weatherhead offered the school's support in any other way and when, in December, the government decided that the Kampala police force must be sent to the Tanganyika frontier, he agreed to try to provide a temporary force from the school. Of his remaining 76 students, 50 volunteered. He selected a squad of 25 which, trained and drilled, formed the Kampala police force for the next year. So for the whole of 1915 the school had only about 50 students and some normal sporting activities had to be curtailed. Other high schools and central schools were losing teachers to the army; seven senior Budo students volunteered to suspend their studies to go to teach in them.

In spite of all these depletions the annual leavers' supper and prizegiving was still held in December, with guests including the Kabaka and two government education officers, H.O. Savile and D.G. Tomblings, who in the 1920s were to become the first and second principals of Makerere College, Uganda's future university. After a drill display by members of the Budo Kampala police force, Weatherhead reported on the year's work and said how delighted he was to have round the tables so many Old Budonians from distant parts of the country. He had often hoped that one day they would form a gathering big enough to fill the schoolroom and now were they were.[16] Secretary Serwano Kulubya however had a stern word for the gathering:

> Many of us despise certain jobs and hanker after clerical jobs and interpreting, as the only fit work for educated men. This is not the educated man's attitude.[17]

Public debate about the purposes of Budo education was re-opened early in the new year.

The mission had realised that its provision for the effective training of teachers was inadequate and demand was rising every year. There was no training college to which boys could proceed from the high schools. Although the Normal School at Mengo trained teachers at a low level, mainly for the bush schools, it was still to Budo that the higher grade schools looked for their staff. All the central schools in Buganda now had Old Budonian headmasters and there were CMS high schools at Mengo, at Mbarara in Ankole, at Kabarole (Fort Portal) in Toro, at Kamuli and Mbale in Eastern Province and at Gulu in Northern Province. In March 1915 CMS convened a conference at Budo, with teacher training the main item for discussion.

The headmaster of the Mengo Normal School, Revd J. Britton, read an opening paper. He believed the present provision was outdated and that unless the Mission's schoolmasters all had a good all-round education - which they could get only at Budo - they would be badly left behind in competence and social position.

> What is painfully obvious at home [in Britain] is found to be true here. It is a sound general education that brings out the true educationalist, and not a poor education filled out with desperate efforts to create a mechanical educationalist on some approved pattern.[18]

He proposed that his own Normal School should be closed and that all teachers for the high and central schools should be trained at Budo.

The prestige already accorded to a Budo education, after only nine years, was reflected in his assertion that if the conference accepted his proposal:

> All our teachers would be able to bargain for proper salaries, just as Budo boys do now.[19]

His proposal was approved by the conference and the Church Board of Education established five grades of teacher; those at the top of the scale were to be called simply "Budo teachers". A few days after the conference the high school at Mbale moved to its present fine site at Nabumali and re-opened with an Old Budonian headmaster.

The conference had not yet finished with Budo. Some missionaries remained unhappy about the aims of the school. E.S. Daniell, although an admirer of the Weatherheads and Bishop Tucker, and friend to many Budo students, put the case forcefully in a paper on "Education and the Sacred Ministry". In his anxiety about ministry he seemed to ignore the dominant contribution Budo was already making to teaching in the Mission's many schools:

> Budo is our highest school and one from which we had looked to obtain clergy and teachers and have so far looked in vain. One would ask "Why is it?" ... Should Budo become a feeder to the theological colleges, as other schools feed Budo? The existence of Budo depends upon the junior schools sending on their best scholars. Is it too much to ask for Budo to send on its best too? In theory one agrees fully with the broad principle adopted at the outset by the founders of Budo - the healthy Christianity, the bringing of religion into daily life in any honourable calling, a principle that must do the school and nation incalculable good. But at the same time we must remember ... that if we raise up an educated community alongside a poorly educated ministry, then the Church will get into disrepute.[20]

Four generations of Ugandan Christians have sometimes been painfully aware of the truth of his final sentence. But he had undervalued Budo's achievements and over-stated his case for a change of direction. In spite of shared anxiety about the ministry, the conference did not accept his paper. It was a turning point for the King's School: from then on the Weatherhead/Tucker objectives have gone unchallenged.

H.T.C. Weatherhead responded enterprisingly to the expressed wish for even more Budonian teachers and in the third term of 1915 launched a specific "Normal class". CMS Uganda decided that any teachers who had trained at the old Mengo Normal School and had gone on to teach at high schools would have to join the Normal class at Budo if they wished to continue teaching at high school level. This would be particularly difficult for married men with families and Weatherhead appealed for funds to provide scholarships.[21]

The annual Letter for 1915 was positive and optimistic in spite of wartime pressures. More students had joined the army, but some of their places had been filled by keen ex-teachers joining the Normal class. The results in the final leaving examinations, for a certificate which now had considerable status in East Africa but was not yet officially recognised overseas, were the best so far. Two students gained First Class certificates and ten Second Class. It was therefore a surprise when the Katikkiro, who continued to be a strong supporter of Budo, took his two sons away from the school and sent them to Trinity College, Kandy in Ceylon, where A.G. Fraser, a co-founder of Budo, was now headmaster. H.T.C. was clearly indignant, but chose his words carefully:

> The experiment of sending two boys to Trinity College, Kandy will be watched with great interest. I cannot say that I was consulted about it.[22]

Another experiment which has had more permanent results was the introduction of cricket at Budo, in 1915. The school has the longest continuous cricketing record among Uganda schools, though the game was played first at a school in Hoima the year before. H.T.C. deserves all the more credit for his far-sighted sporting enterprise because H.W. had considered the possibility in 1908, revealing his apathy and terminological ignorance in words which must sear the soul of any devotee: The "plant" was too expensive.[23]

Other notable events of 1915 were an informal visit from Governor Sir Frederick Jackson, the presentation by Captain Douglas Tomblings of a prize for Luganda composition and the gift to Sabaganzi Weatherhead of a leopard skin, subscribed for by 75 Old Budonians and to be shipped to England for him. H.T.C. had been able to do many more school visits on his motor-cycle and had organised a schools guild, which brought the schools together - usually at Budo - for exhibitions, competitions and sports.

The years 1916 and 1917 were difficult for the mission and its schools. Budo seems to have gone along quietly, with its reduced population, though early in 1916 the first expulsions occurred. Three boys were permanently excluded for misconduct during the holidays; the CMS report noted a difficulty which remains for many boarding schools in the twenty-first century:

> The general tone of the school is good, but the temptations of the holidays are great.[24]

Many missionaries served in the ambulance units or the army for as long as they were needed, returning to their own or other mission stations when they could. The headmaster of Mengo High School was at Budo for a few months in 1916 and again in 1917, while Weatherhead was on leave. There were heavy demands on the school in that year. The Board of Education was satisfied that the Budo Teachers scheme was running well, and the up-country schools wanted as many Budo trained teachers as they could get.[25] Again several students volunteered to suspend their studies and went, alone, to teach in schools which had lost all their staff. A Gayaza girl commended them:

> The boys of Budo are better than we are at giving themselves. They do not leave a school unless there is someone to take their place, and of course they have more places to fill in the high schools and central schools.[26]

In mid-year there was more fighting in Tanganyika and the African Native Medical Corps was re-formed. The entire second and third year classes at Budo volunteered, with their teachers, and were accepted. The force was 1000 strong and the adjutant was Captain Douglas Tomblings. Budo students, many of whom did not return till the end of 1918 when the war was over, served in hospitals as far afield as Turkana and the Zambezi. For a year the school was half-empty.

Ernest Millar had been a generous and energetic supporter of the school throughout its first eleven years. He had cycled from Mengo to Budo almost every Saturday afternoon and knew every student personally - during his leave in 1916 he had written to every student and to a good number of Old Budonians as well. In January 1917 he was taken ill while on the way to Budo and had to be carried up the hill to the school. He died a few days later. The thousands of Ugandans who attended his funeral justify the inscription on his grave - *Omukwano gwa Baganda* - Friend of the Baganda.[27] So did the sum of £2000 which he left to Budo for buildings and scholarships. The clock on the Big School building, given in his memory by Old Budonians in 1924, was re-installed in the new Big School 30 years later; the Millar scholarships have enabled many students to complete their studies at the school.

September 1917, while the war still raged and the issue was still in doubt, saw a development which would be crucially important to Budo and to all Ugandan education. H.R. Wallis, chief secretary and Acting Governor pending the arrival of Sir Robert Coryndon, was a keen supporter of the mission schools and convened the first conference on education to be attended by members of all the missions and of the government. The Mill Hill Fathers, White Fathers and the CMS were well represented and there were three far-reaching outcomes. The government defined its policy on education, which was that it would recognise and, where possible, support any educational efforts by individual organisations which were in line with general government policy. It established a permanent Advisory Board on Education to assist the mission boards; and it increased its annual grant from £1250 to £2000, of which the Native Anglican Church - which for educational purposes meant the CMS - was to receive £1000.[28]

Weatherhead returned in November 1917 from leave in England. He had been away eight months - two and a half of which had been taken up by the tortuous journey back in wartime conditions. For the next three and a half years, until 1921, he and his wife were the only Europeans at Budo. For most of 1918 the school was forced to "mark time", with so many staff and students away. But the Old Budonians, of whom there were now 198, gathered strength. They held weekly meetings, with an average attendance of 40, met daily for Bible study, and ran a successful football club with a regular fixture list. The Budo teachers were now a strong force in Ugandan education, distributed among ten high schools. More than 30 of them attended their first conference at Budo late in 1918.

By the end of the year the staff and students who had served in the war were trickling back. Weatherhead had promised that any student whose course had been interrupted, could if he wished return to complete it. January 1919 saw 102 students in accommodation designed for 92, one classroom having been converted to a dormitory. Reports and letters during the year were optimistic, but Weatherhead wrote of a problem which would recur more potently 30 years later. He sensed that many students had been disturbingly informed by their war experiences and were reaching out to a nationalist feeling, very keen on national progress and not yet wise to distinguish between externals and essence.[29]

His 1912 catalogue of the responsibilities of a lone European at Budo was even more resonant seven years on. He badly needed experienced help with teaching and administration and the Kabaka wrote to Bishop Willis, appealing for a second European teacher to be appointed.[30] But the mission was still understaffed so soon after the war; only two of the ten high schools had a European teacher. E.S. Daniell would have been an ideal choice - he wrote years later that H.W. had wanted him in 1905 and he had wanted to go, but Bishop Tucker needed him elsewhere. He was now Warden of Bishop Tucker College, Mukono, the one CMS advanced Theological College.

The annual letter for 1920 shows Weatherhead planning for the future and as keen as ever about technical education. There were 120 candidates for the entrance examination and though he judged 70 of them to be good enough there were places for only 30. He was convinced that only about 30 students each year should be going out to clerical and administrative jobs and he still hoped that the government would soon give a large grant to set up a full technical school, at Budo or elsewhere, and also a training unit for technicians and craftsmen for the growing Public Works Department.[31] Fees had been raised again to 150 rupees and because the government scholarship fund had remained at £ 200 there were now only 7 scholarships instead of 10. He praised the continuing enthusiasm of Ugandan parents for education but warned that young men would have to start school younger. He wanted them to enter Budo at 16 instead of the present 18 or 19.

There was a positive side to the shortage of European staff. Ugandan education was already considerably "Africanised". Weatherhead had four Baganda assistant masters and thought highly enough of them to appoint each to the headship of a subject department throughout the school and give them each the full responsibility for a house. As secretary of the Church Board of Education, he outlined a plan for future development.[32]   Taking a realistic view of the huge expansion required and the relatively small resources of the missions, he stressed that the Protectorate government must now take more interest and reponsibility. He acknowledged that if government provided most of the finance it would properly expect to exercise a good deal of control. The final stage would be for the nation itself gradually to assume financial responsibility and to take control. It was the natives of the country who would be best able to plan a system of education suited to their own needs.

In January 1921 Weatherhead received some well-earned assistance. Garrett returned to the school for nine months, before going on to Ankole where the high school at Mbarara was going well under the headship of Revd H.M. Grace. For the whole year Weatherhead also had the help of Revd John Lea-Wilson and since, in May, 18 students left, numbers were a manageable 90. He must have felt almost luxurious. Fourteen of the May leavers became teachers. In the annual Letter for 1921 he welcomed the news that the government was to open a big technical school, at Makerere, and that a long-standing friend of Budo, H.O. Savile, would be running it. Budo would therefore not now expand its own technical work, though printing and carpentry would continue. A feature of the year, reflecting a dramatic worldwide development, had been a special fourth-year course for potential telegraphists, who had studied by themselves beforehand and had some special training from a Muganda expert from the Post Office. Two Budonians had already passed the course at Voi, in Kenya, after leaving school and four more were now going on to it. Budo was continually being asked to mount specialist courses but Weatherhead thought that, on balance, this should not form part of its programme:

> It after all seems the most practical plan to give a good general education here, adapted to the present needs of the country, for with this many of our Old Boys can make progress in particular directions afterwards.[33]

He welcomed the government decision to provide an inspector of schools.

Among Budo successes this year had been the winning of the two top scholarships to the government training school for medical assistants; Weatherhead noted that many Budo students still thought that the English word "Cook" was another term for "doctor" - such had been the impact of the Cook brothers at Mengo Mission Hospital. There were now 303 Old Budonians and the Association had opened branches in Busoga and Bunyoro.[34] Old Budonians, and particularly Budo teachers, had taken the influence of the school well beyond Buganda and in 1923 further branches were opened in Toro and Ankole.

Weatherhead had no European colleague again for the first term of 1923 but in April he was joined by Lieut. Commander Edward Callwell, who had met Grace in Kenya and been persuaded by him to come to teach in Uganda.[35] Grace had by then become headmaster of Mengo High School and knew of Budo's needs. Callwell was a handyman, as he was later to demonstrate fully in the difficult early years of Nyakasura School in Toro. He soon made his mark at Budo, teaching mathematics, supervising the building of staff houses, making the swimming pool hold water again, and mending the Millar clock. He planned and supervised an extension to Canada House, which enabled Weatherhead, who was perturbed at the number of strong applicants he was having to refuse, to admit 40 new boys at the start of the 1923 school year, instead of the usual 30. The annual Letter reported that academic progress had been satisfactory, with six students gaining First Class certificates. Athletics and football continued to flourish and there were now inter-house competitions in tennis and swimming.[36]

In his speech at the farewell supper for school leavers, Weatherhead spoke of the importance of "public opinion" and how a strong and right one could help to mould the nation. He stressed what a force for good Old Budonians ought to be and urged them to keep up their support of one of their most original initiatives - the financing of Budo's own missionary, Revd Kosia Shalita, an Old Budonian at that time working in Teso and later to become Bishop of Ankole-Kigezi.

The Letter for 1923 concentrated on the future of education throughout the country. Weatherhead believed that government must now either give much larger grants for the expansion of the mission schools or establish some of its own. He had been glad to have visits from the government education adviser in December and when in the same month the news reached Uganda that the Phelps-Stokes Fund of New York was to send a commission to East Africa, similar to the one it had previously sent to West Africa, to report on education needs and recommend future development, he decided to postpone his overdue leave in England and stayed to help.

The commission arrived in Uganda in March 1924. It was led by Dr Thomas Jesse Jones, an American educationalist who had led the commission to West Africa. Among the members was Dr James Aggrey later a co-founder of Achimota College, and Dr Garfield Williams of the CMS. They visited Makerere College and the Roman Catholic and CMS schools. In his report Dr Jones wrote:

> An educational system which branches out into the whole Protectorate has been brought into being in co-operation with the native chiefs but without any supervision from the Colonial Government, and until recently without any financial support. It is an educational achievement of which the missions can be legitimately proud. Considering that educational work began in the Kingdom of Buganda only thirty years ago and that in some of the areas of most rapid development, in Eastern Province, education was introduced only a dozen years ago, the progress is amazing.[37]

But there was constructive criticism too:

> With full appreciation of the services of the past, it is now generally
> recognised by missionary societies and government alike, that
> educational facilities must now be enlarged and better adapted to
> the needs of the native people... The type of education has been too
> exclusively literary... and there has been practically no provision
> for agricultural education... It is sad to see that the technical work
> of the CMS in Uganda seems to have fallen on evil days.[38]

The commission made six specific recommendations, two of which
had already been partly implemented. The government was urged to
appoint a director of education; to set up a department or board of
education; to give immediate, generous grants to the missions for the
improvement of their schools, and to set up, in consultation with the
missions, a wide system of school supervision and inspection. A re-
grading of the schools into four groups was proposed, along with the
speedy introduction of classes in hygiene and agriculture.

The Weatherheads had tried hard to develop education along the
lines that the commission was proposing, though there had been
disappointments and omissions; Budo had its agricultural projects
but sometimes the boys had not done enough of the work.[39] The
government's sensible decision to concentrate technical education
initially at Makerere, made it unlikely that strong technical education
could also be funded at Budo, as the Weatherheads had hoped.
With a government education department and the Phelps-Stokes
recommendations in support, Budo was to make great progress in the
next few years, but this should not be allowed to imply that the school
had been in a bad way.

This tribute was the more remarkable, as was well-known, King's
School, had fallen on evil days.[40] The Commission's severe comment
about CMS technical education was applied, 40 years later, specifically
to Budo, in C.K. Williams's *History of Achimota College*. He seems to
have assumed that Budo was mainly a technical school, and to have
been unaware of the Makerere development. Of Julian Huxley's 1931
compliment to Budo under Grace (see chapter 4) he wrote:

The twelfth year of Weatherhead's taxing headship the Commissioners recorded its impressions.

This institution, situated about ten miles from Kampala, is for the general education of boys. Its staff nominally includes two Europeans and four or five native teachers. The subjects taught are the Bible, arithmetic, geography, history, English, hygiene and manual training. Typewriting and printing are taught to a few boys. The buildings and general arrangement of grounds are attractive. The spirit of the school is good. The institution has developed standards of behaviour and traditions of loyalty that are effective in their influence on the character of the students. Even without the necessary facilities for training in teaching, the school has produced some of the best teachers in Uganda.

It is hoped that the new educational plans of the CMS and the Government, will enable Budo to relate its instruction and training more nearly to the needs of the people. It should be possible to preserve the best traditions of the institution, to raise the standard of instruction as the lower schools improve, and to train teachers who shall be the leavening influence for a service related to the health, the agriculture, the industry, the home and the character of the people.[41]

It was an emphatic vote of confidence in Budo, but one that made heavy demands. The key ambition - to raise the standard - also raised a key question: Would not specialist teachers be more useful to the future education service than the general all-round handymen who did their best to meet whatever challenges arose - and often became teachers by accident? Garrett, for example, often said that he was a missionary first and an educationalist second. One of his fellow CMS missionaries, H. Gresford Jones, who became Bishop of Kampala in 1920, had no doubt about the way forward. His comments on the Phelps-Stokes commissioners' high praise of the womens' educational efforts, notably at Gayaza, recalled H.T.C. Weatherhead's plea of 1912:

The less settled regime in the boys' schools, which is criticised by the Commissioners, is easily traceable to the circumstance that the clergyman in charge of a school may also have to be in charge of everything else on the station - agriculture, finance, transport, building, road-making, to say nothing of that which presses on him daily, the care of the churches in his district. It is open to question whether the new educational proposals, together with the government offer that accompanies them, do not create a demand for a serious restatement of missionary service. The very word "missionary" - so convenient professionally - is infelicitous in other respects. It obscures the line of demarcation between the different vocations that have come to the aid of the church overseas in recent years. We need today bishops, clergy, doctors, matrons, nurses , schoolmasters, engineers, technical instructors. Why not call them so? Their professional work is, in the main, the same abroad as at home. Yet if they cross the straits of Dover they are all classified as "missionaries", and the result, if unhelpful in other cases, is perhaps especially unfortunate as regards the new educational developments.[42]

The change of attitude he appealed for was only slowly achieved and although Budo did fairly well in this respect, standards in Ugandan schools might have risen faster if the missions had recruited more specialist teachers. Some clergy - Protestant and Catholic - may have believed that more important influences in their schools could have been weakened by this strategy.

H.T.C. Weatherhead went on his postponed leave in England soon after the commission left Uganda. Like his brother in 1912, he expected to return to Budo, so Garrett was asked to be acting headmaster for six months. At the end of the year, however, after 24 years with Uganda CMS, Weatherhead resigned, partly for health reasons. Like Sabaganzi he never saw his school again. He had led Budo calmly and skilfully through many difficult years, particularly during the First World War, when he had always put the needs of the country before the convenience of the school, managing Budo with badly depleted resources. His relationships with students, teaching colleagues, parents, Old Budonians, government officers of both the Protectorate and the kingdom of Buganda, church leaders and individual clan chiefs, all seem to have been friendly and creative, with no record of even minor disagreements - his occasional blunt statements apparently neither disputed nor resented. He made a huge contribution to the King's School and - through his many tours of inspection - to many other schools all over the country.

Garrett, who was ably supported by Callwell, reported that 1924 had been a peaceful year. There had been a record number of applicants and though he could admit only 30 he thought at least 100 had been worthy of places. Six leavers had gained First Class certificates and the report of the examiner in English had been particularly encouraging:

> The marks are much higher than in previous years, the average being 63%. It was noticeable that in Oral work the standard had improved considerably, especially in ability to understand spoken English. This is probably due to the greater amount of teaching now being done in English instead of the vernacular.[43]

Garrett shared the Weatherheads' conviction that the school must be "outward looking" and twice in the year students and staff from fifty bush schools in the area had been invited to spend a day at Budo, for sports and competitions; the school had "fed a vast horde".[44] In an attempt to combat drunkenness, the students had also entertained men from the nearby villages to tea and coffee parties. Garrett urged the students and all Old Budonians, of whom there were now 450, to be aware that change was inevitable and to help to make it successful. In particular he asked that there should be no foolish talk about Budo competing with the Government College at Makerere, which deserved support from all the schools.

> When we hear of their success we shall be delighted.[45]

The Phelps-Stokes report, the progress of Makerere and the promise of government support encouraged the Church Board of Education to plan the expansion of Budo. Grace at Mengo and Garrett, with enthusiastic support from Bishop Willis, were keen to build up the complete age-range of preparatory, middle and senior schools, all on Budo Hill and under one headmaster. The preparatory department would be new, taking boys from age 7 to 13. The middle school would be created by transplanting Mengo High school to Budo. The senior department would be formed by the present Budo students, studying to higher levels in preparation for entrance to Makerere College.

In October 1924 a meeting held in the Katikkiro's office and attended by the Kabaka, Omuwanika and Katikiro of Buganda, Grace and all the leading Protestant chiefs, agreed that the school should have a much larger and more influential Board of Governors, almost all African; that all three departments should have a European in charge, under the overall direction of the headmaster; that Baganda teachers who were given overseas scholarships to train as teachers for Budo, should first have to pass a local examination and sign an agreement to serve on the Budo staff for a specified period. Finally and most importantly, it was agreed that the money needed for the many new buildings required, should be subscribed by the Baganda.[46]

The sum needed would be 546,000 shillings - £ 27,000 - and an advertisement was circulated, explaining how it would be raised over the next four years.[47]   The Kabaka and every Protestant chief would all give 20% of their annual rates; every chief with fewer than 10 ratepayers would give $1/_{80}$ of his annual rates; every Protestant who had any ratepayers was to give 2 shillings a year. Chiefs and landowners from Ankole, Busoga, Bunyoro, Bukedi and Toro were also invited to subscribe, because the school would continue to admit boys from all over Uganda. The Katikiro, Sir Apolo Kagwa, was elected Treasurer of the fund which was to be administered by the headmaster of the re-constituted King's College, Budo.

It remained to appoint the overall headmaster. The choice lay between Garrett who had spent most of his 13 years in Uganda in pastoral work, and Grace who had served 12 years as a teacher and been headmaster of Mbarara and Mengo High Schools. Early in 1925 the Board of Governors appointed Grace; a period of rapid expansion and prosperity seemed to lie ahead.

Notes

[1] Annual Letter for 1912, KCB archives

[2] *Uganda Notes*, No 11, Vol. 13, October 1913, p. 236.

[3] *Ibid* No. 12, Vol. 16, January 1915, p.296.

[4] Church Missionary Gleaner, CMS London, 1 November 1912, p.12

[5] Annual Letter, 1912

[6] C.M. Gleaner, *op. cit* p. 13.

[7] *Uganda Notes*, no 13, vol. 15, January 1914, p.21

[8] *Ibid*

[9] Proceedings of CMS 1913-14, CMS London, p. 70

[10] Roscoe J. *op.cit* p. 193

[11] *Uganda Notes*, No. 12 Vol. 15, December 1914, p. 266

[12] Annual Letter, 1912

[13] *Ebaluwa eri Banabudo abe* King's School, January 1913, KCB archives

[14] *Ibid*, February 1915

[15] *Ibid*

[16] *Ibid*

[17] *Ibid*

[18] *Uganda Notes*, No. 16, Vol. 16, May 1915, p. 391

[19] *Ibid*, p. 388

[20] *Uganda Notes*, Vol 17, July 1916 p. 102

[21] *Ibid*, Vol. 16, December 1915, p.554

[22] *Ibid*

[23] *Uganda Notes*, June 1908, p. 95

[24] Proceedings of CMS 1915-16, CMS London, p. 58

[25] *Uganda Notes*, vol. 19, January 1918, p. 2.

[26] Proceedings of CMS 1919-20, p. 33

[27] Cook, A. *op.cit.* p. 321

[28] *Uganda Notes*, Vol. 19, January 1918, pp 27-28, and July 1918, p. 63

[29] Proceedings of CMS 1919-29, p.33

[30] *Uganda Notes*, Vol. 20, July 1919 p. 55

[31] *Ibid*, Vol 21, October 1920 p. 91

[32] *Ibid*, pp. 144 et sqq.

[33] CMS Uganda Annual Report, Budo Press, 1921, p. 30.

[34] *Ebaluwa eri Banabudo* 1921 KCB archives

[35] Grace, H.M. to McGregor GP 20 July 1964, KCB archives

[36] *Ebaluwa eri Banabulo*, 1922

[37] Education in East Africa, Phelps-Stokes Fund, New York; London, Edinburgh House, 1925, p.151.

[38] *Ibid* pp. 162-3

[39] Annual Letter for 1912

[40] Education in East Africa, *op. cit pp. 156-7*

[41] Jones, H. Gresford, *Uganda in Transformation*, London CMS 1926, *pp. 188-9*

[42] Williams, C.K., *Achimota: The Early Years*, Longman Green, 1962, p. 94

[43] *Ebaluwa eri Banabudo* 1924

[44] *Ibid*

[45] *Ebaluwa eri Banabudo* 1925

[46] Minutes of Meeting 24 October 1924, KCB archives

[47] Printed copies, KCB archives.

4

Visions and Disappointments
1925-1934

Harold Myers Grace was another Cambridge man, from Queens' College. He had come out with the CMS to the high school at Mbarara in Ankole in 1914 and though he had to be away from it for much of the war period, serving with the Labour Corps, he had quickly built up its reputation for lively and useful learning. Gresford Jones wrote of the CMS high schools:

> The spirit is the thing. It is the spirit of the school at its best, as we have breathed it in England after generations of experiment - the spirit of the team, of discipline, of local patriotism - and very remarkable has been the translating of it into the heart of Africa.[1]

Grace believed that such a spirit at Mbarara had been largely fostered by the scout troop which he had founded at the school in 1915 - the first troop in Uganda. When therefore he was persuaded, reluctantly, to become headmaster of Mengo High School in 1921, one of his first proposals, to raise morale, was to start a school troop there. But times had changed. As H.T.C. Weatherhead had noted, there was a new spirit of nationalsim and it was among the men who had returned from war service. The Mengo chiefs, knowing that the scout movement had been born of Baden-Powell's experiences in the Boer War, believed that Grace wanted to train their sons for Britain's next war and that the Scout Promise might make them liable to be "called up" by the government. Grace was convinced that mutual trust between students, parents, staff and governors was the only sound basis on which to run a school. He later told the rest of the story:

> I said that it was not so and that they must trust me and give me time to prove it, but that until they would trust me I would resign the headship of the High School. I was absent from my duties

for three weeks, until Sir Apolo Kagwa wrote and said that they were prepared to take my word. I think the result today, as far as the Scouts are concerned, is satisfactory.[2]

In Grace's four years as headmaster, Mbarara High School had recovered much of its earlier prestige and numbers rose from 35 boys to 175. During the visitations of the Phelps-Stokes Commission, Dr Aggrey stayed with Grace for two weeks and, appreciating his qualities and potential, took a step which helped to mould the future of Budo and later of Achimota College as well.

Grace was due for leave in 1925 and Aggrey invited him and his wife to visit the southern states of the USA, to see the progress that had been made in Negro education. They were greatly impressed by the high standards of the institutes at Hampton in Virginia and Tuskegee in Alabama, by the shared happiness and culture of many of the Negro homes which they visited with Aggrey, and by the way men and women worked side by side, in the professions. Mrs Grace wrote an account of their visit for the *Uganda Church Review* and was clearly going to affect the reorganised Budo in at least two ways. They would set the highest standards, because they had seen them achieved in the southern states; they also now believed - in spite of the strong contrary tradition of the English public schools - that co-educational boarding schools might be right for Africa.

> As English people the idea does not come naturally to us... if we could devise some method by which the same end could be achieved without the actual bringing together of the boys and girls in the same school, this would be more in accordance with our English traditions. But the question is "can it be done?" And also, may it not be true that English traditions need revising for Africa?[3]

Mrs Grace ended diplomatically, suggesting that even if Uganda was not quite ready for co-education, it would be useful to get reports from Achimota and any other schools in Africa in which it was already being tried.

Partly because of his working tour in the USA, Grace's leave extended into 1926. Garrett was again acting headmaster; he not only kept the school running smoothly but, with the support of Bishop Willis - and the subsequent approval of Grace - took a farsighted and nationally valuable initiative. There was concern and division among the strong Muslim community in Uganda about the post-elementary education of the eighteen-year-old Prince Badru Kakungulu Wassajja, whose father, Nuhu Mbogo, was the brother of Kabaka Mutesa I, and leader of Uganda's Muslims. In his fine biography of the prince, ABK Kasozi records:

> Kakungulu was groomed for leadership from the start. He was often taken by his father to the Kabaka, Sir Daudi Chwa's palace, and allowed to see and listen to elders at court. He introduced him to many leaders, as well as issues, and made sure that he became the leader of the Muslim community, by briefing the Kabaka, Sir Daudi Chwa on the matter.[4]

For hundreds of years religion had been a powerful political and social force in the kingdom of Buganda. The arrival of the two alien world religions, Islam and Christianity, strengthened and complicated this influence. Kakungulu, as both senior member of the royal family and a religious leader of a large community, was a young man of great potential influence.

The young Kabaka realised the importance of a sound and broad education for Kakungulu, but there was not yet a school which could teach young Muslims a secular curriculum in a Muslim environment. So in April 1922 a large, newly built house on Kibuli hill, close to Kampala, was converted for that purpose and in June the prince, a month before his 15th birthday, joined 25 other students - the pioneers of what would gradually become a much-admired Muslim education complex, comprising primary and secondary schools and an advanced college of education for student teachers. By the end of 1923 he had completed all the courses Kibuli could then offer. The decision on what educational experiences should follow was important, not only to the Muslim community but to the governments of both the Protectorate and the kingdom of Buganda; Kasozi skilfully untangles the political and social intricacies.[5]

Governor Jarvis wrote to his counterparts in Sudan and Zanzibar, asking if they could offer a suitable facility which would be free from anti-British and anti-Islamic influence. Both regretfully turned down the request. At this point, Kabaka Daudi Chwa suggested that the prince should receive his secondary education at King's College, Budo:

> He was of the view that the Christian missionaries could be dissuaded from converting the prince to their religion. But the Muslim leaders categorically refused to have Prince Badru go to Budo. In this, they got support from an unexpectedly powerful source. In a special Lukiiko [Buganda Assembly] session, the Governor pointed out that he was of the view that Kakungulu should not be sent to Budo. He agreed...that the young prince should be taught by a private tutor.[6]

Governor Jarvis received a formal letter of thanks for his support, signed by 34 prominent members of the Muslim community. But the Kabaka was not to be denied. He consulted the prince, and obtained assurances from CMS Namirembe and from Garrett that there would be no attempts to convert the prince. He proposed special facilities for the prince - at the expense of the Kabaka's government. These would include a separate house on the edge of the school compound, servants and an educated Muslim cleric to instruct him further in the faith and lead him in prayer. Kakungulu himself wisely assured the leading signatories of the letter to Jarvis that he would remain faithful to Islam and in January 1925 Kabaka Daudi Chwa personally escorted the prince to Budo hill. The governor was pleased that the Kabaka had skilfully ended a "perplexing situation" and had relieved the Protectorate government of the responsibility.[7]

The solution was splendidly successful. The young prince proved an able and popular student and became an outstanding athlete and footballer. He was a regular member of the Budo XI, playing - in his first year - in a famous match in which King's College defeated Makerere to win the Kabaka's Cup, and later for several years captaining the strong Old Budonians Club. In athletics he quickly proceeded from the Budo team to the Uganda national squad and in 1927 beat the national 220 yards champion in a new record time which stood for several years.

He remained at Budo for the full three years, never abusing the liberal priveleges which Garrett, and then Grace, accorded him - including visits to the Lubiri for official functions. He became fluent in Kiswahili and Arabic as well as English, which greatly helped him in guiding and unifying the Muslim community in his 75 years of leadership. He made many Christian friends at Budo and the effects of his experiences there, in improving Muslim/ Christian relationships throughout Uganda, have been invaluable.

The Graces returned to Budo in April 1926. During their year's absence heated arguments had developed about the plans for Budo. Garrett had tried to counter the suspicious rivalry with Makerere, but an announcement that the government college was to launch a course of general education "to follow the pattern already established at Budo and Kisubi"[8] did not help. Like the founders of Budo, however, Grace looked ahead to eventual university education in Uganda and insisted that this could not come until the country had schools which could send on students with a high standard of general education. This, he was convinced, was the work that Budo could and should do. But it was hard to persuade the Baganda, justifiably proud of Budo, that it was Makerere rather than King's College, which should eventually become the University College of Uganda. Ham Mukasa's prophecy of 1906 may have cut deep.

Within a few weeks of his return, however, Grace seems to have persuaded everyone that a start should be made on the new scheme of turning Budo into a school for boys from junior to senior level and he and his wife moved house to Budo hill. The next six months must have been hard-going as he was headmaster of two sizeable schools ten miles apart. He went into Mengo by car on three days a week and his wife went with him, to work with and advise the masters who would be coming to Budo when the Mengo students transferred to form the junior department. They both found solace in the beauty of Budo Hill - a compensation for many a hard-pressed teacher and student for a hundred years. Molly Grace enthused in a circular letter to friends:

> Let me tell you about this hill... There are two great trees to mark the spot where the Kabakas are crowned and it is by these trees that

you can distinguish Budo from other hills for miles around. Lake Victoria is to be seen in the distance and between it and Budo and all around in every direction , great stretches of hills and valleys. In the early mornings the valleys are filled with mist, the hills rear their heads out of these misty seas, the sunlight on trees, flowers and paths makes the dew sparkle like diamonds and the place is a veritable fairyland. We are about eleven miles from Kampala and two miles off the main road, up a steep and winding track that curls up the side of the hill and eventually brings you out at the top in a breeze that we think peculiar to Budo, and a view that takes your breath away.[9]

There were six months in which to get Budo ready for the amalgamation of the two schools, and the hill, which had passed several tranquil years without major building projects, was rudely disturbed. Mrs Grace again described it vividly:

Straight ahead is the present school compound and to the left of this are rising the buildings of the future, forming four sides of an entirely second quadrangle. The bricks to build with are made in the valley below and all day long a Ford lorry is bringing them up from one set of hands to another. Quite a village has sprung up around the brick kilns; a hundred or so men work there and have built themselves little round mud huts, and many have their wives and children with them.[10]

Grace wanted people to know about the developments at Budo. In spite of the heavy workload of the two schools he remained chaplain to the English Church in Kampala, kept up his membership of the Kampala Sports Club - he played in goal for the First XI as often as he could manage - and so built up, through many friendships, the interest and co-operation of missionaries, government officials, businessmen and individual supporters, which became both a strength and a pleasure to the school.

It was some years since Budo had put on a show for the public, so in June 1926 the Graces helped to produce a shortened version of *Twelfth Night*. It seems to have been greatly enjoyed by the students, staff and a crowd of several hundred Ugandan and European guests, sitting on the slopes of the open-air theatre - its "backcloth" provided by a huge mango tree. One highlight of the performance came when Maria, unable to locate the letter for Malvolio in the folds of "her" flowing red dress, pulled up the dress and produced it from the pocket of "her" school shorts. But the year, which had promised so well for the school, ended gloomily.

First, Grace was taken ill and had to give up the work at Mengo and most of the supervision at Budo. Then, after a period of failing health and political difficulties with both the Protectorate government and restless Baganda chiefs - many of them Old Budonians[11] - Sir Apolo Kagwa resigned the post of Katikiro of Buganda, which he had held for 37 years. He died five months later, in February 1927. He left King's College 300 acres of land, fifty miles to the west, at Namutamba, which Grace was later able to put to good use. But for the present this generous bequest was small compensation for the loss of Sir Apolo's determined and perceptive support of Budo, and particularly of the Building Fund, at a critical time. His last statement as treasurer revealed that, of the £ 27,000 promised in 1924 over the next four years, only £ 2000 had been subscribed by November 1926 - most of it by the Kabaka and Sir Apolo himself. Already more work had been done than could be paid for. Finally, Commander Callwell, who had loyally supported Grace's vision and specific plans, was so disillusioned at the lack of support for them that he resigned from the school staff. He asked and received permission from CMS to found a secondary school in Toro on the Budo model. Like Miller, he was a man of private means and offered to meet some of the capital costs of the school himself. Under his able leadership the project flourished and became Nyakasura School, one of the best in Uganda. But his departure was a serious loss to Budo.

The expanded King's College, with its new junior, middle and upper school divisions, was due to open in January 1927 and in spite of these setbacks it did. Grace had been too ill to attend the last Leavers Party of the old school in December, but by mid-January he was much fitter. The 1925 building schedule had been for four new dormitories, each for 40 boys, and two large common rooms, all to be ready for the opening. In fact, one dormitory was ready and another, with one of the common rooms, well on the way. The rest would have to await further donations. Mrs Grace was undaunted:

> We have to see the funny side of it and picture a squirming mass of little boys squeezed into one building for the night a la Black Hole of Calcutta. But at any rate they will all have beds to sleep on and that is a great thing. They will also, we hope, have plenty to eat, but nothing to eat it with or on. Owing to the [General] Strike in England such details as plates, knives, forks and spoons are still on their way here.[12]

When the development plan had been agreed in 1924, the CMS had undertaken to provide the European teachers needed to maintain high standards in a school that would have over 300 students.

Many Old Budonians and parents seemed to think of more European staff solely as the means to more academic study; at the 1924 meeting there had been a proposal that Latin and Greek classes should be started at once. But Grace kept the Phelps-Stokes recommendations firmly in mind and in his report for 1926, published a few days before the school re-opened, he stressed that Budo was to remain a school, had no aspirations to become a university, and would be an African school in a real sense. The European staff would certainly be sent, but the support must come from the Baganda:

> You will realise that we are attempting to make a complete Public School, properly graded, with a Junior School attached. To do this the two most important schools in Buganda have been merged... We shall have, I hope, five European teachers this year ... and next year some of the Baganda now in Europe will be with us. So I am convinced that in a very few years you will see much greater progress coming from Budo and the high school than in the past - though let us not despise the past for without it we could not advance now. When we have this graded Public School, well staffed and well equipped, we shall quickly be able to attain the standards of Europe, even though some of our methods may be different, as we do not wish to de-nationalise Africans but, while giving them the wisdom of Europe, also keep them proud of their native traditions and race. For this reason we have the Budo Governors, of which committee the Kabaka has graciously agreed to act as chairman. The governors will, I hope, enable us to

keep the school African, and above all make your people realise "that it is their school and on the 'bataka" [sic] which is the most sacred in the country.

We Europeans who work with you will be amply repaid if we can see African Christian statesmen, lawyers, politicians, clergymen, farmers and businessmen coming from the school.[13]

By March 1927 the CMS had more than met its obligations to the development plan and Budo had six European teachers - having had a total of six in all its previous 21 years. Tom Harrison, a graduate in agriculture, and Stephen Wright, a graduate engineer, arrived late in 1926. With Grace, they were to share most of the senior school teaching. Joyce Evors from Chelsea Teacher Training College came in January, in time for the launch of the junior school which she was to lead, and Fred Robinson, an engineer and scientist, arrived in March from Mengo Hospital to teach in the middle school with Revd Lucian "Ginger" Usher-Wilson, an arts graduate, who some years later was appointed Bishop on the Upper Nile. Grace had also taken great care over the recruitment of eleven Ugandan teachers - all Old Budonians. Each was form-master of a whole class and Grace took pleasure in the quality of their work. Some moved on quickly to headships but Grace seemed able to attract excellent replacements. Among this first cadre he specially prized *Omwami* Nkata in the jumior school and *Omwami* Kaima who was to serve 22 years in the middle school. (Grace disliked the peremptory European habit of calling all Africans by their surnames only; he insisted that African colleagues be called *Omwami* (Luganda equivalent of "Mr") and their wives *Omukyala* (Mrs).)

Throughout 1927 this "team" - which was how Grace spoke and thought of them - concentrated on doing well the things that were already being done, and planning for the future. The Leaving Examination was now supervised by the government Education Department and known as the Government Final Examination. At the end of 1926, a disjointed and understaffed year, only 25 percent of Budo's seniors had passed. In December 1927 the figure was 75 percent. The leavers also excelled in a Luganda composition competition - which seemed to please Grace almost as much.[14]

School health was good throughout the year, helped by the skills of the new teachers. Wright had installed a "ram", which produced a much-improved supply of water; Robinson had taught classes in hygiene, and Harrison in simple bacteriology and health aspects of agriculture. All this was intended to influence Ugandan homes as well as individual students, and Grace did not hide his disappointment when the Protectorate government ruled that the regular health inspections of the school, which were being carried out by Mulago Hospital staff, were too expensive and must be withdrawn:

> I am not sure that the economy is an economy in the long run, in spite of other pressing needs. Large boarding schools, in which regular habits of health are instilled, ought to be one of the chief starting points of all the preventive medicine in the country; the more so in a backward country where the homes of the people cannot be so easily influenced by propaganda as in England.[15]

Games and athletics were taken seriously - but not fanatically as in too many English public schools - and made an important contribution to the programme of health education. The Budo football team had a good year, losing only a single match.

Discipline however was a problem in this first year of amalgamation. Although Grace's previous leadership experience at Mengo was an asset to the new college, each of the two former separate schools had its own traditions and the boys tended to resent the loss of any of them. Some friction was inevitable, and the Old Budonians Association did not help. There was a long dispute about whether former students of Mengo High School should be eligible to join the Association, now that their old school was part of Budo. It was only resolved when the Weatherheads and Garrett wrote a joint letter from England, urging Old Budonians to join with the Mengo Old Boys for the good of the school and the country:

> Your old "kitibwa" [prestige] of belonging to the Old Budo no one can take from you. We three think of you and of the old school with pride and affection but we also look forward to the College - to give it its new name - going forward to still greater "kitibwa" under Mr Grace... We advise you to work together loyally in one united Old Boys Union for the united parts of the new King's College.[16]

The Association was renamed The United Budonian Association, but even in the late 1960s there remained a few former students - then in their seventies - who proudly distinguished themselves as "real" Old Budonians.

Discipline was not helped either by the severe shortage of buildings and consequent over-crowding. The failure of the 1924 Building Fund was having a damaging effect; among other shortfalls it was exasperating for Grace to have two good science teachers on the staff and not even the most rudimentary of laboratories for them to work in. But he was patient:

> In three years we have only £3000 odd, but we are not downhearted. African psychology is very difficult. The African wants to see a good show before he will put money into it, but if he can't have his good show until he has paid, matters become complicated and a great deal of talking has to be got through... Also there was a short cotton crop this year with very low prices... but even if we only get the money in at £1500 to £2000 a year we shall have finished our building programme in about eight years, for a school of 400 boys, and as most things that are worth doing in Africa move slowly at first, we are not yet in despair. It will be better to go slowly and let the Baganda feel that the school is their own and African, than to attempt to rely on outside sources.[17]

At the first Speech Day of the new Budo, however, in December 1927, he put matters more sternly. It was attended by the Kabaka, Governor Sir William Gowers, and about 300 Ugandan and 150 European visitors. Grace outlined the progress so far and the plans still to be fulfilled. He urged parents to send their boys to the junior school younger. At present they were coming aged 8 or 9, unable to read or write. Budo needed them at 7, able to do both. Though the school was mainly geared to the Makerere entrance examination, it would introduce in 1928 a course for boys who would not go on to Makerere:

> That there are needed African leaders in the professions I know, but one of the greatest needs also is the development of the land. I think of the European planter in this country. What he can do the Muganda can do, if properly trained, and there need be no opposition to the white planter, but only mutual benefit. Again if

we can instil the right spirit into our boys they will have the ability and the desire to help the peasantry.[18]

He outlined the curriculum that Wright, Harrison and Robinson had planned for training African planters, including classes in the theory and practice of planting, animal husbandry, basic building, iron work, carpentry, book-keeping and business methods:

> During the second year what the Americans call a "project" will be done by each student.

> He will be given money to attempt an experiment on his own and any profit from the experiment will be his. If he fails, he will not only return the money he has lost but, if the fault is his own, he will have to do another year's training before he will get a certificate of competence from us. Honesty, industry and common sense are I think the only qualities needed for boys who take this course, but they are essentials. Then I hope the European planters will take them on for two years. One has already offered to do so.[19]

It was probably unwise and inaccurate of Grace to imply that the new agricultural course would be less intellectually demanding than the current curriculum. Old Budonians were - and are - intent and shrewd listeners; the generation of the 1920s and 30s were alert to any hint that a new programme might be second best to the academic courses they so highly valued. But Grace moved on to the thorny subject of money:

> We believe that the Government has done its share at Budo, by inspection, advice and grants in aid. We believe that the CMS has done its share, by arranging for the staffing of the school and its leadership until such time as the African can do it himself. We do not believe that the Baganda have done their share, and until they do they cannot expect the government or missions to take them seriously.[20]

He spoke of the generous voluntary giving which had built up the English public schools to their present high standards, and ended bluntly:

> I have been told that no pressure must be brought to bear upon the Baganda to build this school. I can assure you that if the school

> cannot be built by the free self-sacrifice of the well-to-do Baganda,
> then my interest is gone.[21]

Hard words - and it may have been that Grace was too sharp and that the 1924 committee had set themselves an impossible target. Those present at that meeting had certainly been carried away by the enthusiastic insistence of Grace and Callwell that King's College would be truly their school only if they paid for it. But Grace was a courteous man and he was, typically, paying the Old Budonians and other Ugandan supporters of Budo the compliment of treating them as he would have treated any responsible European group which had failed to meet an obligation. He assumed that they had done so from choice, not inferiority. That is more than some subsequent benefactors of Africa have done.

Sir William Gowers' speech seems to have surprised everyone. He was not noted for enthusiasm for mission work and had not met Grace before. He began by saying that he had prepared a speech and now wished that he hadn't, because the headmaster's report had raised so many questions in his mind that he would have liked to get on to discuss them at once. He was sorry to hear that money was not coming in as fast as it was needed because he was sure that there was nothing that the Baganda could subscribe to that was more worthy than this educational effort. Other similar schools were going to be started in other parts of Uganda and he predicted that Budo would rapidly become a school for Baganda pupils only and that this would be a very suitable development.

Happily, the Baganda proved wiser than their governor and broad-minded enough to maintain and extend the mixture of students drawn from the whole country at Budo, which has proved one of its strengths and its best contribution to national development. From the 1927 re-opening at least 20 ethnic groups have usually been represented in the expanded school and often nearer 30. In a Colonial Office book on Uganda, published in 1960, Harold Ingrams was to write of Budo:

> I met men who spoke of the benefit they had received from being
> at school with boys from regions other than their own.[22]

At the 1927 Speech Day, Gowers went on to say how pleased he was to hear of the new agricultural course, and that he wanted to quote something - obviously part of his abandoned written speech - said by a far-sighted teacher in Uganda to the Phelps-Stokes commissioners:

> If the school can turn out yearly a number of sons of chiefs and other landowners, with no particular leanings towards learning and perhaps no immediate means of paying the costs of higher education, but with some sort of vision and knowledge of what they could do with a 100 or 200 acres of land, it requires little vision to see that, in the course of five or ten years, the whole country would be lifted to a higher level. This method of education for the sons of chiefs will not only supplement village education, but in many districts will be the source from which it will flow strongly.[23]

The governor added that not only did he believe that this was true, but he now realised that it must have been said by the man who had since become headmaster of King's College. He was right.

Grace was now a strong influence on education in Uganda and was not alone in his enthusiasm for agricultural education. For thirty years there had been a few teachers in the mission schools who supported the aim of Fraser and the Weatherheads for a large practical element in the curriculum. But they had not achieved it. Behind much of the dissatisfaction about to erupt for the next few years against Grace's idealism, lay a conviction that, whatever the white man might 'say' about practical education, his own wisdom, administrative skill and therefore his power, had been learnt from books: It was, after all, academic education that 'really' mattered and Ugandans would not be denied it. In 1928 Revd T.C. Vincent of Bishop Tucker College wrote, in an article on the training of teachers:

> Parents send their children to our schools with the hope that they will escape from the routine of village life to which they themselves are subject, and not that they may return to it with new knowledge and ideals that will make that life acceptable and of worth to them. This seems to be flying in the face of nature. There are no serious indications that Uganda can ever become a highly industrialised country, supporting a big population in cities, and yet the tendency of the school is to unfit boys and girls for life in the country... We

cannot excuse ourselves on the plea that the natives want the kind of education we are giving them. We have been responsible for educating their taste.[24]

In the same edition of the *Uganda Church Review*, Callwell wrote from Toro, urging that more attention be paid to linking school education to home influences and opportunities. He, like the Graces, now believed that co-education should be started, carefully, in CMS boarding schools and was willing to try it at Nyakasura.[25]

Nineteen twenty-eight began cheerfully at Budo. The governor's supportive speech had lifted spirits, as had the good examination results. At Makerere the new student intake from Budo had made a good impression and Principal Douglas Tomblings warmly supported Grace's rejection of rivalry between the two colleges. With the help of friends in England, the Graces had established a scholarship fund to support boys whose parents could not pay the full fees which were now 420 - 500 shillings a year, according to seniority.

Students and staff felt that discipline had improved in the first year. Grace dealt severely with bullying which, according to students of the period, had become an unpleasant feature of the old Budo in the early 1920s. Any boy found guilty of bullying was made to wear, for a week, a placard reading "I am a bully". Twenty-first century psychologists might deplore this; students and staff of 1928 said it worked - and quickly. Apart from this, there was little imposed discipline. Occasionally, if things seemed to be getting slack, Grace would announce that for the next week the school would work "Under law not under Grace" and restrictions would be imposed. Normally, discipline was, as the Weatherheads had believed it should be, a matter for the boys themselves. There had been a prefect system since the early years but there now grew up a tradition called *kyama* ("corner" or "secret"). It laid an obligation on every boy to be responsible for the behaviour of his fellow students; if he saw anyone behaving in a way which could damage the reputation of the school, he was expected to take him quietly aside and correct him. The principle was that a strong public opinion for good was a more powerful influence than an efficient system of reporting. Budonians of Grace's time talked proudly of this.

The two main innovations of 1928 were the agricultural course, which went ahead as planned, and hobbies. Every afternoon from 3.30 to 4.30 each boy followed, with as much help as he needed from the master or master's wife in charge, a hobby which he had chosen from an impressive list: metalwork, motor maintenance, carpentry, leatherwork, shoe repairing, knitting, sewing, flower and butterfly collecting, animal husbandry, chicken farming, bee-keeping, gardening, piano, harmonium, school band, printing, dispensary and school shop. A hobby, once chosen, had to be worked at for at least a year, and although the aim was to get the boys to enjoy practical skills, no slacking was tolerated. The staff did not want them to "play at it but to learn to do it really well."[26]

Grace was satisfied that the standard of academic achievement was rising at the same time. The boys who left at the end of 1928 were on average two years younger than the leavers of 1926, but he was sure that they knew more. Yet the handicap of unfinished buildings persisted and the school finances were now in crisis. There had been a serious famine throughout the country; there had been no early rains at all and the second rainy season had been slight. With food prices high, even the previous trickle of contributions to the building fund had virtually stopped. The school was £3100 in debt and Grace wrote to the Board of Governors, which had undertaken to clear the debt the year before, to say that he could not continue overspending. The school's creditors were becoming understandably impatient. The only course would be to reduce the services provided by the school and, slowly, to redeem the debt from fees.

He had been heavily criticised by some members of the Board for extravagance; yet at the same time there were complaints that the conditions he had established at Budo compared unfavourably with those at Makerere. He pointed out to the Board that whereas Makerere maintained 80 students on £9000 a year, he had £7000 for 270. (Numbers had fallen below the desired 300 because, as a result of the famine, some parents could no longer pay their fees.) His statistics are important because almost all the subsequent criticism of Budo was comparative. Makerere was certainly better staffed and equipped than Budo. So was the very good White Fathers' school, St Mary's College. This had recently relocated from Kampala to impressive buildings at Kisubi, 12 miles along the Entebbe road, where the Fathers also ran a technical school. Grace readily accepted this, but stressed again and again, that Makerere received all its funding from government, and the Catholic missions almost all theirs from overseas sources. These were fine schools for Africans. But the CMS was trying to create an African school and believed that the Baganda were mature enough to want this and to help to build it. Yet the tide of criticism mounted, and Grace's vision of mutual trust began to fade.

The Board of Governors, with its majority of Ugandan members, had no help for Grace. There was not enough money - and that was that. One member actually suggested, in spite of Grace's financial analysis, that the most urgently needed building – a dining hall for the middle and senior schools - should be built at once, out of fees. Grace introduced stringent economies, some of them rather deflating; no prizes and no farewell party. Yet 1929 was a year of steady progress and letters from members of staff suggest that morale remained high. It was ironic that in this year, before the opposition to Grace erupted, the school was paid a remarkable tribute.

Early in the year, Dr – later, Sir – Julian Huxley, in his early forties already an eminent scientist and authority on science education, was invited by the Colonial Office to visit East Africa to advise on some aspects of native education. He spent an October afternoon at Budo, having visited Kisubi the same morning. He seems to have been too interested in people, curricula, and ideas, to notice the unfinished buildings and inadequate equipment. In his subsequent book, *Africa View*, he wrote:

> The same afternoon, the better to make comparisons, I went to the King's School at Budo, a Church Missionary Society school, corresponding to Kisubi, but comprising younger boys as well. This school interested me for three reasons. First and foremost,

I thought it the best school I saw in Africa; second it was such an interesting contrast in atmosphere and methods to the admirable Catholic school I had seen that morning; thirdly it was a testimony to the power of a headmaster to make or mar a school ... Mr Grace, by his broadmindedness, energy and uncanny knack of persuading the best type of young masters to come and work under him, has put a new spirit into the place.

We all know that the English Public School system is not ideal; but there are many things in its atmosphere that are pleasant and good - the independence of the boys, their feeling that in some intimate and enjoyable way, they belong to the place and the place to them, the delegation of discipline to the senior boys, the companionship and co-operation. At Budo I had the impression of such an atmosphere ... and this seems to me a remarkable achievement.

The contrast with the White Fathers' school was interesting. The Catholic institution probably stood higher in pure academic achievement; but here you felt a much greater freedom, more give and take, a system that perhaps thought less of souls and brains, but more of human beings. One excellent institution at Budo is that of hobbies. Each boy is free to choose one of a number of hobbies, to which, under supervision, he devotes so much time every day. Most of these hobbies are utilitarian ... there is also "general utility" which consists of keeping the school tidy, adding coats of paint where needed, and undertaking special jobs of improvement from time to time. Printing is an interesting hobby. The boys can learn to be quite good compositors and set up all sorts of programmes and what not. The only non-utilitarian hobbies are the collecting of wild flowers and insects. I was much interested to see the extent of the collections that had already been made and the way in which almost all the specimens had been named.

... At nearly all African schools the fees are almost nominal; but here in Uganda, a good many natives are quite prosperous, through cotton and other crops, and the Budo authorities felt that it was time to make the parents pay something more substantial for what the boys were getting. A few years ago, in the face of a good deal of opposition and gloomy prophecies that attendance would fall off, they raised the fees to the sum, very considerable for Africa, of £ 25 a year, and the applications for entrance are more numerous than ever.

I went home inspirited by the high standards of which I had been witness.[27]

It was unfortunate for all involved that nearly two years passed before Grace's critics could be confronted with this distinguished tribute to his work and the quality of the school. Because of Huxley's extensive travels, his book was not published until 1931.

By the end of 1928 Grace was again unwell. Early in April 1930 he and his wife went on leave to England, leaving Tom Harrison, who was now married to the junior teacher Joyce Evors, as acting head, and the school - at least according to the students, staff and Huxley - in good shape. For several months letters of complaint and criticism from members of the Board made it difficult for Grace to relax and enjoy his leave - though some of the letters ended by hoping he was doing so. Finally, in November, he received the minutes of an antagonistic Board meeting and a fiercely critical letter from the chairman, Kabaka Sir Daudi Chwa. The recurring criticisms were that money had been badly used and no clear statements published, that the tone and discipline of the school were bad, and that the academic standards were not rising as promised. The Kabaka concluded:

> I myself consider that the standard of education is very low in comparison to the fees charged ... there is certainly no doubt that the boys who were educated at the Budo of the time of the Weatherheads are infinitely better educated than any of the boys being educated at the present time... At the same time, two Roman Catholic schools have taken a very keen interest in the education of the natives and ... the standard of education in these schools is infinitely higher than that in any of our schools, with the natural result that some of the Protestant chiefs are now sending their boys and girls to these schools. Unless the standard of education and the general tone of the school at Budo are improved, I have no hesitation in telling you that the majority of the Protestant chiefs will be sending their sons to the Roman Catholic schools.[28]

It seemed not to occur to His Highness that the main attraction of the Catholic schools for some of his chiefs might be that they charged virtually no fees. The Board insisted that Budo needed more European teachers and had too many African ones, some of whom were not well enough qualified. The Kabaka, who had himself gone on contributing loyally to the building fund - he had given most of the £ 5000 contributed in 5 years, which was less than one fifth of what was needed - now tacitly admitted that the fund had failed, by suggesting that it was time to forget about buildings and equipment and concentrate on raising academic standards. That nobody referred to the undoubtedly successful agricultural programme and hobbies, suggests that Board members thought them peripheral to Budo's true purpose - academic excellence. Lastly, the letters left no doubt that the superior status of Makerere was bitterly resented.

Grace wrote two long letters in reply - one to the Kabaka, as chairman of the governors, and the other, with copies to the Board and to all the staff, to Bishop Willis, as head of the CMS in Uganda. His responses to the criticisms are important to this history of the school, not simply as an apologia for his own efforts at Budo, but because they have been read and respected by subsequent headmasters and staff, and have therefore left their mark on the Budo of the new century. On the use of school funds he reminded the Board that in a circular of September 1928 he had invited any member of the Board to visit the school at any time without notice, and to inspect the accounts. Very few had bothered to do so but the offer remained open because he knew there had been no extravagance. On "tone and discipline" he readily acknowledged that the merger of the two schools had not been easy, especially in the first year. But the present solidarity of the staff, who had nearly all been new to the school in 1927, the good work of the prefects of the past year, and a growing spirit of co-operation and honour among the boys, showed that the methods had been sound:

> Of course, I could have expelled all the boys who might have deserved it, and ruled by fear, and the external results would have been splendid. But they would have been superficial.[29]

On academic standards he stood firm. It was true that the boys at Budo were not "crammed" for examinations, so they did not always pass into Makerere as highly as students from some other schools. What they did when they got there was more to the point. In the Makerere first year examinations that year, a Budo student had come top and there were four others in the top ten. The other five places had gone to two boys from Zanzibar, and three from the Catholic schools with which Budo was being so unfavourably compared. Moreover, Grace had recently had a letter from an Old Budonian of H.T.C. Weatherhead's time, who had left with a first class certificate. He had just joined Makerere and wrote to say how hard he was finding it to keep pace with the students who had just come directly from Budo.

As to the criticism of his African colleagues, Grace said the school had always tried to take only the best and he believed they were very good indeed. He wanted more, as soon as he could get them, from the newly established Teacher Training Department at Makerere, but he was not being helped by the refusal of some of the brightest Baganda students to enrol at Makerere. Some of Budo's present experienced staff were in fact going back to do the new Makerere course, but qualifications were not everything. He believed, for example, that Mr Nkata was a genius with the younger Budo boys and he would willingly send his own son to be taught by him when he was old enough. [In due course, he did.] About the building fund Grace was restrained. He simply observed that if the long-promised buildings could be provided, the maintenance costs on old, delapidated premises which could be abandoned, would be saved. The school would then run much more economically.

There remained the comparisons with the Roman Catholic schools and with Makerere. Grace acknowledged that the Catholic schools were excellent. It would take time for the Baganda to build, with the CMS, a school of their own which would in all respects be as good. But to the Kabaka's tendentious threat of defections to the Catholic schools he returned a ringing reply:

> I am of the opinion that the Protestant Faith is too free and too hard for many of your young men and women, and that they would be better as Catholic Christians.

> The Protestant freely gives himself to be disciplined by the hand of God, with no mediating priest between ... and this is hard, very hard. If many Baganda go over to the Catholic Church because

they cannot be either polite or patient in the Protestant Church, or because they are not able to pay the cost, they will enter a discipline which will be good for them, and the Protestant Church will be left with fewer but stronger Christians.[30]

He insisted yet again that any idea of competition between Budo, a public school, and Makerere, a future university college, was absurd. If the Baganda did not want their sons to go to a government college for higher education, they would have to build their own, later. That was not the way forward he would choose:

Personally, I should prefer Dr Aggrey's great ideal to prevail: Government, Africans and Missions co-operating for the uplift of the African to rule his own country; Missions and Africans - with government inspections and grants - for all education up to university standard; Government to do university, with Africans and some missionaries on its Board of Governors, on some such lines as Achimota, and university being entirely out of direct Government control.[31]

Grace concluded his letter to Bishop Willis with a firm refusal to allow things to continue as they were:

If we had Dr Aggrey with us today [he had died aged only 52, in 1927] I should not be writing this letter. I feel so strongly that it was by him that I was led to make this experiment in the closer co-operation of the Missions and Africans - that is the Budo Board of Governors - and it is heartbreaking that this is how it has ended.

This final burst of criticism sent me by the Board - only a sample of what has been going on for two years or more - has brought me to the parting of the ways ... I repeat, I cannot return to Budo unless I am trusted and the Governors so consolidate themselves that mutual trust is the foremost thing in our minds.[32]

In its first hundred years King's College has on several occasions been in danger of breakdown and consequent closure, or drastic reduction. This 1930 crisis was the first. Bishop Willis helped to save the day. He wrote back at once to Grace urging him to dismiss any thought of resigning. He had continually asked Board members not to go on making groundless criticisms, and had refuted in detail the complaints that had been raised. He believed that the future of Budo depended on Grace. For the following five months Harrison (as acting head)showed his mettle. He had found the Board so unsympathetic that he informed the Bishop that he was going to run the school according to Grace's ideals - and without any consultation with the Board - until Grace returned, if he did.

The combined rebuttals of Grace, Bishop Willis and Harrison seem to have startled the Board. Many of its members liked Grace, respected what he was trying to do, and were dismayed at the possibility that he might not return. Too many had probably written to him as individuals, without consulting colleagues on the Board, and had therefore been unaware of the cumulative force of their bombardment. Others were genuinely confused.

The 1924 meeting had established the new Board on such a spontaneous wave of emotional support that it paid no heed to important details of composition and responsibilities. Any interested chiefs had been free to attend meetings, which soon became unwieldy and had little continuity of membership. The relationship between the governors and the headmaster had not been defined and was soon misinterpreted by the more assertive Board members, most of whom knew a lot about Kiganda traditions but very little about institutional education. Grace may have persuaded the 1924 meeting to move too soon towards the kind of Board that Aggrey and Fraser had inspired at Achimota, a college which differed profoundly from Budo in one crucial respect. It had, in its early years, no financial constraints of any kind, being lavishly funded by the government of the Gold Coast, to be a showpiece of British colonial education.[33]

Bishop Willis now proposed, and the Board readily accepted, a firm separation of the governing body from the Building Committee and any other necessary committees, so that problematic details could be debated by small groups of regularly attending enthusiasts, who would make recommendations to the whole Board. Grace, through the historian D.C. Somervell, consulted William Temple, then Archbishop of York but formerly headmaster of Repton School, for guidance on the precise relationship between heads and governors in English public schools. Temple's reply was masterly:

> The governors exercise a general control over the finances of the school, and if the headmaster for instance wishes to appoint an assistant at a higher salary than usual he has to get their consent... He lays before them all plans affecting buildings and it is they who make the decisions about these. He reports to them from time to time on the general running of the school and would hold himself ready to answer any questions so that they may be well informed. But the governors exercise no control over the day-to-day running of the school, of any kind. They do not for example, control the curriculum... within the limits mentioned above the headmaster's control is complete.

> The Governors, having selected him, should give him their full confidence and never on any account criticise him otherwise than privately, to his face... The relationship is not unlike that of the Admiralty to the captain of a man-o-war, or of a great shipping line to the captain of a liner. The Admiralty or the shipping line lays down the general conditions of service, but within these the captain has absolute authority and is subject to no interference, though if he forfeits confidence he may be dismissed.[34]

Three years of wrangling had their results. Headmasters of Budo since 1931 have usually worked harmoniously, along these lines, with their governors and the importance of mutual trust has been widely understood.

April 1931 saw Grace back at the school, in good health and with fresh ideas. His European staff had been working together for four years. They were now all married, as were several of the African staff and Grace considered the family life which students saw and shared on the hill to be a great strength to the school. In addition, Amos Sempa had joined the staff from the Makerere teachers course, and Kenneth Bisase and Ignatius Musazi had returned from their training courses at Selly Oak College and St Augustine's College, in England. With the lessons of the long arguments much on his mind, Grace must have pondered the conclusions of an article by Bisase and Musazi in the *Uganda Church Review*:

> May we close with the hope that this enterprise of educating the
> African will still be left in the hands of those who will and can do
> it: either government officials, missionaries or individuals. It is
> becoming too big a task and responsibility to take on ourselves. But
> it must be borne in mind by the African that however good non-
> African teachers, officals and financiers may be, the problem of true
> emancipation will still be in his own hands. Thus the importance
> of co-operation in all directions.[35]

And these were not young inexperienced reactionaries; Musazi was
soon to become a key figure in the development of the co-operative
movement and the first political parties in Uganda.

The worldwide financial depression of 1931 left its mark on East
Africa. Within a few weeks of Grace's return, Budo student numbers
dropped to 200 - and below 240 the school had to run at a loss. The
staff voluntarily gave £100 from their salaries to pay fees for some of
the most deserving boys whose parents could not afford them, but
school expenses had to be pared below even the 1929 levels and many
workmen and servants were paid off.

Other CMS schools were in worse difficulties. Callwell had struggled
on at Fort Portal, and then at the healthier site of Nyakasura, but first
his sole African colleague died and then the European who replaced
him had to be invalided back to England. He had been forced to close
the school for most of 1929 while he returned to England to recruit
staff. By 1931 he had 53 boys from 8 different tribes. Like Grace, he
was trying to foster discipline rather than impose it, but was finding
it hard-going.[36]

Kamuli High School had endured ill-health for many years on its
badly chosen site. In 1930 it had three outbreaks of bubonic plague and
its veteran headmaster, H.A. Brewer, was invalided home to England
where he died of blackwater fever. The government then gave approval
for the school to move to its present healthy and dramatic site at Mwiri,
with the new title Busoga College. Meanwhile, from 1931-32, until the
Mwiri buildings were ready, Budo provided refuge for its 50 students,
along with 30 more from a recently closed government school - an
unwieldy addition to take into an established school still short of
accommodation.

However, 1931 ended well and Grace and his staff were optimistic. In the senior school they kept their promise that African traditions would be maintained. There were courses in African history, African social geography and African folklore, while Luganda was taken seriously as an academic study. The junior school had been strengthened by the arrival of twelve new boys. Grace followed Fraser's policy in Achimota junior school, of not introducing English as the language of instruction from the first year, but striving to teach English well so that a smooth transition to English-medium could take place after four years. Mrs Harrison had built up handicraft and drama and the juniors also had a cub pack, with regular camps. There was frequent football and cricket coaching, and chickens and rabbits to look after, as preparation for animal husbandry in the middle school.

In spite of Baganda scepticism, the agricultural programme continued, though Grace was baffled and disappointed when the government refused support for his scheme for a farm school, to which middle school boys could proceed after a solid grounding from Harrison. He had Sir Apolo Kagwa's gift of good farming land at Namutamba and the support of Mr Lea-Wilson, the most experienced planter in Uganda. Many of the governors were now keen on the scheme too, but he had to be content for the present with the plantations on Budo hill, and with his beloved herd of Ankole cattle. Even these sometimes overreached themselves. A cash book of the period recorded cryptically:

> To Saulo Tibasuboke - Twenty-two shillings: Our cows ate his *lumonde* [sweet potatoes]

But Grace easily forgave and indulged them. His wife wrote in her next circular letter:

> You would have been amused to see one of our cows, reclining gracefully on the side of the hill, clad in a mantle of green canvas. She is recovering from a terribly bad snake bite and Myers [Grace] was so concerned at the way the wretched biting flies were attacking her, that he requisitioned a ground sheet from our safari outfit and had her robed in it.[37]

It had been another good year also for Budo sport. The athletics team won the King's African Rifles Cup for the first time, beating Makerere in the final, and the Old Budonians, captained by Prince Badru Kakungulu, again won the Kabaka's Cup for football.

The December Speech Day was an important opportunity for the recovering school and Grace decided that a little money should be spent on smartening the place up. It was well known that Budo, like almost all schools, was struggling, and a good show in front of visitors and Old Budonians would repair damaged confidence. But they certainly didn't splash out. Miss Dorothy Stubbings, who had just arrived to take over the junior school, was allowed some whitewash to re-decorate the dormitory, but funds would not stretch to grey distemper as a contrast. So she made her own, from wood ash, cassava roots and cow-dung, and it was much admired.

There were the usual 500 or so guests, including Edward Mutesa, son of Kabaka Sir Daudi Chwa. He was already living with the Graces and taking some lessons in the junior school, but this was one of his first public appearances. The Makerere staff had just released the entrance examination results and Grace was able to announce that of Budo's 29 candidates, 22 had won places. Drama and music were two of the Graces' gifts to Budo, and on this occasion, Housman's *Sister Gold* was presented in the open air theatre. There was also a nativity play performed by the junior school, with the senior school choir singing carols in the background. After the Old Budonians had joined the leavers for supper, there was a concert of Kiganda plays, and of European and Kiganda music. The whole festive day made its impression and the school year ended, three days later, with a farewell carol service, for which a large crowd of Old Budonians returned to the hill.

Early in 1932 contributions to the Building Fund began to come in again. The school was at full strength - nearly 300, not counting the temporary guests from Mwiri and elsewhere - so fee income was healthy. Grace announced that all the old dormitories would be renovated. The Old Budonians had set up a memorial fund for H.T.C. Weatherhead, who had died in 1930, and hoped to build a school library. They now had enough in the fund to make a start and the imaginative decision was taken to build it over the 1926 archway into the second quadrangle. But Budo still had no dining hall and with the increasing numbers the need was urgent. Grace had always insisted that the skills acquired from hobbies were meant to be put to serious use and he now decided that, since a new dining hall could not be afforded, the students themselves, led by the "skilled masons" on the agricultural course, could enlarge and convert the Mackay Memorial Workshop, which the Weatherheads had hoped might one day house a technical school. It was a sturdy, central building and with kitchen and dining accommodation problems solved it would be easy to find rooms in which the carpentry and metalwork hobbies could be continued. Stephen Wright was architect and project director:

> The boys are pretty inexperienced and don't get a great deal of supervision, so that the walls went up rather crooked in places. This gave us the idea of making the hall in a sort of Ugandan-Elizabethan style of architecture. We made lattice windows along the front and deep-eaved verandahs at the side. Inside there are red-brick pillars holding up the roof, and all the beams of the ceiling have been left exposed and blackened, the rest whitewashed. There are red window curtains and we have red and white check cloths ... We are slowly making heavy refectory tables to replace the heterogeneous collection that are being used at the moment. The whole hall is about 70 by 30 feet and so holds the 300 boys comfortably. [38]

It is a tribute to the work of the students, and their training through hobbies and the agricultural course, that, more than 70 years later, the Mackay building remains, one of the most attractive on the main quadrangle, having survived two further large extensions, and is still the school dining hall, familiarly known as "Mess".

The swimming pool has been a perennial construction challenge since the time of the Weatherheads. Once again it was overgrown and leaking, but it now became a project for the whole school community, to Mrs Grace's delight:

> A gang of boys worked at clearing the vegetation and then followed a scheme which we hope will go on for always, though in different directions. Every Friday evening, the whole school, including masters and wives, turned out, to carry stones to make the new

walls of the bath. It was great fun and really a great sight to see
the long column of stone carriers, winding its way from the spot
where the stones abounded, to Nansove, about half a mile of rough
walking ... The bath is now practically finished. It has been filled
and we have had glorious bathes in it.[39]

In July, A.G. Fraser from Achimota College came to stay with the Graces.
Achimota College was now well established, with nearly 400 students
in classes from kindergarten to post-matriculation levels. Fraser felt that
he was not fit enough to carry on much longer as principal and asked
Grace if he would consider succeeding him. It was a seductive prospect:
Aggrey's dream of co-operation realised; a massive annual budget of
£ 80,000; splendid buildings, of the scale and quality of European
university campuses; each House with a European housemaster and
an African deputy, both living in quarters connected to the House by
covered passageways, and with only 30 boys and girls in each House
- all the things, in short, that Grace knew Budo would never be able to
afford. But he told Fraser that, much as he would like to, he could not
go to Achimota yet; there were too many unfinished projects which he
wanted to entrench, if not complete.

Fraser's visit resulted in another adventurous development for
Grace to nurture. Some of the most progressive Baganda, including
Board members, were impressed by his account of co-education at
Achimota - and Grace pounced at once. There was no school for girls
in Uganda offering the range of studies or the higher education entrance
standard of Budo. In January 1933 twelve girls were admitted to the
junior school; Grace and his colleagues looked ahead ten years, to the
prospect of young women students at Makerere. It was a bold initiative
and - as Rhoda Kalema later recorded - was vehemently opposed by
some prominent Ugandans, including churchmen.[40] But it made a good
start, largely because the Graces had prepared the ground slowly and
carefully, launching the development only when they were confident
of warm support from the educational community that Budo had
become.

Colin Walker, who joined the staff at this time, left a vivid impression
of the welcome he received and of Grace's style of leadership. He

described his delight in the beauty of the hill, his snug first base - the rondavel guest room in the Graces' garden - and then his introduction to school routine:

> That first evening Myers Grace put me in the picture of how he ran Budo. He said that the first mission station he was on after the First World War was such a miserable place that he determined that when he became head of a station, he would ensure that Africans and Europeans were happy, and as far as possible, one large family. For a start, Europeans were to use Christian names or nicknames. so I never called my headmaster anything but Myers, and his wife, Molly. In return he decided that I was to be "Johnny".

> Fred and Elsie Robinson were always "Robbie" and "Mrs Robbie" ... I remember Myers then telling me "You will take over the English in the senior school - the VI will be taking the Makerere College entrance exam in two month's time. You will be in charge of the clothing and bedding store, and the book store. Tom Harrison will show you the ropes. You will be Housemaster of South Africa House with Omwami Kaidzi as under Housemaster. You will take overall control of the Cubs and Scouts.

> Omwami Magambo is Scoutmaster and Omwami Barlow runs the Cubs ... Mrs Robbie will start to give you Luganda lessons when she returns from leave. You are down to preach in chapel in three weeks time - I shall expect you to do it in Luganda in a few months. Those are your main responsibilities. Organise things in your own way; if you get into difficulties, ask. We have to set the African staff a standard of efficiency. If you are slipshod there will be hell to pay" - or words to that effect.[41]

The Christian life of the school continued vigorously. Usher-Wilson was chaplain and while he was on leave in 1932 Musazi deputised ably. Grace took a weekly quiet hour in chapel on a weekday evening; attendance was voluntary but never fell below fifty. When he once suggested, at a busy period before examinations, that the meetings might be suspended for a few weeks, he was glad to meet strong opposition from the students. The chapel was no longer big enough to hold the whole school so Miss Stubbings suggested that the juniors should have simple services and talks on their own. She raised £ 20 among friends in England, and under her direction, students and porters built a little reed church at the junior school end - white reed work, with black binding and simple wooden furniture. It was much loved until it was accidentally burnt down years later. Grace revived the idea of local schools being invited to meet at Budo, and early in 1933 parties of Budo boys went out to the schools to build, repair, whitewash, dig and even to teach reading and writing, in schools which, Grace said, "were dying, for want of someone to take an interest in them."[42]

A little more building was possible in 1933. A kitchen and store were added to the Mackay building and a small dormitory built for the girls. The great event of the year was the government's approval of Grace's plan for the Namutamba Farm School. He immediately asked Harrison to plan a course for the boys who would be going on to it from the middle school. Perhaps as a result, there was greater enthusiasm for the agricultural hobby; the boys built a new kraal for the cows and started cutting a small dip for them out of the rock on the edge of the hill. Grace felt that agriculture was on the move at last at Budo. Confidence in the school seemed to have been restored and there were 60 new entrants for the new year.

The first students went on to Namutamba early in 1934. Fraser sensed that one big obstacle to Grace's acceptance of Achimota had been removed. He tackled another one himself, by proposing that the right man to succeed Grace would be Revd I.J. Gaster, who had been deputy to Fraser at Trinity College, Kandy. Grace's educational ideas and methods were so similar to Fraser's that Gaster should find Budo congenial and familiar, and the school probably needed a few years of consolidation of all that Grace had initiated. Gaster agreed to come, the Board approved his appointment, and Grace became principal-elect of Achimota. He was to receive a much higher salary than at Budo, but accepted the post on condition that the extra salary should be used to bring members of Budo staff across to Achimota for further experience and training. Among those who served Budo and Uganda all the better for this generous offer were A.K. Sempa and E.M.K. Mulira, who were with Grace at Achimota from 1936 to 1938.

About the same time a further link was forged with Achimota when Revd C.E. Stuart, who had been chaplain and first librarian at the college, came to Uganda, first as Assistant Bishop and then the following year succeeded Bishop Willis. He and his wife were to be staunch friends of Budo for forty years.

In June 1934 the Weatherhead Memorial Library was officially opened before a large crowd of Old Budonians and friends of the school. It was Gaster's first appearance at Budo and one of Grace's last. As he watched the formal completion of the "King's Quadrangle" by the addition of a fine library, he should have felt that he had led Budo some way towards the ideal that Aggrey had set before him. He had been trying, with his colleagues and students, to create a school that would be good enough to keep bright Ugandans at home for at least the first part of their education. Six years before, he had written:

> Aggrey was not a miracle. There was a cause, or causes, which made Aggrey what he was. We believe that one reason why Aggrey never ceased to be a great African, even after he had spent twenty-five years of his life in America, was because he had his early education for twenty years of his life, in his own country and among his own people. So we believe that the African leader will never be soundly educated if he is sent out of his own country during his early years. He must get his education, and a liberal education, in his own country. But where? ... We know that the highly polished and cultured African is desperately needed today in Africa. Aggreys are not easily replaced. And we wish to try to lay at Budo, the foundation of a school that will produce future Aggreys.[43]

The last project started in communal work during Grace's headship was the terracing of the sloping King's Quadrangle. Stephen Wright described how it was finished.

> The last terrace needed a little more work done on it and Canon Grace happened to say that he would like to see the finished grass growing on it before he left. The boys called for volunteers, of their own accord, to get up and work on it from 5 am until 7 on the last few mornings of the term. When you realise that digging is an everyday job to these boys and not done with the air of excitement that English boys might bring to the job, it shows what real love was behind the work.[44]

Wright drove the school lorry round each morning and shone the lights on the terrace for the boys to work by. The job was finished in time; Grace left Budo and never saw the school again.

Ernest Sempebwa, who studied at Budo 1929-36, returned as a teacher in 1940, and again, as deputy head in 1960, expressed his enduring admiration of Grace's leadership, in 1996:

> Canon Grace had plenty to teach us in our physical, spiritual and academic growth ... the chapel was the school's focal point ... He believed in the development of the whole person, that is body, mind and spirit. He laid firm English language foundations, starting right down in the junior school. He introduced hobbies for the whole school ... Agriculture was done more as an ordinary class subject than as a hobby ... It can be clearly seen that all this talk by ignorant politicians, that the early missionaries prepared us for only white collar jobs is rubbish... Our education at Budo had been geared to the development of the whole person. So Budo gave us a good start in life.[45]

Though himself an influential Muganda, he greatly valued the "unifying influence" of Grace's Budo:

> The boarding element made a great contribution to Uganda. We came as Baganda, Batoro, Basoga and so on. We became Budonians. We went out as Ugandans. He was right to press ahead with co-education - it was a great force for good. We called him "Kalondoozi" (everywhere) and "Kabora" (the priest).[46]

Timothy Cobb, headmaster in the 1950s, summed up:

> Canon Grace is usually looked upon as the second Founder of Budo.[47]

And rightly so.

Notes

[1] Jones H. Gresford *Uganda in Transformation*, London: CMS, 1926 p. 181

[2] Grace H.M. to Bishop Willis, 30 October 1930. KCB archives

[3] *Uganda Church Review*, Vol. 1, No. 4 October 1926, p. 116

[4] Kasozi A.B.K., *The Life of Prince Badru Kakungulu Wasajja*, Kampala: Progressive, 1996, p. 6.

[5] Ibid, pp. 8-60

[6] Ibid, p. 55

[7] Ibid, pp. 56-7

[8] MacPherson, Margaret, *They Built for the Future*, London; CUP, 1964, p. 10

[9] Grace, Mrs M., circular letter, 24 July 1926

[10] Ibid

[11] Low, D.A. and Pratt, R.C., *Buganda and British Over-rule*, London: OUP, 1960, pp. 238-9

[12] Grace, Mrs M., circular letter, 11 January 1927

[13] *Ebaluwa eri Banabudo*, December 1926

[14] *Uganda News*, 23 December 1927

[15] Ibid

[16] *Ebaluwa eri Banabudo*, December 1927

[17] *Uganda Church Review*, Vol. 1, No. 9, March 1928, p. 14

[18] *Uganda News*, 23 December, 1927

[19] Ibid

[20] Ibid

[21] Ibid

[22] Ingrams, H, Uganda, London: HMSO, 1960, p. 124

[23] *Education in East Africa*, op. cit, p. 163

[24] *Uganda Church Review*, Vol. No. 9, March 1928, p. 9

[25] Ibid, p. 21

[26] Grace, Mrs M. Circular letter, 13 August 1928

[27] Huxley, Julian, *Africa View*, London Chatto 1931, pp 282-286

[28] HH Sir Daudi Chwa to H.M. Grace, 1 Noveember 1930 KCB archives

[29] Grace H.M., to HH Sir Daudi Chwa, 29 December 1930 KCB archives

[30] Ibid

[31] Grace H.M., to Bishop Willis, op.cit

[32] Ibid

[33] Williams, C.K., *Achimota: The Early Years*, London: Longman, 1962

[34] Temple, Archbishop W., to DC Somervell 10 February 1931. KCB archives.

[35] *Uganda Church Review*, Vol. 1 No. 18, June 1930 p. 55

[36] Ibid No 23, September 1931, p.82

[37] Grace, Mrs M. Circular letter, 28 April 1928

[38] *Uganda Church Review*, Vol. No 35 September 1934, p.62

[39] Grace, Mrs M. circular letter, 9 May 1933

[40] *The Budonian – 90 years*, KCB 1996, p.43

[41] Walker Colin, unpublished typescript circa 1960

[42] Grace Mrs M. op.cit, 9 May 1933

[43] *Uganda Church Review*, Vol. 1, No. 9 March 1928 p.13.

[44] Ibid December 1934, p. 87

[45] *The Budonian*: 90 years, 1906-1996, pp. 12-13.

[46] Sempebwa E.K.K. in personal conversation with the author, Makerere, March 2002

[47] Cobb, T.H. A Note on King's College, Budo. 1950. KCB archives.

5

Consolidating: 1935-1939

Revd. J. Gaster took over from Grace in December 1934, having visited the school several times in the previous six months. Gaster had first gone out to Trinity College, Kandy, in 1910, had taught at the expanding CMS school there for 20 years and had then become Secretary of CMS Ceylon for four years before coming to Uganda. Fraser, who had headed the college, had been away from Ceylon a good deal on war service from 1915 to 1919 and again in the year before he went to Achimota. As Fraser's deputy Gaster therefore had good experience both of running a large boarding school, and of the administrative and financial constraints of the CMS missions. He had taught the sons of Sir Apolo Kagwa, and several other Ugandan boys who had been sent to Trinity during the war and in the early 1920s, so he already had influential friends in Uganda, and knew something of the style and traditions of Budo. Grace would have told him of the long-running disputes about the purpose of the school, and his opening statement in a prospectus, published in his first year, was careful but unequivocal:

> The aim of the school is to provide a higher form of education for those who are likely to fill positions of trust and influence, and to become leaders of thought among their own people; and to inculcate a spirit of Christian service, influencing pupils to become living members of the church.[1]

Gaster was several years older than Grace and, years later, Stephen Wright wrote that Gaster had found the job a good deal more taxing than he had expected.[2] Illness and a leave in England cut into his four and a half years at Budo, yet he made notable contributions to the buildings, to maintaining high academic standards, co-education, the self-discipline that the Weatherheads and Grace had fostered, the teaching of art - which he started - and of science -which he strongly supported - and finally to the public image of the school.

In 1935 he visited many Baganda chiefs all over the kingdom and did much to ease away the vestiges of resentment which some still seemed to feel - ostensibly at Grace's blunt speaking, but more likely at their own well-publicised failure to support the Building Fund. If Grace ever saw Gaster's prospectus, he must have raised a wry smile at its tactful flattery:

> When Mengo High School was merged with Budo ... the new buildings required for this enlargement were provided by the generosity of the Baganda people, who have collected more than £ 8000 for the purpose. [3]

The common rooms and science laboratory, planned ten years before, were still not built and the old buildings which housed the junior school were in a bad state. Yet Gaster's praise made friends for the school, he had no trouble with the Board and he raised money when he needed it. A less fortunate result of his easier personal relationships with leading Baganda was that he was not as rigorous as Grace had been in selecting students for the middle and senior departments. There had been an entrance examination for Budo since 1907, but in 1927 when the junior school was opened it was, understandably, decided not to set a formal examination for boys - and subsequently girls - of seven or eight. So it was now possible to study at Budo up to the age of 13, without an entrance test. Gaster allowed some boys to continue into the middle and senior departments, but in some cases their wealthy home backgrounds had not given them the enthusiasm and perseverance that the Budo curriculum demanded. They were to give trouble to the next headmaster, some years later.

At the end of his first term, Gaster lost his senior master, Tom Harrison, who was appointed head of the re-located Busoga College, Mwiri. Callwell was still at Nyakasura, so all three CMS secondary schools had "Budo" headmasters, and followed the Weatherhead - Grace line on self-discipline.

Gaster modified this further in his first year, and the *Uganda Church Review* took an interest:

An experiment has been tried at Budo during the last year, of giving the boys themselves more power in the organisation of the school. The prefects have always had great power as regards discipline, but not with the programme. This year the games have been run by a games committee, and community work handed over to a Social Service Society, with schoolboys as its officers. One of the Houses has even tried a communal method of ruling, power being in the hands of a body of "elders", elected by the house, instead of in the hands of a prefect. This latter is of particular interest, as many government officials are of the opinion that the rule by elected chiefs, which is general throughout Uganda, is unsuitable for those tribes where the elders of the family, in council, were in the old days dictators of authority. [4]

There were now two scout troops in the senior school, as well as Cubs and Brownies for the juniors, and 1936 brought a striking result of all Grace's efforts for the movement in Uganda. This was the first national jamboree, held at Budo, and attended by the Chief Scout himself, Lord Baden-Powell. He later wrote, with obvious pleasure:

> The camping was excellent and unique. I have never before seen a camp entirely of huts, nor have I seen anywhere such well built shacks, made as they were from local materials and within a 24 hour time limit ... The main thing that I had hoped for has actually been developed in the Scouts, and that is the appreciation of the ideals of the Scout Law, especially as shown in the sense of service to others.[5]

With the firm establishment of the separate farm school at Namutamba and the departure of Harrison, who had been the mainstay of the agricultural course, came growing awareness that the scientific talents of Robinson and Wright were not being well employed. They had to keep the agricultural course going, but would be able to do much more science teaching with some decent facilities. Fred Robinson felt strongly that it was the business of Christian schools to teach science honestly and well. In an article on "The Teaching of Science in Mission Schools" he observed tartly:

> It has been said that there can be no conflict between science and religion, and to the present writer this seems profoundly true, for

the amount of scientific knowledge at present implanted by the mission schools of Uganda is practically negligible.[6]

He noted that the chief secretary of the Uganda government had recently been urging the appointment of a biologist to the staff of Makerere. It was obvious that Africans with a sound biological training would be able to fill posts in the medical, veterinary, forestry and agricultural departments. The right kind of training had been begun at Budo eight years before, with high hopes of a laboratory from the Building Fund. He believed they could make no further progress without it.

He had at least one responsive reader in Gaster, who was a talented amateur architect and had designed the chapel at Trinity College. In consultation with Robinson he now designed a building which was to be sited next to the Budo chapel, to house a science laboratory and the first properly tiered lecture theatre in Uganda. The plans were approved by the mission early in 1936. All that was needed was the money.

When the Weatherhead Memorial Library had been completed in 1934, a number of Old Budonians had been keen to erect some kind of memorial to Sir Apolo Kagwa, and money had already been subscribed. But the Kabaka, Sir Daudi Chwa, had expressed his disapproval of the idea, to the annoyance of many of the subscribers; an unpleasant showdown at the Board seemed inevitable. Gaster skilfully defused the antagonism by suggesting that, as Sir Daudi had made Kiganda custom the ground of his objection, it should be respected. Sir Apolo had always been a practical man, and if the funds already subscribed were put towards the new laboratory, his work for the school would be tacitly commemorated in a very appropriate way. This was agreed and with an additional small grant from the government, the building went ahead. Robinson himself supervised the work and he was teaching in his new laboratory by the middle of 1937. It remained Budo's only lab for 24 years, and the building still graces the main quadrangle, with both laboratory and lecture theatre well used.

The year 1936 brought an important curriculum development when the government gave approval for Budo and Kisubi to provide courses leading to the Cambridge School Certificate, which, introduced in

England in 1917, was well-established, and recognised worldwide. Budo was now thirty years old, and the government Education Department ten years. The state of education throughout the country, and the position of Budo within the developing system, was reflected in the Annual Report of the Education Department, which presented a clear, and in some ways curious, picture.

One immediate impression was how much of Hattersley's late-Victorian system had survived. The terminology had changed but the ideas remained much the same. There were believed to be 750,000 children of school age in Uganda and two-thirds of them were receiving no education at all. Of the roughly 250,000 at school, 228,000 attended unaided "sub-grade" schools, almost identical with Hattersley's "bush schools" of nearly 40 years earlier. From this foundation an educational pyramid rose steeply. 13,000 children attended 218 aided sub-grade schools; 20,000 attended 208 aided approved elementary schools; 4,258 went to 46 unaided approved elementary schools. There were 2,303 at 54 central schools; 1,839 at 22 middle schools; and at the apex of the pyramid, 248 pupils at the 5 schools which the government designated "Junior Secondary Schools".

Of these five, three were CMS schools: Budo with 96 boys - none of the girls having yet reached the senior department; Nyakasura with 30, and Mwiri with 11. The other two were the Roman Catholic schools, Kisubi with 75 boys and Namilyango with 36. So in 1936, five mission schools were the only places of secondary education for Ugandan children, and only the CMS was providing secondary education outside Buganda. The total government expenditure on education for the year was £82,373 - almost exactly Grace's 1936 budget at Achimota College.

The Annual Report had one appendix to the figures for children at school, which recalls - with a jolt - the recommendations of the Phelps-Stokes Commission, 12 years earlier. In addition to the 250,000 children at ordinary schools, there were at technical schools - 449. The report also recorded the results of the Makerere entrance examination. In 1936, out of 31 Budo candidates, 17 passed into Makerere college and in 1937 the number was 15 out of 28 - both being the best results in the five secondary schools. Finally, the report had this to say of Budo:

> King's College, Budo, maintains its reputation for the liberal nature of its education, for all round development and excellent tone. It has acute building needs, the chief problem being the replacement of the present temporary school block by more permanent buildings. The present headmaster is alive to these needs and has not only designed working plans for particular buildings, but has visualised their harmonious grouping in a manner most suitable for the restricted hill site upon which the school is located. This is particularly welcome, in a country where, with encouraging exceptions, the average mission station is singularly lacking in anything resembling an orderly "lay-out."[7]

The report exposes that by 1936 - whatever the excuses - very little progress had been made along the practical and agricultural lines of education so strongly recommended by the Phelps-Stokes commissioners. Thomas and Scott, in their authoritative survey of the Uganda Protectorate, noted with concern the widely held view that it was the business of the middle schools - many of which were the old "high schools" of Hattersley's network - to work towards School Certificate courses as soon as they could:

> It is obvious that such a course cannot be suitable for all boys attending the middle schools and that only a limited number could hope for employment with the British or Native Government after completing the course. The owners of the middle schools have been given therefore complete freedom to experiment on a more practical education for the majority of their pupils, who will not proceed normally to Makerere, but will be employed in their districts, either as chiefs, or with native administrations or possibly in minor appointments, as for example, medical orderlies, or agricultural and veterinary inspectors with government departments.[8]

The Education Department had two day schools for Asian students but no schools of its own for Africans and, as reflected in the Annual Report, it had very limited funding. So it could not demonstrate the kind of education that was needed; it could only advise, exhort and give "complete freedom to experiment". How much experiment went on is suggested by the authors' choice of examples:

Most successful work on these lines has been organised by the Anglican Mission at Nyakasura School in Toro... King's College, Budo, with an excellent hobby scheme, and a miniature farm, has demonstrated also the value and necessity of a wider curriculum.[9]

In short, the kind of work that the middle schools ought to have been doing could be exemplified only in two of the CMS secondary schools.

Institutionalised education in general, and Budo in particular, had now been established for a generation. What had been the effects on and for Ugandan society? Kenneth Ingham noticed some socio-political development:

> The Protectorate authorities welcomed students at all levels of education, since it was only they who could fit into the increasingly complex pattern of modern administration. So there began to emerge a new class, an Aristocracy of Education, which in time tended to usurp the positions of importance formerly occupied by men who had led the religious factions in war and had won their place in a peaceful land, by their strength of character, by their experience and by their powerful following.[10]

But David Apter implied that "usurp" was hardly the appropriate word; the work of the Weatherheads, Grace and their colleagues towards an education that would not estrange the African from his home and from the land, had made an impact:

> Characteristically, in rapidly changing societies, those who come into the greatest conflict with the forces of tradition, are the newly educated groupings. In Ghana and parts of Nigeria, for example, the young educated elements often competed and conflicted with the chiefs. This pattern did not emerge in Uganda. For one thing, the younger, educated elements did not move to towns and cities, removing themselves from the way of life of their families and friends. Quite the contrary, it was common practice for a highly educated Muganda to be a farmer. Also, just as large numbers of educated Africans from Budo and Makerere, were becoming prominent, a considerable turnover in chieftaincies and clerkships was making its appearance. A Makerere generation became a

political force. But it was not alienated in manners and morals from the rest of the country.[11]

He went on to consider what were the best qualifications for office in this changing society:

> It was not enough to claim descent from an important family ... Prestige came to be based as much upon participation in Church, Old Boys' association activities, lecture and literary societies, as upon family itself. Many of the new chiefs and many who came into clerical and functional positions around Mengo, the Provincial Commissioner's Office, and the country and district offices, were drawn from these new and important associations such as the United Budonian Club, or were Makerere College graduates.[12]

In fact there were, as yet, no other old boys associations "such as" the United Budonian Club, of anything like comparable size and influence. At least two reasonable conclusions could be drawn from the varied evidence available in 1936: first, that the government Education Department had neither an adequate policy for African education, nor the funds to implement one; secondly that Budo was fulfilling at least some of the hopes that Bishop Tucker and Sabaganzi Weatherhead had held for it in 1904.

Education in Uganda now had an enthusiastic supporter in the new Governor, Sir Philip Mitchell, who was to do much to forward the development of Makerere. As can be deduced from the 1936 report, Gaster had quickly built a cordial relationship with the Education Department and it did not take him long to obtain a grant for a new junior school building which he had designed. Sir Philip laid the foundation stone in 1936 and the building was in use by the end of 1937.

Meanwhile, Gaster also gave energetic and imaginative support to the co-education experiment. It was regarded as experimental for years by its many strident critics, one of whose ill-considered arguments against it was the undoubted excellence of the CMS girls' school at Gayaza, which - still only a Junior School - had predictably few disciplinary problems. It took the efforts of five headmasters, five girls' wardens and a generation of able girls to entrench confident co-education, and Gaster's enthusiasm was crucial. The girls were still relatively few, young and small. Gaster insisted on a high level of courtesy from the boys. They were encouraged to help with games at the Girls' End, Scouts were to help with the Brownies camps, and all were to try to draw the girls fully into the life of the school. Old Budonians of Gaster's time still talk with admiring amusement of his own eccentric courtesies, notably during heavy rain when he would himself make four or five return journeys in the school van to ferry all the girls to the classroom block so that they would arrive dry and punctual for lessons. The boys, on their shorter walks, could fend for themselves.

In 1938, however, staff and parents were cheered when the first three girls passed the highly competetive entrance examination for the senior school. Makerere bachelors trembled, but the Education Department rejoiced:

> The co-educational experiment [at King's College, Budo] promises to be successful.

> For the first time in the history of the Protectorate, girls are taking the same academic subjects as boys in the first form of a secondary school and have been well placed in the termly tests.[13]

Gaster was quick to press his advantage. He secured from the Education Department a grant to build a large dormitory, to his design, for the steady flow of girls who could now be expected to join the senior school. Lady Mitchell laid the foundation stone of Grace House in August 1938 and Gaster saw it completed before he left. It may not have been the most graceful of his three major buildings - themselves a rare, perhaps unique, contribution by a current headmaster of any school - but it has been good enough to warrant considerable recent extension and still stands, in the twenty-first century, softened in outline by adjacent new dormitories.

The Budo staff remained stable throughout Gaster's headship, though in 1936 Usher-Wilson left to direct CMS pastoral work in Busoga and was then consecrated, with the romantic designation Bishop on the

Upper Nile. In 1938 Miss Dorothy Gayer arrived to take over as Girls' Warden. In the same year, the future Kabaka, Edward Mutesa as he was known throughout his schooldays, entered the senior school, and Captain Freddie Crittendon was appointed to the staff as his personal tutor. The Buganda government paid for the building of a large house for the future Kabaka, his tutor and servants, but Mutesa took part fully in the normal curriculum and activities of the school, excelling at football and debating.

The out-of-class activities which had become a much-praised feature of the school - hobbies, drama, music, which now included tuition in the violin and cello, and voluntary work for neighbouring bush schools - all continued strongly, in spite of a growing preoccupation in the senior classes with the School Certificate courses. Gaster added art - in and out of the classroom. He was a keen water-colour artist, particularly of landscape, for which Budo Hill gave him splendid scope. Boys and girls were quick to take an interest and, from a hobby, formal timetabled classes had developed by 1938. Stephen Wright enthused:

> As a talented artist himself, he inspired a great deal of enthusiasm among many of the boys and girls. His type of Art was not approved of by many artists in Uganda, as being insufficiently individualistic. At the same time, the formal designs, by some of the pupils, based on the indigenous flowers and shrubs of Uganda, received a very good "press" when they were shown at an exhibition in the UK, and some were sold for commercial designs.[14]

Budo has since had several enthusiastic art teachers whose work has inspired imitation. It has been a recurring but perhaps unwarranted criticism of the school's art that it has no recognisable style and "lacks individuality". Ever since Gaster's time the study and practice of art has certainly not lacked enthusiasm.

Gaster felt that if the first candidates could perform well in the Cambridge examinations, then Budo would have "arrived" as a full secondary school. He would have been pleased by what they did. In December 1939, five boys out of the seven entered, obtained their School Certificates, two of them with three "distinctions" and five "credits" each. It was certain that the courses would continue, and likely that entry to Makerere would, before long, be dependant on the results of the Cambridge examinations.

Gaster never knew of this success. He was due for home leave in December 1939 and would then almost certainly have retired, having completed the five years that Fraser and Grace had suggested might be most helpful to the school. But he was unwell through most of the first term of 1939 and late in March was ordered by the mission doctors to return to England, where he died in June. His short headship had been by no means an interim or "caretaker" assignment; in his four years he had done much to - literally - build up Budo to its position as Uganda's premier African secondary school and had faithfully nurtured all that his predecessors and the host of Old Budonians most prized in their school.

Stephen Wright, who had been teaching at Budo for 13 years, was acting head for the rest of the year and in December yet another link was forged with Achimota College when, on the strong recommendation of Canon Grace, Dennis Herbert was appointed from his staff to the headship of King's College. Gaster's plans for further new buildings on the Hill had not been completed when he was invalided home. Within a few months of Herbert's appointment, the effects of the Second World War were being felt in Uganda, and ensured that they never would be.

Notes

[1] King's College Budo: a Prospectus 1936-37. KCB archives.

[2] Wright S.H. to McGregor GP, 9 November 1964. KCB archives

[3] A Prospectus. *op. cit.*

[4] *Uganda Church Review*, No. 41, March 1936, pp. 23-24

[5] *Ibid.* No. 42, June 1936, p. 38.

[6] *Ibid.* No. 43, October 1936, p. 71.

[7] Annual Report of Uganda Education Department 1936, pp. 21-27.

[8] Thomas H.B. and Scott R., *Uganda*, London: OUP 1935, pp. 317-8.

[9] Ibid.

[10] Ingham K., *Some Aspects of the History of Buganda*, Kampala,

Uganda Society 1956, p.11.

[11] Apter D.E., *The Political Kingdom in Uganda*, Princeton/London, Princeton UP/ OUP 1961, p. 199.

[12] Ibid. p. 201

[13] Annual Report of Uganda Education Department 1938, p. 21.

[14] Wright S.H. *op. cit.*

6

Crisis and Convalescence: 1939-1947

Dennis George Herbert was the son of the first Baron Hemingford and had gone straight from Oxford University to teach at Achimota from 1926 to 1939. He had learnt about Budo from Fraser and Grace and had seen their educational ideas in action. Two years after joining Budo he was invited to be the principal speaker at a national education conference held at Gayaza. He chose the theme 'Character Training' and shared some of his convictions and ideals. Like Grace he thought mutual trust was paramount:

> My old headmaster, Sanderson of Oundle, used to say, "No man knows that by which he does the highest good." Certainly he himself must soon have been oblivious of an incident that won my heart. I was told by a master to go into town and buy a syphon of soda water for a visiting examiner. As I marched from the shop, carrying the syphon, I met the headmaster. I took off my cap, he acknowledged the greeting, and I passed on, bursting with pride that he so trusted me that he never even questioned my curious occupation.[1]

He believed that the Christian teacher should not only be a happy person but should show himself to be so. He should be willing to give time to explain to students why he wanted things done in a certain way, and to listen to their explanations. Another key principle was what he called "Expectation":

> A.G. Fraser has said "We do more for our students by expecting virtues from them than by inculcating them"... May I give a warning against lowering our standards for Africa? It is insulting and unnecesary to expect less of a person because he is an African, and it is a denial of the power of Christ. It is true that he that is faithful in little things is faithful also in much, but in my experience

it is not true that he that is unfaithful in little things is also unfaithful in much. Africans fail in many things that we think important because to them they do not seem important. A man who cannot be relied upon to post a letter, may be thoroughly capable of taking charge of a House of thirty boys - a responsibility which catches his imagination. We are sometimes slow to give responsibilities of this kind.[2]

Herbert warmly supported the varied out-of-class activities that flourished at Budo. During his headship the School Certificate became very important, but he resisted the preoccupation with academic study which it tended to induce in students and their parents:

Many of you will have heard of Kurt Hahn's school at Gordonstoun in Scotland. Kurt Hahn believes that every boy has, perhaps lying latent, some great passion - it may be for mathematics or gardening or sculpture or organisation - and that it is the school's duty to discover and satisfy that passion, and that its satisfaction is the surest way of leading the child safely through the disturbing period of adolescence.[3]

He stressed the importance of striking the right balance in a school between firm control and desirable freedom. Obviously teachers had to try not to be irritable and angry about trivialities, however personally exasperating they might be:

But we need not be too much afraid of anger. Sanderson once set a question for discussion, in an examination for student teachers: "Never punish except in anger." The Principal of the college returned the paper suggesting that the question should read "Never punish in anger". Sanderson replied that he had meant what he had written. He believed pupils disliked a cold judicial weighing of their misdeeds and were greatly helped by the realisation that they had infuriated some warm-hearted person whom they respected.[4]

The Education Department's Annual Report for 1940, Herbert's first year, emphasised that every activity had already been badly affected by the war. Fourteen CMS teachers and 5 Roman Catholic teaching brothers had been called up for military service. Budo lost Crittendon, and Clement Pain who had joined the staff in 1936. At Nyakasura,

Callwell re-joined the navy and was temporarily replaced by Douglas Tomblings who, after 16 years as principal of Makerere, gave up his retirement leave, to save the school from closing. Agricultural education was badly hit. The farm school at Namutamba was closed because of difficulties over staffing and funding - which could almost certainly have been overcome if the Education Department had believed that agriculture was important in the secondary curriculum. Even worse, the successful Catholic counterpart, run by the Verona Fathers at Gulu, was also closed - because the Italian priests were interned for the duration of the war.

Yet there was a brighter side to 1940. Government expenditure on education was £136,000, representing over 8 percent of the total revenue and twice the figure for 1936. Sir Philip Mitchell's personal support was also reflected in detailed proposals for expansion and improvement, to which he had given hard thought, troubled by

> ... the problem of overwhelming numbers of poor and illiterate peasants beginning then to clamour for education, for any book learning; a clamour that has since then become almost deafening and which cannot be satisfied, for there are neither the teachers nor the funds to do it.

> The answer that I saw was that my duty lay in promoting to the utmost the development of university education, including of course advanced teacher training; of technical education and of secondary schools to supply both with teachable pupils in sufficient numbers and of teachable quality. If this meant that the education of the masses must remain for a while - a while that might be a generation - the muddle that it then was, I could not help that. I had not the power to stop it.[5]

In 1937 the De La Warr Commission on Higher Education, which Sir Philip had requested, had reported briskly and realistically. As a result Makerere College was expanded, largely rebuilt, and provided with an endowment of £500,000 - which many English university colleges of that time would have coveted - provided by the governments of Uganda, Tanganyika and Kenya and the newly established Colonial Development Fund. H.B. Thomas was appointed to chair an African

Education committee to recommend future structures and patterns of co-operation. Its report [6] was much in line with Governor Mitchell's reflections:

> I was convinced that a Departmental, secular school system was not a suitable way of doing what we had to do, and equally convinced that the missions had an indispensable contribution to make. But the staffs of schools must not be constantly changed, nor their headmasters and mistresses under the direct authority of a society's headquarters in Europe, or of ecclesiastical superiors in Africa, in matters of education. Nor was it right that the schools should be in continuous financial difficulties and teachers grossly underpaid.
>
> This last point involved serious difficulties for the missions for the Roman Catholics, who lived as religious communities and had objections to personal salaries - while legislatures did not like other forms of subsidy. And most of the Protestant missionaries, especially the older ones, had always themselves worked for the merest pittance and felt strongly that there was a spirituality about poverty and personal sacrifice which must be preserved. They had much right on their side; but the fact remained that the salaries offered, both for recruitment from Europe and for African masters and mistresses, were not getting the staff required by places like Budo, in sufficient numbers, or of adequate quality.
>
> So an offer was made to the Bishops that Government would make itself responsible for capital expenditure on approved buildings, and for recurrent expenditure, to the extent of the difference between income from fees - and any other sources of income there might be - and the sums needed to run selected schools as they ought to be run. In return, the schools were to become more or less independent foundations, each under its Board of Governors, on which government would be represented; headmasters and mistresses were to have much more independent   authority, and staff were not to be transferable from school to school as vacancies occurred. After much negotiation an arrangement on these lines was made and has I hope given satisfaction ...[7]

For these enlightened improvements, Budo and the other selected secondary schools - the CMS schools at Nyakasura and Mwiri, and the Catholic Kisubi and Namilyango - owed much to the Thomas

Committee, and particularly Sir Philip, who left Uganda in 1940, as soon as they had been agreed. He was to take charge, in Nairobi, of the Governors' Committee of the East African colonies, including Northern Rhodesia and Nysasaland, which were co-operating closely in the war effort; but he had not seen the last of Budo.

In response to the much increased government involvement in education, the missions accepted a government suggestion that, to facilitate administration, there should be Protestant and Catholic secretariats. CMS made a wise choice, but Herbert lost his most experienced teacher, when Stephen Wright left Budo in 1940 to become the first Protestant "Educational Secretary General", a post in which he served African education well, and continued to offer good advice to Budo, until 1948.

One valuable development, which resulted directly from the war, was reported by Herbert in 1941:

> The absence of members of staff on military service has hastened the proper process whereby our African colleagues take an increasing share of the leading positions on the staff. Little but good has resulted. An African Bursar was appointed at the beginning of 1940. At the end of that year the excess of the college's assets over its liabilities was five times what it had been when he took over. At the same time the post of Caterer was made a whole-time job and given to an African. He has greatly reduced expenditure, and yet - even in the opinion of the pupils - has improved the diet... We have an African supervisor for the primary school, and all their out-of-class activities are organised by Africans.[8]

Four of the five school houses, the Departments of Geography, Mathematics and Luganda and the organisation of scouts, games, music and physical training were all led by African teachers. In spite of the recruitment difficulties which Governor Mitchell had highlighted, Budo was fortunate to welcome back Ernest Sempebwa, fresh from success at Makerere, for the first of his three teaching stints over more than 20 years. The closure of the Namutamba Farm School was eventually to prove fatal to the growth of Agriculture as a full academic and practical study, but fortunately it did not mean that classes at once became all academic. In 1940 Ellis Hillier joined the staff to head a three-year commercial course leading to the Certificate of the London Chamber of Commerce. Similar courses were launched at the same time, at Kisubi and Namilyango.

The most remarkable development of Herbert's first two years was not, however, scholastic. In 1939, after a reign of 25 years as Kabaka of Buganda, Sir Daudi Chwa died. He was immediately succeeded by his son, Kabaka Mutesa II, who remained a student at Budo, as Edward Mutesa, for two more years, until he had completed the Cambridge School Certificate course.

In 1941 the Education Department mounted its first full inspection of the five secondary schools and found that all were satisfactory, except Nyakasura, which was struggling with impossible staffing shortages. The inspectors made only one specific comment on Budo:

> In the case of King's College, Budo attention is particularly drawn to the need for new buildings, to replace those built many years ago, which do not conform to modern standards.[9]

It would be thirteen years before the dire need for a main school block was met - twenty years after Gaster had first urged it. The inspectors also suggested that the headmasters should try to keep daily log books of notable events, successes and difficulties. Herbert began to do so in 1942 and his log books, with those of his successor, Cobb, have been valuable primary sources for this history, and have been preserved in the school archives.

The year 1942 began well with the admission of the first girls to pass into Budo senior school from another junior school - three girls from Gayaza had passed the entrance examination well enough to win places. After Budo's first 1939 successes it was regrettable that this fine junior school had to wait another 13 years for its first "Cambridge" passes; but Budo benefited from a small but steady flow of very able Gayaza girls. The commercial course had begun its third year, so Budo had its first "Commercial Sixth" form, which stretched classroom accommodation to the limit. When therefore, following the inspection, Budo agreed to take in the two top classes from Nyakasura, to complete their School Certificate courses, a temporary classroom was created under the library arch; the floor was concreted and canvas curtains were hung across the two entrances, to keep out the wind and rain.

Herbert invited a small committee of the governors to inspect the school; where the Education Department had pressed for more spacious modern buildings, the governors committee asked that, at the Girls' End

> ... a smaller, more humble building, be placed alongside the new domestic science house, so that the students may produce, under conditions nearer to native home life, the lessons that they learn in domestic science.[10]

The governors were not being perverse, but responding to Grace's injunction to "keep the school African". The problem of reconciling the two cultures seems ever-present; it was highlighted in a log book entry for April 6th:

> The headmaster gave a lecture to the Junior Secondary classes on "English Table Manners", Mr Kaima gave a lecture to the Primary Classes on "The Keeping of Tribal Customs."[11]

Herbert was trying to run a badly overcrowded school, with a wide age range, in unpredictably difficult war-time conditions. Political tensions did not help. Budo had never been the preserve of the "sons of chiefs" and the highly competitive annual entrance examination had now entrenched its openness. Yet it remained true - and still does in the twenty-first century - that many of its students came from the culturally advantaged homes of prominent, politically involved families. For its first hundred years the school has remained sensitive to political unrest in Buganda. Ingrams expressed one viewpoint on that in 1960:

> Politics unfortunately seem to be too much a feature of Budo. One member of the Buganda Government said to me that the significance of Budo was that it led to political interest by those who left.[12]

The Buganda minister was in a sense complimenting the school on achieving Bishop Tucker's and Weatherhead's aim for it; but the tendency for some senior students to follow - and act out - the political animosities of their elders, has not been helpful to the school. Apter linked the serious disturbances at Budo late in 1942 with other signs of political unrest throughout Uganda.[13]

For these, the effects of the war were partly to blame. Like the schools, the Protectorate administration had lost many staff, particularly in the districts, where officers therefore toured less frequently. So government often appeared remote and abitrary. Many Ugandans had served with the army in the Abyssinian campaign and - like Weatherhead's young men of 1919 - had returned with less respect for European civilisation, and a strong spirit of nationalism. Meanwhile, the Buganda government had been finding it difficult to resist the encroachments of the Protectorate government within Buganda. Low and Pratt noted:

> Such factors increased the tensions in the society. They did not alter their basic nature. Suspicion and fear of the European and hostility and jealousy towards the chiefs and ministers who had authority under the British, continued to be the main source of political unrest... As the power of popular agitation became more evident, tribal factions within the ruling hierarchy cultivated the suspicion of things European, in an effort to divert it against the Baganda leaders whom they wished to overthrow.[14]

It was not easy for politically alert senior students living in such a hostile atmosphere to remain loyal to a European headmaster.

Budo had another peculiar difficulty. In 1941 the Namasole, widow of Daudi Chwa and mother of the Kabaka, announced that she wished to marry again. There had been a long-established tradition in pre-Christian Buganda that the Namasole should never re-marry, but the Native Anglican Church solemnised the marriage, and incurred the hostility of many Baganda by doing so. Extremists rejected the Anglican Church along with all other European institutions - and Budo was an Anglican Church school. The first manifestation of Baganda solidarity at Budo in 1942 is whimsically registered in a log book entry of April 11th:

> Cricket match: the Baganda beat the World, by sixty runs to fifty.[15]

In May a committee of staff and senior students considered the problems of reconciling African and European manners; in June two teachers, E.M.K. Mulira and E.Z. Kibuka, lectured to the senior school on "The Importance of the Vernacular" and the Katikiro lectured on "The Role of the Subordinate Chiefs in the Buganda Government". The senior school, in a debate conducted in Luganda, carried the motion "That Uganda should have One United Native Government". In July attention was focused on Kiganda tradition when the Katikiro and senior chiefs paid several visits to the school to make the preliminary arrangements for the coronation of Kabaka Edward Mutesa, which was to take place on Budo Hill in November when he had completed his senior school course and had "come of age". So in spite of its largely European curriculum, Budo could be seen to be making genuine efforts to value Ugandan culture and to keep itself "a Christian, African school".

Yet it had become increasingly difficult to maintain good discipline throughout the school. A number of the boys who had been unwisely admitted to the Junior School from the Primary, without any entrance examination in Gaster's time, were now at the top of the senior school. This was also the ninth year of co-education and the staff were therefore, for the first time, responsible for advising young women and men in the senior classes - nearer to their twenties than their adolescent years - how to relate to each other in a boarding school, in a country in which still relatively few people firmly believed that girls were worth educating to a high level.

In February, seventeen of the African teachers - mostly Old Budonians - had submitted a memorandum to Herbert. Entitled "A Desired Reform of the School", it recorded the view of "many outsiders" that the behaviour of Budo students had deteriorated, and stated that most staff agreed. They believed that the whole staff was at fault and must work together to improve matters. Particular criticisms were that there was too much drinking and smoking by boys and that neither offence was punished severely enough; students were generally untidy and often rude; the dormitories, kitchens, and washing facilities were inadequate and dirty; general school maintenance, the water supply and the housing for African staff were inadequate; and relationships among staff and between staff and students were too distant. Finally, they asked the headmaster to consult them more, and to leave them more often to take their own disciplinary action.

Herbert met the whole staff to discuss the proposals, and also met the prefects to sound their views on the condition of the school. As a result the beginning of the second term, in early May, saw a general tightening up on the observance of school "bounds", on attendance and behaviour at meals, on dress and on general courtesy. In August there was a brief British interlude. The Education Department presented a framed portrait of King George VI to the school, and a Budo "Warship Fund" concert in Kampala raised £50. Among highlights of the entertainment were extracts from the speeches of British prime minister, Winston Churchill - declaimed by Daudi Ocheng, who 20 years later was to be a successful lawyer and member of parliament - and the singing, twice, of "Rule Britania". The year moved uneasily and with growing excitement, towards final examinations and the coronation.

Early in November, one of the European mistresses discovered some boys at the Girls' End after dark, which was forbidden. When she approached them they threw stones at her and escaped. Herbert consulted his head prefect, who thought that discipline was still uncertain; he believed Herbert had been too lenient with boys who had been drinking and should have expelled them all immediately - which recalls Grace's difference with Kabaka Daudi Chwa in 1930.

On 6 November the school staged its formal farewell to Edward Mutesa. The committee of prefects and staff which had planned it had agreed that they wanted to honour him as a distinguished Budo student rather than as Kabaka of Buganda. The day was declared a half-holiday, with numerous group photographs, a feast for the whole school and many visitors in the main quadrangle, and the customary farewell concert. These end-of-year concerts usually lasted about two hours though headmasters had sometimes had to ask the organisers to cut some of the later items to avoid running too late. For this occasion the programme had been left entirely to the boys, but after about two and a half hours, Herbert went backstage and asked them to draw the concert to a close. They did, and after a farewell speech by Herbert, who told Mutesa that whatever the future might hold for him he could always be certain of the love and support of those who had been with him at Budo, the day of celebration ended.

Next evening there was a debate, at which Mutesa and the Resident of Buganda were the main speakers. In the surprisingly small audience there were no girls and hardly any Baganda. During the debate a gang of boys caused a disturbance in the school, and the African teacher and two sub-prefects who went to restore order, were stoned. Herbert met the prefects next morning and they told him that the ugly mood of the school was the result of his "insult" to HH The Kabaka, in cutting short the concert in his honour. The school had expected at least three hours of entertainment for a person of such eminence. Herbert later reported to the governors:

> One prefect expressed surprise at my considering twenty items too numerous for a concert for the Kabaka, and said he supposed that a concert for the king of England might contain thirty or forty items... I said that there was a real difference of outlook between us as to the nature of the concert; that they appeared to think that the longer the concert the greater the honour done to the person for whom it was given, whereas English people valued quality above length and would be extremely anxious that a concert should not be so long as to tire the person in whose honour it was given. I said that if the King of England had been present on Friday I should most certainly have cut the programme as I did... I admitted that I had not understood their depth of feeling about the concert, and blamed myself for not having sensed it ... I tried, but evidently failed, to assure the meeting that, whatever I had done, I had certainly not intended any slight to the Kabaka.[16]

Herbert needed the support of the prefects if the crisis was to be negotiated, so when they asked him to discuss some other general points he readily agreed. They spoke of the condition of the school in much the same terms as the African staff had written, but made one quite contrary criticism which must have baffled him. The staff had thought him remote and arbitrary. The prefects took a different view:

They disliked my knowing too much about the school and said they would prefer to have a headmaster who lived in his house and walked about his lawns and smiled to the pupils. I remarked that they and I had different pictures of what a headmaster should be.[17]

Late that evening the school carpentry shop was set on fire and destroyed. Many of the boys worked voluntarily to save tools and materials from the blazing building. Early next morning the head prefect brought to Herbert the remains of the portrait of King George VI which had recently been hung in Big School. The glass was smashed and the picture torn. It had been found in the middle of the cricket field. Herbert called a staff meeting which elected a sub-committee to advise on the next steps in a serious situation. He accepted its advice that he should announce that the school had 24 hours in which to produce the names of the culprits. Later that evening one of the boys warned him that a group of senior boys was planning to destroy several other school buildings, including staff houses. The carpentry shop and the king's portrait had been first on their list. Shortly afterwards some boys stoned a sub-prefect suspected of giving information to the staff, and Herbert sent a message to the police in Kampala. Four of the boys suspected of leading the disturbance were ordered to report to him and did so, smelling strongly of beer.

A police patrol soon arrived, accompanied by the Katikiro and the regents of Buganda, for throughout all these events, the Kabaka, as a student of the school until the end of the term, had remained in residence on the hill. On the following day, 11 November, two of the four ringleaders were publicly expelled for drinking. After a long staff meeting, at which the Katikiro and the regents were present, the Director of Education and the Resident of Buganda arrived. With the agreement of all, except one member of staff, the Director announced that the school would be closed immediately for an indefinite period. By midday on the 12th the students had left for their homes. They came from all over Uganda, so many could not be present a week later, as they had all hoped to be, when the coronation of HH Kabaka Mutesa II was solemnised in the school chapel.

Herbert had trusted his senior students and they, subjected to very difficult pressures, had let him down. Worse followed. Next day he received a copy of a letter sent to the Bishop as chairman of the governors by 18 African members of his staff. They wrote that now that the crisis was past they felt released from their obligations to the headmaster. They believed that the outrageous behaviour of the students had no political significance but had been directed entirely against the headmaster, and that if a new headmaster was not appointed, they would resign from the Budo staff on 31 December.

The Board of Governors asked for a government commission to enquire into the disturbances and to make recommendations on the future running of the school. The first result was that on 31 December Bishop Stuart accepted the resignations of the 18 members of staff. So an experienced and talented body of teachers were scattered among other schools, and Herbert, after three punishing years, had to begin again. Some of the eighteen names make interesting reading sixty years later.

Among those who resigned were E.M.K. Mulira and A.K. Sempa; Y. K. Lule remained. Among new recruits to the staff were J.L. Zake and A. K. Kironde. In the years to come these five would become respectively: Founder of the Uganda National Movement and member of the Uganda parliament; Minister of Finance, Buganda government; Principal of Makerere University and, briefly, President of Uganda; Minister of Education, Uganda government; Uganda Permanent Representative, United Nations, New York. All were Old Budonians. Apter noted that the schools to which they dispersed, particularly the Aggrey Memorial School, became centres of the nationalism and political activism which were essential precursors of the formation of political parties in the 1950s. Even in disaster Budo seemed to serve its purpose.[18]

The government commission recommended that the school should re-open in mid-February 1943, with numbers reduced from 380 students to 290. The number of classes was to be reduced by having only one "stream" in each of the last three senior years, to facilitate closer relationships between senior students and staff. Grants were made for renovations to the buildings, with a special grant for improved facilities for the girls. It was confirmed that Budo would remain one of the chosen "self-governing schools" - a remarkable vote of confidence. A letter sent to all parents explaining the new proposals ended with a message from the Director of Education, urging them not to listen to advice to remove their sons or daughters to other schools. The commissioners, governors and Education Department were all convinced "that the re-opened Budo would be a far better place than the former Budo".[19]

Bishop Stuart wrote in his 'Annual Charge to the Mission' that, though he might be criticised for concentrating on education at the expense of pastoral work, he would do anything in his power to give Budo a chance of full recovery. It had not been a simple disturbance; governors, staff, parents and students must all bear part of the blame. But close co-operation between Africans and Europeans was now vital - because he believed that Budo would not get a second chance.[20]

Such co-operation could not be easy because the political tensions in Buganda remained. Moreover, the Director of Medical Services had just reported to the Legislative Council that staff shortages and the difficulty of taking essential leave had certainly affected the health of European officers, including teachers.[21] Still, the school opened again as planned. All the old house affiliations were cancelled, the students were re-distributed and new prefects appointed. The re-opening service was attended by the Kabaka, the Bishop and Ham Mukasa - who had been present at the Foundation Service in 1906. In a brief speech - which certainly impressed student Edward Kalanzi, who reported it to me sixty-one years later - he took a pencil from his pocket, held it up, snapped it in half and threw the pieces over his shoulders saying "Now we must all put the past behind us and go forward together."[22]

During the service the new prefects publicly made a promise, which has been made by their successors ever since:

> I accept the office of Prefect in this College and solemnly make this promise, which with God's help I will keep. I promise to do my duty, seeking not my own comfort, glory or popularity, but sacrificing myself for the good of Budo. I promise to be loyal to the headmaster, the staff and those in authority in the College. I

promise to protect those younger than myself and to deal justly between pupil and pupil, making no distinction for the sake of tribe, house, or private friendship. I promise to govern my life so that none shall learn evil from me in word or deed; to fight against sin wherever I see it, and to stand for that which I know to be right.[23]

After only a few days of optimistic activity the school began to feel the effects of a serious food shortage in Buganda. On 24 March, after a promising month, Herbert was forced to close the school again because the food supply was so uncertain. Only the sixth form students were able to remain on the hill. Not until 1 June, when supplies had improved and prices fallen, was the whole school able to return.

The government then formally announced the names of the schools which were to become self-governing and - true to form - the Old Budonians greeted the news with suspicion. Strong government representation on the Budo Board of Governors sounded ominous. Herbert talked to the United Budonian Club about the advantages of the proposed new school constitution, and the Protestant members of the Buganda Lukiiko actually debated the scheme over three days before, at the end of October, approving it, for an experimental period of five years. The United Budonian Club had no legal right to interfere, but it was the most influential non-government body in Uganda and strongly represented on the Board and the staff, so its support was essential if the new scheme was to succeed.

At the beginning of the third term of 1943 a new classroom block for the commercial class was completed and a new dormitory for the girls begun. Both had been designed by Robinson, and the government gave a grant of £1900. In October, while Herbert was discussing with the Director of Education a ten-year plan for building development, a half-completed shed was deliberately set on fire and a new portrait of King George VI in Big School was damaged - both in obvious imitation of the protests of 1942. One boy was expelled and Herbert wrote a letter of apology on behalf of the school to the Governor, who responded by according to Budo the dubious distinction of being the only Ugandan school in which the king's portrait should not be displayed.[24]

Governors and staff had continued to discuss possible improvements and in November the Board decided that one of the school's greatest difficulties - its age range of roughly 7 to 22 years - must be overcome. The primary school should be removed to a separate site, and King's College become entirely a secondary school. A new primary school could not be built at once, however, because there was no money available, and simply to close the present school would cause great hardship. The decision was to be implemented "as soon as possible".[25] It took seventeen years.

The year 1943 ended quietly and the achievements of governors, staff and students were summarised in the Annual Report of the Education Department:

> At King's College, Budo it was extraordinarily disappointing that five weeks after the school had been re-opened under new auspices it had to be closed again because of the acute food shortage. In spite of this, of the shortened year that resulted, of the uphill task of retrieving the good name of the school at a period of abnormal difficulty, the year has been one of most creditable achievement. This has been reflected in the administration, the academic work, the games, athletics and future planning. It bore testimony to the resolution of purpose brought to bear on the peculiar challenge of the year. Building improvements have been carried out and apart from the varied activities of school societies, the year was characterised by visits arranged for groups of students to a wide range of institutions and demonstrations, and by talks given by visiting lecturers.[26]

The praise of the academic work was later justified by the success of all six candidates for the Cambridge School Certificate, and by the only comment made on the Makerere entrance examination by the principal of the college which was that the candidates from King's College, Budo had done notably well.[27] A suitable last word on a testing year might be a log book entry for 4 December:

> Debate: That this House believes that a politician is more useful to his country than a scientist. The motion was lost, by 35 votes to 70.

1944 was another good year. The temper of the school can be judged from three events: Communal work, which had faded away in the emergency and staff losses of 1939-40, was voluntarily revived by senior boys. Three non-Baganda boys asked to join the classes in Luganda - the first ever to do so. A group of senior students revived the voluntary classes for porters, which had been a feature of the early years under the Weatherheads. All this was in spite of the still increasing pressure of examinations, about which Herbert spoke at length at the first Speech Day since 1941, which was held in July.

He began by thanking Governor Sir Charles Dundas, for allowing Budo to become one of the self-governing schools. He was confident that this would prove a wise decision, but under the circumstances it had certainly been a generous one. He regretted that there was not better support for the commercial classes; too many parents still believed that only academic education was of real use. Turning to examinations he cited the case of a Budo boy who at the end of his final year had sat for the Cambridge School Certificate; then for the Makerere entrance examination because, although Oxford and Cambridge universities recognised the Cambridge examination, Makerere did not; then for the Senior Secondary Leaving Certificate, which alone would qualify him for a certain grade of civil service appointment in Uganda; and finally for the special examination of a particular government department - which he might wish to enter should he fail to gain admission to Makerere - and which recognised none of the other examinations. This kind of final year strain made it difficult to arouse enthusiasm for all the other interests which a good school should foster, and Herbert appealed for a rationalisation of the examination system.[28] The governor promised to do all he could to promote more sensible recognitions and when the student in question, Edward Kalanzi, introduced himself, Sir Charles congratulated him, saying, "I think you are the most important person here today!" Three of Kalanzi's examination ordeals proved superfluous; he won a place at Makerere and had a successful career in Government service.[29]

Budonians of Herbert's time recall that he seemed to know all the senior boys well - one claimed that the headmaster could actually recognise any student in the school, from behind - and was aware of almost all that went on in the school. We have noted above, the contrary views of staff and students about that. The students seem to have been unanimous that, though Herbert was sometimes too lenient, his punishments were just - and usually very appropriate. Two 1944 log book entries illustrate:

> January 25th: W.S. Kajubi was punished for tricking a new boy into carrying water for him. He is to work as a porter for a week, carrying 25 buckets of water a day from Nansove...
>
> February 10th: S. Bengo is to sweep one of the quadrangle lawns every afternoon until half-term, for writing on a Mulago Hospital chit, a request purporting to come from the Medical Officer, that he should be excused sweeping.[30]

Kajubi became one of Budo's most distinguished educators, being director of the Makerere Institute of Education, twice vice-chancellor of Makerere University, and founder vice-chancellor of Nkumba University. Bengo maintained his interest in medical matters by becoming a dental surgeon.

Martin Aliker, who became a dental surgeon, and later Minister of State for International Cooperation in the Ministry of Foreign Affairs in the NRM government, looked back nostalgically to his four years at Budo under Herbert (1944-1947). Like his elder brother Daudi Ocheng - a celebrated Budonian (1933-44) – he was from Acholi and greatly valued the ethnic diversity of the Budo student community:

> I believe that Budo was the first institution to try to bring Ugandans together. We had no senior secondary school in the north and in my time all 18 districts of Uganda were represented in the school... When I arrived it was still an offence not to speak English, but Mr Herbert wisely modified that, allowing use of the vernacular in leisure time. A lot of non-Baganda - including me - took the trouble to learn Luganda and I think this had a further unifying influence - so Budo had two common languages!... I thought that the Christian influence was strong but not aggressive - good Christian guidance was always available from the headmaster, chaplain and staff ... looking back I think my years at Budo were the happiest of my young life - I enjoyed them more than prep school or Makerere.[31]

By this time the Old Budonians had become reconciled to the new status of the school and in August they came back in force for their first reunion for four years. More than 200 members spent the weekend on the hill. Herbert invited two members of the committee to talk to the sixth form about the aims and activities of the Association, and suggested that this should be done every year to encourage students who were leaving the school to join.

Makerere had now introduced a range of "higher courses" - the forerunners of subsequent degree programmes - and also a new "preliminary course". This was to meet the needs of students with good entrance results, who were not yet ready for the higher courses but should be after a further year of guided study. In November 1944, Catherine Senkatuka was accepted from the sixth form for admission to the preliminary course and so became the first woman student to enter Makerere College. The school staff - and the government Education Department - were jubilant, but because of a rumour that Catherine had been admitted only "because she was a girl", Herbert wrote to the college principal. He replied firmly that Catherine had been admitted "by merit of her work."[32] The boys of Budo did their best to appear unimpressed. On the evening the results of the entrance examination were announced, the school debated a motion that "Agriculture should be the chief subject of women's education in Uganda" - and carried it by a large majority.

Six Ugandan secondary schools, including for the first time Nabumali High School, entered a total of 47 candidates for the Makerere entrance examination. Of the 23 who passed, 12 were from Budo. In spite of this success, the staff were so concerned at the still growing shortage of staff and equipment that a staff meeting in December agreed that the school should not present candidates for the Cambridge School Certificate the following year.

The school opened a week late in 1945 because of a strike by porters, influenced by political disturbances in Buganda in January. In February the new girls' dormitory was officially opened by Lady Hall, wife of the governor. It was named Sabaganzi House after H.W. Weatherhead, who wrote from England to thank the school for so honouring him. He was then 74 and had just retired from a parish in Sussex. Sir Albert Cook, who had walked up from the coast with him in 1896, was present at the opening ceremony. Sabaganzi House was much superior to any of the boys' dormitories, but the boys may have salved their pride a few days later when, in the first debate of the term, they overwhelmed a motion "That women should receive equal pay with men for equal work."

Easter celebrated during term will remain an outstanding memory for hundreds of Old Budonians - students and staff. One of the best of Budo traditions was initiated in 1945 when for the first time a voluntary choir sang Easter carols around the hill at dawn on Easter Sunday. [My wife, Jean, and I arrived at Budo in January 1959. This was the heyday of the "Nightingales" - but no one had told us about Easter. At about four on Sunday morning I woke to the glorious sound. Jean was a few moments behind me but then sat bolt upright in bed and said, with great conviction, "It's Angels!" This fine tradition flagged during the violent years 1971-86, but is alive and well in the twenty-first century.]

Later in February 1945 serious rioting against the Buganda government broke out in Kampala and other parts of the kingdom. It was proof of the good work done in the previous two years, that Budo remained calm throughout. Even in September, when the Katikiro, Martin Luther Nsibirwa was assassinated at Namirembe Cathedral, there was no school demonstration. Nsibirwa had been a governor of Budo and was succeeded as Katikiro by E. Kawalya-Kagwa who was the first Old Budonian to hold that office. In spite of the staff decision of the previous December, the continuing high standard of work in the sixth form seemed to justify entering four candidates for "Cambridge" - and they all passed.

The Allied victories in Europe and the Far East and the end of the Second World War were quietly celebrated at Budo, but 1946, the first year of peace, opened more bleakly than any of the wartime years. Herbert had gone to England for his first leave after six years as headmaster. Nyakasura School had again been closed because of lack of staff, and again the senior class had transferred to Budo to complete the School Certificate course. Food was in short supply and the water pump at Nansove was unreliable. Most disappointing of all, the hopes for a new Big School block and for the removal of the primary school to its own site, were dashed when the Education Department announced that there could be no new building grants to existing schools until 1948. Yet government expenditure on education in 1946 was a generous £ 263,000, which reflects how much leeway there was to make up in maintenance, staffing and renewal of equipment, after the war. In August, Robinson received several cases of chemicals and laboratory equipment; he recorded gleefully that they were the first since 1939.

Early in the year, George Turner, who was retiring after seven years as principal of Makerere, had undertaken a review of African secondary education in East Africa, to assist the governments to plan expansion and to improve standards. In his report, presented in December, he wrote of the Protestant mission schools, comparing them with the Catholic schools in terms reminiscent of Huxley's impressions of 1929:

> Protestant and non-Roman Catholic schools present wider variety, as the tradition which they share is less positive and authoritarian. At their best they have great educational merit - a robust independence and free co-operation between staff and boys... Their buildings are often poor and rather ill-kept ... and shortage of competent staff often leaves the teaching patchy. But African teachers are given, on the whole, better scope in these schools, though the conditions they work in are often unsatisfactory. Budo has some special status and tradition which gives it a momentum peculiar among African schools.[33]

He endorsed the reforms of the Thomas Committee, and the self-governing schools scheme, but warned that there were gaps in the missionary education which the government must fill:

> In general the picture of African education in Uganda is encouraging. From the early vigour of missionary enterprise it has acquired more tradition than is found elsewhere. But as Government assumes larger responsibility, it needs to correct the casual distribution of the mission schools, to concentrate fragmentary and sporadic efforts which do not make for economy or efficiency, and to demand more strictly a return of competent service for public expenditure.[34]

When Herbert returned, in August, he found that Revd K. Edmunds, chaplain and teacher, who had been at Budo throughout the war, was returning to England, and that several teachers were ill and unable to work at the beginning of the third term. For the first half-term, twelve senior boys who intended to become teachers, took classes in both the junior and senior schools. Throughout the 1940s and 50s, Herbert and his successor found illness among staff a major problem. In their time, a day on which the whole staff team was fit and on classroom duty was remarkable enough to be recorded in the log book.

Two events saw 1947 off to a good start. The first was the celebration of the 50th anniversary of the arrival of Sir Albert Cook, the first Protestant medical missionary to Uganda. Sir Albert himself took vigorous part and reminisced on the early days of Budo, which he had known and supported well through all its 41 years. The second was the re-appointment to the staff of Mrs Essesa Makumbi, who had been one of the teachers who resigned in 1942. Herbert may well have felt that the recovery of Budo was complete.

Behind this gradual success lay the work of dozens of ancillary staff, without whom the best efforts of teachers and administrators would have been ineffective. Two such retainers of Herbert's years deserve mention. In 1947 *Ebifa* published a poem by an Old Budonian in praise of *Omwami* Katetemera who had been school messenger for more than 20 years. His feats of conveyance to and from Kampala - with a vast wooden crate fixed to his bicycle - were legendary. Herbert himself capped this by reminding Old Budonians of the marathon contribution of a school mason Antonio Tabula, who had joined the staff in 1905 to help build Big School and was still at work in 1947 having assisted on every building the school had erected.

All the classroom work went well throughout 1947. Domestic Science for the girls flourished in a new Homecraft Cottage; all four candidates for the London Chamber of Commerce Examinations were successful, as were all six for the Cambridge School Certificate. Yet again the Makerere entrance examination results were the best in the country.

In June, Herbert gave notice that he would be leaving at the end of the year, returning to West Africa to become the first rector of the newly separated Teacher Training College of Achimota. In appointing his successor, the Board of Governors broke with two traditions. Timothy Cobb was a housemaster at Bryanston, a reputedly liberal and progressive English public school. He was the first headmaster of Budo to be appointed from an English school, and also the first who was not a CMS missionary.

In October 1947, an era in CMS education in Uganda came to an end, with the death, at Nyakasura School, of Commander Callwell. Only then did the mission and the government realise how much of his own money he had put into keeping the school open and developing its curriculum and ethos. It was a fitting tribute to his work that, after consultations with the CMS, the Protectorate government agreed to take over responsibility for the school, with an assurance that the Christian character of its education would be maintained.

Cobb arrived at Budo early in December and Herbert left two weeks later. Like Canon Grace, Herbert had led the school through great difficulties and left it in good shape. He later became the first former headmaster to make a return visit.

Notes

[1] *Uganda Church Review*, No. 66, October 1942, p. 113.

[2] *Ibid*, pp. 114-5.

[3] *Ibid*

[4] *Ibid*

[5] Mitchell, Sir Philip, *African Afterthoughts*, London: Hutchinson, 1954, p. 180.

[6] Report of Uganda Education Department 1940.

[7] Mitchell *op. cit.* pp 182-3

[8] "A Letter to his Friends from the Headmaster of an African School." KCB archives

[9] Report of Uganda Education Department 1941, p. 8.

[10] KCB Logbook, 23 June 1942.

[11] *Ibid*, 6 April 1942.

[12] Ingrams H, *op. cit.* p.124.

[13] Apter, D, *op. cit.* p.207.

[14] Low and Pratt, *op. cit.* pp. 273-4.

[15] KCB Logbook 1942.

[16] Herbert D. The Closing of the Term at King's College, Budo,

[17] November 1942. KCB archives.

[18] *Ibid*

[19] Apter D. *op. cit.* p. 207.

[20] A Letter to Parents, January 1943, KCB archives.

[21] *Uganda Church Review*, No. 67, September 1943, p. 10.

[22] Report of Uganda Education Department 1943, p. 1.

[23] Kalanzi in conversation with the author, Namirembe, March 2004.

[24] KCB Logbook, 16 February 1943.

[25] Ibid, 9 October 1943.

[26] Ibid, 17 November 1943.

[27] Report of Uganda Education Department 1943, p. 19.

[28] *Ibid*

[29] KCB Logbook, 8 July 1944.

[30] Conversation with the author, March 2004.

[31] KCB Logbook, 25 January and February 10th 1944.

[32] Alliker, Dr Martin, in conversation with the author, Makerere, March 2002.

[33] KCB Logbook, 25 November 1944.

[34] Turner, G.C., A Review of African Secondary Education in East Africa, December 1946. p.16.

7

Towards Maturity: 1948-1957

Timothy Cobb found much that he admired and enjoyed at Budo, but throughout his ten-year headship his affection for the school did not blind him to its faults and shortcomings. In an account of the school in the early 1950s he wrote:

> The school motto forbids complacency. It is "*Gakyali Mabaga*" which, I am told, means "Though we may have done something there's still an awful lot more to do." But I may have invented the first part, for I am unashamedly proud of Budo. [1]

He was keen to preserve good traditions and build new ones, but had little patience with the Budonian habit of defending worthless traditions merely on the grounds that they had always been there.

An early log book entry captures much of the spirit of his leadership. It is not easy for a newcomer - of whatever status - to find out how things work at Budo, and it was only on the first Saturday of his first term that Cobb learnt that the school normally staged a concert on that day. He recorded:

> January 31st. The headmaster decided that the first Saturday evening must not go without some effort at entertainment. He summoned any members of staff to meet him, if interested, at 2.30 pm; only Mr Katana [Music] turned up, at 2.45. The entertainments monitor was sent for and an entertainment planned at 3 pm. An assembly was held and the school informed at 5.00, and an hour's entertainment given at 8.30. The school did not appear to enjoy it vastly, but the performers did. The headmaster was hit by bird droppings from the rafters, as usual. Some scheme must be devised for preventing A......... from singing again in public. [2]

He soon discovered some of the exasperations of Budo life. The sanatorium was still a dream and a boy who caught measles early in the term had to be covered in eucalyptus oil and isolated in a dormitory.

In April it was discovered that Big School, two of the dormitories and two staff houses had been badly damaged by termites. Some of the domestic facilities were still primitive. A note in the log book refers to the arrangements for accommodating some Makerere student-teachers, which included laying fresh cowdung on the floor of the house they were to live in. A prospectus commented sardonically on the lighting of the school by oil lamps:

> A dormitory for thirty boys, illuminated by one hurricane lamp, is one interpretation of Darkest Africa.[3]

Co-education remained problematic. Numbers were still depressingly unbalanced - in the senior school there were 40 girls to 200 boys - and many of the girls were weak in academic subjects. Some members of staff felt that, in spite of the extensive work in domestic science, the course for the girls was too academic and not related nearly enough to the domestic situtations to which most of them would return. On the other hand Budo's reputation was increasingly academic - perhaps inevitably as the education system expanded and some schools became more specialised. It was argued that Budo's main purpose in admitting girls was precisely to demonstrate that they were capable of holding their own with boys in academic studies, and should be given the chance to do so. In December Cobb wrote:

> A man whose daughter we have admitted to the school next year, and whose son we have refused to admit, came and asked if we would give her place to the son. The headmaster refused. Parents often talk of "wasting money" on their daughters' education.[4]

There was plenty of social contact between boys and girls but opinion among parents and teachers was sharply divided on the subject of ballroom dancing at school. Such dancing was alleged to be contrary to Kiganda social custom; it came close to causing a crisis in Buganda a few years later. Cobb took the view that as the boys and girls would certainly dance in the holidays if they wanted to, they might as well be taught to dance gracefully at school. So the dancing classes continued.

By the middle of 1948 Cobb had decided that there were at least three things he wanted to improve. He set up a "Brighter Weekend Committee" to suggest activities through which Budo could celebrate the sabbath in a fashion "somewhere between the Black Sunday of the Protestant churches and the Continental Sunday of the Roman Catholic."[5] Communal work again seemed in danger of slipping out of the routine - perhaps for want of a project - so he called for volunteers to excavate a site for a new pottery kiln. More radically, he announced at a prefects' meeting that any form of "fagging" was to stop at once, and that in future prefects would no longer have their clothes washed by the school porters. (All other boys and girls washed and ironed their own clothes.)

In June he acted on one of the recommendations of the Turner Report and convened the first meeting of the headmasters of the Protestant self-governing schools, to exchange information and ideas about future development and co-operation. They soon christened themselves "The Robbers" - presumably because they "stole" each others' best ideas - and the meetings continued fruitfully for the next 20 years.

As a result of the first one, Cobb produced a circular on the relationship between the self-governing schools, their Boards of Governors and the Education Department. He suggested that the schools could well look after themselves, though they would welcome advice from the government, provided it was not couched in imperatives. Financial support came two-thirds from government and one-third from the parents, but this should not be thought to reflect the division of authority over the schools. Freedom from government control was vital.

> If the Government could delegate its authority as the mission had done in the past, the path to education, in which it was interested, could be as unhampered as the advance of Christianity , which was the chief concern of the mission.[6]

Other notable events of the year were a successful Speech Day in July, celebrations on the return of HH The Kabaka from his university studies in England, and - less welcome - the raising of the school's fees. These had been reduced in 1945, at the request of the Director of Education, from 430 shillings a year to 300. At the end of the war Uganda had appeared to be on the verge of a period of prosperity and it was expected that the cost of living would fall, as peace-time conditions returned. In fact prices rose steadily and when it was revealed that 300 shillings did not cover the cost of just food and uniform for one pupil, government approved the restoration of the fees to the old level.

The year ended gaily with the production of Cobb's first pantomime, *Hansel and Gretel*. He revived the interest in music and drama which had been a feature of Budo under Grace, but had been difficult to sustain through the war and its after-effects. The annual pantomimes were not only enjoyed for themselves but were useful experiences for actors and audiences, towards more taxing performances. In his report to the Governors on the year's work Cobb recorded that the Cambridge School Certificate results - 26 passes from 28 candidates - were the best in Uganda, and the admissions to Makerere - 15 out of 27 candidates - the best in East Africa. But apart from academic achievement he had most valued the school's ability to entertain itself:

> Nearly every Saturday night there is a show of some sort in Big School, and these are nine-tenths produced by the boys themselves. There are three or four concerts a term, consisting of music and plays. Debates are popular and impromptu speeches very popular. The performances are rough but vigorous and the vitality on and off the stage - the audience hardly ever stops talking - makes me glad to be among a people who can still entertain themselves because they live in a pre-cinema age.[7]

He believed that school societies were doing well and should be encouraged. Their members were being urged to do more for themselves and not just sit back and listen to visiting speakers. His report ended with a crisp summary of Budo discipline:

> Petty discipline is sloppy and the pace is a jogtrot. Punctuality is not in our vocabulary. I believe that the causes of this are that there is no 100% effort made at anything; there is a dislike on the part of the prefects and of some staff of seeing that an order is carried out; and the Greek vice of thinking that "to obey" is synonymous with "to be persuaded".[8]

Early in 1949 Cobb visited Nyakasura School, now led by Edward Cooper, and on his return he let it be known that he had been highly impressed by the standard of "petty discipline" there, by the achievements of communal work and by the general smartness. To be compared unfavourably with another school was a new experience for Budo, but a salutary one which needed repeating occasionally throughout the century - and still does. Budo was at this time one of eleven full secondary schools and, though the system was growing steadily, Budonians still tended to feel the same sense of obvious superiority as their predecessors of 1906; "conceit" remained no less of a danger than when Weatherhead first feared it.

In May there was more political unrest in Buganda. The violent opposition of the Bataka party to the Buganda government culminated in a series of riots which threatened to involve Budo. Mona MacMillan, who chose the critical day to visit the hill, wrote in her book, *Introducing East Africa*, an account of the response to the emergency, and an interesting view of the temper of the school:

> Dr Huxley in 1930, admired the public school spirit it displayed, with prefects and houses. The grounds were less beautifully laid out than Kisubi, but there were more playing fields. The buildings... are growing a bit worn and repairs to old buildings are beginning to eat up the funds which should go to new ones. The dormitories are crowded and bare of furniture as usual, and boys must sit and study on their beds ...the classrooms are inadequate. Some of them are open-sided, pretty and good in a dry climate, but complained of as cold by the children on top of this hill, in a humid one. Budo receives a Government grant of course, but it shows signs of the crippling lack of funds that affects all Protestant missionary institutions. The general difficulty of recruiting European staff of the high quality needed, was vexing the headmaster...
>
> We arrived unannounced and waited under a tree laden with weaver birds' nests, like large fruits. These nests are pear-shaped, made of leaves, and it is fascinating to watch the bright coloured little birds flying in and out of the neat entrances. The headmaster was finishing a letter in his small office beside the modest bungalow in whose garden the weaver birds' tree stood.

That letter was certainly an urgent one ... sending word to the police and the authorities of an alarming situation. The school had reassembled the day before and many of the children had arrived in tears because of a poster displayed by the organisers of the recent rioting, which announced that vengeance would be taken on the chiefs, by attacking Budo, where many of their children were gathered. The road to Budo is a cul-de-sac, and there is no telephone. A single road block would have cut off assistance - road blocks were among the tactics of the rioters, who had learnt this method in [wartime] Burma. It was a frightening situation for the head, who had only two or three European men to help him and a number of women and girls to protect.

He showed us a stack of firewood which had been piled near the gate and from which the boys were to arm themselves; drill with these weapons was being organised mainly to keep up morale, but it needed strong nerves to give it any reality. The head was relying on the hope that a show of determination would be enough; the rioters were out for loot and arson, not for fighting. Fortunately his faith was not put to the proof, for the cowardly threats against the children proved empty. We drove away from Budo feeling as if we were deserting a beleaguered camp, but impressed by the spirit shown by all, which was worthy of a school with the traditioon that Budo undoubtedly has. [9]

The crisis passed for Budo and for Buganda, and Speech Day two months later found the school in high spirits and presenting, as well as the usual exhibitions, a production by Cobb of *The Magic Flute*, a musical directed by Alan Walker, who had arrived in 1948 from Bryanston, to teach mathematics, and all the parts were taken by students. *Papageno* was sung by Michael Sozi, who later became Chief Education Officer of independent Uganda.

Governor Sir John Hathorne Hall spoke of the importance of self-discipline; a school which was trying to teach it could lay a foundation in the life of each student which would not easily be destroyed. Cobb took up the theme in his annual report. He said that discipline in a school was founded simply on Love: Love for each other, Love for the school and ultimately Love of God. He admitted that he had found the sixth form, as a whole, " rather arrogant and trying" though they had done well as individuals. He appealed to the visitors not to be too critical of Budonians:

> When our pupils come on to you they will be full of faults. They may not be as humble as you would like. I admit that, though I think that much that is taken for lack of humility is really the effect of awkwardness. They may not stick to their jobs; they may not be reliable; they may have a hundred and one other faults of character which you may notice. You would also find the same faults in a bunch of English boys fresh from school, though I doubt if you would notice them so keenly.
>
> It is not for want of trying on our part that they have these failings, when they do, and I ask you to treat us with charity... If you are really friends of Budo, a great service you can do us, and schools like us, is to think twice before condemning us with adjectives which neglect the fact that we are men and women engaged in what we believe to be one of the most important tasks in the world, and the most rewarding.[10]

The Board of Governors had agreed in 1943 that, as soon as possible the primary school should be moved from the Hill to a separate site; meanwhile it was in some ways an embarrassment. There was by this time little need for a boarding school for primary pupils in Buganda, but Budo Primary School had acquired considerable snob value. There were usually about 200 applicants each year for the 25 places in Primary One, and most of them went - on merit, as far as this could be assessed at the age of seven - to children from the leading families. Parents then tended to assume that admission to the primary school had conferred the right to continue at Budo to School Certificate level. There were usually hard feelings, and sometimes personal antagonism towards the headmaster, when pupils were refused admission to the Senior School because they had failed the entrance examination. Cobb sometimes envied the heads of government schools in this respect. When they refused to admit a child it was assumed that the decision came from government and it was not disputed. Self-governing status brought its problems as well as its privileges.

In September the school was once again visited by Sir Philip Mitchell, former governor of Uganda, now governor of Kenya. Sir

Philip had supported Budo in Gaster's time and Cobb now asked his advice about new buildings, as the state of many of the old ones was alarming. He recommended that Cobb should send a full report, with specific requests, direct to the governor; when the money came, the school should build really well, without being extravagant or "going in for marble halls."[11] This was encouraging, as were Sir Philip's parting words:

> I have always loved your school. It is one of the few places here that has a soul - and it has found its soul.[12]

In his annual report Cobb noted that the School Certificate results - 24 passes out of 33 candidates - had not been as good as the previous year's. Communal work and societies seemed to be developing well, but he felt that appearances were sometimes deceptive:

> The pupils need more urge to creative activity. A few show good drive ... but the majority are content to do nothing but idle away time, lying on their beds gossiping.

> Budo often gives the impression of a place of great activity, but that is because of the activity of a few. I think it is a place where some great opportunities are missed, but it will take some time to convince people of that.[13]

The year 1950 was, however, good for drama and music. For Speech Day in July, Cobb produced *Dido and Aeneas*, and in August the Dramatic Society produced *Hassan*, without staff assistance. In October the African Music Society, with the help of Walker and Cobb, produced the first performance of an opera in Luganda, *Omuwalajjana Kintu* and the *Magic Horn*, by teacher and musician Solomon Katana - the first of three of his operas to be presented by the school. Best of all, this year was the formation, on the initiative of Michael Sozi, of a select school choir of 24 voices - students and staff - who called themselves The Budo Nightingales. The founder members elected Alan Walker as their first president and conductor. They drew up a formal constitution, the first clause of which reads "The purpose of the Society is to sing." With a few silent years in the violent 1970s and 80s, they have continued to sing into the twenty-first century and have given some truly distinguished performances.

Girls and boys who came to Budo Primary School and won places in the senior school spent twelve years on the Hill and it was not surprising that some of them came to their last year with relief - the traditional title for a sixth former being "A Goer".

With this in mind, some sixth forms became completely absorbed in their own examination challenges and contributed little to the school in the very year in which they had most to give. Cobb's 1950 log book contained a deceptively simple entry, for the first week:

> The sixth form has voluntaryly renounced the "goer" name and mentality. They cannot know themselves, how much this means to the school.[14]

He was still concerned about discipline and in his Speech Day report, referred to rumours about punishments at the school. It was not true that he had abolished corporal punishment, but he had refused to issue prefects with canes and had also dissuaded several masters from using them. What mattered most was earning respect, and seeing that an order was carried out. When he arrived at Budo he had found masses of rules that nobody had obeyed. Now a proper check was being kept, on fewer rules, and discipline was improving - though he still did not believe it was good. The essence was not that the child should be "sat on" but that (s)he should learn to take responsibility for personal self-discipline.

He welcomed the Old Budonians' generous gesture of endowing several prizes for the products of leisure activities.

> Life at Budo is less regimented than at many other schools in Uganda. But because of this I believe it is more usefully active... The large amounts of leisure time are of immense value if we can educate the pupils to use them advantageously. They give scope for enterprise and initiative, two very difficult things to inculcate, and two of the most important in any scheme of education. That kind of thing can only be caught like an infectious disease and it is our business as staff to see that conditions are right for catching

and spreading the infection. 1950 has been an extremely good year for this. [15]

In an article for an East African journal he said that he was proud of the school's ability to come up to scratch, and of its wideness of range, but he diagnosed a quality which Budo had long before he came, and has certainly not lost:

> We are always ready to make a special effort, though we are not
> so good at making an ordinary effort.[16]

Mona MacMillan had observed in 1949 that it was hard to get enough good teachers, and in 1951 resignations and leaves left big gaps. Mary Stuart, wife of the Anglican bishop, came to the rescue and so, as ever, did Douglas Tomblings. It was not easy for outsiders to understand that staffing was a genuine problem, not one which the governors or head were creating by insisting that good staff meant European staff. During a visit to the school, the Katikiro proposed a radical "solution": Budo, he said, should admit 500 pupils instead of the current 230, thus eliminating the need for some of the smaller secondary schools and the consequent dispersal of competent staff. It should then rely on the best available African teachers, so overcoming the difficulty of recruiting good Europeans.[17] The glum response of the governors can be imagined; they were only too keen to recruit able Ugandans, but faced stiff competition from other government departments, commerce and higher education. Within a year of the Katikkiro's sage advice, the school had lost all four of its African graduate teachers. It was as well that the governors and staff could not know that fifteen years later the position would be even worse.

In 1952 the political atmosphere in Buganda was again uneasy, with the Mau Mau rising in Kenya having an unsettling effect. Many Old Budonians were involved in a disturbance at Makerere College. Cobb recorded that the school had "gone sour" and that he had met the staff to try to reassure them that he was neither anti-African nor weakening in his commitment to strong discipline.[18]

The school suffered two heavy losses at the end of the year, with the retirements of Bishop Stuart and Fred Robinson. The bishop had been chairman of the Board for seventeen years. By the light of oil lamps he and his wife walked slowly down Budo Hill - as they supposed, for the last time - and shook hands with every student and teacher and with the many Old Budonians who had come to bid them farewell. They were in fact able to visit Uganda three more times over the next decade, each time spending many hours at Budo.

Fred and Elsie Robinson had been on the staff for 25 years, with four successive headmasters. Fred's fine work as science teacher and builder has been recorded above. His wife's contributions were at least as valuable and she must rank as the most remarkable of the many wives of teachers who helped to shape Budo. She had come to the school from Mengo Hospital, where she had been a dispenser, and she soon became Budo's medical expert. She organised the nursing of the school through a major 'flu epidemic, nursed countless individual pupils - with primitive facilities - and was revered by staff and pupils who were in residence on the two separate occasions when she resuscitated boys who had been struck by lightning. Such was her expertise in Luganda that even after retirement she went on serving Budo and other Uganda schools, as Cambridge School Certificate examiner. What the Baganda thought of Elsie Robinson was reflected in the honour bestowed upon her of membership of the Monkey clan - with the clan name *Nakabugo* - and by the enormous congregation at her funeral on Namirembe Hill, twelve years after she retired. The "Robbies" shared with Douglas Tomblings the distinction of being the only Europeans who were presented by the Kabaka with plots of land on which to build their retirement homes; they were much visited by affectionate Budonians for the rest of their long lives.

In March 1952 the governor appointed a Uganda Education Commission, under the chairmanship of Mr (later, Sir) Bernard de Bunsen, principal of Makerere College, to examine the educational system and make recommendations for development in the light of the report of a group of experts, led by A.L. Binns, which had visited East Africa the year before. The de Bunsen commission, which included two influential Old Budonians, S.W. Kulubya and Y.K. Lule, presented its report in December.

The section on secondary education recorded that there were in 1952, 13 full secondary schools mounting 4 year courses, with a total of 1837 pupils. The commission recommended a careful expansion to 2850 pupils by 1957, including 500 in the final year of the course.[19] It favoured the establishment of more denominational schools, making the startling assertion that:

> True education in the fullest sense must be based upon religion.[20]

Since in the twenty-first century many intelligent educators argue that denominational schools encourage prejudice and bigotry, the commission's minority report on the issue is particularly interesting. It proposed that future policy should be based on non-denominational schools, which should assist the development of a national community as well as ensuring a more balanced regional distribution of schools. It was the work of three former students from denominational schools - the two Budonian members and one from Gayaza.[21]

The year 1953 began well, with an exhibition of Budo Art at the Geffrye Museum in London. No one from the school could be present but the Curator cabled, "Great success. Everyone delighted."[22] Approval was also received from a surprising source. A Dutch art critic, Dr Italiaander, who was writing a book on African Art, visited the school:

> He expressed more appreciation than is normally required by good manners, of the results of Miss Carney's teaching, laying special emphasis on the variety and originality of the products, which he said was rare outside French colonies. Particularly he stressed that the art was not stamped into a mould by the teacher.[23]

In March 1953, the American political commentator, John Gunther, visited the school. He was preparing material for his substantial book, *Inside Africa,* and he and his wife asked if they might take away a copy of *Current News,* a wall newspaper, written and edited by the students, and allowed considerable "freedom of the press" by the staff. They said that they were impressed by the maturity of the views expressed. The extract, which Gunther quoted, referred back to the school dilemma over ballroom dancing. Budo's problems have often been Buganda's - in miniature:

> The Katikiro had outlawed western dancing because the bars had become haunts of vice, and an editor who called him a fool for doing so was imprisoned by Mengo Court and released by a British judge. The Lukiiko [Buganda Parliament] supported the Katikiro, and the ban remained. the student journal at Budo had this to say:

> The Baganda always boast that they are the most progressive people in Uganda and East Africa, but this is a fallacy of the greatest order. They are still under the yoke of feudal lords, and these lords are the people who are directing the machinery of the country. Instead of thinking of ways to develop the country they engage themselves in political manoeuvres in order that they may be enabled to stay in office for a longer time.

> After throwing the editor of the *Uganda Post* into prison on political grounds ...the Katikiro introduced a bill banning all western ballroom dancing. The Lukiiko, in a state of frenzy, coupled with the fear to oppose the bill on the part of the chiefs, lest they should lose their posts, passed the bill with an overwhelming majority. Incidentally, the Lukiiko failed to say which was western dancing. It seems we can still carry on with the Samba Rumba and Konga.[24]

In June the Education Department conducted a four-day inspection of Budo. They found much that they approved of: a wide range of activities, students polite and helpful, co-education going well - but plenty to criticise. They thought the tempo slack, the library inadequate for subject reading, textbooks inadequate and badly used, teachers' timetables too light, and the school compound untidy. This last impression was formed on arrival, when a dirty cricket pad lay conspicuously across their path to the staffroom. It was still there when they left and its offending presence ran, like a leitmotif, through their report. They supported Cobb's own view that though there was discipline there remained a lack of order, which was a real brake on the school's progress.[25]

Meanwhile, earlier in the year, work had begun on the construction of a new main school block, and the Big School which had served for nearly fifty years had been demolished. Cobb had acted on Sir Philip Mitchell's advice with the result that Budo and three other secondary schools had each received a grant of £ 40,000 for capital development. There were many needs and it must have been tempting to spread the grant over all the school's facilities and try to improve everything a little. But governors and staff accepted Sir Philip's simple advice to "build well". The whole grant was spent on a new Big School block with a main hall to seat 500, and ten classrooms; and on one new dormitory. They were strongly built and in spite of the ravages of violence, fire and time, remain well used fifty years later. The whole project was completed in 18 months and the classrooms were in use by September. At the same time there were further discussions with the Education Department about the long postponed removal of the primary school to a separate site. In November the project at last became more than a pipedream when HH The Kabaka offered the school the use of 30 acres of land, two miles down the Hill, at Kabinja.

In spite of all this progress the year ended wretchedly. On 30 November, after growing friction between the Protectorate and Buganda governments, Kabaka Mutesa II was deposed by order of Governor Sir Andrew Cohen and deported to England. Anyone who has read this far will understand something of the impact this had on Budo. Cobb's personal position was particularly sensitive because he was Sir Andrew's cousin and was therefore suspected by some Baganda of collusion in the removal of their king. It says much for the responsibility of students and staff, and for Cobb's leadership, that in the two years of the Kabaka's exile there was no disturbance at Budo. It is one of the big achievements in the history of the school.

When the staff and students reassembled, at the end of January 1954, Cobb made a statement, summarising the issues and how they were to be confronted:

> The school, as a school, has no politics, and its business is to carry on with its work in the quietest conditions it can secure. Therefore neither the headmaster nor any member of staff will make any

official pronouncement. But every individual is entitled to his own view, and may voice it privately, so long as he exercises the ordinary discretion of a schoolmaster. The pupils will not be allowed to hold public meetings, but no check on private views or the talking about them is desirable, as long as no one is attempting to incite others to disturb the school. For the present both the Political Society and the Current News should avoid discussing the "Deposition", but this ban will be lifted as soon as this appears desirable.[26]

For several years political activity in Uganda had been moving towards the formation of parties. In 1952 the Uganda National Congress was founded, and elected as its first president general, Budonian Ignatius Musazi, who had been politically active for fifteen years. As president of the Uganda Farmers' Federation he had been a strong influence in the discontent that provoked the riots of 1949, which had threatened the safety of Budo. The first secretary of the Congress was another Old Budonian, Abu K. Mayanja. Soon after the deportation of the Kabaka the Congress organised a deputation to London to protest to the British government. But it did not have the field to itself for long. Analysing the growth of political parties in Uganda, D.A. Low wrote:

> Within two days of the Kabaka's deportation in 1953, the political initiative was seized, not by Congress ... but by a tiny group of "advanced" western educated men who had just been elected to the Buganda Lukiiko. The most prominent of these was Eridadi Mulira. During the following months it was he and his companions who steered the Lukiiko through the prolonged crisis which ensued; and it was this same group which dominated the Buganda Constitutional Committee in 1954 and laid the foundations for the resolution of the immediate dispute...

> Early in 1955 ... they formed themselves into the Progressive Party. This was a genuine attempt to form a "fifth phase" political party. It represented in the main a largely Protestant group of schoolmasters, prosperous farmers, and African entrepreneurs, who had not found a niche for themselves within the Buganda government hierarchy... Many of them were old boys of the leading Protestant school, King's College, Budo, which had earlier replaced the Kabaka's own household, as the main seminary for the country's elite.[27]

Low mentioned many other Old Budonians who influenced this formative period of Ugandan politics, and Ingham particularly stressed the part played by Paulo Kavuma, then Katikkiro, in guiding the Lukiiko through the complex negotiations which led to the return of the Kabaka in 1955.[28]

Ernest Sempebwa had been a teaching colleague of both Musazi and Mulira at Budo and retained his admiration for both, sixty years later:

> Musazi had founded Bazzakulu ba Kintu as early as 1939 and incurred immediate opposition from Mengo. He was a very impressive and courageous politician. Mulira was less forceful - quiet, very truthful, and always refusing to make rash promises. He was very inclusive - always trying to heal divisions and bring people together.[29]

Among Budo's pressures in 1954 were several anonymous threatening letters to Cobb, an anonymous accusation against the Girl Guides who had attended the Queen's Birthday celebrations, and an attempt to organise a boycott of Speech Day because Sir Andrew Cohen was to attend. But none of this was allowed to disrupt normal routine and in mid-year the school had a double celebration. On 30 June a mains electricity supply to the Hill was switched on - and so farewell to hurricane lamps, though the office of "sublamper" remained for many years an honoured sinecure in each of the school Houses. On 3 July Sir Andrew Cohen formally opened the new Big School hall and classroom block, and was courteously received.

Discipline remained a contentious issue not just for the inspectors but for staff, students, Old Budonians and a headmaster who never flinched from expressing disapproval and demanding higher standards. Cobb had plenty of critics. Boys sometimes complained that they had not been given a full hearing; staff that pupils were allowed too much freedom to comment and question. But whatever its faults Cobb's system embodied two fundamental requirements of good discipline: the ability to make a difficult decision and stick to it, and the willingness - for which he often appealed in others - to give time to ensuring that orders had been carried out. This year saw a good example of each.

For fifty years staff and students had shown periodic reluctance to follow Weatherhead's plan for communal work. Cobb now decided that it must either become an accepted part of the regular timetable or be abolished. Some staff and many parents wanted it retained, so it was made compulsory, in spite of the tense political situation in which it could easily have been misinterpreted as a deliberate flouting of Kiganda tradition. The work was done in groups during games time, with the headmaster and staff joining in. The first job was to clear ground for a sanatorium and the next to recover the old open- air theatre.

On 6 August a few minutes after lunch had begun, Cobb was informed at his house that the school had refused to eat the maize *posho* provided. Food prices were up again and the school could not afford to buy *matooke* and *lumonde* in the usual quantities. At an assembly earlier in the week, Cobb had explained the situation and asked for co-operation. He now went to the Mess and announced that no boy would leave until he had eaten the lunch provided. (The girls took lunch in their own dining hall.) There was little response, and when the food was cold Cobb ordered the mess stewards to heat it up and serve it again. He recorded that the prefects and monitors "behaved with great dignity, firmness and helpfulness", in keeping order as the meal proceeded. By the end of afternoon school many of the boys had eaten their lunch and left, but at two o'clock the following morning five remained, asleep, before their untouched posho. Cobb had remained in the mess the whole time. He had the boys woken and told them that they would either eat the food or be sent home from school that day. Two boys stood out and were suspended; the others eventually completed their "lunch" and the meal ended at ten minutes to four in the morning. Cobb noted that "the good temper of everyone throughout the operation was remarkable." Many of his African colleagues expressed strong appreciation of his action, and there were no further incidents over food. The end-of-year report included a piquant postscript:

> The finding of a middle way between rigid regimentation and endless persuasion is one of our hardest and most interesting tasks.[30]

Cobb was on leave in England for six months of 1955 and Ellis Hillier was acting head. Voluntary activities - clubs, societies and sports teams - flourished, but the curriculum was continuing to develop in academic rather than practical directions. Staff were concerned that the farm was not flourishing and it was agreed to ask the government Agricultural Department to inspect it. The firm advice was that the farm should now dispense with livestock and concentrate on the production of staple crops. Staff were also critical of the results of their own teaching of English and decided that the examination classes should in future be taught in three sets rather than two forms, to give more opportunity for individual tutoring.

Cobb returned in September and in October Lord and Lady Hemingford returned briefly to Uganda and visited the school. Hemingford wrote, in a warm letter of thanks:

> The assembly was the perfect climax to our visit. The boys and girls looked neat and smart, asked good questions and were very friendly to us. We both felt very happy about them.[31]

A few days later there was rejoicing at Budo - as all over Buganda - when the Kabaka returned from exile to resume his responsibilities. A new Buganda Agreement was signed and a long period of tension and disruption seemed over. It must have been all the more exasperating for governors and staff therefore that at a parents' meeting held in November, Cobb's report on the state of the school was severely criticised and a motion was passed calling on the governors to set up a committee "to enquire into the recent deterioration of Budo". When Cobb reminded the parents that it was the Board of Governors, not the Parents' Association or the United Budonians who ran the school, there was general disagreement. The meeting produced nothing but bad feeling all round and, at a time of national rejoicing, confirmed Budo's disconcerting capacity for producing the unexpected. The last entry in the 1955 log book reads:

> The headmaster was too dispirited to write his usual Annual Report and was confirmed in his view that the Governors did not read it when no one asked after it during the year.[32]

It may well have been that the following year brought enough pleasant compensations to enable the governors to live contentedly in the present rather than return to past contentions.

The year 1956 began with further erosion of practical, work-based curriculum activities. A staff meeting decided that the new, greatly increased rent demanded for the land on which the farm was located, could not be afforded. After years of gradual decline and diminishing enthusiasm it was, regretfully, agreed to close the farm. Support for the commercial classes had also been disappointing for several years; the investment required to maintain them was significant, so - for commercial reasons - it was decided that this would be their last year.

By contrast, enthusiasm for games and sports was high. Almost all students found something available during games periods which they could enjoy, and matches with many other schools brought new social experiences and friendships, often beyond Buganda. There were regular fixtures at football, cricket and tennis and occasional ones in athletics and swimming. The standard of Budo cricket had risen steadily under the enthusiastic coaching of Dick Drown - chaplain and teacher of English since 1947 - and 1956 proved an exceptional year - with Cobb himself a keen supporter and organiser of fielding practices. The First XI, unbeaten throughout the season, was captained by all-rounder John Nagenda, who later played for Uganda, and also for East Africa in the 1975 World Cricket Cup. But - as he always insisted - the star player was his vice-captain and great friend Pesuery Nyangabyaki, who made centuries in two successive matches for the school and another in the Uganda Trial, after which he became the first Ugandan to play for the country - against the touring Pakistan Test XI - while still at school.

Nagenda went on to a successful career in publishing, journalism, farming and government - as a Senior Presidential Adviser to President Museveni. He wrote a perceptive article on "Budo in the Fifties" for the 1996 *Budonian 90*, paying tribute, forty years on, to Cobb's leadership and particularly his personal kindness and insight:

> My parents thought I was too young, at around seven, to go away
> to boarding school. So I went to our village Primary School, the

expectation being that after P4 I would go to Budo. It did not happen. The Headmaster said to my parents that he was being most unfair, since my father and all his brothers had been to Budo, as indeed had my mother's father... I only reached Budo by open competition [in 1950, aged nearly 12]

... Timothy Cobb, by his actions and character, was a true colossus of Budo; a defining figure... His mission in opening up Budo to a wider audience was the best thing that could have happened to the school and to the country ... Cobb was also very alert to those in his charge, as I can attest personally. When, at the end of 1952, it seemed to him that I had reached a cul de sac in my maths studies and in my behaviour too, he wrote a very nice letter to my parents saying that to safeguard my future, I should be sent for a year to a school as far away as possible and a place at Budo would be waiting my return. Who knows where I would be today if he had not done this? My parents chose Kigezi High School, where I spent 1953 before returning to Budo in 1954. (My Bakiga friends aver that this year in their company was the making of me.) ...

What a golden time our generation at Budo enjoyed in the 1950s.[33]

The year 1956 was strong, too, for music and drama, with a successful initiative to enable more students to take part. This was the inter-house drama competition, for which the plays - some of them musical - were written, produced and acted by the students, with a specifically limited amount of advice from members of staff. The keenness and quality of this first competition were such that it became an annual event for many years - a valuable experience and also a training ground for the successful major productions which drew large audiences to the Hill every year.

The year 1956 also had its troubles. Relationships between boys and girls - always uncertain, partly because there were still so few girls - were particularly difficult. After more than 20 years, co-education at Budo was still widely regarded as "an experiment" and some thought it a foolish one. The Director of Education chose to include the opinion of one of his officers in the Department Annual Report:

The Provincial Education Officer for the Northern Province comments very unfavourably on the effects of co-education at the senior secondary stage, on the girls. He considers that they become frustrated and feel inferior, and that therefore the CMS, which relies on co-education, cannot hope to achieve solid progress.[34]

There had also been some drinking detected and three boys were expelled. Yet, on the whole, the students and staff felt - as Cobb expressed it in his annual report...that the cloud they had been under in 1955 was lifting and that the school was a closer community.[35]

There can be no doubt that students, staff, parents, governors and Old Budonians were drawn together in the celebrations, on 7 July, of the Golden Jubilee of the school. Cobb described them vividly:

> It was not easy to foretell how this celebration would turn out, because a lot depended on things we could not measure... For days before we had reports that every Old Budonian who could reach Budo would be coming. The dispute about whether the Kabaka should take part in the procession was settled by the Kabaka most graciously consenting to do so and giving us every help with the planning. The Old Budonians are capable of great solidarity and if they joined in heartily they could make the afternoon a real Golden Jubilee celebration. But they are stern critics too, desperately jealous of the past, and if they felt that their "Sabaganzi" or their Myers Grace had not been honoured enough, or if they thought that the glory of the school was not upheld enough by the preparations for the afternoon, there would be ill-feeling and long lasting trouble...

> Before tea, from 2.30 till 4.00, visitors - about 2500 had turned up - were left to the garden party atmosphere of talking to each other, and the numerous exhibitions for them to see. They were much like all school exhibitions, but I do maintain that the Art, under Rita Carney, is outstanding, and the Pottery, taught by Mr Kasirye is the best I have seen in the country... Everyone seemed to get a cup of tea and a plate of food, and though most people had to sit on the grass, they all looked happy. I have never seen so much talking going on. We had four Kings at the high table - The Kabaka of Buganda, The Omukama of Bunyoro, The Omukama of Toro and The Omugabe of Ankole - three Queens, The Governor and

Lady Cohen, The Bishop and Mrs Brown, and the Kabaka's mother. I do not know when last the four Abakama were here together. There is an instance recorded in 1908, when the Omugabe arrived, carried by sixteen men, in a basket.

After tea we went to the open-air theatre for speeches. We did not attempt to provide seats, and all except about twenty people sat happily on the grass. The stage was decorated with the coloured House pennants below, and a huge Budo lion flag on a reed fence behind the speakers' table. There were three speakers. I had regarded speeches as a necessary evil - something which we had to have, even on a Golden Jubilee Day. they were kept short. What I had not been prepared for was the way people afterwards made a point of saying how much they had enjoyed them. One of the boys said to me "Your speech was surprisingly interesting."

We then went to the procession. The present school and staff had been rehearsed and it was a question of marshalling about 1500 people into years and categories. We had boards on poles, with the years painted on them back and front, and there were many brightly coloured boards respresenting special events or phases: Mengo High School, the start of Scouts and Guides, the start of Co-education, eleven times winners of the Kabaka's Cup for football, the Coming of Electricity, and many other landmarks, ending with the great Golden Jubilee Board at the back. The procession was a mixture of set pieces and marchers by years. At the head came the Budo lion, an animated scarlet beast, from the school shield. Behind him the party that opened the school on March 29th 1906 - Kabaka Daudi Chwa, Bishop Tucker, the Namasole, about 20 pupils, in *kanzus* and fezzes, representing the original pupils and some of their wives, with "Sabaganzi" among them. The Acting High Commissioner was pushed in a rickshaw, with his ADC. With this party were seven old men, the survivors of the class of pupils who were here that day fifty years ago. Some of them had tears streaming down their cheeks.

Behind them marched hundreds and hundreds of old boys, through the years, under their banners. Many were wearing their school caps, or had put replicas of the Lion badge onto fezzes; many had robes of office, for they are high up in the State. I saw two barristers, several university men, churchmen, ministers of governments and two kings in this early section, walking quite simply with their classmates. They were wildly excited and most of the groups were singing. The scene at the marshalling was one of the happiest crowd scenes I had ever been in. The next set piece was 1942, the Kabaka's Coronation, and Mutesa was carried on the shoulders of his offical carrier, with drums, spears, an enormous umbrella and a whole jeep-load of paraphernalia grouped around him. This part of the procession of course aroused terrific enthusiasm.

Close behind, the first Self-governing Board of Governors on a flat trailer, and with the banners of successes crowding thick: Winners of the Namirembe Music Festival - the Choirs of 1951 and '55, singing lustily on a lorry - winners of all the relays in the Protectorate Sports of 1951, the Class of 1955 with 100% success in "Cambridge", and the Jubilantes - the present top form. Then the school, by houses - a babel of songs - the staff, the headmaster and Jubilee 1956. When I was passing the mango trees to start on the processional route, about four rows had already come to rest on the library field ...where we formed up in rows. There must have been about a thousand visitors watching and cheering from the steps and terraces by the Primary School. We broke into the Martyrs' hymn and the Bishop blessed us - and that was the end.

It was not the end however of the Jubilee celebrations, because next morning we all went down by buses to Namirembe Cathedral to give thanks to God for the first fifty years. The cathedral was quite full of old boys and girls. The Budo choir joined with the Cathedral choir for the service and sang an anthem on its own, Vaughan Williams's "Let us now praise Famous Men". The head prefect and Bishop Tomusange, an Old Budonian, read the lessons, the school chaplain Mr Drown, read the prayers and the Bishop preached. Benoni Lwanga took the service, himself an Old Budonian, governor and father of five Budo boys. After all the shouting and excitement and glorification of the day before, it was part of the beauty of holiness to come humbly to the church, and give the glory to God.[36]

Early in 1957, Cobb announced that this would be his last year at Budo. Like most years it was one of progress and problems. The buildings for the new primary school at Kabinja were begun in March, but to temper any false sense of affluence, the school fees had to be raised to

480 shillings a year. In May Kosiya Shalita, who had for many years been Budo's missionary, was consecrated Bishop of Mbarara, becoming the third Old Budonian bishop. At the same time, the Christian life of the school was enlivened by the challenge of reconciling the extreme evangelical position with the orthodox Anglican one. Since the Rwanda Revival of the 1930s the influence of the *Balokole* ("saved ones") has been strongly felt at Budo. In August the Dramatic Society produced *Tobias and the Angel*, important as the first in a long series of annual major productions - occasionally two in one year.

In October Cobb was appointed to the headship of Dover College, in England, with effect from April 1958. After a series of farewell parties from school, staff and Old Budonians, he left in January, with his wife Celia who had been a great support and a popular and generous hostess. In a last speech to the Old Budonians he said that although more than six hundred boys and girls had gone out from the school in his time, he hoped that they would think of themselves as Old Budonians and not as Old Budonians of the Cobb era - which recalls H.T.C. Weatherhead's admonition of 1914. He considered that Budonians were very generous and kind in welcoming a newcomer, and in saying "goodbye"; it was the period in between that was sometimes difficult.

Twenty years later, in an autobiography published posthumously only in 1995, Sir Bernard de Bunsen paid a fine compliment to the influence of Budonians on Makerere in the 1950s. He was commenting on the international mix of students at the college and the influence of the Baganda:

> I admired many of their personal qualities, their style and their own institutions evolved through time. Their major school, King's College Budo, with which Makerere had long had so special a relationship... was now under Tim Cobb's stimulating leadership, full of the enjoyment of life, of African music and acting, and of a sense of assurance in itself. With such assets sometimes went the wholesome ability, found in the more ancient Public Schools in England, to relax. Budonians did not fight for position; they had it. In the days when the struggle to reach school and Makerere and so enter a profession, was so intense, it was good to have

among us those who could relax, see some fun in life, even doze off occasionally in lectures. Budonians came the nearest ever to pulling our legs - alas, never hard enough![37]

But the last word was with one of his students who, sated with farewell speeches, observed:

Praising Mr Cobb is like flogging a dead horse.

Notes

[1] Cobb, T.H., "King's College, Budo" in *East Africa Magazine*. KCB archives.

[2] KCB Logbook 1948

[3] Some Notes for Visitors. KCB archives.

[4] KCB Logbook 1948

[5] Ibid

[6] Ibid

[7] Ibid

[8] Ibid

[9] MacMillan, Mona, *Introducing East Africa*, London: Faber, 1952, pp. 40-42.

[10] KCB Logbook 1949.

[11] Ibid

[12] Ibid

[13] Ibid

[14] KCB Logbook 1950.

[15] Ibid

[16] Cobb T.H. op. cit.

[17] KCB Logbook 1950

[18] Ibid 1952

[19] African Education in Uganda, Entebbe, December 1952, Appendix.

[20] Ibid. Minority Report.

[21] Ibid. Introduction.

[22] KCB Logbook 1953.

[23] Ibid.

24   Gunther John, *Inside Africa*, London: Hamish Hamilton 1955, p. 425.

25 KCB Logbook 1953.

26 Ibid. 1954.

27 Low D.A., *Political Parties in Uganda 1949-62*, London: Athlone Press, 1962

28 Ingham, K. *The Making of Modern Uganda*, London: Allen and Unwin, 1958, p. 273.

29 Sempebwa E.K.K., in conversation with the author, Makerere, March 2002.

30 KCB Logbook 1954

31 Ibid. 1955.

32 Ibid.

33 Nagenda, John, "Budo in the Fifties" in *Budonian 90 Years*, Kampala 1996, pp. 17-18.

34 Report of Uganda Education Department, 1955.

35 KCB Logbook 1956.

36 Cobb TH, Budo Golden Jubilee Speech Day, 1956. KCB archives.

37 de Bunsen, Bernard. *Adventures in Education*, Kendas (UK) Titus Welson, 1995 p. 103

8

Through Independence Towards the Gathering Storm 1958-1970

The Board of Governors invited Ian Cameron Robinson to apply for the headship and he came into residence, with his wife Dorothy ("Do") and young daughter and son, a week before the school opened for the new year in 1958. Educated at Repton School and Emmanuel College, Cambridge, where he read engineering, he had served with the Friends Ambulance Unit in Ethiopia and Austria from 1940 to 1947. He had then volunteered to serve the CMS as a school teacher, and joined the staff of Busoga College, Mwiri, where he had taught for ten years before coming to Budo.

His engineering expertise was soon in demand. The new Primary School buildings at Kabinja were almost finished when heavy rain and close inspection exposed serious construction faults; every building had to be re-roofed and the opening of the new school was postponed. Another troublesome roof was that of the 1912 chapel, in which bats had become permanent residents, in spite of ingenious efforts to dislodge them. The swimming pool - inherited liability of every Budo headmaster - had cracked yet again and been unusable for almost two years. An even bigger building problem was on the way.

In 1956 the government Education Department had promised to launch, as soon as funds could be provided, the first Cambridge Higher School Certificate classes in Uganda. The aim was to relieve Makerere College "of a heavy commitment to its Preliminary Course, which by current British university standards was not a university-level course." In 1958 government announced that HSC classes would begin the following year, at Budo, Kisubi and the government secondary school at

149

Mbale. This would require additional classrooms and accommodation for staff by March 1959. It seemed doubtful that Budo could be ready in only twelve months; the government grant seemed meagre and, as usual, experienced staff seemed hard to recruit. The establishment of sixth forms in schools brought another difficulty.

Students would be drawn from secondary schools all over the country and many would have been prefects - some perhaps head-prefects - in their former schools. Because the results of the November examinations for the Cambridge School Certificate were not available in Uganda until mid-February, the HSC students would be unable to join their new schools until early March, six weeks after the school year had begun, and being unknown could not be appointed "officals". They would therefore be in the difficult position of being at the top of the school but having no authority in it for at least a year. St Mary's, Kisubi decided to solve the problem by building an entirely separate sixth form block and allowing the new seniors considerable freedom from the out-of-class routine of the rest of the school. Mbale was a day school so did not have the residential disciplinary problem. Budo staff decided that the sixth form should have similar status to that accorded in most English boarding schools, be expected - with some concessions - to conform to normal routine, and to contribute to the life and activities of the school community.

This issue was further complicated by the announcement that Makerere was to admit one more preliminary course. Guy Hunter summarised the problem as follows:

> Until 1959, the Sixth Form was, in effect, the Makerere pre-university course, with its environment of university buildings, gowns, better food, pocket money, freedom and adulthood. It was certainly a comedown to remain, instead, at school. Moreover some overseas scholarships, and some places at the Royal College, Nairobi, were offered at form four; more recently, Catholic boys could go to Strathmore, a Sixth Form College near Nairobi - all these were more luxurious and exciting than school. It is self-evident that if one or more of the East African university colleges offered entry, or if more Strathmores were built, or if more overseas scholarships were offered at form four, it would become impossible

to hold students in the sixth forms - the comparisons would be too sharp and widespread. It was remarkable how at least some boys did in fact opt to remain at school (for example at Budo College in Uganda) during the brief period when there was actually a choice between the school sixth form and the Makerere pre-university course; but this attitude could only be exceptional.[1]

During 1958, Robinson personally visited the secondary schools in Uganda which seemed likely to send sixth form students to Budo. He talked to the fourth formers, explaining exactly what they could expect, and what would be expected of them, if they came on to Budo.

So there was a great deal to be planned for the coming year, but there was plenty done in 1958. Early in the first term the staff presented *The Barretts of Wimpole Street* - and at the end of term the students presented the Red Cross with 43 pints of blood. Giving blood was a new form of social service for Uganda schools, strongly supported by Robinson, from his wartime medical experiences, and it has continued at Budo. On this first occasion the enthusiastic donation - a record at the time for any institution in Uganda - was so unexpected that the Red Cross Unit ran out of bottles.

In June the Primary School moved at last to its fine new premises two miles down the hill. But with it went two-thirds of Budo's experienced Ugandan teachers - to the consternation of many senior school students who had previously taken little note of the balance of staffing. In the same month, the newly formed Uganda Development Corporation sponsored a visit by 22 Budo students to Toro. They were shown round the copper mines at Kilembe and toured the Queen Elizabeth National Park, gaining insights into their country's abundant wild-life and tourist potential. Communal work continued, voluntarily, with the planting of new grass on the games fields - for which footballers and athletes were grateful - and the regular cleaning of the chapel - to which the bats remained impervious. In October the Literary Society presented *Macbeth*, with an encouraging number of fourth formers sparing time to take part only a month before "Cambridge". Discipline and staff/student relations were good, with the prefects a strong influence, led by Apolo Nsibambi who Robinson believed must have been one of the best head prefects Budo had ever had. Perhaps he had a head start - his father and grandfather had been Budo head prefects before him. A good year ended with the triumphal re-opening of the swimming pool, sealed and renovated at a substantial cost met largely by staff contributions. This was the start of one of its longest periods of continuous use.

In mid-January the first of the newly appointed staff arrived from England. Victor Gilbert (History), Douglas Hare (English and RE) and Gordon McGregor (English) were in good time for the start of HSC and were joined in August by Cyril Truran (head of Geography) and Bryan Wilson (Maths). We all had young wives and children, so what little we may have added in intellectual prowess, we hugely offset with family hubbub. George "Mac" Bolton (Physics) had arrived the previous October, as the sole newly- recruited bachelor - but that did not last long. This welcome augmentation was sadly offset in the same long vacation, when Ellis Hillier was diagnosed with terminal cancer. He was lovingly nursed in Mengo CMS Hospital for three months, much visited by colleagues and students, who worked together on a recording he had asked for, of parts of Dorothy Sayers *The Man Born to be King*. It was played for him over Easter, and a few days later he died. He and his wife Lorna had served Budo for 20 years.

The school lost two more, crucially experienced, teachers in the same month, when senior Ugandan colleagues, Erisa Kironde (English) and Senteza Kajubi (Geography) - both outstanding Old Budonians - were appointed to lectureships at Makerere. With the departure also of Albert Maleche on a post-graduate scholarship to America, we were left with a single Ugandan graduate teacher, John Kisaka (Art, Football and a Budo Nightingale). Within nine months, while the country was looking for increased Africanisation in industry, commerce and the professions, Budo staff had become overwhelmingly white.

Of the 300 students in residence at Budo by the middle of March 1959, 100 were new to the school. In the reorganised national system pupils spent 6 years at primary school, going on - if they passed the competitive entrance examinations - to two years at junior secondary, and four years at senior secondary, to School Certificate level. The

Department had decided that junior schools should not normally be attached to senior ones and the intention was to move Budo Junior to Kabinja as soon as funds could be found. For the present however it remained on the Hill, so King's College was admitting new students into Junior One, Senior One and the first Senior Five. Moreover, very few of the J1 admissions had been to a boarding school before. To add to the general unsettlement, the increase in overall numbers made it necessary to form an additional boys' house. Some newly admitted students were allocated to "Ghana House" and the members of the other houses drew lots to make the number up to 45. Most students co-operated willingly, but some strong house loyalties had to be broken.

In spite of such turmoil, the year began well. The new staff settled quickly, three fine new staff houses were ready by the end of 1958, and five more were to come over the next two years. Work began on three new HSC science laboratories and space was made in old buildings for sixth form study cubicles. In February Queen Elizabeth the Queen Mother visited Uganda and at the banquet and reception at State House, Entebbe, the Budo Nightingales were chosen to provide the only formal entertainment. Their final rehearsal, on the floodlit lawn of the headmaster's house, was a memorable experience, especially for those of us new to Budo.

The new fifth formers arrived in March; there were several of the previous year's Budo fourth formers among them - most notably former head prefect Apolo Nsibambi and girls' prefect Elvaniya Namukwaya - but they had strong competition from able former students of Nabumali, Nyakasura, Gayaza and Ntare schools, who had gained confidence from excellent "Cambridge" results. They seemed to settle to work quickly but many confided to their HSC teachers that they found the new level of study daunting. Some of the fifth form staff were also modestly apprehensive about this first two-year programme at "A" level - as it was now known in UK. It was unfortunate that at a time when a relaxed and confident approach was needed to a new challenge, the words "too busy" were heard too often and some teachers felt that they now had little time for the informal social contact with students which had been a hallmark of Budo life.

A happy result of the introduction of Higher School Certificate studies was close co-operation between Budo and the Roman Catholic St Mary's College, Kisubi. Individual teachers met for discussion and exchange of teaching methods, and visited one another's libraries, laboratories and subject rooms. Budo staff were entertained informally by Kisubi staff and returned the compliment. The fifth forms also exchanged visits and the resulting friendships broke down the sense of isolated endeavour among students and teachers. Makerere College supported the HSC schools generously, arranging an inter-territorial planning conference and advising on the structure of courses, subject combinations, and the selection of books and equipment. Aware of the dangers of over-specialisation for these pioneer students, Budo staff mounted a substantial General Studies programme for the fifth and sixth forms, with an evening lecture and two seminars each week. Most of the lectures, for what proved a successful and long-lasting programme, were given by Makerere staff, and fourth formers were sometimes invited to attend.

During 1959 the political atmosphere in Uganda was warming up. After a number of splits in the early political parties, from 1955 to 1958, Musazi and Mulira founded a new group, the Uganda National Movement. Supported mainly by other leading Baganda politicians, it quickly became the most powerful political party Buganda or Uganda had ever seen.[2]

It protested against a Protectorate government proposal that there might be special representation in the Legislative council for the non-African minority, and it called for a boycott of non-African trade. Low described the outcome:

> Before long the latter had led in a number of places in Buganda to violent and destructive attacks upon trade, people and property. The Protectorate government eventually decided to intervene, and on the 23rd of May 1959, declared the UNM an unlawful society. Its leaders riposted by changing its name, and in reply to further government proscriptions, changed it again; but within a week, six of them, headed by Musazi and Mulira, had been deported by the Protectorate Government to Northern Uganda, and the death knell of the movement, though not ... of the boycott, was sounded.[3]

Meanwhile, in concerned response to the series of Protestant-led political initiatives in the early 1950s, the Democratic Party had been founded in 1956. Looking back forty years later, A.B.K. Kasozi suggested its main motives:

> Catholics in Buganda perceived that Mutesa II was not looking out for their interests. In 1956 they formed a political party of their own, the Democratic Party, to fight the Protestant Oligarchy in the pre-independence elections. The DP sought fairness in the distribution of official positions between Catholics and Protestants and the democratisation of Buganda's political institutions. Like most Buganda politicians, they believed in the kingship and wanted to uphold the integrity of the monarchy. But they wanted it to be a constitutional monarchy ... It was vital to the institution of the monarchy in Buganda that the Kabaka be impartial, or perceived to be so.[4]

They were not alone in this last aspiration, which many politically involved Protestants shared. Eridadi Mulira had in fact been barred from the Lukiiko in 1956 for asserting that the Kabaka was actually a constitutional monarch. Nor was DP membership limited to Catholics; Senteza Kajubi was prominent among its influential Old Budonian members.

Less than a year after the deportation of Musazi and Mulira, and the effective end of the UNM, the Uganda Peoples' Congress (UPC) emerged from a regrouping of activists, including some prominent Protestants and Old Budonians, led by Apolo Milton Obote. They were alarmed at the prospect of Buganda dominance of an independent Uganda:

> Where most political parties are governed by an ideology or ideas that represent the interests and views of their members, the leaders of the UPC were divided in their aims; they had different ethnic and religious loyalties; they were power hungry and, for the most part unprepared to act honourably towards one another and the nation ...

> Most of the UPC leaders were notables who derived their authority from colonial appointments, as traditional chiefs or civil servants. Many were lineal successors of chiefs or clan leaders, the majority

were Protestant, and a number had gone to boarding schools based on the British public school system...

For the most part the UPC leadership wanted to rectify regional inequality, especially the uneven development that favoured Buganda, and contain the speed at which Baganda educated elites were taking up posts in the country's civil service. Beyond that, little united the party leadership. Few acknowledged or wanted to correct the rural/urban income disparity and other sources of conflict... None sought a fundamental transformation of the economy, such that domestic rather than external needs might be served or wealth shared with the masses.[5]

As in 1942, many Budonian families were involved in the political events leading to the banning of the UNM, which were widely interpreted as representing the interference of the Protectorate government in the internal affairs of Buganda. The school political society was addressed by two members of the Lukiiko, and the ensuing discussion was heated. But there were no incidents and the term moved steadily to Speech Day in July, at which the Guest of Honour was the Governor, Sir Frederick Crawford. He complimented the school on its rapid progress to HSC level and reminded the students that among them were many of the future leaders of Uganda. In his report to the governors, Robinson stressed that the last three years had seen great changes at Budo and that it was much to the credit of the staff and students that these had been accomplished quietly. But he sounded a warning:

The Minister of Health was recently reported as regretting that the shortage of qualified local candidates was inevitably leading to a process of de-Africanisation in the expanding medical services. We are being equally hard hit in the senior secondary schools. We advertised recently in the local press and in the UK for an honours graduate to replace Mr Kironde. There was not a single reply from an African. In a rapidly expanding economy such as ours this stage may be inevitable, but we must hope that it will be short-lived. A school, if it is to do its job properly, must provide an education related to the needs of the country and integrated with the surrounding community. With few Africans teaching at the top of the school, this integration is in danger.[6]

At the end of the term, several experienced teachers expressed concern about discipline. The perennial Budo weaknesses of lateness, lack of attention to detail, and failure to ensure that orders were carried out and punishments done, had lately been accompanied by personal rudeness which seemed to be more than "the effect of awkardness" - for which Cobb had asked indulgence. The girls' warden, Mary Jewell, and her supporting housemistresses were disturbed about relationships between girls and boys, and the old problem of imbalance of numbers. For some years it had been forecast that there would "soon" be much larger numbers of girls passing with high grades in the Senior Secondary Entrance Examination, and that Budo would then have more strong girl applicants. But it had not yet happened and some disenchanted staff urged that Budo should revert to being a boys school, and Gayaza be asked to admit the thirty girls.

For many of these reasons 1959 was a hard year for the prefects. The school had needed another outstanding group - like the one which had supported Robinson so well in his first year - sensitive to the unusual position of the fifth formers, and also of the third formers who had expected to be at the top of the school in 1960 but would now have to wait two further years. The new HSC prospect also created more anxiety than the former Makerere preliminary year and, with a few notable exceptions, the prefects for the year were diffident, and preoccupied with the School Certificate course - the key to a fifth form place in 1960.

Considering all these difficulties, however, there was still a sense of confidence and progress. The Chapel Appeal Fund stood at £ 1500, and it was decided to organise a fete, a previous one in Cobb's time having raised about a third of the fund. It was a popular community project, and students and staff worked cheerfully together, galvanising the school - in spite of imminent examinations - to provide a range of stalls and activities. The occasion drew about 3000 visitors to the Hill on a glorious October day, to spend a jolly afternoon - and raised more than £ 700 towards a new chapel. Once again the school had demonstrated its capacity - while its daily routine showed many shortcomings - for "making a special effort."

Two weeks later, one of the fourth form boys, who had already had a severe warning from the headmaster for breaches of discipline, was involved in an angry argument with a girl during an Art class. After the staff had considered the case, bearing in mind that he was taking the School Certificate examinations, he was suspended and sent home. When the news spread around the school, there was an unpleasant demonstration by a gang of boys against some of the girls, returning from lunch. Early in the afternoon, the prefects sent a letter to the headmaster, signed by all except the head prefect, James Nsubuga, stating that they had resigned their prefectships. The headmaster announced that afternoon classes would begin at the usual time, but the school did not respond. A group of boys summoned a meeting of students on the main football field. To the noise of its speeches, bell-ringing, and general imitation of a political rally, the staff discussed the next move. The headmaster ordered the school to assemble in the main hall. As teachers walked up to the hall a few boys threw stones, but without much conviction or accuracy. The school, well marshalled by a few senior students, then sat down on the grass outside the hall, refused to join the staff inside, and proposed that the headmaster should come out and speak to them.

So far there had been more noise than significant activity, but when Robinson was informed that there had been some premeditation about the demonstration, and that some boys had drawn up a list of the teachers and wives they intended to "beat", he sent a message to the police in Kampala. A patrol arrived, to find the staff sitting inside the hall in the gathering gloom and the school still sitting quietly outside. With the staff were Erisa Kironde and Senteza Kajubi who had heard rumours of a disturbance at Budo and had come at once from Makerere to help. Two entertaining interludes followed. The first was when one of the British police officers suggested that the college simply had a bunch of naughty boys to deal with, went out to address them but returned after two or three minutes, conceding that the problem was much as the staff had explained, and that "something must be done". The second was provided by Do Robinson who had been stranded alone at home, but now strode with slow dignity through the main quad - where the school remained, but now restive - disguised as a night-watchman, with full-length ex-army greatcoat, felt hat and stick, to join the staff in the hall.

The police patrol had reported to headquarters and a full detachment was sent from Kampala. With the headmaster's permission they quietly broke up the crowd of students who were ordered to bed, and to assemble in the hall at 8am next day; the police remained on the Hill all night. In the morning Bishop Brown and several other governors arrived, with officers from the Department of Education. They found the school plentifully decorated with chalk slogans inviting the headmaster and staff to return to Britain, and the students sitting quietly on the grass outside the hall, displaying a blackboard message urging the headmaster to resign. The bishop announced that the Board of Governors was closing the school immediately and indefinitely. Transport would be provided that day to take all students to Kampala. They would receive letters in due course, telling them whether and when they would be allowed to return to Budo.

It was a sad and quiet morning, as cases were packed, dormitories cleared and buses loaded. The closure had clearly astonished almost all the students. With "Cambridge" so near they had not considered it possible. Housemasters were bombarded all morning with the same incredulous - and for the moment unanswerable - question: "But what about our examinations?" By tea-time all the dormitories and studies were deserted and Budo was eerily silent.

Why had it happened? It was now obvious that - in spite of Robinson's sincere congratulations of July - the welter of swift change had been too much for the students. They had, understandably, misinterpreted the sudden de-Africanisation of the senior school. It was hard for them to believe that the governors truly wanted more African teachers when they had recruited only young Europeans. Discipline had deteriorated partly because once again - as Cobb said he had found in 1948 - too many rules had been allowed to spring up, there were few clear distinctions between rules and procedures, no list of either, and too many officials. When the staff discussed this later they were all surprised to discover that there had been 26 prefects and monitors and no clear distinction between the two levels of responsibility.

Probably more influential than all these weaknesses had been the rapid deterioration of the easy social relationships between teachers and students. This was revealed to my wife and me by one of my most gifted S1 students of English, Shadrach Davis Sebukima, who had passed through Budo Junior School and was to prove, in the late 1960s, a courageous president of the Makerere Students Guild in opposition to the extremes of the Obote regime. He was used to dropping in casually at our home and had persuaded me to try to pass on to him my rudimentary knowledge of French. (He later did post-graduate studies at the Sorbonne.) He told us that whereas visits to staff houses had formerly been relaxed and leisurely, teachers had lately tended to ask, after only a few minutes, "Well now, what can I do for you?" In a sentence, which I can still repeat verbatim because it was such a sharp cross-cultural lesson from a student to a teacher, he said, "And you see, when someone calls unexpectedly at my father's house, my father may not discover what he has come for until the next day, or even the day after that." We pondered ruefully the impact such courtesy and hospitality would have on social life in England.

The alleged influence of Busoga College, Mwiri had also offended many students. Budo had grown used to having its headmasters specially imported from "overseas" - Cobb from England, Herbert from West Africa, Gaster from Ceylon. To have an assistant master from a neighbouring - and of course, inferior - school, appointed headmaster was a blow to Budo *kitibwa*. A new covered and properly seated Budo lorry, adapted from a design by Robinson, was simply a safer and more comfortable vehicle than the old one, but was resented as a Mwiri importation. Blue paint on the woodwork of the lower school block, was regarded not as the bargain consignment it actually was, but as the Mwiri colour plastered over Budo buildings. A few days after the closure I recalled a sensitive comment made several weeks before, by Apolo Nsibambi, then an outstanding student in my fifth form English Literature class. In a sympathetic tone he had said that he felt rather sorry for Europeans coming to Uganda at this time, "because you are going to have to put up with a great deal of willingness to misunderstand." It was a shrewd intuition. Budo in October 1959 was in a situation that could easily be misinterpreted - and was.

There were similarities with the disturbance of 1942, but at least Robinson, unlike Herbert, did not have the devastating experience of a mass resignation of staff. Most of the teachers stood strongly with him. There was encouragement, too, in prompt letters of support from Cobb and Lord Hemingford in England, where *The Times* had taken brief note of Budo's plight, and from Bernard de Bunsen at Makerere, who was sure that personal relationships and confidence in the school would be quickly restored. There should have been some consolation also in the knowledge that he had not applied for the headship, but had been invited by the governors to take it on.

The governors asked for a commission of enquiry which in due course produced a written report on most of these causes, though some of the lesser irritations were understood only after subsequent discussions with students. It recommended that the governors and staff consider very carefully the value and organisation of co-education at Budo. The staff met daily under Robinson's tolerant chairmanship for several weeks and almost the whole period from October to mid-January was spent re-examining the way the school had been run.

Four boys were expelled for leading the disturbance; they were all helped to find places in other schools or colleges. The staff decided that none of the fourth formers should be re-admitted, even though this meant that in 1961 the school would have no prefects who had been at Budo more than a single year. Arrangements were made for all the fourth formers to sit the School Certificate examinations in Kampala, and school staff travelled in daily to supervise and invigilate. Apolo Nsibambi did not return to Budo. He had been a moderating influence throughout the disturbance, advising strongly against any violence. But he had also informed the school authorities about staff influence on the train of events, and because his evidence had not been acted upon he assumed that it had not been believed. Having been such a respected head prefect the year before, he was not willing to continue in the school if he was no longer trusted. This was a great disappointment to his family, as his father and grandfather had also been Budo head prefects. He studied privately and by correspondence for his Higher School Certificate, and won a place at Makerere.

After long and outspoken discussions, the staff agreed to recommend to the governors that co-education should continue. The performances of the fifth form girls in their first six months had impressed their teachers. All five would continue into the sixth form in February. Their teachers felt there was a good chance that they would do well in the HSC examinations in 1960 and that if they did this might raise the aspirations of girls in secondary schools all over the country as well as improving recruitment to Budo. A steady stream of able fifth and sixth form girls ought surely to increase the willingness of parents to take girls' education seriously. Even the colleagues who were least optimistic, recognised that to send the girls away after nearly thirty years of the Budo "experiment" would be a public rebuff for the cause of women's education and advancement, and might set back co-education many years. This remains one of the most thoughtful and democratic debates on education I have known in more than fifty years as a teacher - and I believe, one of the most important. Governors, parents, Old Budonians, and the many prominent Ugandans whose opinions we asked, overwhelmingly supported the majority staff view that the girls should stay.

After the long staff discussions and much informal conversation with students, there were many minor overhauls. Rules were fully codified for the first time in the history of the school. Rules and procedures were clearly distinguished, punishments regularised, the numbers of prefects and monitors were reduced and their responsibilities defined. Perhaps most important of all, the staff came to understand how relationships with students had deteriorated and what could be done to restore them. Altogether, we tried, with as much advice as we could get, to preserve the best traditions of Budo and to root out the spurious ones.

A final dimension to the political background must be recorded. As has been indicated, independence was in the air and anti-European feeling was widespread and understandable. The UNM trade boycott continued with sporadic violence and not only aroused resentment against the large Asian communities; it also separated the political leaders of the Baganda even more sharply from those of the other kingdoms of Uganda. Headmaster and staff were anxiously aware of all this. What they did not know until after the closure was that fourth former Sam Nsubuga, who had planned and led the disturbance, had been distributing Communist Party books and pamphlets on the Hill. Within a week of the closure he was in Cairo and shortly after in Moscow, where he studied for several years.

Robinson's clear warning, only six months before, that the school could not do its job without African teachers, was now widely understood and accepted. Staff and students were impressed and encouraged when HH The Kabaka readily agreed to second Ernest Sempebwa - Old Budonian, former Budo teacher and father of three Budo boys - from his senior post in the Buganda government, to join the staff as Second Master. His wisdom and humour were invaluable during the period of convalescence.

The year 1960 was excellent for the school. From the start students seemed determined that things should go well. A few murmured that Budo had been changed - which it certainly had - but they seemed glad to have clear rules, more written guidance and generally to know where they stood. Headmaster and staff had given time and care to the selection of the officials, and the new prefects were strong and responsible, with head prefect Matthew Rukikaire and girls' prefect Elvanyia Namukwaya, outstanding. Rukikaire was a Muhororo and his success and popularity in a school half of whose students were Baganda, reflected the easy relationships between students of more than twenty ethnic entities, which even a bad breakdown had left undamaged. The thirty members of the first sixth forms were drawn from fourteen of these groups.

Studies were resumed enthusiastically, especially by the sixth formers who now had to complete a taxing two-year HSC curriculum in only eighteen months, having started three months late and lost another three months during the closure. But out-of-class activities did not suffer. Apart from the Political Society which was closed, school clubs and societies continued to discuss, organise expeditions, sing, present plays, and entertain visiting speakers. The Nightingales gave concerts and the school band continued to shatter the nerves of the first cricket XI (and the teachers who coached them) near whose nets they practised. The sixth form refused to let their studies swamp them and produced a spirited version of *A Midsummer Night's Dream*, with Rukikaire an athletic Puck. Scouts and Guides flourished. And so did the girls.

As expected, the sixth formers gave a strong lead and were soon well supported by more good recruits from Gayaza, Nabumali and Budo, in a capable new fifth form which arrived in March. As their juniors realised that it was possible for girls to be outstanding members of sixth forms, both academically and socially, the girls' morale and classwork improved noticeably throughout the school. It was at last not true - and never would be again - that "girls allow the boys to do all the answering".

The enjoyment of games and athletics was a feature of the year. The near-fanatical belief in the efficacy of team games which still characterised many English public schools had, happily, not taken root in Uganda. Budonians enjoyed matches and competitions with other leading schools, but the main aim of the games programme was not to win matches but rather to help as many students as possible to find a sport that they could enjoy. That year about sixty new students learnt to swim, and in the cricket team, in spite of a shortage of pitches, nearly 100 volunteers were able to play and be coached regularly. The football season was similarly successful, with a high level of participation, but it remained disappointing that - perhaps because soccer is regarded as the national sport and one which Ugandans really know how to play - the boys still responded reluctantly to coaching, so their standard of play was not as high as their combined natural talents should have produced. Meanwhile, the girls swam and played netball and tennis enthusiastically, and a few made their debuts on the running track.

It was through athletics that sport did most to help restore a communal spirit in the school. Games time was from 5.15 to 6.45 each weekday evening and, with limited playing fields, it was only for athletics that the whole school could be actively involved, in two shifts, on one evening. Under the enthusiastic and well-organised coaching of chemistry master Don Crawley, this happened on three evenings each week. Standards had been improving through the 1950s and in 1959 had compared favourably with those at the annual Oxford and Cambridge athletics meeting in England. But they rose dramatically that year with the arrival from Nabumali of two outstanding sprinters, Erasmus Amukun and Aggrey Awori. Their selection to represent Uganda in the Rome Olympic Games in August, delighted us all, but more important to the school was their eagerness to coach anyone, from youngest junior to teacher, who was willing to learn. Both later won university scholarships to the USA and had successful careers, Amukun in education and Awori in politics. Their example, in making really hard training and practice seem enjoyable, was widely followed at Budo and standards remained high. Chris Eswau and William Kamanyi represented Uganda in the 1962 Commonwealth Games, and Kamanyi in the Tokyo Olympics of 1964.

The year came to a happy end with a spate of house parties and a farewell party for the first sixth form, organised entirely by the students, all but one of whom gained entrance to university courses in 1961. The staff also gave a "concert" for the school. It was, no doubt, not as uproarious as we believed at the time, but seemed to be enjoyed by a packed hall. One highlight was our mixed staff choir, modestly entitled "The Budo Hornbills" to signal our intention to avoid any competition with "The Budo Nightingales". It was unanimously agreed that we succeeded.

The year 1961 was notable for good examination results at School Certificate and HSC levels; the visit of the Archbishop of Canterbury, Dr Fisher; an innovative production by Susannah McRae, recently arrived from England, of the *Antigone of Sophocles* in a Kiganda setting; and the loss of two fine teachers - Mary Jewell who had been senior history teacher and girls' warden for nine years, and Alan Walker, senior mathematician and inspiration of Budo music for thirteen. The Budo Nightingales' imaginative parting gift to Alan was an LP recording of their farewell concert for him, still nostalgically heard in Old Budonian homes around the world, more than 40 years later. What had been a contented and surprisingly settled year for Budo had, however, been anxious and unpredictable for the country.

Under Protectorate government supervision, elections had been held throughout Uganda to form a provisional administration, to exercise what the British called "internal self-government", as a short stage towards independence. The Democratic Party, with a majority Baganda membership and strong Catholic influence, won a comfortable majority over the Uganda Peoples' Congress, largely northern and Protestant in sympathies. The DP, led by a politically experienced lawyer, Benedicto Kiwanuka, therefore, had the potentially huge advantage of forming the interim government. The party, and Kiwanuka personally, showed poor judgement, however, in paying scant respect to Kiganda traditions, particularly those of the Lukiiko and the Kabakaship, thereby alienating thousands of Baganda voters, including some of its own party members. Within months the formation of a third political force, *Kabaka Yekka* (The Kabaka Alone), changed the balance of power. When the elections for the government of a fully independent Uganda were held in 1962, the UPC had entered into an improbable and entirely expedient alliance with Kabaka Yekka, jointly winning 58 seats in the National Assembly. The Democratic Party with 22 seats formed a chastened opposiiton. As the British prepared to withdraw, having governed for 60 years, largely through the long-established traditonal tribal structures, the "problem of the hereditary Kingdoms" had been shelved, not solved.[7]

Buganda was not only geographically central in Uganda, it was by far the most populous, prosperous and powerful of the kingdoms. Obote understood the danger of this imbalance early and clearly. He eventually became a scourge to his country and, at best, a mixed blessing to Budo. But he should be given credit at least for his foresight and candour as a young and inexperienced politician. In his maiden speech as a member of the Uganda Legislative Assembly , in May 1958, he referred bluntly to Protectorate government policy - or lack of it - towards the kingdoms:

> If the Government is going to develop this country on a unitary
> basis, how on earth can the Government develop another state
> within a state? Does the Government really think that when
> self-government comes to this country, the State of Buganda will
> willingly give up the powers it has got now, in order to join with
> other outlying districts or provinces? I do not think so.[8]

A possible emollient for the Baganda was the creation, for the
Kabaka, of a constitutional position in a unified independent Uganda.
Such a role would have to be precisely defined and meticulously
observed. Douglas Tomblings predicted, before independence in
1962, that this would be virtually impossible.[9] Though long retired,
he remained alert, well-informed and devoted to Uganda, Makerere
and Budo. He was a personal friend of Kabaka Mutesa but believed
that any such arrangement would be facile, and that Mutesa himself
and the Baganda political elite would eventually be unable to accept
the constraints that it would impose. But the attempt was made and
Tomblings' prophecy was to be fulfilled - certainly in the opinions of
Obote and his UPC government.

So October 1962 brought independence to Uganda, and Sir Frederick
Mutesa, an Old Budonian, still holding the Kabakaship of Buganda, was
sworn in as constitutional - but virtually ceremonial - president of the
new nation in 1963. Independence brought immediate expansion for
Budo. Through a grant of £ 70,000 from the United States government
the school was able to plan for 140 more student places over four years.
Additional buildings at Kabinja enabled the junior secondary classes at
last to move down the Hill. The senior school built two new Houses,
"Grace" for girls and "Nigeria" for boys, two more staff houses, an
additional laboratory and - at last - a sanatorium. The old chapel was
well converted into the main library. Over the four years a complete
new "stream" was added to the school so that by March 1965 the total
enrolment was 439, of whom 85 were girls. In 1958, the year before
the HSC classes began, the total had been 207, including 24 girls. Budo
had more than doubled its intake within seven years.

Growth had not been only in buildings and student numbers.
Activities too had multiplied and the school was taking much greater

advantage of its closeness to Kampala. Robinson proclaimed this in his 1964 report:

> There is now in Kampala a quite astonishing variety of activity - educational in the widest and best sense - art exhibitions, science exhibitions, courses of lectures at Makerere and at the National Theatre, plays, concerts and recitals, elocution competitions, drama festivals, choir festivals, TV and radio quiz programmes, seminars and forums, as well as the various cups and tournaments and competitions for all games. To all these the schools in and around Kampala are invited... such schools must be selective and attempt to strike a balance between all this outside activity and a vigorous internal school life.[10]

Among the new developments in Budo's "internal life" from 1962 to 1965 had been the establishment of the school zoo, made possible by another generous American gift, and several more stage productions, two of which - *Saint Joan* and *The Merchant of Venice* - were taken by invitation to the National Theatre. Another production, in an African setting, was a prize-winning entry by a Budo boy in a national play-writing competition. The games' programme had been extended, with the additions of basketball, netball and hockey to the regular schedule, and occasional forays into sailing and mountaineering. When the first mixed Budo group climbed Mount Elgon, co-education had "arrived" beyond all dispute. It had owed much to Susannah MacRae, who led that expedition and, who as girls' warden, had built enterprisingly on the work of Mary Jewell and her predecessors. Many girls acquired new confidence from taking part in her drama productions.

The most striking development of these years, however, was the new chapel. In 1961 the staff had regretfully decided that the plan to enlarge Sabaganzi's chapel was no longer realistic. Estimated extension costs were high and the site could not contain an enlargemnent that would accommodate the doubled student numbers, already projected to rise to 540. Since 1959 daily and Sunday services had been held in the main hall and many Old Budonians were keen to restore Sabaganzi's principle that the centre of school life should be the chapel. With £ 3000 already subscribed, the target was raised to a formidable £ 12000. Through the efforts of staff, students, governors, Old Budonians, friends of the school, the English Diocese of Bath and Wells and finally of two anonymous donors, the fine, prominently sited chapel to seat 600, which has served Budo so well for more than 40 years, was consecrated in 1964. [It was not until 2002, while I was researching this history, that my friend and former colleague Bryan Wilson, who was treasurer of the chapel fund, confided that the two anonymous donors had in fact been Ian and Do Robinson. Unlike some earlier Budo benefactors, they had no private sources of income, yet gave more than half of the cost of the new chapel. Bryan and I agreed that in Budo's centenary year, this most generous gift should be publicly acknowledged.]

In its early years Budo had been a training ground for headmasters and this tradition was resumed in the early 1960s. Ron Wareham, senior English teacher and housemaster of Ghana, took over at Nabumali High School near Mbale, and Don Crawley, senior science teacher and housemaster of South Africa, went north to Sir Samuel Baker School near Gulu. Dick and Gwyneth Drown, after eighteen years of fine work for Budo Chapel, English teaching, England House, cricket, hockey and humour, went to Kenya to take over St Andrew's Preparatory School, Turi. Another sad loss was Eapen "Johnnie" Oommen, who retired to India after ten years' science teaching. In sixty years he had been Budo's only Asian teacher and with his wife Mary, and daughters Soosie - an outstanding student at Budo and Makerere - and Anna, had made, by example, a fine contribution to African/Indian relationships. In 1963 I moved from Budo to a lectureship in the teaching of English, in the Faculty of Education at Makerere, where I was joined in 1965 by senior Biology teacher John Hall.

Such departures were the kind that any lively school must sustain, but during Robinson's first seven years the staff had changed at an alarming pace, and had remained overwhelmingly European. In 1962 we had lost our two senior African teachers, Ernest Sempebwa, deputy head, and John Kisaka, head of Art, both moving to senior administrative posts in education. In 1963 the school said farewell to one of its truly remarkable retainers when school caterer, *Omwami*

Kangave - a fount of wisdom and kindness to students and teachers for 30 years–was appointed head caterer at the new Mulago hospital.

Enoch Mulira was a valued senior colleague for the next two years but when he was appointed to a post with UNESCO, Budo faced its sixtieth year without a single African teacher. In his Speech Day report in 1964 Robinson echoed his own appeal of 1959 and Cobb's as far back as 1952:

> There is a world shortage of teachers, and until Uganda can produce enough of her own, schools are going to be difficult to run, because the expatriates are mostly birds of passage nowadays, staying for only one or two tours [which meant 2 to 4 years].[11]

This bland generalisation concealed the harsher reality that, with a teaching staff of 24, Robinson had endured more than 40 staff changes in the previous 5 years. Of the staff who had launched the HSC classes in March 1959, he was the sole survivor.

Yet a report by the Uganda Education Inspectorate, halfway through this unprecedented staff movement, suggested that the school was surmounting the unwelcome changes, because it had established a sound tradition of all-round education which new, inexperienced teachers, however transient, could respect and maintain:

> Budo is doing its best to give its pupils a liberal education in the widest and best sense.
>
> Based on Christian foundations, as it is at Budo, such an education represents the best that Western Civilisation can offer. The Inspectorate feels that this aspect of Budo's life is of tremendous importance. Art, music, handicrafts and a number of school societies, lectures and extra-curricular activities, are a prominent feature of Budo life, necessitating a great deal of work by staff outside teaching hours. In fact a whole-hearted effort is being made to provide a full education for a full life. We know that this state of affairs could only have been attained by the whole-hearted effort and co-operation of all members of staff.[12]

The period 1964-5 was good for this kind of balanced education and also for Budo social service. The senior students took the Cambridge examinations in their stride. Of the 43 School Certificate candidates

38 won HSC places at Budo or other schools and 31 out of the 33 HSC candidates went on to university. At the same time, communal work was revived, on the initiative of a sixth former who had spent two years in England and been impressed by the work of his school's Voluntary Service Unit. Budo's VSU members gave up part of their Christmas vacation to social service on the Sesse Islands and laid a pavement around the new chapel. They were the first voluntary manual workers the school had produced without any prompting from the staff.

Another notable Budo contribution to the local community at this time was the weekly child welfare clinic which my wife Jean - an experienced paediatric nurse and midwife – ran voluntarily in our garden for two years. Thirty to fifty mothers, some expectant, others with their babies or young children, assembled every Tuesday for examination, advice and treatment, if necessary. The Red Cross provided scales and medicines, UNICEF supplied dried milk powder, and Sarah Kisosonkole, sister-in-law of the Kabaka, drove out from Mengo and gladly spent many hours translating and helping. Complications in pregnancy were detected early and the mothers taken to one of the Kampala hospitals. With breast-feeding strongly urged and the right - and wrong - uses of powdered milk explained, the health of many babies and mothers improved. A number of mothers' and babies' lives were saved by early diagnosis and prompt hospital treatment. The villagers knew that Budo cared about their families.

Two published estimates of Budo about this time are worth recording. In a major study commissioned by the British government, *Uganda: A Crisis of Nationhood*, Harold Ingrams wrote in 1960:

> To some extent at least Budo has fulfilled the hopes of Bishop Tucker ... But it seems to have had its ups and downs and, perhaps for historical reasons, does not seem to be achieving all that might have been hoped for it.[13]

This was faint praise. Three years later Elspeth Huxley, a distant relative of Sir Julian who had praised Budo in 1929, was effusive. But she was also culpably ignorant of the achievements of the many Budo girls and women teachers.

> Budo was founded about half a century ago for chiefs' sons and
> since then anyone who is anyone has sent his sons there to be
> shaped into true Uganda gentlemen by its first-rate academic
> discipline - only the best masters have taught there - and its
> muscular Christianity in the Dr Arnold tradition. Now, Uganda's
> establishment is almost solidly Old Budonian.[14]

Both judgements should have embarrassed Budonians of the 1960s but
it was Ingram's that they needed to keep in mind. Post-Independence
Budo was still a long way from Weatherhead's ideal of the Christian
African school. It urgently needed Christian teachers who would stay
and - as many Budo staff had tried to do - live Christianity rather than
preach it. In the new Uganda, Bishop Gresford Jones's appeal for less
sense of "mission" and more of straight professional service, still had as
much force as when he had made it forty years before. Christians could
be quietly glad that they had done something for education in Africa,
but they needed to understand that many Ugandans were alert to some
destructive effects of the collusion between colonialism and mission.
They would have applauded the sharp judgement of contemporary
African writer and academic Ezekiel Mphaphele:

> To us the Church has become a symbol of the dishonesty of the
> West. [15]

Budo and other mission-founded schools could counter this charge, only
through the work of men and women who would teach with relaxed
enthusiasm and enjoyment and with none of what one of my own Budo
students dismissed as "that bloody and awful sanctimoniousness with
which some teachers do their work."

It needed teachers who would persevere in what seemed to me a
good Budo tradition, to work and speak out for what was right rather
than conform to what was there. In fact Budo had not been founded "for
chiefs' sons" as Elspeth Huxley had claimed. Mengo High School had
been. But Weatherhead's insistence on manual labour for all at Budo
- "There is no difference here between prince and peasant" - made that
clear. But it was a fair criticism of the Budo of the 1960s - as of other
secondary schools I had visited in East Africa – that it tended to make
too much of its role of training an elite to lead the country. I felt that,

during my four years at the school, there had been enough visitors preaching and lecturing about leadership to last for the next forty. But it had also had teachers who tried to educate for a full and active life in the community and for service to it. It will always need more.

Above all, in the early years of Independence, it needed African Christians. It was fashionable but futile to criticise past European staff because the school was not more African. They could bring it only the best that they knew. In his Inaugural Lecture as Professor of Education at Makerere, Eric Lucas spoke about English traditions in East African Education:

> Before a tradition is carried over into another situation, another country, another race, ideally it should be examined and its relevance to the particular set of circumstances assessed. This has rarely been done, not so much from lack of common sense or shortage of time, as from the unrecognized assumption of traditions. When this has happened, as it has in education, the best we can do is to make periodic appraisals of the traditional elements and try to assess their value.[16]

Budo headmasters and teachers had often tried to fulfil those hopes but with incomplete knowledge of the traditions of the society for which they were building. By the end of 1965 it was clear to all that it must be Africans who eventually determined what would best serve their countries and their schools. It was also clear that it might be some years before this could happen in Uganda.

The school's 60th year began promisingly at the end of January 1966 and plans were laid for the celebration of the Diamond Jubilee in June. Uganda's first three years of independence had brought progress in many fields, notably in swift expansion of school education, with wide popular support. But Robinson and his colleagues knew that Budo remained a peculiarly sensitive microcosm of the volatile political antagonisms aroused by the actions which had led to the formation of the new government.

The year 1965 had passed quietly but anxiously, with the Baganda chafing under alleged favouritism towards Northerners by the UPC government, and with Obote first widely suspected and then publicly accused of corrupt dealings in gold and arms, across the Congo border. In February 1966, he suspended the national constitution, claiming that the actions of the president, Sir Edward Mutesa, were endangering national security. Tension mounted throughout the country and in May, Mutesa as Kabaka of Buganda, demanded the withdrawal of the national government from the kingdom. On 23 May Obote declared a national state of emergency and on 24 May it became known internationally that Uganda government forces had bombarded and virtually destroyed the Lubiri. Robinson's terse account of what followed at Budo remains a key document towards a true understanding of the later problems and successes of the school.[17]

> On the Monday, May 23rd, our telephone lines were cut and roads were blocked. On Tuesday the gunfire at the Lubiri could be heard. The main road was opened again and some immediate supplies were brought from Kampala by school bus. By Tuesday evening it was clear - from broadcasts from Uganda, Kenya, the BBC and South Africa - that the Palace had been taken; there was no news of the Kabaka.

> On Wednesday morning there was a growing number of absentees from classes. Those Baganda who did attend were mostly barefoot. A meeting of Baganda, with a few sympathisers, formed in Mutesa quad. When, by break, it had become somewhat noisy, I went to speak to them. They were 80-100 strong, perfectly friendly, and said that they could not settle to work... I told them that I had no objection to their missing classes that morning... but that I must insist that they kept quiet and did not disturb the rest of the school. Between 100 and 150 missed lunch.

> I was assured by John Nsubuga (last year's head prefect, now a student teacher and the only Muganda member of staff) that this "mourning" would finish at lunchtime and that normal school routine would be resumed. This may indeed have been the wish of the seniors, but the rank and file had other ideas... Incidents that afternoon showed that events could easily have taken an unpleasant turn. First a number of groups left the hill for Kasozi, with sticks but without uniform; according to the Northerners they had gone to fetch the villagers, to beat them up ... At tea-time, a number of the group "jumped the drum" and went to tea early, eating more

than their share of "slices" [bread]. This was an unexpected act of provocation to the rest of the school who had hithertto in the main shown a tolerant and even sympathetic attitude.

There were reports of intimidation ... for example a middle-school Northerner brought me a piece of paper he had found on his bed, inscribed "Keep away - Death" I was now told that ... they would like to be given some firewood so that they could sit up in the quad with their photograph of the Kabaka, in traditional mourning around the fire.

In assessing the anxiety about possible violence it needs to be remembered that most of the 150 senior students in S5 and S6 were aged 18 to 21, and a number were well into their 20s. They were young men and women, not boys and girls. Altogether, Robinson and his colleagues were responsible, on an isolated hill, for 450 students aged 14 to mid-20s. On Wednesday morning, 25 May, Robinson, still without a telephone line, made a brief visit to the Ministry in Kampala, to alert Ernest Sempebwa, now Deputy Chief Education Officer for Uganda, that Budo might need his help. Early that evening, Do Robinson drove in to confirm the request, and Sempebwa responded immediately:

The fact that someone in his position was prepared to leave his wife and family for the night and come out alone just before curfew, was a measure of his friendship for Budo for which we shall always be in his debt. I believe his presence with us that night was decisive and that without him events might well have got out of control. In the meantime I had called a meeting of prefects and some senior staff... The prefects, both Baganda and non-Baganda, were clearly most disturbed. They reported bitterness of a tribal nature which had never been overt at Budo in their experience. It was increasingly difficult for a Muganda prefect to communicate with the Northerners in his house, and vice-versa. They were agreed that there was no anti-staff feeling and were confident that the leaders of the Baganda group did not intend to be violent. We decided to discourage the bonfire. ... I made it clear that at the first hint of violence I would be obliged to call the security forces, curfew or no curfew. I believe this had a deterrent effect, as it was the last thing any of us wanted. I am sure too that John Nsubuga's moderating influence was most valuable.

When Mr Sempebwa arrived we heard that there was firewood in the quad and agreed that the bonfire session should be allowed to continue, patrolled by staff ... At 9 oclock I was told that a group of young Northerners wished to see me. Mr Sempebwa and I met 80-100 of them in a classroom. They insisted they were really frightened. They regarded those round the bonfire "armed with sticks, knives and bottles" as a threat ...I said that they could sleep in the hall, guarded by staff. A staff rota was therefore arranged.

After this meeting, at 9.30, Mr Sempebwa and I went to the bonfire, where about 150 were gathered listening to the news. I went on to prayers in chapel, leaving Mr Sempebwa with them. He stayed there till well after midnight.

When he returned he reported that all seemed quiet, but the Baganda group had requested that for the next few days the whole school should refrain from playing music and from dancing. Robinson had already decided that the school must be closed. The assurances given by students about times of dispersal had not been kept; the request for prohibition of music and dancing was "not reassuring"; the school had no reserve supply of basic foodstuffs, and it was unlikely that much useful work would be done if term continued, given the disturbed state of the whole country. A break would give time for tempers and bitterness to cool.

The nub of the matter was the realisation of all of us that if there were news of the Kabaka's death, or even arrest, violence was more than likely. In the circumstances that would then obtain in Buganda, help from outside would be impossible. The maintenance of law and order would depend on 15 European men whose authority would be inadequate to control the situation ... It was clear that we must act at once.

At 1 am on 26 May Robinson asked Ernest Sempebwa as Deputy CEO, to approve his decision, since it was impossible to consult the governors. He then called a meeting of Housemasters, which endorsed the decision, planned the procedure, and adjourned at 3 am, agreeing to announce the decision to Houses at 7 am.

The first bus left at 8 am. By midday 350 of the school's roll of 450 had been transported to Kampala, having been given transport money. Fifty more left in the afternoon and another 30 the following morning at dawn. A member of staff - sometimes two - conducted each of the seven trips in the school bus ... About a dozen boys remained - either Sudanese or Rwandan refugess with nowhere to go, or those who went to Kampala and found their families missing. The smoothness of this evacuation, carried out under conditions of uncertainty and urgency, was in my view a remarkable tribute to the efficiency of my staff, and I wish this to be put on record.

Some weeks later it became clear that the evacuation had been completely successful, all the students reaching home without serious injury. Many journeys had taken several days by roundabout routes because the state of emergency, which extended well into 1967, brought road-blocks and rail disruption. After consulting with colleagues, Robinson recommended to the governors that the school should remain closed for a full month, but that the closure should take the place of the August vacation. Because of the state of emergency the planned Jubilee celebrations were abandoned. Budo re-opened at the end of June and the sixtieth year continued until early December, with a short mid-term break.

Throughout this five-and-a-half-month period the school lived up to Cobb's accolade "willing to make a special effort". Obote's government aroused further resentment by presenting a new constitution, appointing him executive president, and proclaiming that Mutesa would not be allowed to return to the country as Kabaka of Buganda. In spite of this provocation Budo continued calmly with its full range of activities and the end-of-year examination performances showed no traces of the turmoil that the school and country were enduring. The largest School Certificate entry so far, 113 students, produced the best results - 68 First Class certificates, 32 Seconds and 9 Thirds. The HSC results were even more impressive because the sixth formers had taken so much responsibility for school discipline throughout a tough year: of 31 candidates, 21 achieved 3 or 4 Principal passes and 9 gained 2 Principals, which was the minimum university entrance requirement.

As Makerere and other Commonwealth universities matured and higher education became more international, there was growing interest in the academic standards of the feeder secondary schools. Comparisons were made with standards in Britain and the USA, partly because able expatriate teachers were more likely to be attracted to schools of demonstrably good quality. Lewis Dodd taught English at Budo from 1966 to 1971 and was well placed to comment, having taught for many years at Malvern College, a well reputed English public school:

> The culture shock involved in the move from Malvern to Budo was inevitably major; perhaps the most immediately noticeable difference was the extreme seriousness with which the boys and girls regarded examinations. In England there had been a more relaxed attitude and consequently more fun (and possibly more real education) in the classroom. In Uganda, where at the time there were a mere 8000 secondary places for each year's 80,000 primary school leavers, the competition was severe and future prospects depended on good academic qualifications. They must pass their examinations. The syllabus became a sacred cow. I had to work harder than I had been!
>
> The next striking feature of the work done by sixth formers was the high quality of their written English, which compared more than favourably with what I had been receiving at home. There was an understandable tendency to parrot learning ... but their work was extraordinarily good in general and I was amazed at their grasp and enjoyment of English Literature, and the quite tough diet of Milton, Hardy, Chaucer and Shakespeare still set before them in those unreformed days.[18]

English was a key subject, but by no means the only one in which Budo worked hard to keep in touch with international curriculum developments. New Mathematics curricula were being developed in the USA, UK and Ghana. Bryan Wilson and Colin Davis incorporated aspects of these into Budo Mathematics, beginning with an S1 class in 1964. They later helped to develop an East African version of the School Mathematics Project Course. Nine of the students selected in 1964 were included in the "Express" class which was to complete the School Certificate programme in three years. In 1966 they became the first Commonwealth students, outside the UK, to complete the SMP course, which all three S1 streams followed from 1968. "Express" School

Certificate classes for some students continued until 1973.

Robinson was the first scientist to lead Budo, giving the science department enlightened support and himself contributing to the teaching of Physics and Maths. In Chemistry, Biology and Physics the staff tried to keep the syllabuses up to date and to relate students' learning to their life experience. A new Biology syllabus for East Africa was devised by study groups in Uganda, Kenya and Tanzania. It made radical departures from the Cambridge course, putting much stronger emphasis on experimental work and encouraging students to make their own biological discoveries by observation and deduction. John Hall's experimental research on the weaver birds which nested around Budo hill, set a fine example as well as earning him an MSc degree.

In January 1967 Budo was one of 12 schools in Uganda and Tanzania to launch a new East African Chemistry syllabus in S1. The course was designed with particular reference to the natural resources of East Africa and incorporated some of the latest innovations in Chemistry teaching from the UK and USA. A similarly adventurous programme for Physics, launched in 1968, included many topics entirely new to school Physics in East Africa. As Budo rose to the challenges of higher academic requirements for university entrance, and for the narrow and competitive range of post-secondary employment opportunities, it continued to try to relate the curriculum to the social and personal needs of the students. The Sixth Form General Studies programme was still supported by a range of high quality lectures and demonstrations by visiting speakers, some of whom were international experts.[19] It included a laudable innovation:

> A feature of sixth form work in recent years has been a course in Sex Education, taken by Arts and Science students. This has attracted the interest of medical sociologists, as it is believed that, at school level, nothing as detailed and comprehensive has been tackled elsewhere in East Africa. A course on the anatomy and physiology of human reproduction, illustrated by filmstrips, is followed by a study of sex in relation to society:
>
> Marriage and parenthood; prostitution, venereal disease and infertility; discussion of the values involved in differing forms of

sexual relationship; and an introduction, through the subject of family planning, to the wider issues of world population control and the need for positive national policies. In this, Dr and Mrs George Saxton of the Family Planning Association, have been of great help, both in lecturing and providing films.

This study has been extended to include problems arising from drug-taking, alcohol and tobacco, where specialists have visited the school to lecture; also other subjects of a public health nature, such as the prevention of kwashiorkor and the understanding of mental disease, assisted by visits to Mwanamugimu Clinic at Mulago and to Butabika Hospital.[20]

This programme and the attitudes it encouraged was intended to alert Budo students of all ages to the difficulties of the vast majority of Ugandans, who had no opportunity for formal education or for paid employment. In Robinson's report on the years 1964 to 1968, a section entitled "Service to the Community" issued a challenge and followed it with a brief account of Budo's current contributions to communities in and around Kampala:

No school community can afford to be an ivory tower, selfishly going its own way. An active contribution must be made to the world at large... Budo social workers number about 90 students of whom 50 go to seven centres in Kampala on alternate Wednesday afternoons. The group at Sanyu Babies Home is engaged in maintenance work. The groups in the children's wards at Mulago hospital and at the Save the Children Fund home, run play groups for the afternoon and the children are encouraged to find creative and emotional outlets in painting, modelling, paperwork, toys, sand and water. (The Sisters at Mulago encourage painting and work with clay - in bed!)

One group goes to the Salvation Army hostel where the inmates, aged between one and eighty, need entertainment and occupation. Another group goes to the Naguru Remand Home where they and the fifty or so children in care are experimenting with art and construction work.... joining in ball games, building their own equipment and discussing the techniques of playing with children in care... Other students sponsored a Kisozi Youth Group and responded to appeals from Mulago Hospital and the Ministry of

Community Development, co-operating for example on a Spring [water] Protection Project.[21]

The two years which followed the 1966 coup were calm and successful for Budo. There may not have been - by Malvern standards - much "fun" in the classrooms, but there was plenty outside them. The full sports programme continued, with Budo teams competing well, but the main aim still being to encourage every student to enjoy at least one physical activity. In spite of chronic water problems the swimming pool was valiantly maintained, and drama and music flourished, officially and informally. Robinson identified eight different "pop" groups, though they did not own many instruments between them. Occasional dances, and frequent film shows were exuberantly enjoyed.

Such diverse and fulfilling activity should not be thought to have reflected a settled national atmosphere. It was a creditable achievement by staff and students, in this and in other Ugandan schools, to maintain enthusiastic studies and social activities in a political scene of rampant distrust and creeping corruption. Even before the overthrow of the Kabaka, the marriage of convenience between the UPC and Kabaka Yekka had collapsed. Some of Kabaka Yekka's most influential members had joined the UPC, which had become so powerful that it virtually ignored the DP opposition and was bolstered by Obote's autocratic detention of opponents and interference with the Judiciary. It was obvious to the politically concerned - who included most of the Budo community - that, as Yoweri Museveni recorded 30 years later, Ugandans' high hopes for a People's Democracy were being betrayed:

> The basis of political affiliation at the very beginning of Uganda's independence was... opportunistic and sectarian, with divisions along religious and sectarian lines. These divisions clouded the real issues and prevented the electorate from distinguishing between important issues and trivial ones.
>
> The interests and needs of the people were therefore not made a focal point, because opportunistic, ideologically and politically backward politicians had so fragmented society that common interests were lost sight of. The peasant in Lango, Northern

Uganda, did not regard the peasant in Buganda as his ally; he was persuaded to believe that the Baganda were arrogant, while the Baganda were told that the Langi were "primitive and cruel". This atomisation of the masses into sectarian groups served the interests of the politicians, who divided and ruled the people. Sectarianism gave them an automatic and cheap exploitative political base ... Political awareness among the masses was anathema to this type of politician.[21]

The ethos of Budo remained strongly anti-sectarian, but it was no easy task to maintain it, against such a political background. Student recruitment still drew on all the peoples of Uganda, with the Baganda still much the largest cohort, but rarely an actual majority. It was an appropriate time to review, and if possible strengthen, the influence of the school's Christian foundation and continuing affiliation to the Church of Uganda.

Robinson's Report 1964-1968, which was presented to all who attended the 1969 Speech Day, attempted this, making no extravagant claims, but describing impressive activity. The opening of the new chapel had coincided with the departure of a popular and effective chaplain, Dick Drown, who had been well succeeded by Hugh Sylvester, a gifted teacher, preacher, counsellor and musician, whose approachable manner, and innovative evangelical style, won him many enduring friends and admirers at Budo and beyond. Most of the teaching staff were practising Christians, of various denominations from Roman Catholic to *Balokole*, and a watchful Board of Governors supported the school's continuing Christian commitment. There were still some compulsory chapel services, but Robinson had encouraged debate on the merits of voluntary attendance. At this time a vocal majority of Old Budonians favoured compulsion, but chapel arrangements offered scope for students to exercise choice on a range of optional services and activities.

The Chapel, completed at the end of 1964, has had four years good use. Apart from the regular morning prayers, taken by different members of staff, and the main Sunday services, there have been weekly voluntary services of Holy Communion and mid-week evening prayers. The numbers confirmed in the four years 1965-1968 were 17, 20, 24, and 29.[23]

A long list followed of visiting preachers: archbishops, bishops, university professors, medical doctors, up-country clergy and laymen, but, as yet, no women. Chapel collections had supported a wide range of international charities including ones for the deaf, blind, cancer research, and also many village projects. The chapel choir had developed a repertoire ranging from Elizabethan motets to African settings of the canticles, and plays had been produced in the Chapel every year:

> The 1967 play-cycle culminated in a voluntary service of Holy Communion on Monday, Thursday, at which half the school communicated. The chapel is admirably suited for drama, with open spaces on both sides as well as at the front. In May 1966 an informal meeting at the chaplain's house, called "Sunday Night at Eight" was launched, for singing, prayer and Bible study. Weekly attendance of 80 to 100 has been a regular feature and the record stands at around 140. Special holiday Christian conferences have been arranged for Budonians: 1967 at Mukono; 1968 at Nabumali and 1969 at Nyakasura. [The latter two venues each about 200 miles from Budo.]

> Opportunities for outreach from the Christian community have included a Christian Literature Group, writing small booklets for publication by the Africa Christian Press; Sunday School for the local villages; teams visiting churches to take services, and social work in Kampala. There have been many visits and exchanges with other local senior secondary schools.[24]

Many chapel members also took part in the various social and community projects listed earlier in the report. So it could fairly be said that Budo Christians were awake.

Early in 1969, after eleven years as headmaster - a stint second only to H.T.C. Weatherhead's twelve - Robinson announced his intention to resign with effect from August. He and Do wanted to rejoin their daughter Mary and son Nicholas, both senior students at public schools and hoping to go on to university in England. The news seems to have been greeted with general consternation and Robinson would probably have endorsed Cobb's whimsical analysis: the years in between might sometimes be difficult but Ugandan welcomes and farewells were extremely generous. Founders Day, 29 March, was the first of his public farewells and provided a chance to review Budo's progress in his time. While the invitations were being sent out, President Obote, who had been a student of Robinson's at Mwiri, made it known that he would like to come. He was invited to be Guest of Honour and to address the influential assembly of Old Budonians and friends of the school, as well as present students and staff. Robinson gave an account of an extraordinary occasion, in a personal letter to his daughter, Mary, at Headington School.

> Speech Day, though topsy turvey, was a great day. Fine weather, everyone in a good welcoming mood, bunting and flags everywhere, plenty of visitors, plenty of tea. But at 3pm a message from the President that he'd be at least an hour late, as there was a debate on the Emergency, in Parliament, which he couldn't miss. When it was clear that he'd be two hours late, we had tea first and then waited for him. By the time he arrived and everyone had been presented and the Bishop and I had made our speeches, it was obvious that it would be dark by the time he had finished his, so we had to get the emergency lamps from the Chapel - luckily it was a perfect evening and sunset.[25]

In his own speech, Robinson ranged over the activities and achievements set out in his printed report for 1964 to 1968. He welcomed the president and applauded his faith in education:

> You are, Sir, no stranger to this hill and I know that you count many of our products among your most trusted advisers and servants. But this is your first visit to us as Head of State of the Republic of Uganda ... Those of us who have served the schools and colleges of Uganda through the 50s and 60s ... will, I know, be eternally grateful for one most important fact: We have never had to spend time and energy persuading our leaders that education is important. This, in Uganda, has been recognised by Government and People alike... We have, throughout the education explosion of these past years, been able to rest assured that you, Mr President,

were personally aware of the importance of what happens in our schools - and the priority you give to meeting with students has made your position plain.

On occasion, we have been reminded by visiting economists from some over-developed countries, that education is a non-productive service - that we are all consumers. That may be commonsense to an economist but it seems to me, as an engineer, to be uncommon nonsense. Surely the schools are the most productive institutions in society? We are the primary producers. I like to think that over these past twenty years I have been as productive as a schoolmaster as I would ever have been as an engineer.

He took some satisfaction from Budo's responsible use of taxpayers' money by thrifty "productivity", and he rebutted the frequently levelled charge that, to maintain its high standards, Budo must have received generous additional funds.

Our fees are lower than those of most boarding schools, and our recent expansion has been achieved with surprisingly little capital expenditure... Our recurrent grants are no more than elsewhere; our staffing ratio is the same and in fact we pride ourselves on making the best use of available resources. As you look around, you will I hope find nothing on a lavish scale. Our food costs are the lowest in the country; we have no blazers, no school caps, no terrazo floors. Our Chapel, built entirely by the private help of friends of Budo, was specially designed for economy of maintenance. Even the equipment for our new Language Laboratory [given by the Madhvani family], which some, in their ignorance, might label a luxury, has been designed for maximum efficiency at minimum expense.

He paid warm tribute to the work of all the school staff and to staff wives, in sustaining the wide range of curricular and out-of-class activities, and he thanked Makerere staff for so much help freely given. He then paid a typically sensitive compliment to the students:

A word of praise for the members of the school themselves. In these years, first of expansion and then of consolidation, I have met with a great deal of constructive comment, positive thinking, responsibility willingly accepted, initiative intelligently grasped, and mature appreciation of the realities of boarding school life. The result has been that the staff and I have had to spend a minimum of energy on solving disciplinary "sharis" and been able to concentrate on the more productive aspects of education. I am not suggesting that we have a school of 500 angels ... but this sense of responsibility, found in so many, is an incalculable asset.

I have tried to indicate that the image that some people hold of the traditional Budo - living in the ancient past of 1906, stuffy and remote ... a relic of a paternalistic colonial era - this image "is" only an image and is therefore in fact imaginary.

The president responded by referring warmly to his acquaintance with Robinson at Mwiri, to his teacher's genuine interest in his students there, and through them his deep affection for Uganda. He promised to return to this theme. But he then proceeded to contradict his former teacher, upbraiding the students for tribalistic tendencies. He seemed unconvinced by Robinson's deft demolition of the Budo "image" and unsympathetic to the school's peculiar tensions of May 1966. He may have persuaded himself that the closure and dispersal had reflected Budo's dissent from his violent solution to the problem of the kingdoms - and he may have been partly right. But he seemed to ignore the prime concern at the time, which had been the safety and well-being of the students and the country. Three years later he seemed unaware that he was preaching to the long-time converted:

Uganda can only be happy and stable if her people move away from the pre-independence position, where communities in the form of tribes, were unable to see their fellow countrymen or compatriots as "we", but only as "the others"...

Budo was the only school in the country which closed during the 1966 crisis, when it was stated that "tribal tension" was the reason. I am surprised that you young Ugandan boys and girls should in this age be thinking of 1900 rather than 2000! The question is whether Budo is with Uganda in the march forward to one, united, prosperous and peaceful republic.[26]

It seems unlikely that the presidential analysis convinced many Budonians. Several who had been present, told me 33 years later that

Obote's patronising censure had been bitterly resented and, coupled with his very late arrival, had been construed as deliberately insulting behaviour. Martin Aliker offered the only convincing explanation for this. As a schoolboy, Obote had applied for a place at Budo and had done well in the entrance examination. As always, however, the competition had been severe. He had not been offered a place, and believed that the one he should have secured had been given to a member of a prominent Kiganda/Budonian family with the same examination grade as his own.

> He was bitter about this. The later history of Uganda and the relationships between tribes after Independence, might have been very different, if Obote had become a Budonian.[27]

But if that is true, the rest of Obote's speech must be thought remarkably generous. He had promised to return to the subject of the headmaster and did so, with an oratorical coup:

> Speaking now as Head of the Uganda Government, I want to tell the Society of Budo - past and present - a secret. Your present headmaster, Ian Robinson, apparently wants to run away when Uganda still needs him. I have never been at Budo, but Budo remains in my present responsibilities, a prodigal son. I first met Mr Robinson - or more accurately he met me - more than 20 years ago. I think he is a Ugandan, in spite of his skin and origin.
>
> I am not a member of the Budo Board of Governors and I am not Minister of Education. But if I had that horizon of power, in Mr Robinson's house and heart ... I would say that you, Mr Robinson, Headmaster of King's College, Budo, [should] remain here to advance education in Uganda. You cannot leave now, and you must stay and continue. I ask you, Budonians past and present, to assist me in this endeavour.[28]

The word "unique" is used sparingly in this history, but it must be doubtful whether any other national president has ever publicly asked a long-serving expatriate head teacher to withdraw a resignation and stay, because the country could not yet do without him. These were the last word's of Obote's address and their impact can be deduced from the following day's headline and account in the *Uganda Argus*.[29] He had shown courage, if not tact, in making his surprise appeal, with no prior consultation with Robinson. He was in process of trying to guide UPC and national policies sharply to the left, advocating a one-party socialist state - which he in fact proclaimed a year later. He must have had real convictions about the importance of national education and of Budo's role within it, to have risked such an apparently retrograde step at this point. Robinson was astonished. His account of the rest of the evening carries - in the light of what was to come for Uganda and Obote - tones of both appreciation and pathos.

> After he had opened the Language Laboratory, he asked to come to the house and talk, and we sat in the sitting room with the Head of the Civil Service, the Bishop, Mr Sempebwa and his Private Secretary. There he made the appeal more specific. He said that if I really had to go now, the problem of who would be the next head here would really be very difficult. However, if I could by any means agree to stay just an extra year, he was quite sure the position in a year's time would be radically different, and there would have been time to find someone and train him up if necessary.

> From our house he left offically - police band playing the National Anthem and the school cheering him off - but he took me in the car with him, to show him the way round to Mrs Ntiro's [Budo's senior woman teacher] as there was a TV programme on Anguilla which he particularly wanted to watch. So we stayed there for more than an hour, very informally and happily - he was obviously feeling in a very relaxed mood.

> He left finally, in a flurry of police and security cars, at about quarter to ten. Before he went I told him that of course I would give every consideration to his request, and let him know after the weekend.

It was not an easy decision. The Robinsons had given it careful thought before notifying the governors - and the president personally - the previous December, that it was time to go. Now, after a quiet weekend of reflection in the Kenya highlands, "asking ourselves who we would be hurting by either course of action" they returned to Entebbe and next day personally gave a letter of acceptance to a contented president. They were to go on leave as planned, in April, returning in September to stay a further year. In fact, they stayed until the end of the school year in December 1970.

What kind of leadership and school ethos had prompted such a presidential gesture? Twenty-seven years later, Stephen Kamuhanda wrote for *The Budonian* about his years at Budo under Robinson. He had since read History at Makerere and been assistant master at Budo and in Lesotho, deputy head at Budo and finally head of another of Uganda's leading schools, Ntare, in his Ankole homeland:

> With a mixture of great excitement, high expectations and deep-rooted anxiety about what lay ahead for a boy like me from the rural cattle area of Nyabushozi, studying at King's College, Budo, I travelled unaccompanied from Mbarara by bus ... I had only a metallic suitcase for a few belongings... At first I was not impressed by Budo's old buildings.
>
> I soon became rather frightened to see so many white teachers, though later proud that I was being taught by Europeans with degrees ... The first weeks of term one became difficult because I could not communicate easily with teachers due to my inadequate English. I had to rely heavily on interpretations of my fellow pupils ... children of some Uganda Kings and middle-class civil servants ... who were already used to the European accent. One very important aspect of Budo life was the role of the teachers. Most of them were very committed to their job. They were always close to us anywhere we were.
>
> They loved and cared for us ... and gave us the best they had academically. Because of their devotion and interest in us, we liked and respected them. The headmaster, Ian Robinson (now retired Reverend) was regarded as a father figure. We affectionately and respectfully nicknamed him "U Thant" - in comparison with the then Secretary General of the United Nations - a sign of his great authority and to show how much we respected him. Or we simply called him "Rob". A good number of these teachers have remained very good friends of my family. The Ugandan teachers were equally good - I shall never forget Mr E.K.K. Sempebwa ...
>
> Historically, Budo has always taken a clear academic lead, not only in Uganda, but in the East African region as a whole. Budo students regarded themselves as natural leaders in the country.

Becoming a possible failure was not considered, as we always looked to our successful predecessors ... My student days at Budo were very happy and enjoyable. I took an interest in many things - like everyone else. Great ideas fascinated Budo students; we read newspapers and magazines, both local and international. Sad events saddened us - the assassination of US President John Kennedy in 1963, and his brother Robert in 1968, and the murder of the Congolese Nationalist, Patrice Lumumba, in 1961. On these occasions we marked the event by removing our shoes for a whole day, as a sign of mourning. The Cuban missile crisis of 1962 and the British election victory of the Labour Party in 1964, were exciting events which were debated by the junior classes ... The sad events in Uganda, 1964 - 1967, followed by the abolition of the Kingdoms, nearly tore the school apart on tribal lines, but for the wise leadership, firmness and neutrality of Ian Robinson and his staff ...

The spiritual side was the centre of Budo life. Chapel services were most enjoyable and enriching. The present Chapel, to which we all contributed money, was consecrated on Uganda Martyrs' Day 1964, with Sir Edward Mutesa, President, as Guest of Honour.

I was proud to have been chosen, as one of the leading Scouts in the school, to act as a bodyguard to Sir Edward. This Christian -centred life was remarkable to me... the most precious gift that Budo gave me.

One of the most exciting periods in Budo life was the end of the school year. We looked forward to the farewell House parties ... with dancing, fun and plenty of good things to eat, and finally to the last school supper of the year. This was a general farewell for the whole school, but especially to S4 and S6 leavers and to teachers returning to their home countries in Europe. Robinson had a fitting farewell message for everyone. At times these were sad occasions because they involved friends - even boy/girl friends - parting for good...

What did and does Budo mean in the lives of Budonians? It is hard to describe satisfactorily ... the experiences I have described briefly, shaped my life into what I am now. To me and my family, Budo has come to symbolise everything good and valuable in our entire lives.[30]

Second Master, David Weston, was acting head, while Robinson was on leave. Robinson spent part of his leave undergoing tests and treatment in Hammersmith Hospital. He was diagnosed with Coeliac disease, which required the future complication of a gluten-free diet, containing no wheat products. But he did not allow this to postpone a prompt return to Budo in September. Meanwhile, the Board of Governors had been active.

They had invited Daniel Kyanda - Old Budonian, Makerere graduate and, until 1968, Deputy Head of the Lubiri Secondary School - to consider applying for the headship. He was in the first year of a two-year commitment in Nairobi, with the Pan African Fellowship of Evangelical Christian Students, but as the governors were willing to offer the post from January 1971, he had felt he should accept, suggesting a briefing overlap with Robinson in December 1970. So the future seemed settled, as the Robinsons began their final "tour" in Uganda.

Within weeks of their return, the country's complex political enmities were further embittered by an assassination attempt on the president. Attending the annual conference of the UPC at Lugogo Stadium in Kampala, to present further proposals for socialist reforms, Obote was shot in the jaw. He was rushed to Mulago Hospital, where a successful operation - carried out with armed guards outside the operating theatre doors - removed smashed teeth and repaired facial damage. He made a rapid return to work, but even his considerable self-confidence must have been badly dented by the attack. The gunman was never identified, but it was thought unlikely that he had planned alone. Most observers considered that from this time, presidential and Government anxiety about security became obsessive.

But the third term of the Budo year ended quietly, with the seniors again achieving very good HSC results and a large university entry. Robinson seems to have enjoyed the sort of constructive final year he deserved. He summarised it, 30 years later, with his usual brevity and throw-away wit:

My recollection is that 1970 was a good year at Budo:

"No shipwrecks, nobody drowned Not much to laugh at at all!"[31]

David Weston was enjoying the new Language Laboratory. We built a pantry extension to the Mess. Communal Work - on its own initiative - paved and built low walls round the chapel approaches. Another tennis court was levelled and wired in. The new - compulsory - School Council behaved responsibly. Relationships with Nabbingo [a highly reputed Catholic girls' school about five miles away] were particularly warm; their Father often came to celebrate Mass in the Martyrs' Chapel. The new Sick Bay/Sanatorium was ably manned by Lewis Dodd and Nurse Mary, with a weekly visit from a Mulago doctor.[32]

One of Robinson's many valuable contributions to the development of Budo had been a big improvement in health-care provision, including many innovations and one piece of dogged but inspired conservatism. There had been frequent requests throughout his headship for the introduction of water-borne sanitation. But as an engineer who had spent years ingeniously maintaining a temperamental hillside water supply - and incidentally ensuring by far the longest period of continuous use of the swimming pool - he judged that this could never be adequate to support such a demanding refinement. (Jean and I had ourselves once arrived at a distant school on the evening when, after the flush toilets had failed for several days, a boy had died of typhoid fever.) In view of the disruption of public services which Uganda was later to endure for many years, this proved a crucially sound decision, sustaining health and avoiding temporary closures. It has to be conceded that deep pit latrines, often dank, smelly and dangerous - to young children - are unlikely ever to become endearing.

Robinson's twin concerns for science and health were gratified by a research project conducted at Budo, in his final year, with international benefits:

> Dr Denis Burkitt was a regular visitor to the hill, researching with the Medical Research Council on intestinal transit times. He had already established that African diets, high in unrefined fibre, had

half the transit time of European ones: He expected Budo's mixed diet would fall between them. He asked for twenty volunteers from the 6th form to swallow X-ray opaque tablets and collect their stools in plastic bags. Mary [Robinson] then labelled them with name, date and time of passing, and took them down each week to Mulago in our tin trunk - not, she said, the most welcome visitor to the Radiology Department!

Denis's obituary in the *British Medical Journal* said that he had been proved largely right, and millions have benefited through the change in Western diet that he pioneered. "He changed the breakfast tables of the Western world."[33]

Robinson's final year came to a celebratory end with a sequence of farewell events which softened the sadness of parting, after 13 years at Budo, 24 in Uganda and 30 in eastern Africa. The achievements during his headship speak for themselves. Those of us who taught and learned with him knew that we had been privileged. He had valued and trusted all members of the school, and his brisk, good-humoured, confident manner veiled his respect for the opinions of colleagues and students. He remained committed to democratic processes, however exasperating and time-consuming he knew they could sometimes be - a rare quality in a man who was by nature decisive. He willingly shared power and exemplified the old adage "When the good leader has been at work the people say 'Didn't we do well?'" Budo's twelve leaders in its first hundred years have all served it well. His was the longest headship - through a period of rapid change and frequent crises - and one of the most distinguished.

In mid-January 1971, the Robinsons went to State House to say their personal farewells to the president. He thanked them for all that they had done for Uganda and confided that he was particularly busy, as he had, reluctantly, to leave the country in a few days, to attend a rather inconvenient Commonwealth Conference in Singapore. It was to be a fateful journey.

Notes

1 Hunter G. *Education for a Developing Region*, London: Allen and Unwin, 1963, p. 74.

2 Low, *op. cit.* p. 32.

3 *Ibid.*

4 Kasozi A.B.K., *The Social Origins of Violence in Uganda 1964-1985*, Kampala: Fountain Publishers, 1994, pp. 66-67

5 *Ibid* p. 60

6 Speech Day Report 1959, in KCB archives.

7 In February 1959, when I had been at Budo only a few weeks, I asked senior colleague Erisa Kironde, how he saw the future political settlement of Uganda. "The hereditary kingdoms must go!" was his startling reply. It was a sharp political lesson for a novice.

8 Martin, David, *General Amin*, London: Faber and Faber 1974, p. 129

9 Tomblings D.G. in private conversation with the author, June 1962

10 Speech Day Report 1964, in KCB archives.

11 Uganda Argus, 22 July 1964.

12 Report of Uganda Education Deptment Inspectorate, March 1961. in KCB archives.

13 Ingrams, H. *Uganda: A Crisis of Nationhood*, London HMSO, 1960, p. 124.

14 Huxley, Elspeth. *Forks and Hope*; London, Chatto and Windus, 1964. p. 222.

15 Mphahlele, Ezekiel. *Down Second Avenue*. London, Faber and Faber, 1959, p. 221.

16 Lucas, Eric. *English Traditions in East African Education*. London OUP, 1959, p.3

17 Robinson, I.C. Headmaster's Report on the situation which led to his Decision to end term on Thursday 26 May 1966. In KCB archives. (Source of The 4 following quotations)

18 Dodd, Lewis: "Dr Dodder", unpublished typescript of Uganda Reminiscences 1966-71. p. 93.

[19] Robinson, I.C: A Report on King's College, Budo 1964-68, March 1969, p. 10. In KCB archives.

[20] *Ibid*, p. 7.

[21] *Ibid*, p. 9.

[22] Museveni, Yoweri K. *Sowing the Mustard Seed*, London: MacMillan 1997, p. 36.

[23] Robinson, I.C., Report 1964-68. p. 8.

[24] *Ibid*

[25] Robinson I.C. to Robinson Mary, 31 March 1969.

[26] Obote, President Milton: Address at KCB speech Day March 1969. In KCB archives.

[27] Aliker, Dr Martin, in private conversation with the author, Makerere, March 2002

[28] Obote, *op.cit.*

[29] *Uganda Argus*, 28 March 1969.

[30] Kamuhanda, S. "Budo in the eyes of a Student in the'60s." *The Budonian* 90, 1996, pp. 26-29.

[31] Holloway, Stanley: *The Lion and Albert, in The Stanley Holloway Monologues,* London, Elm Tree/EMI, 1979, p. 29

[32] Robinson, I.C. Personal letter to the author, 5 October 1998.

[33] *Ibid*

9

School Democracy Under National Tyranny: 1971-1975

The new headmaster, Daniel Kyanda, had been a student at Budo from 1947 to 1958. He had therefore experienced the whole of the Cobb era and the first year of Robinson's, when he had been an HSC student. He had admired both his headmasters and greatly enjoyed his Budo years. At Makerere he read for a BA in English, history and geography. Returning to Budo as a teacher for one term in 1964 he was then appointed to the Lubiri Secondary School where he quickly became head of geography and then deputy headmaster. In 1967, he had moved to Kenya to become travelling secretary of the Pan-African Fellowship of Evangelical Students and also one of the chaplains to the University Nairobi.

> It was a strenuous job, with a parish stretching from Khartoum to Lusaka, but I very much enjoyed it. Then came the bombshell![1]

The Budo governors invited him to apply for the headship of the school; like Ian Robinson before him, he found the challenge neither welcome nor straightforward. He spent six months thinking and praying about it, having advised the governors that he could not abandon his present responsibilities at short notice. At length he accepted the offer, subject to the agreed starting date being January 1971. He was by then encouraged to learn that his appointment had the support of the national president. Aged thirty, he remains the youngest headmaster in the school's 100 years.

He had particularly requested a period of handover before the new school year began, and found it very helpful. Robinson briefed him fully.

But he made no attempt to suggest Dos or Don'ts. I then tried to follow the best that I believed Herbert, Cobb and Robinson had created for Budo.

Though the governors realised that he did not see headmastering as a long-term career, his commitment to Budo was obvious and the appointment was popular. His wide travels and contacts throughout eastern Africa had kept him well-informed of political developments in the several newly independent countries. As a Muganda he was keenly aware of tensions in Uganda arising from events of the past four years and of Budo's particular sensitivities. But the school was in good heart and prospects for the coming year seemed promising. Before that year had even begun, however, its political context had been irrevocably changed.

President Obote had left for the Commonwealth Conference in Singapore, uneasy and reluctant but with a measure of altruism. He felt an obligation to support Presidents Nyerere of Tanzania and Kaunda of Zambia in their efforts to persuade the Commonwealth to embargo sales of arms to South Africa. Before he left he warned General Amin that he would expect, on his return, an explanation for the deficit of £ 2.5m which had been reported in the armed forces accounts. He never received his explanation.

On 25 January 1971, in a swift and bloody coup, Amin deposed Obote and seized power as leader of what quickly became a military government. At first there was widespread jubilation at the fall of Obote. Kasozi recorded that:

> The Baganda rejoiced and applauded the change not because they loved Amin but because they hated Obote. It was more a negative vote against Obote than a positive one for Amin. Violence was the only way left to change the government, and though the Baganda were not part of the army they were still a strong social force in the country.[2]

During the early weeks of the new government there were promising developments. Amin lifted the much resented state of emergency and released hundreds of political prisoners. They included prominent Baganda: Ben Kiwanuka, the former prime minister, Nalinya Ndagire, the Kabaka's sister, and Prince Badru Kakangulu, leader of the Muslim community and caretaker of the Buganda royal family. In a dramatic gesture of apparent conciliation he had the body of Kabaka Mutesa ll flown back from London for burial in the historic tombs at Kasubi. Unlike the wary Obote, he mixed freely and often with the people in public gatherings and communicated easily with them in Luganda, several Northern languages and some Kiswahili and Arabic. Moreover, there was widespread optimism that he would not want to remain for long in overall charge but would prefer to return to his army command.[3]

The new Budo year therefore began without disturbance. Kyanda's log book and the recollections of many staff reflect an effective and uneventful first term. The British government recognition of the new regime on 4 February probably implied relief at the fall of Obote rather than informed approval of Amin. But it ensured the continuance of British Aid programmes with their heavy subsidies for expatriate teachers, who still formed the majority of staff in Ugandan secondary schools and at Makerere. It was especially reassuring for Budo with only six Ugandan teachers and seventeen British. But by the end of the term a different impression of the new government had emerged.

Having promised political freedom Amin angered his small cabinet by announcing on Radio Uganda that the military government would be in power for five years, though when ministers protested he assured them that it would be only a "caretaker government".[4] He refused to restore the hereditary kingdoms so recently abolished by Obote. In view of his early concessions this incensed Baganda traditionalists but more sinister was the quiet re-introduction of detention without trial. After only six weeks of "amnesty" the prisons held several hundred detainees by the end of March.[5] Budo's first crisis under the new regime came the following month.

After a major overhaul in 1970 the school's main water pump had failed again but this time, with the national supply situation already affected by political events, there were no spare parts available in Kampala. Three weeks of attempts to make them had failed; so Kyanda convened an emergency staff meeting on April 24th to consider whether the start of the second term should be postponed. The reserve pump could supply little more than half the minimum need of 2000 gallons a day, so the reluctant decision was to readmit years 3,4,5 and 6 but postpone the arrival of S1 and 2 until a full supply could be restored. The immediate public announcement on Radio Uganda stressed that strict water rationing would be imposed. The emergency lasted several weeks and was compounded by a shortage of matooke and potatoes. During a protest in the Mess a lot of crockery was deliberately smashed, the Houses responsible being charged for its replacement. The simmering unrest was a setback after a promising start to Kyanda's headship. But it was only a symptom of what was soon to afflict the education system.

By the end of the second term the government's budget estimates revealed an appalling change of priorities. Expenditure on defence had been £ 7.3m in Obote's last year; in Amin's first it was to be £15.2m with an additional £ 8m of the national development budget also earmarked for defence. The health development budget had been cut by 60 percent to less than £ 1m and education by 40 percent to £ 2.1m - for a service publicly committed to rapid expansion. So while an already huge defence estimate had been tripled, the relatively tiny health and education provisions were to be halved.[6]

Such were the priorities of the articulate but illiterate president. Martin later quoted from a long memorandum sent by one of Amin's ministers to several African heads of state:

> His abysmal ignorance has made him hate education, educated people and educational institutions.[7]

And Mutibwa trenchantly depicted the situation created in the early years of Amin's terrible regime as follows:

> In the general "degeneration of morality" violence had become endemic and children accustomed to the sight of corpses. Life was cheap. There was a widely experienced devaluation of education and of the professions:

> Education ceased to be a passport to anything and therefore lost much of its attraction... What came to be valued was money, and it did not matter how it was made. Drop-outs from school were

catapulted into positions of influence through violence, theft or simply influential allies in government. Makerere became a laughing stock and a symbol of the misguided, of those who would never make it in life.[8]

Budo, like other long-established schools with national reputations, probably suffered less and later from these negative attitudes than many less well supported and equipped schools. It maintained most and actually expanded some of its activities throughout 1971, with a good set of examination results and a strong entry recruited for 1972. The athletics and football seasons went well, though students grumbled that roadblocks and security risks made fewer teams willing to travel out to Budo hill.

The year 1972 began well but by mid-year there was concern at staff meetings about persistent large-scale cutting of classes - a new problem for Budo - and a big increase in vernacular speaking. After much discussion staff accepted Kyanda's advice that individual students should be warned but there should be no drastic threats or action. Similarly, with the serious offence of drinking alcohol, for which the penalty was slightly reduced from "automatically expelled" to " liable to expulsion", he decided not to expel a girl who had been found drunk after receiving warnings and staff support. There was some dissent from this but most colleagues shared his sympathy with the pressures and fears under which most students now lived. He met with the *Gombolola* chief to discuss the danger to students from an illegal distillery just down the hill from the school. This was promptly closed and Kyanda expressed his appreciation by announcing that nearby villagers should not hesitate to ask for support from the school which would be given whenever possible.

Rapidly rising costs, particularly of food, forced the school to apply to the Ministry of Works for more time to pay some maintenance bills, and to the stores department for the restoration of the credit facility which had not been needed for several years. Both requests were accepted and in spite of stringencies there was a large attendance at the inaugural meeting of the French Club in July followed by strong support for its activities. The Budo Nightingales flourished, celebrating their 23rd birthday, now led by Dennis Chisholm, and in August the school was cheered by a very good production of St Joan. But hanging over a hard-pressed staff was the impending loss of six expatriate teachers including the deputy head Jonathan Watson. The ministry had promised four replacements from an expected new cadre of British secondments, but Kyanda was sceptical. It was not known in the school that he himself had been offered by USAID an internship in an American university for the next semester, but had regretfully postponed acceptance. He confided to his log-book:

> If the teachers we need do not come because of strained Anglo/ Ugandan relations, there can be no question of the headmaster going. This would be tantamount to abandoning the school at this critical juncture.

It was to prove a wise as well as unselfish response.

On 4 August 1972 Amin announced to troops at Tororo barracks that the previous night he had had a dream in which God had instructed him to expel all Asians - of whom there were more than 60,000 - from the country within ninety days. He proceeded to do it. Kyemba summarised the impact:

> Asians almost totally controlled Uganda's trade, factories, plantations and industries. They were the managers, the bureacrats, the accountants, the technicians, the doctors, the engineers, the lawyers. They formed an affluent middle class, a distinctive element in the population, with their own language, behaviour patterns, names and occupations. On the whole they were not popular with the Africans ...

> They were in other words ideal targets...

> At the time of Amin's original announcement, nobody thought that he intended to expel both Ugandan Asians and British Asians. But it soon became clear that he did not intend to make a distinction between passports. He wanted the Asians to hand over property to his troops. It was a brutal and thoroughly racist decision, and one that was to deal the Ugandan economy a terrible blow.[9]

Budo felt the full force of the effects of the expulsion, immediate and long-term. First and most dramatic was the collapse of many essential services and the rapid deterioration of the rest. Kenya at once seized Uganda's markets and levied heavy tariffs on the roads to the coast - the death blow to the reeling East African Community and all its hoped-for educational co-operation. The national climate of fear and suspicion deepened. Obote had expelled the Kenyans; Amin had ordered the slaughter of hundreds of Lwo speakers, especially Langi and Acholi members of the army. Now all Asians were to be robbed and expelled. Who might be next? The order was greeted with international outrage, promptly expressed through the closure or suspension of international aid programmes, notably - and most threatening to Budo - the recently agreed further £ 10m UK programme and the "topping up" for salaries of seconded British teachers.

Within a year the removal of the wealthiest sector of the population had also destroyed the government's urban taxation base and placed an impossible burden on an already over-taxed rural African citizenship.[10] At the same time, some 50,000 Ugandan employees lost their jobs and the European expatriate community declined from 10,000 to under 2000. The tourist industry, which in 1972 up to September had attracted 100,000 visitors, was in effect closed down.[11]

National security and morale were further violated on September 17th, when a poorly equipped force of about 1000 Ugandan exiles loyal to Obote invaded the south of the country from Tanzania. The badly planned incursion was quickly detected and repelled. But

> Obote's attack was a pure gift to Amin. His troops were anyway incensed at the invasion, which they saw as an attempt to stop them seizing Asian property. Since the guerrillas were no conceivable threat, Amin could safely exaggerate the danger and show himself to be his country's saviour. He could also, more ominously, use the invasion as a pretext to move against those members of the population whom he saw as a threat.[12]

The September Budo staff meeting was sombre but Kyanda urged everyone to carry on calmly in spite of the political tension. Rumours that the "invasion" had been accompanied by bombing at Entebbe only 25 miles away had proved false but the security situation was dire. Kyanda had arranged for all vehicles on the hill to be provided with KCB stickers for easy identification at the many roadblocks. He advised all staff and students that courtesy and careful speech would be essential at all police and army posts. One cheering event at the beginning of the new term was the return of Eliezer Bawuuba, former Budo student, Makerere graduate and Budo teacher, after three years of further study in the USA. On September 24th he preached at the Sunday chapel service on "True Security". Kyanda recorded in his logbook: "A very good sermon and very apposite indeed."

Four days later, in mid-afternoon, several gunshots were heard in the area of the bursars's office. Staff and students were quickly on the scene to find the bursar, Augustine Yawe, lying badly wounded, following an attack by three *kondos* (bandits) who had made off by car.

Two colleagues tried for some time to revive him but he died shortly before the arrival of a doctor who confirmed that he would have had no chance of surviving his wounds. Police, who had arrived promptly and were efficient and calm, said that such raids were now common; earlier that week they had themselves shot five kondos who had tried to rob a local hospital.

> It is very sad for the bursar's family who live near us. The whole staff went round, as is the Ugandan custom, to the house last night with Dan Kyanda, who expressed our sympathy and sorrow. It certainly has been a difficult first month of term for the headmaster.[13]

This was an early impression for Alan Rayden who had arrived only four weeks before, after ten years at Oundle, an English public school. He was to teach Chemistry and had immediately lost his only subject colleague with the withdrawal of all Peace Corps volunteers by the US government. His wife Eleanor was appointed on arrival to strengthen the English department. In a remarkable sequence of twice-weekly letters to their parents in England over the ensuing eighteen months they offered perceptive impressions of Budo's determined progress under increasing hardship.

The school now has 600 pupils, 120 of whom are girls. From Senior 1 to 4 class sizes are just over 30. The headmaster has insisted that the classrooms are too small for more and already there are few gangways between desks to enable teachers to look at work in progress. It is easier in the laboratories which are spacious. I have two S5 classes of 30 and one S6 of 24, whereas at Oundle my average post O level class has been 10 -15. Because I have to teach all the S5s together lessons just become lectures and since I have to do it in the school hall I can't do any demonstrating. At present there are 27 staff but many contracts are ending and it's likely there will be only three expatriates for our last six months.... 760 Asian teachers have already left and Makerere has lost 60 lecturers....

I would judge that most of the students are just as good as those I have taught in England for the same syllabus. They work very hard.... the standard of English speaking in the school is really very high.[14]

Staff and students appreciated Kyanda's commitment to maintaining high standards whatever the difficulties. He believed that the Christian witness of the school was central to its value and purpose and that it was best expressed in "work well done and in care for every member". Looking back he was convinced that as a Budo student he had been taught to distinguish between mediocrity and excellence in both the intellectual and pastoral life of the school. "At Budo every student mattered." He tried to maintain good relations with all students and to give them easy access to him - which imposed both strains and occasional novelty. A brief logbook entry in October 1972 reads:

The chairman of the School Council visited the headmaster this evening to complain about the food. His supper had been inedible. The Headmaster cooked him an omelette.

To be friendly and open and yet maintain good, reasoned discipline was a hard balancing act as the country descended into lawlessness - all the harder because Kyanda made an early decision that he could best serve the school by spending as much time as he judged necessary representing its needs and interests to Ministry of Education officers in Kampala. He did not seek preferential treatment for Budo, only responses to genuine necessities. But to other schools and even to well disposed colleagues it may have seemed like favouritism by the ministry:

He knows everyone in the right places which enables Budo to run with a smoothness denied to many other schools. We all support him.[14]

But this did not protect him from frequent, severe criticism, most of it face to face at meetings, in the open manner he encouraged. His absences in Kampala were a common cause of irritation although he usually managed to maintain his regular teaching commitments. As supplies and staffing levels worsened, ministry officials were hard-pressed and defensive; his visits frequently lasted all day and into the evening. Some of his colleagues also thought he yielded too easily to student requests for change. Yet logbook entries and staff meeting notes for October and November indicate that he could be both compliant and resolute.

He had publicly disapproved of a fashionable knotted hairstyle which some of the girls had adopted, ordering a return to "the old style". After some dissent and persuasion from female colleagues, he announced that there could be several "approved hairstyles". The following week a deputation from one of the Houses demanded the replacement of their housemaster because he used too many group punishments and "pushed boys around". They astutely suggested that this reflected the growing "culture of violence" in the country and was dangerous. Kyanda refused the request but agreed that the situation should be "monitored"; he discussed the matter privately with the housemaster. Two weeks later a deputation of 5th formers protested about the increase in schools fees. He told them

Economics is the study and practice of using scarce resources. Either fees must be raised or the school must cut expenditure. If you do not trust what I say you should appeal to the highest authority.

They did, but received no response from the ministry.

Four days later, the new edition of a student magazine *Perspective*, a few copies of which were usually circulated beyond Budo, carried an article by a boy whose father had been murdered during the Obote administration. It contained well argued criticism of Amin's economic policy. Kyanda showed both sympathy and decisiveness:

> The Headmaster explained to the editor and writer that he was well aware that many countries had advanced through revolution; he had himself given an upper school lecture in October on "The Gospel according to Karl Marx". He did not believe that evolution always worked best politically. But this article endangered the school which has to identify with national goals and aspirations and pull its weight.

After consultation with senior colleagues and the head prefect it was agreed that all copies of the magazine would be withdrawn at once. There was general approval of the headmaster's attitude and action; the discretion of staff and students evidently prevented any report of the incident from circulating outside the school. Kyanda forestalled damaging rumour at the ministry by confidentially informing the chief education officer, who supported his action. All this took many tense hours of discussion and reflection when just sustaining the physical and academic survival of the school was more than a full-time job for head and colleagues.

While the national government demonstrated its contempt for individual freedom and lives, the staff gave time and care to decisions about difficult students:

> J.C. is academically weak but tries hard. Agreed that he should be transferred to a less academically demanding school as soon as possible.

> J.T. is consistently wasting staff time. Agreed that rather than be suspended he should have a compulsory work chart.

> M.A. also continues difficult. Recommended for a work chart rather than being sent home, because he needs to be protected from his own father.....

> The Headmaster had interviewed several parents one of whom requested that his son should be publicly flogged. The headmaster politely declined.

Staff meeting had recently approved that Id should be a holiday
for Muslim students except for games and prep. It was now agreed
that, if they wished, they could leave the hill after Id.

During the same six weeks, the *Uganda Argus* had published a
government list of prominent citizens who had been declared enemies of
the state. The vice-chancellor of Makerere University, Frank Kalimuzo,
"disappeared" some days after his disappearance had been announced
on Radio Uganda, and chief justice, Ben Kiwanuka, who had refused
to bestow a spurious legality on the government's "policies" was
dragged from the High Court and murdered. The president had
given army personnel authority to arrest any suspected individuals
without warrant, provided they were handed over to the police within
24 hours. Thousands of Ugandans " detained" in this fashion were
never seen again.

The School Council, which enabled students to make suggestions
and criticisms in the presence of the head and members of staff, had
functioned well throughout 1972. In November Kyanda entertained
the whole council to supper, which he described as a "magnificent
occasion". In his speech he asked members to be patient:

> If the School Council seems to be developing slowly. This is
> because I am weighing the consequences of the decisions to be
> taken.

The student chairman - perhaps still savouring his omelette - advised
his fellow-members

> The Headmaster is a liberal man and it is up to the Council to
> make full use of him.

The following day the headmaster caned three boys who had caused
a serious disturbance at prep. But before the caning he had first asked
them whether they would prefer to be sent home.

In considering his many difficult decisions, Kyanda was certainly
not short of advice - except from the group from which he had most
right to expect it.

> The one great disappointment of my Budo years was that I hardly
> seemed to have a Governing Body.

Most of the governors were prominent Baganda, the chairman, Eridadi Mulira, having been active and courageous in the political affairs of both Uganda and the former Kingdom of Buganda for more than thirty years. The governors' inclination to keep low profiles and not parade their association with the school most integrally linked with the history and mystique of Buganda was understandable. But it was not helpful to a young, relatively inexperienced head and a continually changing staff. The governors did not meet to consider either condolence or security after the murder of the bursar. A few months later the school badly needed their support over another student demonstration about alleged increases in fees and costs.

The Higher School Certificate students, of whom there were now 130, published a memorandum to the headmaster, accusing him of raising charges and fees without explanation. The euphoria of the School Council supper seemed to have evaporated and Kyanda was now said to have behaved in a "dictatorial manner", in spite of his attempts to explain how the collapse of the national economy was affecting the school. After consulting colleagues and the head prefect, Aggrey Abate, who had refused to support the protest, Kyanda reported the situation to the ministry. The permanent secretary wrote at once in strong support of all the school's economies, condemning the student demonstrations and warning that he would not hesitate to send in troops. Next day the HSC students boycotted all classes. Police then patrolled the Hill in a show of force and the students met the headmaster's deadline to assemble in the hall. Although he spoke forcefully of a group "who wanted to create maximum disturbance and paralyse the school" he did not take disciplinary action against individual students, judging that corporate defeat and vehement ministry disapproval were enough. In his relief at surmounting the crisis without violence Kyanda confided to a colleague that the students had "gone back to their studies with their tails between their legs". Unfortunately, the comment was relayed to students and gave great offence. Kyanda promptly convened an assembly and publicly apologised, which, as another colleague wrote, "was a big thing to do".

He may have felt that he lacked a governing body but he was in no doubt that Budo still had a remarkable fount of advice on procedures, precedents and traditions. By 1973 Barbara Collins was in her twentieth year of continuous service as secretary to three successive headmasters, having been appointed by Cobb in 1954, when Kyanda had been a junior secondary pupil. Looking back, he believed that most of the counsel and support he should have had from governors actually came from the chief education officer, James Lwabi - and from Barbara Collins who had been most efficient and, with her wide knowledge of Budo personalities and traditions, saved him from many mistakes.

It was not an entirely smooth relationship. Having known many effective Budo Boards of Governors, she was indignant at their current negligence and the virtual impossibility of arranging quorate meetings. Eventually, Kyanda asked her to convene the governors to discuss yet another crisis. Long accustomed by now to having to use her own initiative, she refused, urging him to use his own judgement. In what now reads like a splendid compliment he observed that this was a good example of Budo's customary over-confidence. Finding time and energy to teach voluntary typing classes and to coach the girls athletics team, Barbara was also a perceptive preserver of useful documents, reports, photographs and letters. That it has been possible to write an accurate study of Budo has been in large measure because of her foresight and care.

National and local shortages made it hard to maintain the traditional school publications but in January 1973 a commendably optimistic edition of *The Budonian* appeared. The first page listed the full teaching staff for the previous term - four Ugandan, twenty-three British, one French and one American. It is testimony to Budo's resilience - and Kyanda's - that at the end of the following year the school continued steadily with only two expatriate staff - Colin Davis, head of Maths with 11 years service and Barbara Collins with 22 years. The examination results for 1972 had again been very good. One hundred two students had passed O levels, with a total of 104 distinctions and 530 credits. Twenty-four students in form 6 Arts had gained the Advanced Certificate of Education and 50 from 6 Science; history students did particularly well, all 18 passing, 7 with the highest "A" grade.

The house and sports reports described plenty of success and enjoyment. House rivalries remained keen and friendly, while school teams had done well: The football team had won most of its matches and drawn 2-2 with a visiting English Public Schools XI; the swimming team had won, in both 1971 and 1972, the new Uganda Hotels Swimming Championship; the Hockey Club had won 6 of its 8 matches in 1972 and the athletics team 4 of the 5 championships open to it, with Otim and Njuki representing Uganda in the East and Central African Championships in Zambia. Cricket continued to flourish, with the school XI unusually strong in spin bowling. Bunyaga, Nkonge, Katumwa and Golooba had been chosen for the Uganda Cranes touring side. The Inter-house cricket competition was in good health and had clearly startled Alan Rayden. Any Old Budonian will endorse his impressions:

> Cricket house matches here are in full swing. I must say they make English ones look awfully staid! The crowd keeps up a continual cheering and shouting of advice, comment and wisecrack about what has happened, is happening or may happen. Every run and wicket is cheered to the echo. Immense fun but a bit surprising at first. Its more like a soccer crowd!

Other noteworthy features of this 1973 edition were *The Budonian's* first article and poem in French - now well established as a school subject - and two articles and a story, all suggesting a need for Ugandan secondary schools to modify their highly academic curriculum by including training in practical subjects. Agriculture, carpentry and crafts were thought likely to improve the employment prospects of school-leavers competing in a stricken economy. The theme was taken up in the first report of the newly formed Agricultural Club under the guidance of Patrick Boston, head of biology, who already presided over the flourishing Wildlife Society. The student chairman, Henry Kakande, reported.

At present the club has forty members. It seems not to have enjoyed much popularity in the school because some narrow-minded students treat agriculture with disrespect and contempt. They still harbour the out-dated belief that manual work is for the unfortunate ones who never went to school, or only a form of punishment for the educated.

We hope that these attitudes will quickly die. They must.

Such concern about the best form of secondary education for the country was also evident in the long interview of the headmaster by the head prefect and the chairman of the School Council. Asked about curriculum development, Kyanda, aware of Grace's aspirations in the 1930s, reminded the students

> At Budo there is a strong academic and administrative background. Emphasis on practical subjects, as in the whole of Uganda, will not mean for us a sudden beginning from scratch. Since we have had experience in teaching Agriculture, Carpentry and Pottery we shall merely be picking up where we left off.

The contributors to *The Budonian* could not know that while they were debating the dangers of academic secondary schools producing unemployable school leavers, A.B.K. Kasozi was researching the issues with care and some anxiety. His study suggested that as early as 1945 the aim of most Ugandan parents in educating their children had been economic and that by the 1970s it was probably even more so. In 1960 Uganda had 29 aided senior secondary schools with a total of 6,457 students - an average enrolment of 222. By 1970 there were 73 schools with 40,662 students - including 9,707 girls - and an average enrolment of 557.

Government statistical abstracts showed that over the ten-year period, although the annual increase in the gross national product had been only 5 percent, the annual growth rate of schools and of education expenditure had been 20 percent. The number of Ugandans in employment in 1960 had been 244000; by 1970 this had grown to only 312,000. So an increase in student numbers of 600 percent had been accompanied by an increase in jobs of only 25 percent. In the early 1970s it remained the case that, in a predominantly agricultural economy, the school system

> prepared students for employment in the top sector of society, a sector that is not directly involved in agricultural production. This sector ....is tiny and thus can absorb only a few people. Yet all students are schooled to join this sector.[15]

Kasozi's study was subsequently published under the title *The Crisis of Secondary Education in Uganda 1960 - 1970* and many experienced observers predicted a severe loss of parental and student confidence in the value of education. Remarkably, this did not occur even in the wretched economic and social conditions created by Amin's tyranny; there seems to be little evidence of it more than thirty years later.

The first staff meeting of 1973, with Dennis Chisholm now second master, welcomed the news that a strong first year intake had been selected, but considered a number of disciplinary problems. Kyanda reported several letters of apology from parents and unruly girls who had been disciplined. Drinking, smoking and aggressive behaviour were continual concerns in the boys' houses and increasingly among the "girls" - who were actually young women aged from 14 to 20. Kyanda insisted that offences would not be tolerated but there must be hard evidence before accusations or punishments. The prefects' meeting had asked him why there were relatively few girls in the new S1 entry and he had assured them that it was solely because they had not done well enough in the examinations. He hoped that numbers would grow steadily from the following year. They did.

A three-day ministry inspection of the school resulted in a very positive report and at the next assembly Kyanda thanked everyone for their efforts. But Budo self-esteem was deflated. The following week there was an ugly fracas at "the girls' end" with stones thrown at students and at recently arrived house-warden, Wendy Moore. Kyanda showed his anger at an immediate assembly, protesting that this was a criminal offence and new to Budo (but see October 1959).

> If you feel like throwing stones your target should be the Headmaster - not staff or students.

The school was sobered a few days later. John Inson, who had come out as a volunteer teacher the previous year and had been seriously ill for some weeks, was flown back to England where he died a few days later. At a memorial service in the chapel on 4 March Dennis Chisholm gave a warm appreciation.

"Cleanliness" had been proclaimed as the theme for the term and at a March assembly Kyanda complimented the school on improved smartness and on their patience over food shortages. The School Council had agreed to try to advise the head on how to reduce a budget shortfall of 58,000 shillings. Staff supported by emphasising to their houses and classes that the financial prospect was grim. Founders Day was observed as usual on March 29th. Kyanda suggested

> This should be a day for thanksgiving and stocktaking. All members of the school should consider themselves present Founders of Budo.

April 1st had traditionally provided light relief on the Hill, with occasional damaging excesses. The logbook records:

> The Headmaster dressed up as a night watchman and managed to foil three raids - on his car, the Big School piano, and the Communion table!

He felt less festive the following day after visiting first the ministry, to protest that the promised staff replacements had not yet appeared, and then Makerere, to ask for help. Both returned stony responses. The logbook entry was terse:

> The Headmaster was very angry - and showed it.

His anxiety was not just about the impending exodus of expatriate colleagues and the virtual certainty that the donor nations would send no more. He knew that all schools were suffering similar staffing crises. Gayaza was, for example, losing 15 staff and had been promised only 2 replacements. For Ugandan graduates and school leavers teaching was no longer an enticing career. Teaching salaries were low and had not been increased since 1962. As Mutibwa had noted, education had suffered a sharp loss of prestige, and in terms of essential supplies, many schools were now beleaguered. Moreover they were now competing for a shrinking work-force. Kyemba put the issue starkly:

> Throughout 1973 and thereafter, the country's economic plight was accentuated by a massive brain drain. We had already lost the doctors, lawyers, accountants and other professionals of Asian origin. Now thousands of Ugandan professional men and women, on whose training the government had spent millions of shillings, fled.... ministers, ambassadors, permanent secretaries, fled into exile. Two Vice- Chancellors of Makerere University fled. Professors, heads of department and lecturers fled by the score... Consultants and doctors fled. Nurses, mid-wives, teachers and professionals of all kinds vanished in uncounted thousands.
>
> ... From 1974 onward, signs of economic chaos multiplied.[16]

Within three years of the expulsion of the Asians it was probably true that more of Uganda's professional talent lived out of the country than in it. But many stayed to give loyal service to the professions, including teaching. Eliezer Bawuuba's second period at Budo lasted only a year - far less than the school would have wished - because the ministry wisely invited him to accept the headship of Kampala High School (formerly and now again the Aga Khan HS), one of Uganda's best secondary schools and, until the expulsions, notably multi-racial. But Stephen Kamuhanda joined the Budo staff in 1972, succeeding Dennis Chisholm as second master within a year. In 1973 John Mpagi arrived to take over geography and Robina Mirembe, appointed to teach biology was soon head of the department and in charge of Sabaganzi House. She was to give outstanding service as deputy head and Budo's longest-serving woman teacher over the next thirty years.

In spite of this accession of talent the school was five teachers below strength by mid-year, though Kyanda's show of anger seemed to have induced the ministry to promise three more. Physics, biology and English were in greatest need, even though the number of English periods had been reduced in 1972 because of the high standard being maintained. Colin Davis was now timetabling up to 8 non-teaching periods a week for S1 classes, in which they were expected to continue with supervised projects.

Further strains were imposed by food shortages and huge price increases for equipment - the cost of cups and plates had risen from 4s to 8s, glass bowls from 8s to 23s and brooms from 4s to 12s - all out of a reduced budget. Kyanda decided to increase assemblies from once a fortnight to three times a week, to keep students as well-informed as possible. At a mid-year meeting he congratulated the caterer Mr Kyanku on having managed to find some sugar and salt - he knew that most students would have had neither throughout the vacation. He also reported that beds were now hard to find and very expensive. He reminded students that

> We all thought Africans would not charge exorbitant prices when the Asians went. But it is now clear that Africans can be as exorbitant as Asians if not more so! We are now having to use double bunks. Please do not complain or try to dismantle them. Many in Uganda would gladly sleep on the floor to get the kind of education that Budo offers.

He added in the logbook that the laughter in Big School showed that students knew his comments were absolutely true!

After long-running discussions at staff meetings it had been agreed that mid-week chapel attendance should become voluntary and Kyanda was heartened by the initial responses, with about a third of the school attending and singing well. He explained his support for the move, suggesting

> Compulsory Christianity can easily become soft and flabby. What we need here is a tough muscular Christianity, willing to make a stand.

The year 1973 was proving a bad year for discipline, with more drinking and violence and threats to staff in the girls houses reported. Kyanda again spoke forcefully, demanding full attendance and a prompter start for evening prep, and strict observance of "lights out":

> "Masters on Duty" are to be obeyed at all times. Staff are overworked and no nonsense is expected.

He was himself badly overworked. He was trying, with a teaching timetable of 20 lessons a week, to maintain standards and morale, lobby for staff and supplies, and keep relationships with the ministry "open and supportive". He was mortified when a senior education officer advised him to find an excuse to go abroad and then to recruit staff privately - the ministry would pay. In July, after a chaotic end of term, he was taken ill and was absent for several weeks. Stephen Kamuhanda, as acting head, led two long, well-minuted staff meetings in the August vacation, to review discipline and recommend strong action, including a "staggered" start to the third term. Kyanda accepted this advice and made some stern announcements to the first assembly in September.

One girl was expelled for drunkenness, one boy for stealing and another suspended for smoking. Because of unruly behaviour on outside visits, the school band was "gated" for the whole term and all outside drama commitments cancelled. A tighter system of serving was introduced in the Mess, with the girls at separate tables "because the boys are mistreating them". Kyanda met with the head prefect and deputy who were concerned at the loss of staff.

> They said that the old staff had been custodians of Budo discipline and traditions and were being replaced by young staff who just did not know them. As expatriate staff leave, the headmaster seemed to them isolated, as if only he cared. They believed Budo needed three more Stephen Kamuhandas but that with co-operation things could be put right.

> They also thought it would now be right to make Sunday chapel voluntary. I agreed.

As long-serving British staff left, the national sense of isolation from the outside world - which seemed not to care about Uganda's plight - was keenly felt at Budo. The Western media tended to treat Amin as a cruel but jovial clown. An honourable exception however was British journalist David Martin, whose book, *General Amin*, brought some encouragement. It was the first documented exposure of the evil regime and fiercely critical of the failure of Uganda's former allies to denounce it. Of Britain and Israel he wrote:

> Throughout the remainder of 1971 both countries had considerable influence in Uganda, yet they turned a totally blind eye to the

killing of hundreds of Ugandans when some pressure might have checked the slaughter. The interests of Britain and Israel it seems were limited to their own economic interests and to their own nationals.[17]

He was concerned, as were many Budonians, for the integrity of Uganda and all other independent African states:

Amin's blatant racialism and anti-Semitism deeply affected African credibility. The most important cornerstone of the OAU is the commitment to the liberation of Southern Africa from white minority domination, apartheid and racialism. Africa continuously vocalises about white oppresssion south of the Zambezi, but in the case of Uganda, and the ethnic slaughter in Burundi, African leaders and the OAU with few exceptions have remained silent.[18]

He noted that only Nyerere of Tanzania and Kaunda of Zambia had condemned the expulsion of the Ugandan Asians. (Shortly after his book was published Martin himself was expelled, at 24 hours notice, from Tanzania where he had been a widely admired reporter for ten years.) For Budonians and many other Ugandans his brave book brought encouragement - but no help.

By mid-October Kyanda was again ill, this time in hospital. Several students were suspended for the rest of the term. A senior boy and younger girl had been discovered in a sexual relationship; the boy was expelled, with arrangements made for him to sit his ASC examinations, while the girl's parents were advised to find another school for her because she had" failed to comply with the demands of a co-ed boarding school". Equivalent penalties for boys and girls were a hotly argued concern at staff meetings. *The Voice of Uganda* had been critical of Budo discipline, but had also reported that several secondary schools had already been closed indefinitely because they could no longer maintain order. Severe staff shortages were acknowledged and the ministry announced that it had been given priority - when the Makerere degree results were published - to draft suitable graduates into the teaching service "to close the gap". The ministry had also approved a Budo initiative to limit its 1974 entry to 114 because of staff vacancies. Other teaching strategies included the "setting" of maths and science for S3s and agreement that French, though well established, should become a voluntary subject from S2.

The December staff meeting welcomed Kyanda back from hospital but at the end of an exhausting year it struck some lugubrious notes. The school was being required to host 850 gymnasts throughout the long vacation, while they trained for their performance in celebration of Republic Day early in 1974. It seemed certain that the burden of administration would fall on the school staff - especially Barbara Collins. The school year would therefore not begin until February 7th. Further economies for the coming year were that special diets for students must be abandoned because supplies were so unreliable and that, unless ministry grants increased, there could be no issues of soap or toilet rolls. It was not an inviting prospect.

A month later, to general astonishment, Kyanda returned from another of his Kampala meetings to announce to staff that ministry capitation grants were to be hugely increased - for O level students from 472 shillings to 1450, and for A level students from 840 to 1500. He regarded this as the best news for schools for several years and wrote to congratulate the ministry on winning its battle for better funding. School fees were to remain unchanged at 650 shillings but governing bodies were given discretion on whether to maintain uniform, which would now have to be charged to parents.

At the first assembly of 1974 Kyanda therefore had good news to announce. He rejoiced that in spite of national tensions the school had still been able to recruit from all over Uganda. He stressed the importance of carrying on the "Budo way of tolerance, openness and non-violence" and while acknowledging that the visiting gymnasts had done a lot of damage to school furniture and equipment during the vacation, was confident that students would "continue to have a conscience about school property". The staff was not yet at full strength but four teachers were promised shortly from the ministry and Makerere had offered five graduates for a term's teaching practice.

The year began well and in March the examination results were gratifying - the best in the country. At O level 39 out of the 98 candidates had gained first class aggregates and every candidate had passed in English. At A level out of 99 candidates 44 had gained 3 or 4 principal passes and 29 at least 2; 73 students had therefore qualified to enter Makerere. At both levels the results in maths were so good that the staff were modestly incredulous.

Discipline was better but still not good enough. There was evidence of a drug problem, and alcohol remained a continual temptation. Helen Macdonald, the girls' warden, had written to the head in defence of a girl who had several times been caught drinking over five years. She believed that if Budo could not help the girl through the problem then it would be the school that had failed. Kyanda was sympathetic but firm:

> After a long and distinguished career in alcohol we have told her to go. I hope that she gets a place in another institution of learning, but not in a school.

He also published a dismaying statement about the effects of alcohol on Budo, strongly recommending Alcoholics Anonymous, of which there were now several branches in Uganda.

Staff reports and logbook entries record that the second term also began well, though "lights out" was still poorly observed, and dances had continued beyond agreed closure times. After the restrictions of late 1973, most social events, on and off the hill, had gone well. Gayaza's announcement that its future mixed social events would be held only in the afternoons, reflected the continuing risks with evening attempts. Food supplies remained sporadic; the school lorry had often to scour the Kampala area even for maize for posho - matooke being now quite beyond the Budo budget. The main water pump had again failed and parts had to be made because spares were no longer imported. The games programme had tailed off with the departure of many enthusiastic teachers, but there was still a full programme of Upper School lectures. In May the Minister of Education toured the school and addressed an assembly, wary of Budonians' capacity to think for themselves. Rayden's verdict was

Thoroughly depressing. The basic demand was for unthinking obedience and adjustment to whatever might occur. And remember that posho is as nutritious as matooke!

In July Kyanda's health again failed and he flew to Switzerland for rest and treatment. Some staff complained that he had "gone on holiday" before the end of term. At the final staff meeting Kamuhanda congratulated colleagues on their revival of the athletics programme, the school's victory in the Buganda championships, a fine concert by the Nightingales and the well chosen additions to the library, bought by heads of department with the increased funding. But report signing - still an important process - had been sketchily done and some staff were rebuked for regular lateness and for cutting classes. The national context steadily worsened. Inflation and price rises were relentless and taxes severely increased, though many could not pay them. The Raydens wrote home:

> We feel as if we are watching the classic capitalist society exploiting the masses. The price of a small loaf is now 3s 50 - up a shilling in two weeks. It's said to be due to world commodity prices but no one believes anything in the papers or on radio any more... The Kenya papers are now banned. One simply looks for disintegration. The sad thing is the helplessness of the educated sensible people. As they say, what can you do against guns?

Kyanda was back for the opening assembly of the third term and warned the school not to expect "slices" in the mess - the price of a loaf was now 4s. Other serious shortages were art materials, spares for the Mess cookers, candles and electricity - power cuts now being frequent. Uniform rules had to be relaxed because the khaki drill for shorts was often unobtainable; so was soap to wash it. Kyanda made a short trip to Nairobi to negotiate foreign currency exchange for the school and took the opportunity to visit Alliance High School "to see how we compare with that great institution". He noted that they had a far better staff/student ratio but that uniform was poorly observed. In Uganda most parents now had real difficulty raising the school fees; teachers were sympathetic but even at Budo some students were excluded from classes till fees were produced.

The term proceeded peacefully until late October when some loutish behaviour at a seniors' dance caused the cancellation of any further invitations to girls schools, Namagunga having already refused one. A housemasters' meeting also decided that the reduced house funds could no longer be used for end-of-year parties. At the final staff meeting Kyanda thanked colleagues for their fine efforts throughout a good year and a calm end of term, and congratulated Stephen Kamuhanda on the confirmation of his appointment as deputy head. The logbook records an unusual compliment, from a battle-hardened headmaster, on a pleasant end of term dance:

I have never smelt so little alcohol in my life at Budo!

January 1975 brought a curious mix of surprises. Budo boys were required to return by the 13th to train for the Republic Day celebrations; two new maths teachers arrived from Pakistan; students were driven to Mulago in groups of 50 for inoculation against cholera, about which there were warnings; Stephen Kamuhanda was seconded to Makerere for a full-time Master of Education programme. But most of the reports to the first staff meeting of the year were depressing.

The food situation was the worst yet with very poor supplies of vegetables and meat and even worse of sugar and salt. Sales of food to staff had to be suspended - after sixty years. With only half of the Mess ovens in working order, a badly fed term lay ahead, and though the students were kept informed there was much unrest and complaint. Posho was now the main meal at least three times a week - especially distastful to Baganda students. General school health remained fairly good, but Kyanda, having recovered from an attack of malaria in the vacation, was again unwell and made several visits to Mulago. He was pleased with staff efforts to improve the games programme and with a successful Parents Day, but not with the permanent secretary's sudden demand for a five-year retrospective report and a five-year programme forecast from every school. One of his last logbook entries harks back to Cobb's tart comment of 1948: "Petty discipline is sloppy and the pace is a jogtrot."

> Although the Ministry has co-operated in every way to secure us the staff we need, the school sometimes looks like a holiday camp - with some students hanging around doing nothing.

After four and a half years of tenacious effort to maintain standards in the face of appalling national conditions, Kyanda felt that he had met his 1970 commitment to the governors and gave notice that he wished to resign with effect from the end of the following term, in August. He was "exhausted, sleepless and drained". Continual criticism, much of it from outside Budo, had undermined his efforts. Like Canon Grace in the 1930s, he had realised that "Many Baganda know what they don't want but not what they do want".

He had given energy, patience, teaching skill and much sound judgement to a task which he had not sought and under pressures which, when he accepted the post, neither he nor the governors could have imagined. He had set out to sustain an involved and democratic community at Budo and had largely succeeded. Like all leaders he was not always right; unlike many he was nearly always reasonable and willing to change his mind in the light of new evidence. In a meticulous handover report to the ministry and to his successor he urged the appointment of stronger governors.

> It will be necessary for the Board to meet more regularly. My first three and a half years saw only four meetings.... I therefore took the responsibility for the school... the scars left are still with us... If the board is not active then the headmaster will be isolated as I was...

But looking back, twenty-seven years on, he still spoke generously of his colleagues:

> Throughout my time I had a most able, kind and considerate staff. The expatriates gave me fine support from the time of my appointment.

He also paid warm tribute to the loyalty and shrewd advice of his wife, Victoria - all the more praiseworthy because she had not wished to go to Budo. (Their son Kezi and daughter Rebecca remain the only children born at Budo to a serving headmaster and wife.) Kyanda had deserved such support; he had made a crucial contribution to keeping the school open and true to its ideals.

The governors needed to move fast to find a successor. They did not. Their first choice would have been distinguished Old Budonian Erisa Kironde, former Budo teacher, Makerere lecturer, and chairman of the Uganda Electricity Board. He was now working in Nairobi and, wisely, was unwilling to risk returning to Uganda under Amin. The governors then asked for Eliezer Bawuuba who had been less than two years at Kampala High School, from which the ministry was not prepared to release him. Since the governors had failed to appoint the ministry felt obliged to act. It did so, with a speed and decisiveness that astonished Budonians - and their new headmaster.

Notes

[1] From my verbatim notes on a two hour conversation with Dan Kyanda in March 2002. All the direct quotations of his views come either from this conversation or from his Budo logbook.

[2] Kasozi A.B.K., *The Social Origins of Violence in Uganda 1964-1985*, Canada, McGill-Queen's University Press, 1994, and Uganda, Fountain Publishers 1999. My quotations throughout are from the Fountain edition.

[3] Mutibwa, Phares, *Uganda since Independence: A Story of Unfulfilled Hope*, Kampala, Fountain Publishers, 1992, p.81

[4] Kyemba, Henry, *State of Blood*, New York, Ace Books 1977, p. 42

[5] Martin, David, *General Amin*, London. Faber and Faber, 1974, pp. 56-57

[6] Martin, *op. cit.* p.233

[7] *Ibid*, p.224

[8] Mutibwa, *op. cit.* p.122

[9] Kyemba, *op. cit.* p.56

[10] Kasozi, *op. cit.* p.119

[11] Martin, *op. cit.* p. 235

[12] Kyemba, *op. cit.* p. 58

[13] Rayden. A. and E. to Mr and Mrs R.G. Rayden, 30 September 1972. As soon as it became apparent that some outgoing mail was being

opened, the Rayden's ensured the delivery of the correspondence -
and protected Budo - by using an ingenious code, the key to which
was delivered personally by a friend who was flying to London.
All names were disguised. Amin became "Aunt Agatha" - see P.G.
Wodehouse!

[14] Rayden, *op. cit.* 21 October 1972

[15] Kasozi, A.B.K. *The Crisis of Secondary Education in Uganda 1960-
1970*, Kampala, Longman, 1979, p.104.

[16] Kyemba, *op. cit.* pp. 98-99.

[17] Martin, *op. cit.* p.232

[18] *Ibid*

Official opening of King's College Budo on March 29th 1906 by Deputy Commissioner Mr George Wilson (centre), with the young Kabaka Daudi Chwa (second right front row), Apolo Kaggwa (behind the Kabaka), Nuhu Mbogo (behind, left of Wilson) and Bishop Tucker (extreme right).

Rev. H.W. Weatherhead, 1906-1912

Rev. H.T.C. Weatherhead, 1912-1926

Canon H. M. Grace, 1926-1934

Canon L.J. Gaster, 1934-1939

D.G. Herbert, 1939-1947

T. H. Cobb, 1948-1957

I.C. Robinson, 1958-1970

Daniel Kyanda, 1971-1975

I.J.K. Uryirwoth, 1975-1979

E. K. Bawuuba, 1980-1988

Sam Busulwa, 1988-2000

G. W. Semivule, 2000-present

Staff of King's College Budo in 1967. Front row, fourth right is headmaster Ian Robinson.

Staff of King's College Budo in 1972. Front row, third right seated is headmaster Daniel Kyanda.

*Staff of King's College Budo of 1984 with headmaster Eliezer Bawuba,
front row third left*

*Staff of King's College Budo after a workshop in 2005. Centre is headmaster
G.W. Semivule*

Prefects of King's College Budo in 1925.

Prefects of King's College Budo in 1967 with headmaster Ian Robinson, front row centre; second left is head prefect James Bahinguza.

Prefects of King's College Budo in 1971 with headmaster Daniel Kyanda, front row centre; head prefect Geoffrey Mukwaya, second left seated. G.W. Semivule, the current headmaster, is standing, third left.

Prefects Council of 2003 with headmaster G.W. Semivule, front row centre.

Archbishop of Canterbury Dr Geoffrey Fisher (front, second right) with his wife, visits Budo in 1961. Far right is headmaster Ian Robinson.

President Apolo Milton Obote being welcomed by the headmaster, Ian Robinson, during his visit to Budo in 1969.

Lord Hemingford, formerly Dennis Herbert (headmaster 1939-47), visits Budo in 1971. To his left seated is the headmaster Daniel Kyanda.

The visit of his Royal Highness the Kabaka of Buganda Ronald Muwenda Mutebi II in 1996 on Founders' Day. To his left is Prince Barigye of Ankole and his wife.

The first lady of Uganda, Mrs Janet Museveni (left) with Madame Mitterand, the wife to Francois Mitterand, the French president then, visit Budo on March 20th 1991. Behind Mitterrand is headmaster Sam Busulwa.

H.E. Godfrey Lukongwa Binaisa, former President of Uganda (centre), receives an Order of Merit from Dr Khiddu Makubuya Minister-of Education at the time on Founders' Day of 2002. Looking on is Mr Ntwatwa Kyagulanyi, Chairman Board of Governors.

HRH Nabagereka Sylvia Nagginda (holding plaque) presents Order of Merit to Prof. F. Mirembe on Founders' Day of 2002. Looking on are Dr Kayondo, "Mobiliser" Old Budonians Club and H.E. Godfrey Binaisa, former President of Uganda.

Some distinguished Budonians on Founders' Day in 2003: Front row: Chrispus Kiyonga, Justice B. Odoki, Mayanja Nkangi, Wako Wambuzi, and the late Abu Mayanja. Back row: Behind, seen between Kiyonga and Odoki is Martin Aliker.

Budo students from western Uganda in 1946.

S4 Top Class 'Trojans' in 1958, including Prof. Apolo Nsibambi (second row, fourth left).

School Chior, the Nighingales in 1967.

School football team of 1969.

Girls' cricket team playing against Gayaza at Budo Oval, 2005.

Budo rugby team, 2005.

Inside the School Chapel.

March 2002, Hope Mukasa (first left), Andrew Kasirye (seated), Alan Shonubi (right), hand over music equipment from the OBC to the school music teacher, Mr Katuramu.

The Old School.

The Main Hall.

10 🦁

Keeping the Budo Train on the Rails: 1975-1979

During the final term of Kyanda's headship an international incident developed in Uganda which enhanced Amin's prestige among his supporters, drew amused respect from some ill-informed, influential observers overseas, vindicated Kyanda's caution over the 1972 *Perspective* article and made the national situation even more menacing for the next head of Budo.

Denis Hills, who had been a lecturer in English at the National Teachers College since 1964, had also been occasional correspondent on Ugandan affairs for *The Times* of London. His engaging and frank account of Ugandan experiences, *Man with a Lobelia Flute*, had been published in 1969 and well received both in Africa and abroad. By 1975 he was known to be working on a second book. On April 1st at 2am he was roused in his flat in Kampala by security officers with police escorts, who demanded to see the manuscript. After they had glanced at some pages he was accused of "not co-operating", spent the night in a police cell and was transferred to the maximum security block of Luzira prison, where 94 condemned prisoners were awaiting execution. After two weeks he was allowed a visit from his wife and the British Consul; two weeks later he was formally charged with sedition for describing Amin as "a village tyrant" and was refused bail. The charge was swiftly upgraded to one of treason, which carried the death penalty. He was then transferred to the infamous Malire military prison at Bombo, was tried on June 11th by a military tribunal which questioned him on the meaning of the phrase "the black Nero" - which he had quoted from *Punch* - and found him guilty. He was immediately sentenced to be shot by firing squad, which was on many counts contrary to international law, not least because he was not a Ugandan citizen.

Ten days later Amin arrived at the prison by helicopter, accompanied by British Lieutenant General Blair bearing a letter signed by the queen. He quietly informed Hills that the situation was "most extraordinary" and that Kampala was full of international pressmen. The president then told him sternly that he had seen his book, which was " a bad book and not good for Uganda's relations with Britain."He added that the execution was fixed for the following morning but would now be reconsidered "because the Queen is my friend." Hills remained in a closely guarded cell for 19 more days until on July 11th he was driven to Amin's Command Post where he was astonished to be greeted by the British Foreign Secretary, James Callaghan, and flown back to Britain, to freedom and a hero's welcome. *The White Pumpkin* was published at the end of the year, to wide acclaim.[1]

The incident is recorded here in detail because it exposed worldwide Amin's contempt for all human rights, particularly freedom of speech and writing and therefore all liberal education. But to his supporters the hero of the day was their president, who had induced the personal intercession of the queen and the attendance of the foreign secretary (shortly to become British prime minister). His authority in Uganda seemed further entrenched and the prospect of outside intervention even more remote. Rajat Neogy, editor of the respected African journal *Transition*, had in 1971 welcomed the coup and "the joyousness of the people." Four years on he conceded the reality:

> The result of Amin is anarchy and a reign of terror the likes of which Uganda has never experienced in her history ... Amin has changed one of the most outgoing and liberal regimes in Africa into a closed society.[2]

So it was an unpropitious time for any newcomer to take over the leadership of Budo - even a very enthusiastic applicant. Yet Ishmael Joash Uyirwoth, looking back 26 years, told the story of his extraordinary appointment to the post with much humour and no trace of rancour.[3] He had been appointed the Ministry of Education inspector in charge of Geography in 1973, having previously been deputy head at Lango College and before that acting deputy head at Comboni College, Lira. By late 1974 he had been aware that some parents were concerned about alleged falling standards at Budo, but his inspectorial experiences had taught him how difficult it now was to maintain standards in any secondary school, however prestigious. Early in August 1975 the chief inspector, Y. Y. Okot (who was to be executed by Amin's thugs two years later), had expressed concern about Budo and particularly the demonstrations over the serving of posho. Uyirwoth had been about to leave for Nairobi to attend a geographical conference when he was summoned by the chief inspector, who told him that the Budo governors had failed to appoint a head teacher and that the ministry wished him to accept the post. He was astonished, but quick-witted.

> I told him that there were three good reasons why I should not go to Budo: First I was not an Old Budonian. Second, I was a West Niler, not a Muganda, and third I was very happy in my present post. After a brief discussion the C.I. said I should go off to my conference and the matter would be considered further. I left his office fairly confident that I had headed off the crisis. But when I got back from Nairobi I was again called to the C.I.'s office. Going up the stairs I met Dan Kyanda coming down.

> He was smiling and offered his congratulations. "On what?" I asked. "You're the next headmaster of Budo," he replied. When I went into the office I found the C.I. accompanied by Permanent Secretary Masagazi who told me they were aware of my reservations, but Budo needed a headmaster and they were sending me. My first assignment was to report back to the Minister and the Inspectorate on the state of the school.

The new term began four days later. Dan Kyanda introduced Uyirwoth to the morning staff meeting, which began with only 10 teachers present out of 26, though numbers slowly swelled to 16. Few of the staff had met him before; several who had just returned to the Hill, had not understood why he was there. He briefly explained the circumstances of his absurdly recent appointment. Discussion then ranged widely over the usual topics for a new term and Uyirwoth took a full part, summing up several issues adroitly. At the end of the meeting, he complimented his new colleagues on their ability to discuss the progress of individual students so fully; in his experience many school staffs could no longer do this because they did not know their students well enough.[4] In the evening, a school assembly was well attended by students and a few governors, but only 10 staff. Chairman Eridadi Mulira introduced the new headmaster to the school. There were several interpolations from students - as had now become common at assemblies - but the chairman afterwards said he thought the student reaction "quite positive". The day's experiences had given Uyirwoth plenty of impressions for his report to the ministry.

The following Sunday morning saw a minor crisis just before the chapel service. A bishop who was believed to have been invited to preach had not arrived and there was some doubt whether the invitation had in fact been sent. Seeing an early opportunity to be involved in the Christian life of the school Uyirwoth offered to give the address himself. There was a startled silence from the staff and student group leading the service before his offer was accepted. It transpired, to his amazement and amusement, that they had assumed - perhaps because they thought he was Amin's appointee, or because his name was Ishmael - that he was a Muslim. His address, on the lesson from Nehemiah with which he was confronted, was well received by students, staff and governors.

Late the following Saturday night the headmaster, investigating unreasonable noise, found a group of waragi drinkers just outside the school boundary, boys and girls "in dark corners" and a rowdy party still in progress in Sabaganzi House. He closed down the party and went up to Big School, where an angry scuffle became a fight and he himself was struck by Nathaniel Mulira, son of the Chairman. Uyirwoth believed the blow had not been intended for him but it had been witnessed by a lot of students. After things calmed down, members of the School Council met, long after "lights out", not to consider an apology to the headmaster but to complain about the closure of the party. Uyirwoth felt obliged to report the incidents to the Ministry and the governors, before rumours could exaggerate them. The response was dramatic.

On the following Tuesday morning the permanent secretary, chief inspector, chief education officer Oguli, and provincial education officers drove to the school where Uyirwoth had been requested to convene a staff meeting. The atmosphere was tense but discussion ranged widely over conditions in the school and in the teaching service and about appropriate disciplinary action. The officials were clearly outraged and wanted examples made; Mulira was obviously in danger of expulsion.

> The quote of the meeting came from the Permanent Secretary: "There is no doubt that Budo is going to the dogs!"

At one o'clock the school was ordered to an assembly in the chapel. Uyirwoth began it by announcing a range of measures to improve discipline: "Lights Out" would immediately be brought forward from midnight to 11pm. House parties were forbidden. The rule that dormitories were out of bounds during class time would be enforced. Hooliganism would be severely punished, uniform rules enforced, and only staff patrons of societies allowed to book school transport. Electrical fittings were not to be tampered with, nor school furniture moved without staff permission. The card game *matatu* was forbidden. A Saturday cleanliness competition was announced, and elections for prefects were to be held at the end of the month.

The chief education officer then addressed the students "as if they were still in primary school" and the permanent secretary summed up much that had been said. He then administered a public beating to Nathaniel Mulira and the assembly was closed. The fact that such a punishment had been given in the chapel was widely felt to have been the worst of the day's many humiliations for Budo.

There was, however, a heartening response for Uyirwoth, when Eridadi Mulira immediately expressed his gratitude that the headmaster had not insisted on the expulsion of Nathaniel, which many students and staff had expected. Nathaniel also took the trouble to write to Colin Davis who had suggested at the staff meeting that the punishment should not be too severe. Budo courtesy was not dead.

> I have thought it right to write this letter thanking you for all you did for me on the incident which nearly cost me the whole of my future. I wasn't told directly by my father that you made a considerable effort to defend me. It was just fortunate that I

overheard my father telling an uncle of mine ... I hereby say again that I appreciate very much all you did for me.

Over sixteen days from mid-September Uyirwoth had convened five long staff meetings, three of which went on beyond midnight. They could have left staff in little doubt that he valued their experience and opinions and knew that he had much to learn about Budo. But he had already learnt enough to report to the ministry.

> I told them that the most immediate problem was the huge turnover of staff. Nineteen out of the 26 current teachers had been at Budo less than six months and most of them had received no teacher training. Staff discipline was bad, so student discipline was bad too. There was very little money. I appealed for better staff and felt that the Ministry gave me good support. During my first month at Budo the money available to feed the students was quite inadequate. The Ministry then gave us an additional 9000 shillings, with which Kyanku was able to buy more posho. Of course the students disliked this so I told the whole school that the old days of Budo were past. Posho now had to be part of the school diet, as rice was very hard to find and matooke was too expensive.

Some readers may feel that food is blamed too often in this account of the ups and downs of a famous school. But those who have led a residential school, college or university, in any country, may be ruefully aware that poor food can be a dangerous flashpoint.[5]

Uyirwoth was quick to attend to the problems of staff absenteeism and inefficiency. Early in October he issued a stiff circular to all staff insisting that unauthorised staff absence from timetabled lessons would not be tolerated. There was some improvement in staff attendance, but the third term was always disrupted for several weeks by national examinations and then by staff having to attend examiners' meetings in Kampala. It was also discovered that, with the national shortage of experienced teachers now an epidemic, even Budo was not immune from the growing practice of taking time off, without permission, to teach at Makerere and elsewhere for additional pay. Restoring order and efficiency to the timetable would be a slow process. Uyirwoth later recalled that it took two years to make a significant improvement in the quality of staff, in spite of ministry support.

Another long staff meeting, continuing after midnight, gave careful attention to the choice of prefects to take office immediately. Few of the current staff were aware of the tradition, from Robinson's time and the start of HSC classes, that prefects were in office for the whole of a calendar year and maintained their responsibilities throughout the examination period. There was some unease that the number of additional prefects with limited responsibilities, for example sports, the library and the Mess, might lead to a proliferation of appointments and differing levels of prefectorial authority. Robinson's staff had pruned prefect posts drastically in 1960, for example, but Budo student numbers had more than doubled by 1975. The range and number of appointments that Uyirwoth approved was probably about right for the task ahead.

The wisdom of appointing a mess prefect was soon apparent but he needed plenty of support from house prefects and the master/mistress on duty. One master reflected at the end of his duty week:

> ...the standard at house inspection has been raised by having the competition... Lights out was not so bad, so the HM's efforts have had some effect. The start of prep however was the worst ever... The other awful situation is the Mess. The standard of behaviour at a normal meal and the standard of service is hopeless. Insufficent cutlery, very few cups, water not provided on tables...food slopped on the tables, banging of cutlery before the meal begins, arguments at the mess hatch or in the kitchen, "celebration" of a football victory ill-mannered in its noise, with even the window shutters being made to bang [6]

A staff meeting in September had agreed that internal school examinations should start on November 17th, but Uyirwoth now decided that they should be brought forward to the 10th so that the term could end early. He believed it was wasteful to feed the school when there was so little teaching going on.

He had many major policy issues to attend to but understood that discipline would be restored only by constant concern for numerous details. Staff and prefects must bear the brunt of this but the school needed to know that the headmaster too was involved. A typical example was his published letter to the captain of football following a complaint from a visiting school that there had been no one to greet their team on arrival and to show them where to go. The captain did not apologise, claiming that "it is a Budo tradition to come late". The headmaster refused to accept this and the captain resigned.

The relative calm expected once external examinations had begun did not ensue. There was another serious disturbance in the Mess, over the serving of sour, brown posho. Crockery was again smashed and there was loud argument and unruly behaviour. The headmaster summoned a prefects' meeting at once and asked teaching staff to meet him in the staffroom at 9.30 p.m. He did not arrive until 11.30 and the meeting lasted until 1.30 a.m. It was not until Uyirwoth's full written report on the incidents appeared a week later that his colleagues learned the true reason for his lateness. It was not, as they had supposed, because discussion with the prefects had been fractious and prolonged, but because he had been put under "house arrest" by an officer of Amin's Public Safety Unit, who had accused him, in front of the prefects, of disloyalty. This must have been a frightening experience since the unit was one of Amin's three main agencies of terror, torture and murder - the other two being the Military Police and the State Research Bureau.

Originally it was set up as part of the civil police to deal with armed robbery... equipped with submachine guns and allowed to shoot robbers on sight. The PSU is based at Naguru next to the Police College... much of the activity that goes on in the compound takes place in full public view... to serve as a warning to any potential "enemies" of Amin... The cries of prisoners can often be heard from the roads that run alongside.

A peculiarly sadistic form of death has been developed at Naguru by Ali Towelli. To save ammunition, one prisoner is forced to batter out the brains of another with a heavy hammer on the promise of a reprieve. The "executioner" is then killed in the same way by another prisoner brought from the cells on the same promise... Under Towelli the PSU has become an instrument of terrifying public menace.[7]

A lesser man might have "confessed", apologised and then tried to flee the country. Uyirwoth was able to persuade his interrogator to allow him to join his waiting staff. He then not only proceeded calmly with the two-hour meeting, but the next day, after the school stock of posho had been tested, led a party of prefects into Kampala to scour the city for better quality unsoured supplies. They managed to buy several sacks, which was timely since only seven out of 150 ten kilo bags tested had been found to be still edible.

Headmaster and staff had earned a long break from the strain of trying to keep the school stable. They seemed unlikely to get it when a ministry circular announced in December that several schools, including Budo, were to re-open on the 13th of January instead of the 2nd of February. Some students were to be trained for yet another national gymnastics display and the ministry proposed that those not involved in the gymnnastics should stay in their classrooms and "occupy themselves". Staff who were not training gymnasts were to teach their classes; those who were training were "to organise themselves properly to ensure that all non-participating pupils are fully occupied." It was a prescription for chaos and for expensive extra catering, which would have guaranteed a bad start to the new school year. It caused consternation among those staff who were still on the Hill to receive the bad news.

In spite of his recent encounter with the PSU, Uyirwoth stoutly resisted the proposals and claimed exemption for Budo. He reminded the ministry of the recent demonstrations over food and of plans to buy replacement cutlery and crockery and to introduce a tighter, more civilised system of serving in the Mess. Stationery stocks were low and many fluorescent light tubes needed replacing. None of this could be in place by January 13th. He nevertheless prepared a careful letter to all parents warning them of the earlier opening date and asking for full co-operation. Crisis then turned to farce when the circular could not be reproduced because there was no duplicating ink to be found in Kampala and the school stock was exhausted. His colleagues - and even Uyirwoth himself - did not find his case very convincing. They were all the more relieved and heartened when the ministry accepted it. Budo got its full vacation after all.

The first term of the 1976 school year started reasonably well. During the holiday there had been difficult negotiations on the details of the timetable because of ministry demands and staffing uncertainties. The ministry had decreed that there were to be 40 teaching periods in the school week and that Wednesday afternoons were to be timetabled, in spite of the long Budo tradition that they were available for inter-school and house sports fixtures, for hobbies and for the several cultural societies. Agriculture, Technical Drawing and Physical Education were to be added to the timetable and, for S4 and S6, Art and Economics/Commerce. This was unrealistic and, after a first draft, Uyirwoth authorised Colin Davis to timetable only 38 periods for S3 and above. No additional staff had yet been provided for these new demands and, because three teachers were now known not to be returning, there was already a shortfall of more than 100 periods in Chemistry and Physics throughout the school.

Yet by the second day of term most students were attending classes all day and most teachers were present for all their timetabled lessons. To Budonians of the first sixty years it may seem scandalous to dignify this as a "reasonable start" but in the prevailing conditions it was commendable. Moreover, food was at least adequate and the service in Mess much improved; there were no demonstrations and few complaints. The Christian life of the school seemed vibrant with chapel often well attended and the singing good. Contact, an informal evening gathering for study, discussion and prayer, drew attendances of around 100 and had to be transferred from the Junior Library to the Lecture Theatre. The Scouts resumed activities with new enthusiasm in spite of increasing problems of security and transport for their popular expeditions.

In his first term Uyirwoth had deliberately cut through some urgent issues with authoritarian decisions because he thought that the students, and a few staff, needed reminding that the headmaster was actually in charge. Though there was occasional criticism throughout his four years of leadership, of his tendency to announce policy first and consult afterwards, he held regular staff meetings - always long and usually good - and was often willing to modify his proposals in the light of discussion with staff and with prefects.

In his journal entry for 16 March Colin Davis recorded his impression that "The school seems to be jogging along fairly happily". Bishop and Mrs Usher-Wilson (1927-1933) had re-visited the hill that day and though they must have found great changes from Grace's Budo they would probably have recognised the aspirations and the efforts to achieve them. Two weeks later the 70th anniversary was celebrated with a chapel service attended by about 100 Old Budonians, one of whom, Bishop Shalita, took the rest to task in his sermon for a "lack of Budonian spirit." But at the informal discussion afterwards Davis was warm in his appreciation of all the help Old Budonians were in fact giving to chapel and Christian activities. Sports fixtures, a school play, and supper with Old Budonian guests rounded off the celebrations of Founders Day. A good tradition had been vigorously maintained.

In the last week of the term there was a short but total strike by the school porters. They believed they had been denied an entitled pay increase, because they mistakenly assumed that they should receive the new minimum wage. A remarkable feature of the event was that for two days the students prepared, cooked and served all meals in the Mess, until the porters returned to work. This was undoubtedly a Budo "first" and showed that, far from being a pampered elite, many senior students could respond to the harsh realities of life under Amin. The end-of-term supper passed off well but the final assembly which followed was disappointing, especially since assemblies throughout the term had been well conducted. There were several student interruptions during the headmaster's address and again during the closing prayer, which the teacher leading it therefore decided not to complete. But Uyirwoth held firm. He ordered all present to remain seated until there was silence. There soon was and the prayer was duly completed.

The new term began at the end of May, preceded by an all-day staff meeting. Uyirwoth announced a change to Sunday evening routine, with chapel to be at 6pm, followed by roll call. Some staff thought this arbitrary, but he insisted that it might help alleviate the destructive problem of Sunday evening drinking. The school settled quickly and the easy resolution of a problem on Whit Sunday morning reflected a spirit of cheerful co-operation. The morning service was timed for 10.30 but because of a water supply failure, breakast had still not been served by 10. With a visiting preacher having arrived it was decided to go ahead-with a large and hungry congregation. Shortly before the sermon was due the breakfast drum brought blessed relief. It was quickly decided-though not unanimously, with an assistant chaplain proclaiming "Man shall not live by bread alone!" - to break off for breakfast and hope that the congregation would return. They did and the Whitsun celebration was happily concluded.

Contentment was shortlived however; Budo perversity surfaced in a disciplinary crisis the following week. One of the prefects was caught selling cigarettes and was immediately demoted and suspended, by deputy head John Mpagi. The prefects promptly met and nine out of thirteen resigned. Head prefect Bakibinga was among the four who did not. Uyirwoth was in Kampala examining student teachers, but returned for an urgent staff meeting and accepted the resignations. The staff met again later that evening and received a letter from the protesters, apologising and withdrawing their resignations. Some staff were impressed but others dismayed when the headmaster was willing to accept the apologies and reinstate the defectors. After heated debate the meeting voted 12 to 7 against reinstatement. Uyirwoth democratically accepted this decision. Housemasters then had to give time and energy to justifying the staff decision at house meetings and, to inducting and advising newly elected prefects. The civilised manner in which the whole dispute had been resolved contrasted starkly with a barbaric episode two weeks later at Entebbe airport, which revealed the true nature of Amin's regime to even the most cynical international reporters.

On June 28th an Air France flight from Tel Aviv with over 300 passengers, many of them Israelis, was hijacked by members of the Popular Front for the Liberation of Palestine and landed at Entebbe. Amin gave the hijackers immediate support, exulting to his Minister of Health, "I've got the Israelis fixed up this time!"[8] The hostages were crudely accommodated in an abandoned airport building now used as a warehouse. A doctor and nurses were in attendance and several French passengers were allowed to attend Entebbe hospital. With Amin's connivance the hijackers announced their terms: Unless 53 Palestinians held in several countries were released by July 4th, the hostages would all be killed. Over the next three days many of the hostages were released to their national embassies in Kampala, leaving 106 Israelis imprisoned. On July 2nd Dora Bloch, an elderly lady with dual Israeli/British nationality, was rushed, dangerously ill, to Mulago hospital, Kampala.

Just before midnight a force of Israeli commandos landed at Entebbe and after a swift and bloody engagement flew out an hour and a half later with the hostages, leaving 20 Ugandans and 7 hijackers dead. Amin, with many of his officers and troops, had fled the airport and hidden nearby. The enraged dictator took his vengeance on the innocent Mrs Bloch who, next day, was dragged screaming from her hospital bed, driven away and murdered. Her body was dumped by the roadside 20 miles from Kampala. Famous Ugandan photographer, Jimmy Parma, who was said to have taken pictures of the corpse, was found soon after, riddled with bullets. News of these events caused international outrage and Britain broke off diplomatic relations with Uganda. British nationals, including Colin Davis, Budo's only remaining expatriate teacher, were advised to leave the country. For Budo and all other schools and centres of liberal culture the outlook became even bleaker.

> In Kampala and the surrounding areas anyone who talked about the raid or seemed to belittle the weakness of the Ugandan armed forces was killed. Despite the purges and mass eliminations that followed Entebbe, no Ugandan news media mentioned the event.[9]

This did not inhibit freedom of speech on Budo hill. Davis noted a discussion with members of Contact who deplored "the appalling lack of respect the army has for human life". He also welcomed the unimpeded arrival of his copy of the air-mailed *Guardian Weekly*, the previous edition of which had given a detailed account of the Entebbe raid, roundly condemning the "tinpot dictator" Amin. More serious for Budo than the British government's reaction was the further worsening of relations with Kenya. Essential supplies to Uganda were cut off and the acute shortage of petrol resulted in rationing; in July and August the school vehicles were often stranded.

Supplies of alcohol for tempted students were unfortunately not affected. An emergency staff meeting was convened during teaching hours to consider clear evidence that drink had been given by teachers, in their homes, to students including some girls. The punishment for the students was a period of withdrawal from classes to work at portering jobs. It stopped short of suspension or expulsion because there was strong feeling that the real miscreants were the teachers. Both the headmaster and head prefect condemned their behaviour. Privately, both also expressed feelings of depression and helplessness. If staff could not be trusted how could good discipline be maintained? Uyirwoth, like Kyanda, was often unfairly criticised for leniency or indecisiveness, by senior students and Old Budonians comparing, as Stephen Kamuhanda later observed,[10] their regimes with Robinson's. The stark difference was that they were trying to sustain a school community in a country in which, despite the honest and considerate efforts of many civil servants and local officials, civilised national government had been virtually destroyed.

At the end of July the ministry announced, partly for security reasons, that the secondary school term must end early. The Budo annual Sports Day was therefore brought forward, once school examinations had been completed, from the normal Saturday to a weekday afternoon which unfortunately began with rain. When this cleared, staff and students seemed determined to make the event a success and most of the track and field events were completed before dark. Lamps were then brought and at about 7.30 the final relay races were run. It had been a "special effort" of which Cobb would have approved.

On 11 August, the school having accumulated enough petrol, the bus began at 4 am its usual long sequence of journeys to and from Kampala. Uyirwoth had been up well before the first busload left, to give out travelling money. The ministry, to its credit, acknowledged the danger for travelling students, especially girls, by providing transport from Kampala to all district headquarters. There were no reports of interference. Uyirwoth rounded off the staff term with a well attended and crisply conducted meeting which ended by 7.30pm. Towards the end of August petrol supplies improved and staff were able to leave the Hill as usual during the vacation.

The early weeks of the third term went well and the school seemed calm. Then the head prefect courageously intervened when fighting broke out at a dance, which he closed down. A later dance coincided with a graduation party at a staff house. Drink was yet again the root problem but there was also resentment that Budo girls had been lured away from the dance to the graduation party and village girls brought in to replace them. In October the staff took the unwelcome decision to expel two S6 students, only a month before their HSC examinations, for entertaining girls to drink. Staggered by the severity of the punishment they appealed to Uyirwoth, who remained adamant. There were no general protests and it seemed he had judged the mood of the school correctly. The national examinations proceeded smoothly and the year ended quietly. Davis reflected in his journal, with a mixture of satisfaction and foreboding.

> Looking back to the entries in this diary for about a year ago, the situation in school has really calmed down now... There are more things in the shops these days...The climate looks like turning a bit against the Church of Uganda...[11]

Within a month his prophecy proved tragically accurate.

After the humiliation of the Entebbe raid, Amin tried to reassert his authority by turning on those who he considered "enemies of the State". Following his inept attempts to turn Uganda into an Islamic state - against the wishes of many Ugandan Muslims - these enemies included the Christian churches. Missionaries were expelled and the preparations for the centenary celebrations of the Anglican Archdiocese were publicly ridiculed. Church leaders were accused of preaching hatred. Amin's armed soldiers then raided the house and family of Anglican Archbishop Janani Luwum, assaulting him on the pretext that arms were hidden in the house. Nothing was found. Luwum sent the president an account of the incident and tried unsuccessfully to arrange a personal meeting. Then, on February 10th, with the supporting signatures of all the Anglican bishops, he published a stern condemnation of government-sponsored violence, urging the president to protect his defenceless people. Kyemba, then still Minister of Health, admired the document:

> When I received my copy I was amazed at its boldness... The things that the Archbishop described were commonplace, but it was the first time such a statement had been made so forcefully, to such a wide range of senior officials ....In addition to his outspoken criticism of the regime, Luwum had another fault in Amin's eyes. He was an Acholi... "We did not do very well in the Israeli raid," he told me..." because the Acholi and Langi officers were in contact with the Israelis." [12]

The statement warned Amin that church leaders had intimate knowledge of many murders because they had buried the victims and cared for their relatives. Vengeance was swift. On 17 February, a large gathering of soldiers, diplomats and churchmen was harangued in the grounds of the International Conference Centre, about an alleged plot to assassinate the president. Archbishop Luwum and two cabinet ministers, Erinayo Oryema and Charles Oboth-Ofumbi, who were no longer trusted by Amin, were then driven from the meeting to the State Research Bureau and murdered.

A collision between the two cars in which they had been driven was immediately faked, on the road from the President's Lodge at Nakasero to the International Hotel; this was then officially announced as the cause of all three deaths. Next day Kyemba himself inspected the bodies at Mulago mortuary. All three were riddled with bullets. Amin further outraged public feeling and Kiganda tradition by refusing to allow the bodies to be released to the families. They were buried in their home districts, under military guard so that no one else could examine the bodies.[13]

At Budo, as in Uganda at large, the news of the murders was received with mingled horror at the atrocity, pride in the courage of the martyred

Archbishop, and caution. Any further public condemnations would have invited more execcutions. But there was a surge in the steadily growing loyalty of Christians to their churches and to each other, in response to the increased savagery of the regime. As tribal hatreds were deliberately fostered by the dictator and his assassins, Budo's determination to exemplify a united national community, was stiffened. Uyirwoth remained quietly alert to developments:

> I kept a low profile for myself and for the school. But when in public I thought it important to behave confidently not furtively, especially in the presence of soldiers.[14]

These attitudes are reflected in a staffbook entry he made on 4 March, in relation to disciplinary decisions of a staff meeting. The tribal origins of the students concerned warranted caution.

> The case of the eight students you recommended for expulsion has become political. Hence a political decision has been made: That they all serve one month suspension, receive 6 cuts of the cane, and porter for a week. We expect them back this weekend.[15]

One swift consequence of the murder of the Archbishop was a private warning to former headmaster, Dan Kyanda, that his life was in imminent danger. He had been appointed by Luwum, early in 1976, to be organising secretary of the Church of Uganda centenary celebrations and had necessarily become one of the country's most prominent Christians. Wisely he accepted the advice and left for Kenya where he resumed work with Christian groups and set up a project which accurately recorded details of persecutions in Uganda and elsewhere. Other known opponents of the dictatorship also defected, the most influential being Henry Kyemba. He could no longer deceive himself that he could do more good by remaining in Uganda and trying to spread concern and honesty through at least one government ministry. This proved a crucial decision.

He departed in April to negotiate medical aid for Uganda at conferences in Cairo and Geneva, arrived in London in mid-May and announced his defection. Within two weeks he had written a lengthy two-part denunciation of Amin's regime which was published in *The Sunday Times* in June, in time to influence the Commonwealth Conference of 35 nations meeting in London. Impressed by first-hand evidence from a Ugandan, the leaders declared:

> Cognizant of the accumulated evidence of sustained disregard for the sanctity of life and of massive violation of basic human rights in Uganda, it was the overwhelming view of Commonwealth leaders that these excesses were so gross as to warrant the world's concern and to evoke condemnation by the heads of government in strong and unequivocal terms... The heads of government looked to the day when the people of Uganda would once more fully enjoy their basic human rights, now being so cruelly denied.

This was the first multi-national condemnation of Amin's barbaric regime. Kyemba then worked at exceptional speed on his book, *State of Blood*, which was published only two months later and was a powerful influence worldwide. Words alone cannot defeat tyranny. But his formed a turning point. They encouraged many beleaguered Ugandans, who could now at least be sure that many influential people world-wide knew the truth. How much they would care - or do - remained to be seen.

The Budo year had begun quietly ten days before the assassinations. At a long meeting with teaching staff and prefects the headmaster had called for more effective involvement in and out of class and particularly in the supervision of the houses. The house system had long been one of the school's strengths, but if not well organised would quickly become a liability in a situation still fraught with fears and shortages. Head Prefect Herbert Wamala told me, 27 years later, that he thought Uyirwoth had been wise to try to run the school largely through the prefects, who understood and respected Budo rules and traditions, which most of the rapidly changing staff did not. The new S5s arrived in March, earlier than for several years, and so made a prompt start to their HSC courses. Although both the bus and minibus had been out of action for the whole of February, food supplies were ingeniously maintained, though not to the students' preferred tastes. Davis noted early in March:

> I am impressed by the improved behaviour in the Mess this term.
> Grace has been far more audible. There are no queues. There has
> been very little change of diet from posho, yet the students have
> taken it uncomplaining... But there is a shortage of beds.

There was also a shortage of enthusiasm for games, partly because there
were few experienced sports coaches among the staff. Some cricket
was played in this first term but swimming had been abandoned,
partly because of the uncertain water supply. Davis walked down to
Nansove to inspect the pool, which had been one of Budo's prime sports
facilities in the 1960s.

> It was in a sorry state. Water covering about 40% of the bottom,
> dead frogs lying around. No wood from the diving board left and
> no baati (corrugated iron sheets) left from the upper changing
> room ... the lower pools all overgrown.

The term ended without any further serious incidents, but maintaining
stability was a constant struggle, with staffing in all schools even more
transient and unpredictable. More Ugandans, including teachers,
doctors, nurses and other professionals, were fleeing the country.
Barbara Collins, who had gone to Kenya to explore employment
possibilities, spent part of her last vacation in Nairobi, helping
to receive and settle Ugandan refugees. But many well-qualified
professionals and promising undergraduates were staying, and one
of the pleasures of teaching at Budo remained the receipt of letters of
appreciation from former students. Colin Davis, also approaching his
last term, included extracts from many in his journal. One was from
Winnie Byanyima, the youngest student he had taught for HSC, and
one of the best mathematicians. She thanked him and Barbara Collins
for the many ways in which they had helped her to benefit from a
Budo education. (She went on to become an aeronautical engineer
and later a courageous and outspoken M.P.) She stressed, as other
students did, how valuable the voluntary activities of Contact had been
in strengthening her Christian faith.

Ironically, just two weeks later the Budo Parents Teachers
Association discussed the reintroduction of compulsory chapel. Davis,

who had been co-ordinator of chapel services and music during several periods when the school had no chaplain, spoke strongly against it. But the vote was overwhelmingly in favour. Only 3 staff voted against and a few more abstained. They believed that the effort to build a strong voluntary chapel community was slowly succeeding and that the Sunday evening pattern of voluntary chapel, roll-call and supper was now working well. Since few staff attended chapel and enquiries had revealed that few parents encouraged their offspring to attend church in the vacations, the new decision smacked of hypocrisy. "Do as I say, not as I do" was - the opponents of compulsion urged - an attitude which undermined true school discipline.

Thirty years on, Christian parents and teachers remain keenly divided on this issue, in many church-related schools all over the world and find it hard to disagree amicably. Uyirwoth accepted the advice of the PTA without more debate, and announced that Sunday and weekday chapel would immediately become compulsory. Davis was invited to lead the first Sunday service of his final term but declined, on principle. Some weeks later chairman of governors, Eridadi Mulira, returned to the theme in a chapel sermon which was well received by the school. He recalled that Canon Grace, whose student he had been, had based his leadership of Budo on the ideal of love and consequently there had been little compulsion in the routine of the school. But Mulira acknowledged that the parents, in reaching their decision, truly wanted their children to experience the best of life and they doubted whether students always used freedom wisely. The debate continues, at Budo and beyond.

The school curriculum was now being well supported, with good staff and student attendance at classes, but it was decided to spread the mid-year examinations over an unusually long two and a half weeks. Many classes would not have to be taught, and this would give more time to resolve staffing problems for the second half of the term. No Budo headmasters before Kyanda and Uyirwoth had needed to resort to such short-term "planning".

Tight security, fear, widespread defections and punitive currency control now made the process of legal departure from Uganda complicated and wearisome - though less arduous for expatriates than Ugandans. Davis felt fairly treated and was soon embarking on a series of farewell ceremonies which rounded off his fourteen years at Budo. Staff, Chapel, Contact, Kisozi Church, Scouts, and Canada House all organised rousing send-offs and among his many leaving gifts was a Church of Uganda centenary tie - designed by Dan Kyanda. At the staff party Uyirwoth spoke generously of his fine contributions and bore no ill-will for the many sincere disagreements his last ex-patriate colleague had expressed over discipline, chapel, curriculum and timetable. On 13 July headmaster and colleagues, head prefect, and a large gathering of past and present students said final farewells at Entebbe airport. Davis confided to his journal, "Such a crowd of people. That was a marvellous gesture."

Two weeks later Barbara Collins ended her unique twenty-three years of service under four headmasters and, after many farewells, departed for Kenya. In a reminiscence for *The Budonian* reflecting on the pervasive influence of the school, she wrote:

> When A level work first started, some of the sixth formers who had then spent fourteen years on the hill were known as "The Budo family", but I became particularly conscious in my last few years of the very special bond which exists among all of us who have been at Budo... In my prolonged negotiations winding up my financial affairs I received invaluable assistance from Old Budonians in every government office I dealt with...and I regarded this as the most perfect leaving present I could have had. I have found that this "goodly fellowship" extends even to Kenya... I am now school secretary at St Andrew's School, Turi. A large number of Old Budonians send their children here so Parents Days are often the scene of Budonian reunions ... Instead of starting a new life in Kenya I have been able to strengthen my ties with the place that was my home for so many happy years.[16]

For the third term of 1977 students returned to the first entirely Ugandan teaching staff in Budo's 71 years. Uyirwoth had been badly shaken in a car accident during the holiday; he noted that it had "made me lose interest in almost everything", but he recovered quickly. He found time to write to Davis with news of his latest attempts to improve school diet and security. The former zoo area had been converted into a paddock now grazed by three Friesian cows, providing an additional source of fresh milk. Moreover

> I have done another funny thing. The school is now almost within barbed wire. A few gaps remain but we shall be completely enclosed by the end of December.[15]

He would have had no illusions about keeping the murderers of the Public Safety Unit at bay, but theft from staff houses and school buildings had become endemic. Barbed wire would make a loaded escape more hazardous - and might help to keep the cows at home.

Football flourished this term and the staff entered a team in the inter-house competition. Except in the SCR there must have been general glee when they were knocked out. Teacher Samalie Kirya cheered Davis with the news that Canada was playing very well. She also wrote about chapel developments:

> The compulsory chapel services are still on and students seem to have invented ways of cutting. Recently a number of them were sent home for the PTA fund [required contribution] of 250/=. Some students took advantage of this and cut classes, Sunday services and other activities. Contact is still going on well...At the end of last term we ate chicken for supper - can you imagine that? The problem of essential commodities is now acute. We haven't had anything for about 3 months. [18]

Only two teachers resigned before the end of the year and one was promptly replaced. After a year of relative calm, despite the demoralising atrocities, hopes of better examination results were not disappointed. Of 112 candidates at O level 39 obtained 1st class certificates, while of the 95 A level candidates, 49 gained at least 3 passes at Principal level and 30 more achieved university entry level.

At the end of the year Uyirwoth recorded an agreeable difficulty. Selections for entry to S1 had proved a real problem "because everyone wants to come to Budo." In his search for high standards while continuing to champion co-education, there was one slight reservation. While girls entering Budo for the HSC course were excellent, the very top girls at secondary entrance often chose Gayaza or Namagunga.

In selection processes, and in other matters, he thought he was often helped by not being a Muganda. On one occasion, for example, he had needed to discipline a nephew of Amin and had found the president "quite helpful".

The first term of 1978 started confidently and although by mid-term five teachers had resigned, three replacements, in history, geography and music, were appointed in time for the second term. Among Uyirwoth's priorities for the year were to provide better school transport, to improve the library stock, and to encourage the chapel and other Christian activities with more consistent staff support. Robina Mirembe, who after only four years was already one of the longest-serving teachers, was a strong organiser for both chapel and Contact but as head of Biology and warden of Sabaganzi House, carried a heavy load.

Tom Nabeta, who had been teacher and chaplain at Mwiri, and warden of Universtiy Hall, Makerere, was a long-time friend of Budo, who reported cheering news to Davis.

> Budo, like all Ugandan schools, is going through a difficult financial patch. The Old Boys and Girls came to the rescue the other day, by organising a fund-raising auction. They were all very generous, but I think they were anxious to improve the bookstock in the library and to provide transportation for the staff. The school has had a very big turnover of staff in a very short time, and one of the main reasons, it is said, is that it is very difficult to go into Kampala from Budo... The Bishop of Namirembe has agreed to ordain Laban Bombo [teacher of Mathematics] as a clergyman, and he will act as chaplain.

This certainly achieved the continuity the headmaster was seeking. Bombo was to give great service to Budo chapel for the next twenty years and to remain a senior mathematician long after that. Uyirwoth endorsed Nabeta's optimism in a letter to Davis which was the most positive statement about Budo he had felt able to make in more than three years of leadership. And he was planning ahead.

> We now have two vehicles...a Leyland bus (62 seats) and an 8 ton Leyland lorry. Things are much easier now. The tractor should

be ready by mid -1979 and it is my intention to get a staff car by the end of 1979. Another development is the improvement of the medical facility in the school. Nurse Mary retires at the end of the year and we intend to employ a senior medical assistant. We now have a visiting doctor... You will probably be happy to hear that Mr Ongicha is doing well as a housemaster and as head of the mathematics department. The staffing position is steadily improving but Arts are still in a bad staff position... Namirembe has taken an interest in the chapel affairs now. The Bishop of Namirembe was in the school last month.

By the end of the year he felt well supported by the ministry, the Old Budonians, the prefects, most staff and many students. But not by the governors. He felt that the Baganda members of the Board still distrusted him, some even holding him responsible for the rapid turnover of staff, believing that he was unable to establish good relationships with them. It must have been all the more heartening for him at the end of the year to learn that Budo had achieved the success which was still most valued by governors, parents, teachers and staff. It had obtained the best results in the country at both A and O levels, the latter being a big improvement on 1977, with 55 candidates out of 93 gaining 1st class certificates. After a vacation with no serious incidents or damaging policy changes he would have warmed to the joyful confidence of Robina Mirembe, who wrote, early in the new year, to tell Davis how grateful she was for all the blessings of 1978, "and even more for 1979 - a special year". Within a few weeks all was changed.

After the murder of Archbishop Luwum and the vengeful slaughter wreaked by Amin's troops over the next year and a half, opposition to the dictatorship hardened and began to organise itself in the neighbouring countries, Britain and the USA. Kasozi provides a lucid account of the intricate network of opposition groups - not, unfortunately, working together - and of the unrest in the army and Amin's brutal responses to it. The beginning of the end was unexpected. After a series of army mutinies

...loyal elements in the army quelled the rebellion, pursuing the mutineers to theTanzanian border. Amin then completely took leave of his senses by pursuing the rebels into the Kagera Salient and attacking Tanzanian civilian and military positions. Tanzania responded by mobilising.[19]

The Tanzanian government appealed to Ugandan patriots and exiles to join the struggle against Amin, who had announced that Uganda had annexed the Kagera Salient and that the river would in future form the border between the two countries. The two main Ugandan groups to respond were Obote's *Kikoosi Maalum* (Special Unit) with about 700 troops, and Yoweri Museveni's Front for National Salvation, FRONASA), with about 300.

> As the war progressed, other groups picked up courage in the typical bandwagon fashion of Ugandans. Particularly after the fall of Masaka on 24-25 February 1979, there was need for political direction in case Amin fell...Tanzanian President Julius Nyerere said that "as far as we were concerned, we could have pulled our people out, but the Baganda were going to be in real trouble because Amin, if they were left without adequate forces, would really teach them a lesson and I would be having thousands of refugees in Tanzania."[20]

But the Tanzanian government was also aware that many Ugandan political groups would not accept the return, as leader of their country, of Tanzania's favoured candidate Milton Obote. The admirable Julius Nyerere, in asserting that Obote's was the legal government of Uganda, appeared to overlook the fact that Obote himself had usurped the presidency by violently overthrowing Sir Edward Mutesa, revered hereditary leader of the Baganda, as well as constitutional president of Uganda.

With encouragement from Nyerere a number of Ugandan "freedom" organisations met in conference at Moshi, in Tanzania, March 24-26. They formed a Uganda National Liberation Front (UNLF) to fight Amin and restore democracy to their country. They elected Yusuf Lule, Old Budonian, former Budo teacher, and ex-vice chancellor of Makerere, as chairman of its National Executive Committee. But events moved too fast for them - and for Budo, which would be a strategic vantage point for the Tanzanian army moving eastwards to attack Kampala.

Robina Mirembe wrote a graphic eye-witness acount of the impact on the school community:

> I thank God that he has seen me through the impossible. Early, before the school broke off, Amin's soldiers were stationed at Nsangi. They misbehaved around the villages, including Kitemu and some were making their way to Kisozi - who knows, Budo would also fall victim! These soldiers mistreated women - we all got worried, all females. Then we heard bombs [shells] from afar. That was Saturday night, 24th of March. On Sunday 25th more shelling ... curfew was declared. In the darkness of the small chapel twenty of us went down in prayers for our nation for almost an hour. Then we quietly left for our houses.
>
> On Monday 26th we had the first three lessons. then the emergency drum sounded and we went to chapel for assembly - the most chaotic assembly that I have ever seen at Budo. Parents - some eager to take away their children - and students, were all shouting at the top of their voices... After a struggle to control the frightened students, the Headmaster told them to pack at full speed. For three days students were taken down to Kampala to get means home. Those who failed were returned to school.
>
> On the 27th we went down [to Kampala] to cash our cheques, but the banks had closed. On the 28th we went back. On our way we were stopped at gunpoint by a big group of Amin's soldiers in the forest near Budo junction. From then on I did not go back to town - it was clear that Budo was cut off from Kampala. Shelling continued... and on the 30th they shelled Nigeria house, then my compound and the shells damaged the windows and doors of my house. Then Mr Boston's house... We were on the slope, near Wendy Moore's house, in the bush trying to lie flat. Shelling continued from 12.30, with a short break, until 5pm. Never before had I felt so close to death. Children cried, some teachers cried.
>
> It had been said that Amin's soldiers were near and so that is why the liberation army was shelling this place and Kasenge and Kinawa with long-range artillery. We realised we had been grounded. Then on the 31st Amin's soldiers, thousands, were heading for Budo from Kitemu. We left the school - very few teachers stayed.[21] We all scrambled to get on the lorry with a few

belongings. As we got on, the headmaster, not experienced in lorry driving [Uyirwoth later revealed that he had only driven it once before], tried to drive off while they continued shelling. I couldn't help shedding tears.

Children frightened, students anxious, we drove through the main gate and headed towards Nakawuka. We drove for a short time when we were stopped by villagers who said that heavy lorries couldn't pass through that road due to planted land-mines. So we had to leave the lorry and walk for about three and a half miles - running and falling flat on the ground as they continued to shell Budo from Nakawuka, hitting the spur and damaging Gaster House... We then reached the Tanzanian roadblock. They checked us and told us to pass on and sit in a banana plantation - sort of hiding - lest Amin's soldiers shelled us.

Then we walked on to Nakawuka trading centre where we found very many people. We sat on a verandah not knowing what next. Then some kind village people gave us small rooms. I remember us sleeping in a tiny room - 14 of us - breathing in breathed-out air, children crying. All we had were mats and something to cover ourselves. So on the hard mud floor we slept in very unhygienic conditions. We used to have one meal a day. We were interrogated by Tanzanians, who never trusted our headmaster, because he comes from West Nile. Some were threatened to have their noses cut off and their children tortured if they did not give necessary information.

Every evening we would gather around the small mud houses for prayers and then go on to sleep - hardly any sleep. In the night they shelled heavily... I remember our Palm Sunday service in the market shelter. We had only one hymn book to about sixty people but the Lord blessed us. We stayed there for about ten days. Then two days before our return to our badly hit place they told us that soldiers had opened all our houses and villagers had stolen most of our things. I thought the world most unfair - I cried at the thought of starting from scratch.[22]

As the sixty Budo refugees soon learned, there had been much greater suffering elsewhere. Amin's retreating soldiers left a stream of blood from Jinja, Nakasongola, and Fort Portal. Thousands of people were shot and their property vandalised.All types of motor vehicles were snatched from unarmed civilians. Then, on the 11th April 1979, two weeks after the meeting at Moshi and before the UNLF had crystallised as a political institution or a tried fighting force, Kampala fell to Tanzanian forces and a few Ugandan exile fighters. People who had never worked with one another were suddenly placed in positions of responsibility involving power and wealth and asked to co-operate.[23]

As Budo staff, families and a few students returned to the hill in mid-April they could not know that such co-operation would prove a delusion.

> The sight was terrible. Bullet-stricken houses opened and looted badly. I entered my house to find books and letters scattered, ventilators and drawers broken. But after those thieves had come my people came in and saved some of my things and took them to the village... Some teachers have been reduced to nothing - this includes the headmaster. Over half of the school beds have been stolen and all the school mattresses, a good number of stools and other school property. The Battle of King's College Budo, as the Tanzanians call it, took eight hours - while we were at Nakawuka. It was a gun to gun battle, so many bullets were found at the Gaster end, the battle field.

> Now Budo is a barracks. They are in the classrooms and dormitories and some staff houses. I have them on my verandah and in my guest house...When the students come back they will sleep on the floors. They have missed a whole month. Gayaza was OK and so was Nabbingo. Kampala is no more. They broke windows and doors, got in and stole everything. We can't buy a thing. The army people here (some) have been kind and have given us some sugar and salt... People are walking to town on foot - cars are all looted. Amin's soldiers are still busy killing people and taking their property.[24]

Sadly, in spite of all the care of Uyirwoth and the staff, one Budo student had been killed during the evacuation. Joel Kyeyune, Canada House prefect, attempted a few days after the fall of Kampala, to recover some looted household property. The looter denounced him to a Tanzanian soldier, as a former State Research agent and he was executed on the spot. He had gained a place at Makerere for Agriculture. It was learned later that his contemporary, Godfrey Mutyaaba of England House, had been murdered by Amin's fleeing troops, near Tororo. He too was to have entered Makerere, for a B. Com degree. Many present and past Budonians lost parents and siblings in the carnage.

The devious, violent and precarious sequence of political rivalries which beset Uganda as soon as Amin was toppled and the Tanzanian army began its gradual withdrawal has been admirably analysed by Kasozi.[25] In a brief account of the last weeks of Uyirwoth's Budo, the first incidents were crucial:

> Yusuf Lule had been elected chairman of the UNLF at Moshi and became President in April 1979, after Amin's fall. But after only sixty-eight days of rule, he was violently removed. His inability to contend with Uganda's political forces contributed to his fall.

In assessing Budo's response to this setback it is essential to consider the state of the country at large. The fall of Amin seemed to release a surge of savage destruction of the very kind he had sponsored.

Ordinary Ugandans seemed intent on demolishing the resources and buildings of the State, as if to make the restoration of civilised government impossible. A Commonwealth team reporting later in 1979 recorded that

> Crops were damaged and livestock killed; houses, factories and public buildings were gutted; school supplies, textbooks and writing materials were looted; food, furniture and clothes were taken from houses and shops; office records were lost or stolen; tools and equipment were taken from workshops, and thousands of cars and trucks were taken out of the country to Sudan,Tanzania, Zaire, Rwanda and Kenya.[26]

Even worse were the persecution and murder of many innocent minorities, especially Muslims and the people of West Nile, unjustly assumed to have been supporters of Amin.

> Communal revenge against groups is common in Uganda. The problem is that many innocent peasants find themselves the victims of issues they do not understand. A rural Ankole Muslim peasant in Kashari, or a Kakwa in Koboko had no power to make or unmake Amin as president; but he suffered the consequences of his presidency.

Ugandans were gladdened by Amin's departure. But their pride as a nation was hurt. They had failed to change their own government without the help of external forces. The violence that accompanied the struggle to remove Amin and the destruction that followed have left a permanent mark on Ugandan society and on the country's physical structures.[27]

Having been occupied by the Tanzanian army for more than two months, Budo re-opened in June, with some soldiers still encamped in tents on the bluff, around Gaster House which they used as a store. The girls - to protect them from the soldiers - were moved all together to Africa House, sleeping on the floor. The boys of Australia and Africa Houses moved into Sabaganzi and Grace until the occupation ended. The soldiers - about a thousand - had, throughout the occupation, behaved well towards people but not towards school buildings and property. Classroom and dormitory doors had been wrenched off and used as firewood for cooking. Goats had been tethered inside the chapel and the Mess. The last units to leave the Hill took with them as much school furniture as they could load, including desks and chairs. Gaster House and many of the classrooms were completely bare. Renovating the school would be a task for years rather than months.

Uyirwoth and his senior teachers braced themselves to re-launch the curriculum and to assert discipline. In a fragmented and dangerous political situation the governors made little attempt to influence or assist. Many staff and students were demoralised and disunited. Several long-established schools which had tried to re-open - including Mwiri, Nabumali, Namilyango and Ntare - quickly suffered strikes, with students demanding the removal of head teachers and staff on the specious grounds that they were "Amin's men". A head who had previously tried to assert strong discipline - and came from West Nile - was a prime target. Posters round the school demanded that the Head and Deputy, John Mpagi, be removed. A small group of teachers held an unofficial "staff meeting", passed a vote of no confidence in Uyirwoth and communicated this to the ministry and the governors with a list of grievances. The headmaster stood firm. He insisted that he could manage the school, but only with a staff he could trust. He proposed to the ministry that five of the present staff be removed from Budo. Then came the blow of the overthrow of President Lule - a special affront to Baganda Budonians. Uyirwoth recalled that

> Discipline was poor after the overthrow of Amin and worse after the fall of Lule, which created many problems.

He had already received anonymous death threats from Kabinja village, which had protested to Lule that Budo was destroying its crops. In fact the headmaster had given the village six months notice of the planting up of an extension to Budo farm, on land which the school owned.

The ministry responded wisely to the situation, sending an inspection team to the school for several days, led by Assistant CIS Eliezer Bawuuba.The inspectors reported towards the end of July and the problems seemed close to resolution. Uyirwoth was assured that the troublesome teachers would be removed and Budo would receive six new staff. Greatly relieved, he prepared to go down to Nairobi to try to buy teaching materials. But the ministry took fright at renewed threats to their headmaster's life. On July 30th he received a letter, personally delivered to the school, instructing him to hand over to John Mpagi and return to the ministry - by the 31st!

Uyirwoth had come nowhere near achieving Cobb's parody of "The Budo Experience". He had received scant welcome, no farewell at all, and the "period in between" had been appallingly difficult and personally dangerous. The ministry signalled its continuing confidence in him by appointing him senior inspector for administration in schools. He began his new work the following week, without any leave. Yet he looked back with few regrets:

> I had set myself to continue the real aims of the school, to maintain and raise academic standards. I had set out to maintain and try to raise academic standards, but that was not the only priority. What, after all, was the aim of the school? I wanted to support its Christian activities - which was why I went back to compulsory chapel. But I was also aware of the growing number of Muslim and Catholic students. I was especially keen to maintain co-education,

having been to co-ed schools myself. In my four years at Budo there were about six hundred students and we wanted at least a hundred girls. I did my best to get to know all of them.

My task was to change some attitudes and if you make changes you are bound to tread on a few toes! There was fear and insecurity all over the country and therefore in all the schools too. It was hard and long work. I hardly ever got to bed before 1am and often it was 2 or 3am. I think we had managed to clean up the school compound and strengthen the discipline. I left feeling that, in spite of all the obstacles, the Budo train was still running on the rails.

In spite of all the disappointments and his abrupt removal from his post, he spent many hours during the next three weeks preparing an exemplary handing-over report - preserved in the school archives - ranging widely over 10 pages of close typescript. In it he warmly commended John Mpagi for his competence and strong support, and also the large majority of students for their highly responsible behaviour.

What worries me is that the students lack guidance. Spending nights out without permission, and the increased alcoholism, is a direct result of the irresponsible acts of the staff... All I can say is that the Budo teachers need to think more rationally and behave themselves.

On the Board of Governors, he quoted Kyanda's strictures of 1975 and added his own:

The Board has to think of a Ugandan headmaster ... The white headmasters were never Old Budonians nor were they Baganda. We have to think of "Budo today" rather than of "The Budo I knew". Progressive conservatism is what this school requires. Permanent membership on the Board leads to stagnant conservatism.

It was a resounding Farewell.

Few Budonians, past or present, have heard or read much about the school's trials and triumphs from 1975 to 1979, because the documents, letters and personal testimonies on which this study is based have not been known. The record speaks for itself. It was a skilful, brave and distinguished headship.

Notes

1 Hills, Denis. *The White Pumpkin*. London: George Allen and Unwin, 1975

2 *Transition* No. 42, Accra 1973

3 From my verbatim notes on a three hour conversation with Ishmael Uyirwoth, March 2001. All direct quotations of his views come either from this conversation or his own notices and letters.

4 Davis, Colin. "Glimpses of Budo 1963-1977." Unpublished notes and letters which have been invaluable sources for chapters 10,11 and 12.

5 This was certainly my own experience in Africa and in England. As a result, during my tenure of two university college principalships, 1970 to 1995, I tried to ensure that catering was always good. Then, if students began to grumble about it, my colleagues and I tried to find out what were the real, unpresented problems!

6 Davis *op. cit.* 20 October 1975

7 Kyemba *op. cit.* pp. 113-114.

8 *Ibid.* p. 169

9 Kasozi, *op. cit.* p. 121.

10 Kamuhanda, S. Personal letter to the author in response to a draft of chapter 10, January 2004.

11 Davis, *op.cit.* Jan. 1977

12 Kyemba *op.cit.* pp. 181-2.

13 *Ibid*, p 189.

14 As 3 above.

15 KCB Staffbook 4 March 1977.

16 *The Budonian* 1983 pp. 51-54.

17 Davis *op. cit.* 26 October 1977.

18 *Ibid*, 9 October 1977.

19 Kasozi, *op. cit.* p. 122.

20 *Ibid*, p. 125.

21 In a discussion of these events with some Budo staff in March 2000 it emerged that Bombo not only did what he could to defend school and staff property but also successfully hid a female colleague who had missed the last school lorry to leave the hill.

She was able to leave her "safe house" for only a few minutes after dark each night and was smuggled off the hill a week later.

22 Robina Mirembe to Barbara Collins, May 1979.

23 Kasozi *op. cit.* p. 126.

24 Robina Mirembe *op. cit.*

25 Kasozi *op. cit.* pp. 120 - 132.

26 World Bank: "Uganda: Country Economic Memorandum No. 8". Quoted by Kasozi p. 127.

27 Kasozi *op. cit.* p. 127.

11

False Dawns — Then Uphill all the Way: 1979-1989

As the ministry had insisted, Budo was led for the third term of 1979 by deputy head John Mpagi who gave calm and resourceful guidance to staff and students. But the governors had learned their lesson and this time moved swiftly. Bishop Misaeri Kauma and Chairman Eridadi Mulira invited Eliezer Bawuuba to accept the headship as soon as he could be released from his duties in the inspectorate. Having led the recent short inspection of the school he had no illusions about the huge difficulties of the task. But he accepted the challenge and his appointment was welcomed by governors, Old Budonians, staff and students.

He came well-equipped for the post. He was a Muganda and an Old Budonian (1956-1963) who had been popular as a student and admired for his integrity and strong Christian witness. As an HSC student - and member of the *Balokole* Fellowship - he had been respected for his firmly expressed convictions but also for being a good listener, willing to change his mind and arguing with wit and good humour. His academic qualifications and experience were stronger, and probably more immediately relevant to Budo's needs, than those of any of his predecessors. But he never forgot his humble beginnings and made a point of alluding to them - with a light touch - at his first Founders' Day in March 1980:

> I emerged from a very obscure place called Ngogwe Primary School, to this famous school. Although we new students had arrived two days before the old students came back we were quite a spectacle, particularly myself, because not only was I a newcomer but - worse still - a "saved" newcomer! However I must confess that there was plenty of fertile ground for my faith here, so I was able to grow to spiritual maturity.

He had passed from Budo S6 to Makerere, where he graduated with a BA in English and Religious Studies in 1967 and completed a Postgraduate Certificate in Education in 1968. He then taught at Budo for two years - sharing that advantage with only Kyanda among Budo's twelve headmasters - before being awarded a scholarship to the USA. He followed a joint master's degree programme in TESOL and Linguistics at the University of Ohio, graduating in 1972. He taught again at Budo for the first term of 1973, experiencing the effects of the Amin regime on education and society before being appointed headmaster of the Aga Khan Secondary School, which during his headship was renamed Kampala High School. In 1978, because Amin wanted a Muslim head at KHS, he was appointed assistant chief inspector of schools (secondary).

The ministry, perhaps acknowledging that its treatment of the Budo governors and their headship in 1975 had been harsh, confirmed Bawuuba's appointment not only promptly but also on generous terms which he, with typical openness, publicly acknowledged:

> I have not surrendered my title of Assistant CIS, so that if I am no longer wanted here, by old and young students, I can go back and make a legal claim to my former post. I must add that it was purely for the love that I have for my former school that I accepted this very difficult post at perhaps the most difficult of times. Budo made me what I am. I will therefore sacrifice, to let Budo be Budo once again.[1]

Bawuuba's wife, Christine, was also an Old Budonian, who had trained at the National Teachers' College, Kyambogo and taught maths at Buganda Road Primary School in Kampala, continuing to do so throughout 1980, their first full year at Budo. They had six children and, twenty-five years later, Christine looked back with satisfaction on their crucial decision to bring the family back to Budo hill:

> Eliezer had not applied for the post. It was by invitation and there was no one else interviewed. We knew of course that there would be many difficulties but Kampala High School had given him good experience, which he had enjoyed. Through his work as inspector he had also seen many other schools. We were ready to leave the traffic and crowds of the town and were glad to be coming back

to Budo. But we knew that transport would be a problem and it was, all through our time - though things improved.[2]

Bawuuba visited the school towards the end of the third term to assess the urgent needs. Yet, in spite of the co-operation between ministry and governors, the news of his appointment was slow to reach the staff. As late as 12th November a senior teacher wrote to Colin Davis: "Rumour has it that Erisa Kironde is to be the new headmaster of Budo."[3] The Bawuubas came into residence on the Hill during the long holiday. They had ample time before the new school year to appreciate the extent of the damage.

This has already been summarised in Chapter 10. The state of the country was even more perilous. When Yusuf Lule was forced to resign the presidency after only ten weeks in office, the National Consultative Council next day, 21st June 1979, elected another Muganda Old Budonian to succeed him. But Godfrey Binaisa, well-known and experienced advocate, was no better equipped than Lule to maintain democratic leadership in the face of the conflicting parties - Kasozi identifies nine[4] - now fighting for political control of the country. And Binaisa and the NCC had no army.

> He had to contend with forces that desired Obote's return to power by hook or by crook as well as those that wanted to organise free and fair elections ... The population clearly understood the political nature of the change from Lule to Binaisa and reacted by withdrawing the goodwill it had conferred upon the first post-Amin administration. People stopped voluntarily surrendering their guns and ammunition to the government and kept them instead for the rainy day they now realised would come. Merchants and farmers freed the prices of goods they had initially kept below market levels in a gesture of support for the government... A resistance movement ... met in the suburbs of Kampala to organise strikes, riots and attacks on officials. Crowds released political prisoners at Katwe police station, among them people who had supported or worked for Amin. More than eighty people were killed between June and August 1979 in the aftermath of Lule's deposition. The government imprisoned suspects on a far greater

scale than before ... By September more than thirty thousand people
had become political prisoners.[5]

Such were the bitter realities of Uganda, and particularly of Kampala,
while Bawuuba's appointment to Budo was in process. Worse was to
follow. The power and influence of the National Consultative Council
were undermined by widely active supporters of Obote - some of
them council members - and his rapidly expanding army, the *Kikoosi
Maalum,* soon effectively controlled the Ministry of Defence. They
had realised that the chief obstacle to their takeover of power was
the minister, Yoweri Museveni, and they were able to press Binaisa
- "suspicious of Museveni's charisma"[6] - to remove him, even though
an NCC committee found all the accusations levelled against him
to be untrue. Had Museveni stayed at defence the machinations of
Obote's faction - and six more years of slaughter - just might have
been forestalled, though Obote's influence was already so strong that if
Binaisa had resisted he would probably have been forced from office.

Two other aspects of the national scene must be acknowledged
in any fair assessment of Budo's problems and successes during
Bawuuba's headship. First, the state of the police force, without whose
protection the people could derive little benefit from whatever justice
continued to be administered. In his published account of his long
period of influence in Uganda's judiciary, Justice Peter Jermyn Allen
strongly commended the large majority of his African colleagues for
their courageous persistence in maintaining fair court judgements and
resisting corruption. Having entered the legal profession from the police
force, however, he was also well qualified to assess the development
of Uganda's prime security force. His verdict was dismal.

> One of the many saddening things during this time was the
> tremendous deterioration in every way of the police force over
> the years, which naturally made an enormous impact on the
> members of the public who had hitherto relied on it entirely for
> the preservation of law and order throughout the country. At
> Independence Uganda had one of the finest police forces in the
> Commonwealth (and that is not just my opinion). It was well-
> trained, highly disciplined, smart and efficient ... the required

standard of education for recruits was steadily raised each year
... corruption was dealt with immediately and very severely;
consequently the public had learned confidently to rely upon the
police to keep the peace... During Oryema's nine years in charge the
force steadily deteriorated.... One of the main reasons for this was
the extraordinary and unexplained removal of almost all incentives
to the men to improve themselves and their work.[7]

The compulsory courses and examinations in English and law for
trainees, and the salary increments they conferred, were abolished,
as were courses abroad for senior officers. The law school's offer of
bursaries for senior officers to gain legal qualifications was refused
and the education levels for admission to the force drastically reduced.
Under Ali Towelli both the general force and the Public Service Unit,
whose murderous activities were noted in Chapter 10, accepted illiterate
recruits and known criminals, some with recorded convictions.

The ordinary people lost confidence in the police and often
complained bitterly about their rough treatment in police stations,
even those who were there to report crimes or assist by making
statements, let alone those who were taken there as suspects. Any
of them was likely to be beaten up and locked in a cell, regardless
of why he had come. The delays in bringing accused persons before
the courts grew longer and longer and sometimes they were never
brought at all ... In the courts we complained continually about the
situation but nothing was ever done to improve things.[8]

In such conditions of insecurity and with little hope of anything
but further deterioration, Budo staff and students had to begin the
restoration of their school, knowing that even on a simple return journey
to Kampala they risked violent robbery and even death - possibly at
the hands of the "security" forces.

The second depressing obstacle was the increasing rate at which
trained professionals, including teachers, were quitting the country if
they could. Phares Mutibwa - professor of history and Old Budonian
– commented acidly:

During a period of uncertainty in which nobody believed that
stability could be restored the exodus began with Lule's fall in
1979, increased when Obote returned from Tanzania and Binaisa

was overthrown, and became a stampede when Paulo Muwanga installed his chief Obote in power in December 1980. The net result was to be disaster for the country. The UNLF personnel came, helped themselves to what they could, and left. Those that hung around longer than others did not do so with the true interests of the country in mind. They merely continued to accumulate savings for the day when they would join others in exile.[9]

Bawuuba took over at Budo on 1st December 1979. Ten days earlier, he had written at great length to his former headmaster Ian Robinson - now Rector of Westleton and Dunwich in Suffolk, England - describing the challenge and what he believed were the school's most immediate needs:

> Christine and I were overwhelmed at the magnitude and complexity of the task that lay before us. For one thing, society at large has been dehumanised and lost many of the values and virtues to which many people once aspired. It is an enormous task to try to rehabilitate Budo and its values in such circumstances...

> Students' discipline has deteriorated a great deal. Many Budo students mingle freely with the villagers around and share the same crude waragi, to say nothing of women. Even concerning teachers, a number of them drink heavily and set a bad example. Very few have the commitment that a boarding school demands... Stealing and cheating in one way or another have become commonplace throughout the country and Budo is no exception. Where askaris are employed they do the stealing themselves! ...

> School uniform material is not available and even if it was the prices are prohibitive. As a result students are shabbily dressed in all sorts of clothing...

> Chapel [on Sundays] is still compulsory but the spirit that accompanied it in our days has died... attendance is a mechanical, trivial and childish requirement that is intended for students only and hardly attended by the teachers.[10]

Budonians had been justly proud of the school's academic achievements at the end of 1978, heading the national secondary results at both O and A levels in spite of all the problems and threats. But nobody expected decent results at the end of 1979 with all its traumas for people and buildings - and so much time lost. Bawuuba was also keenly aware of how little the school could offer:

> Even where students manage to do well they do so with a very impoverished kind of education centred on the tactics of passing examinations. The Library has only a few ancient volumes left; the Junior Library is no more! Of the Language Laboratory only the building still stands. No motion pictures, no slides, no charts - nothing but chalk and talk from the teachers!

In describing the state of the buildings he emphasised the leaking roofs and damaged floors of Big School and all its classrooms, which could not be used when it rained; the smashed glass in almost every window and door frame on the Hill - most of the doors having been removed altogether; the ruin of the stage and theft of its huge curtains and all its lighting so that no performances could be held, and the serious damage to the dormitories and most of the teachers' houses. All this was not the product merely of the war and the army occupation. For several years hardly any routine maintenance of buildings had been possible because the school's grossly inadequate funds had largely to be used for an even greater priority - keeping students and staff alive!

> Feeding has become very poor and almost impossible. A sack of beans costs 2000 shillings; meat is 60s a kilo and a loaf of bread 30s. A kilo of sugar is 15s (official government price) but 60s on the actual open market. As a result students are offered just the bare minimum of food - and of poor quality -to enable their continued existence. Meat is eaten once a term! Tea is without milk and sugar. Eating bread is a thing of the past. Despite all these unbelievable prices school income has not increased much from what it was in your time.

Two other areas which concerned him were transport and physical education. He noted a vast difference between his two years as a young teacher at Budo and the present situation. Most of the departed expatriate teachers had owned cars and the school lorry had also been in daily use. Now, with only the large bus - sparingly used because petrol, when available, was costly - Budo had become "an isolated place hated by many of the teachers there". Enthusiasm for games and athletics had also, he believed, virtually disappeared with the expatriates, and the school's sports equipment was worn out or stolen. He realised that little help could be expected from a well- intentioned ministry:

> Naturally one would expect the government to bear the responsibility of repairing and rehabilitating the school. But the government has an enormous task of trying to rehabilitate the various sectors of the country: roads, hospitals, colleges, primary and secondary schools - all of which were severely damaged by the Amin regime. It will take years for government to accomplish this task - if at all. The only alternative left is to engage in self-help projects. In this connection may I suggest that you could appeal on our behalf to Budo lovers and well-wishers to come to our aid at this time?

He made a number of specific suggestions to which Robinson and his former colleagues in Britain were quick to respond. But Budo had first to start the new year 1980.

The staff were encouraged to be led by an experienced Old Budonian determined to restore the best Budo practices and traditions. They had been strengthened too by the removal of several dissident teachers, as the ministry had promised, and by the arrival of William Kayondo. He had been Bawuuba's sturdy deputy at Kampala High School and had acted as deputy to John Mpagi from September 1979. So, with Robina Mirembe as senior woman teacher, there was a strong and trustworthy group at the top.

From the start of the new year, Bawuuba took the students into his confidence and made clear his intention to advance on all fronts. He confirmed his support for compulsory daily chapel, and announced severe punishments for drinking, stealing, breaking bounds, cutting classes and damaging school or inviduals' property. He was frank about the dire food supply, expecting students to respond realistically. He promised that every effort would be made to renovate school buildings and equipment, warning that it would be a long and expensive task. Like Uyirwoth, he was prepared to put great faith in the prefects and to work through them. This was one of Christine's vivid memories: "He valued the prefects very much and always gave them tea at meetings

- with cakes when possible!" He also took great care in the appointment of new teachers, to bring the staff back up to strength for a school of over 600 students. He tried hard to recruit practising Christians, some of them Balokole, and - provided they were the best applicants - Old Budonians.. These efforts were strongly supported by staff and most students, with notable effects. Towards the end of term Robina Mirember wrote cheerfully to Davis, in Lesotho.

> The school is being restored gradually. Students are starting to dress properly in school uniform. Daily chapel is restored - and students behave themselves! Of course a few naughty chaps misbehave but not always - not even when fellow-students are leading. Chapel choir is coming up. Games are back and compulsory. Defaulters are put in the "Black book" and are punished, either on Saturday or Wednesday afternoon. Drinking has reduced considerably, though I imagine the students are fearing the new Headmaster's stand on drinking and perhaps may resume the irresponsible act after some time. The relationship between the HM and staff is apparently healthy ... Sabaganzi and Grace Houses are very tidy - they have a Matron. Sick Bay has a full-time qualified nurse and ward attendant. It has also been restored. Old Budo teachers have promised to help in various ways. Enough on the good side!

> Main hall still leaks badly and the damaged houses. Famine has struck the country - so much that we are finding ourselves almost unable to survive... We had a successful Easter Play. The audience behaved.[11]

In the absence of qualified or interested music staff, Gideon Kasozi, an HSC student and one of Colin Davis's many former piano students, had taken on most of the music responsibilities in the school, while studying for his own university entrance. He shared his new headmaster's view that enthusiasm was the all-important quality for a teacher and he deplored the decline of Budo's former high standards in national music festivals.

> I sincerely believe it is because of lack of encouragement from staff that we have ended up music dwarfs compared to other - even primary - schools. I still conduct the Nightingales who are about to put up an Easter carol service. Chapel choir is also still on my list

of duties ... The piano class is the strongest group I attend to and is gradually improving. Last year one of my piano students did Grade 5 theory and practical and passed very well. I also did Grade 5 theory and Grade 7 practical and passed well - thanks to you. This year two of my students are going for the same (Associated Board) exams. We are continuing with our end of term concerts and I am practising hard for a piano recital ....Mozart sonatas, Chopin nocturne and waltzes, Bach's prelude and fugue and Beethoven's Moonlight sonata...

I hope you've seen last year's results [academic] because I remember you told me you always wanted to know how the school performed. They were both terrible as you can see and Budo was not even among the first five schools in the country as it had always been in your days... We just hope that last year's results were the fruits of war and not of inexperienced teachers, otherwise we are doomed this year - my final one![12]

These relatively poor results had been expected after a year in which Budo had certainly suffered more damage and lost more teaching time than any other leading secondary school. So after a promising start to the new regime, Bawuuba and his colleagues greeted, with optimism and confidence, the large congregation of Old Budonians who, in spite of the risks of the road, assembled on March 29th to celebrate the 74th Founders Day. National morale was sinking and when Obote, from the safety of Tanzania, proclaimed earlier in the month that Uganda was "leaderless" there would have been few knowledgeable Ugandans contradicting him with any conviction.[13] But Budo morale was on the rise and Bawuuba meant to keep it so.

Having begun his first address to his new constituency with the fragment of autobiography already quoted, he struck a historic note:

I stand here to represent all the headmasters of this school that you have known and those that will occupy this seat in the future. That is quite a gigantic position - as you can imagine - for a man of my size... We are assembled here to commemorate the 74th Founders Day... I will therefore continue by making a poor imitation of that great American leader, Abraham Lincoln:

Three score and fourteen years ago, the Reverend H.W. Weatherhead brought forth a new school, based on the proposition that the British and the Ugandans were created equal, so that if the public school was good enough in England, it must be good enough for Uganda.

This was the best that Reverend Weatherhead and his colleagues knew at the time and only the best was good enough for Budo. From its foundations Budo established a tradition of excellence.[14]

He praised and thanked the Old Budonians for having recently provided funds for the school bus and for some books and stationery. But he now appealed for even greater generosity to meet huge immediate needs. He asked for money and gifts of building materials to restore Big School, the dormitories and houses; a mowing machine and tractor to repair and maintain the grounds and playing fields; furniture for the denuded staffroom "which is actually deplorable"; equipment for the Home Economics building, which had been "thoroughly looted so that the girls now have no chance of doing the subject at all"; and a van or small transit to enable regular contact with Kampala for supplies. His most resourceful bid, underlining his emphasis on self-help, was for the school farm:

We are grateful for donations of cattle to our farm. At present we have two cows and one calf, the latest arrival being Nakisunga from Mr Nkambo-Mugerwa's farm. It is our intention to expand the farm, producing enough milk for student consumption. We call for and welcome more donations of cows - even local cattle would be useful at least in clearing our new pasture of ticks! Under the able management of Mr Matembe, a Namutamba Project proponent, I am sure that our farm will flourish. A tractor would greatly enhance our agricultural sector, so that we could grow more food for ourselves.

He appealed also for material for school uniforms, equipment for games and medicines for the sick bay. Finally, he complimented his colleagues and students:

I must state publicly that so far I have found the teachers very co-operative, especially in the areas of discipline and classroom teaching... So far the students too have been positively receptive of good discipline... With such co-operation and with your material and moral support we should be able to undertake successfully this momentous task.

The guests appreciated the school's hospitality in a well organised event and many donations followed.

There was good news too from England. Robinson had convened a London gathering of some twenty-five former staff early in January. They opened a bank account under the title "Budo Response" and set about meeting the most urgent requests. £ 2000 was quickly subscribed and by April supplies were on the way by airfreight - generously negotiated at no cost for a worthy cause. Ten good second-hand microscopes and ten new dissecting kits; a cine-projector; electrical and maintenance equipment; a large parcel of basic medicines with more promised; a range of up-to-date and relevant textbooks; 1000 library books; 100 atlases; a range of sports equipment; and 300 new hymn books for the chapel arrived in a sequence of deliveries through May to September. The bank account appeared elastic because many former colleagues personally paid for items they donated and two schools in which members were teaching, made substantial collections of money and sports equipment. It was a good start with more to follow in 1981-2. Staff were delighted not just with the equipment but the knowledge that friends understood their needs. Bawuuba, Eridaadi Mulira and others wrote warm thanks, knowing that their needs were only representative of the whole nation's:

> The work you are doing for Budo has given us great encouragement. Budo being the heart of Buganda, her suffering is a measure of the suffering of the whole country.[15]

By the beginning of the next Budo term that suffering had intensified.

Binaisa, like Lule before him, announced decisions which he had no power to implement. He dismissed the ruthless Oyite Ojok who was now the effective head of "Defence" and continued to recruit by far the largest army in the country, in support of Obote. On May

10th the Military Commission of the UNLF, led by Paulo Muwanga, denounced the dismissal as "unconstitutional" and the pro-Obote forces took over strategic positions in and around Kampala. The Tanzanian army withdrew from the city to observe developments and on May 12th Radio Uganda announced that

> The Military Commission has taken over all Presidential powers. This is an action of the Military Commission and not of the army.[16]

When this was followed the same day by the threat from Muwanga that the assumption of power was not to be questioned in any court of law, it was obvious that the return of Tanzania's nominee, Obote, must be imminent. After eleven months of ineffectual civilian government Uganda was again under military dictatorship.

Budo's second term of 1980 nevertheless saw some progress with most students keen to study and restore the high standards of success enjoyed before the full effects of Amin's regime were felt. But the continuing lack of windows in most classrooms and houses still played havoc with the timetable, many classes being cancelled because of heavy rain. Bawuuba realised that this must be a priority and gave a brave and resourceful lead. He managed to arrange a significant transfer of foreign currency into the school account, hired a reliable transit van and drove to Nairobi hinself, knowing that window glass, virtually unobtainable in Kampala, was plentiful there. Towards the end of the school holiday he returned, with the van laden with window glass, door and window fittings and some paint, having negotiated numerous roadblocks and examinations of his cargo on the return journey. Christine recalled the jubilation among the staff at the good news: "He got a real hero's welcome!"

The materials were quickly put to use and the students returned in September to a transformed Big School. Robina Mirembe's September letter to Davis mingled rejoicing with harsh realities.

> This way we are pressing on... there is a lot going on. We are in real trouble. Starting from the country - there is chaos. Robbery has increased. From village to village gunmen enter houses and

sweep them clean. We are on the list of those to be visited by these killers. They swept Kitemu [a village nearby on the Masaka road] the other day. In town suburbs people sleep outside their houses - for how long?! Many Ugandans around the centre don't wish for the night to come. Daily, lives are lost.

We are almost through our holidays and a busy term to come for the S4s. S6 will sit next March. This is with our local examinations board - no longer the East African Exams Council. Our former teachers have helped us a lot. The projector arrived - almost every other day there is a film show to teachers and students. (For students it's educative except on Saturdays, when it's entertainment.) Very many books have come - useful for library (at least, most of them). Ten good microscopes with illuminators have also arrived and many other small items. We are grateful to God for this!

The school managed to get a bit of foreign currency and so the headmaster got glasses from Nairobi.. Now our houses, classrooms and dormitories have glass replaced, and they are going to paint some of the buildings as well. There are now enough beds after all that looting. Discipline has also improved - standards haven't... I turned down the invitation to an interview for a job on the Examinations Council. I just fear the town! The extra cash the job offered would all be spent on food - then security.[17]

Samalie Kirya's praise was succinct but she seemed to agree with Robina about academic standards:

Well Budo is quite fine and I think the headmaster is doing a great job. Already they are renovating the school... the students seem to be better behaved. This is very noticeable, especially in chapel. The Senior 6s will do their exams in March next year so still have a bit of time. Generally there is a feeling of relaxation among the students. They seem to see no reason in working hard.[18]

Meanwhile, the preparations for the promised national elections in December 1980 were being murderously undermined by the Military Commission, which had become, in effect, the military arm of Obote's UPC. Supporters and candidates of other parties were intimidated and some brutally killed. In October Yoweri Museveni protested against the violence and denounced Obote's UNLA army as responsible. The leaders of the four largest religious groups, Muslims, Catholics,

Protestants, and Orthodox, petitioned President Nyerere to intervene and send an international force to stem the violence before elections were held. But no action followed; Nyerere insisted that Tanzania must follow the United Nations injunction that no member state should interfere with "the internal affairs of another member".

After helpful pressure by the Commonwealth Observer Group and in spite of gross interference with the Electoral Commission by the Military Commission, which dismissed almost half of the returning officers, elections proceeded on December 10th. By the next afternoon it was clear that the Democratic Party was heading for a handsome victory - actually proclaimed on several international radio stations. That evening Muwanga announced on Radio Uganda that anyone publishing election results before he had personally approved them would be liable to five years imprisonment. That night, after a barrage of unexplained gunfire around Kampala, the secretary of the Electoral Commission and several of the Commonwealth observers fled the country. On the evening of the 12th, Radio Uganda announced that the UPC had "won" 74 seats, the DP 51 and the UPM one. Muwanga later added that the UNLA would be allowed to send 10 members to parliament. All would, of course, be UPC, giving Obote 84 seats with which to construct his second administration.

> Ugandans had not voted for eighteen years. Now their general will as expressed through their choice of representatives, was snatched from them... When the bitter truth registered in the minds of Ugandans, most thought there was no alternative but to fight: the ballot had been tried without success, leaving violence as the only way to dislodge the UPC from its illegal assumption of political power. And fight they did. From February 1981, civil war and chaos raged.[19]

So it was under yet another violent and treacherous regime that Budo staff and students returned to the Hill in January 1981, to try to maintain the democratic school procedures which Robinson, Kyanda, Uyirwoth and Bawuuba had fostered since national independence in 1962. They were met with cheering news. In spite of the reservations of Mirembe and Kirya, Budo had topped the O level result tables for 1980, with 105 candidates obtaining 40 first class certificates, 36 seconds and 21 thirds. This did not equal the successes in Uyirwoth's fourth year, 1978, but, unsurprisingly, the national success rate was low. Robina Mirembe confessed her own underestimate:

> O level results were the best in the country - 40 grade ones - that gives you an idea how poor the results were in the country. Biology was well done - to my surprise. I didn't trust those students![20]

She had accepted Bawuuba's invitation to become acting chaplain for a year - in addition to her considerable responsibilities as head of Biology, warden of Sabaganzi House and leader of Contact - while the chaplain, Laban Bombo, was seconded to England for a year of full-time theological training. It was to be a busy year for chapel because Bawuuba had already announced plans - remarkably ambitious considering the doleful national scene - to commemorate Budo's 75th anniversary with a series of Christian, cultural, and sporting celebrations running from Founders Day March 29th to a weekend of festivities at the end of June. It was hoped that several former staff would be able to come from UK to take part and Bawuuba - always optimistic - appealed for donations in foreign currency.

> For an institution such as ours in Uganda, 75 years of learning is no mean achievement. We intend to celebrate the anniversary in a big way and would like all Old Budonians and friends to join us... The spirit of co-operation, devotion and positive response that is evident throughout the school community is most encouraging.[21]

Unfortunately, the security situation was not, so three former Bazungu headmasters who had hoped to fly out - Lord Hemingford, Cobb and Robinson - were advised in England not to travel to Uganda, though the full extent of disaffection and active rebellion was not understood outside the country for some time. Indeed, the alacrity with which many foreign governments officially recognised Obote's blatantly illegal regime was bitterly disappointing to Ugandans who knew the truth about the "elections" and the machinations which had preceded them.

Seven weeks before the first of the Budo celebrations, however, a first blow was struck against the restored tyranny. It went unreported outside the country, was dismissed as negligible by the Military Commission, but would later be hailed as a turning point for the future democratic Uganda. Yoweri Museveni had openly expressed disapproval of Obote's insinuation towards his former presidency. The overturning of the elections had been his moment of truth. He now believed that only armed conflict could restore honest government. On 6 February, with 27 companions, he made an early morning raid on the military barracks and armoury at Kabamba, north-west of Masaka, hoping to make off with a large cache of arms:

> It seems that neither the UPC nor the Tanzanians believed that we would actually go to the bush and fight . They thought... we would never dare challenge 11,000 Tanzanian soldiers stationed in Uganda ... We knew that we were capable of challenging and defeating them as long as they took an unjust stance against the people of Uganda...

> In the first phase of such a war, survival is success. The Kabamba operation had met this criterion although we had failed to capture the big haul of guns we had expected. We now had 43 rifles... The previous day we had only 27. So we had made a net gain of 16 rifles and one Rocket-propelled Grenade Launcher. This may not seem much but we had not lost anybody and had only one comrade wounded. So in our own terms it was quite a successful operation. [They had also captured eight military vehicles.][22]

Late in March, towards the end of another good term, the first anniversary celebrations went ahead at Budo though not exactly as planned. Erisa Kironde, now returned from Kenya, wrote a frank but cheerful account to the Hemingfords, Cobbs, Robinsons, Kyandas and Uyirwoths:

> Unfortunately we had, at the very last moment, to postpone a major part of our kick-off celebrations after mounting violence. We had planned a fund-raising in the Mayor's Garden, Kampala for Saturday afternoon, but with the felling of major electricity lines,

a broadcasting station, and the disconnecting of telephones, plus the machine-gun spraying of Uganda House - where I work and was at the time - plus the re-emergence of fierce road-blocks and an acute shortage of fuel, we called off the fund-rasing event on the Friday and were lucky enough to get on radio - the external mast based on Soroti... The headmaster wisely insisted that the Service for Sunday stood and we announced a bus service from City Square. It was a very pleasant surprise when at Budo we discovered a much better turn-out than anyone had imagined. Quite a number braved the road-blocks to drive up.

Ernest Sempebwa gave an excellent sermon, while Alex Odong and Jane Kentembwe read the lessons. A marvellous, unprecedented departure was that the service was led by a woman, Miss Mirembe, the acting chaplain and most confident at that... She announced that Queen Elizabeth had sent us a signed present of commemoration - a Bible, brought out by John Wood, a new member of staff.

After chapel we met in the main hall of the Junior School, Old Budonians and some parents, for entertainment - the Nightingales, etc. But the best pieces were by the Junior School, particularly the infants. There were presentations to various groups - oldest Budonian, past teachers, present staff, etc, of the platinum biros you kindly sent. This ended the entertainment and we went in to lunch which, we had insisted, had to be the same as the school's.

So we entered our buses and cars for the journey back.[23]

John Wood, a Cambridge graduate and son of the Bishop of Norwich, had volunteered to come out to Budo for a year - the first expatriate arrival since the mid-1970s - and was already teaching English and history, assisting with chapel, and producing two plays: *Julius Caesar* and *Murder in the Cathedral* were both later taken to the National Theatre and drew enthusiastic audiences. Wood also led the renovation of the Big School stage and the installation of new lighting so that there could be live performances to add to the regular films and discos.

Budo Response continued active from Britain, sending a range of educational aids , and supporting the widening cultural programme - with spare parts for the pianos. One of the largest and most imaginative requests we were able to meet was for an electrically powered maize mill and huller, to serve both the school and nearby villages. Bawuuba and colleagues were delighted:

> We have started the work of installing the maize mill which is going to be housed in the carpentry shop... We look forward to the day when the mill starts functioning, because it is going to be a tremendous money saver as well as income earner... We are actually looking forward to the coming year with confidence now that we are equipped with stationery , electrical items and drugs, all from the Budo Response Fund.[24]

Sadly Robinson had to report the loss of two stalwart supporters, John Hall and Hugh Sylvester. Both had died in their late forties, at the height of their powers, having given loyally of their many talents to the school and then been enthusiastic and resourceful members of the Response, John as scientific adviser and discoverer of good, used equipment, and Hugh as first treasurer.

Robina Mirembe continued to keep Colin Davis in touch with school developments and seemed increasingly optimistic. The Old Budonians had slowly realised that Ishmael Uyirwoth had proved a worthy leader of their school and - a year and a half after his departure - gave a dinner in his honour. Thanks to the foundation he had preserved for Bawuuba to build on, the school was increasingly imbued with a Christian spirit - not without its problems:

> I must say that these days committed Christian students are taking a leading role in the running of the school... All our S6 Contact members have responsibility in the school. On the staff - teaching and non-teaching - there are now many Christians - the only problem is that we belong to different fellowships. [25]

A number of loyal Budonians have spoken of this perennial but rarely acknowledged difficulty. The Balokole are widely admired for their brave and forthright witness to the Faith. Yet they are sometimes insensitive to the hurt given to "ordinary churchgoers" who, because they do not claim personal salvation, are considered inferior and accorded less influence. Bawuuba's Balokole colleagues were undoubtedly a strength to the school but divisions were sometimes created when staff felt that school policy had been formulated at fellowship meetings rather than at full, open staff meetings.

In spite of the dangers of the now entrenched civil war, the June celebrations of the 75th anniversary proceeded as planned. Colin Davis returned to share them, arriving in time to watch a TV programme about the forthcoming events.

> The hill was really looking quite smart ... the grass is being kept under control and lanes were marked out on the athletics field... There are flowers about, notably in Canada's little quad... A greater area is under cultivation, in staff gardens and elsewhere ...cassava is growing on part of a field... the poultry unit is still going. There is more farm at the girls' end and also a section on the Mityana road...

> I was in a way surprised that it was possible to be holding anniversary celebrations at all, but a good number came up in private cars ... Banana trees had been planted halfway along the Budo road to provide an effective welcome...There was drumming as cars arrived. Buses from the Ministry of Finance and Buganda Road Primary School helped with transport.

> The exhibitions were well patronised, including agriculture in the south laboratory... The fundraising auction took the lion's share of the time - a wide variety of goods from farm produce to hoes to radio cassettes to live chickens - the record item being a gas cooker which went for 115,000 Uganda shillings [six months' salary for a young teacher] ... The headmaster's speech included the presentation of cups and pens ... The Minister, Isaac Newton Ojok, spoke without notes and what he said was relevant to the school ... a great contrast with Obote's speech some years ago on a similar occasion.

> The pageant made a happy conclusion to the day's celebrations. Then we were brought back to reality. It was reported by telephone that shots had been fired in Kampala. We were sitting discussing this when the lights went off. One of the buses taking people back was robbed by soldiers who took watches and money ... John Wood spent an uncomfortable night at the National Theatre with one party, while others were refugees for the night at Budo. Monday's story was that there had been a false alarm about guerrillas.[26]

On the Sunday Davis joined a huge congregation for the anniversary service in Namirembe Cathedral and was pleased to hear Gideon Kasozi performing well on the organ. After several days of participation in academic and chapel activities, and renewing many friendships, he flew back to Lesotho early in July, recording in his journal that he had just spent "the best two weeks' of holiday in my life."

In September another former teacher to risk the hazards was Jonathan Watson, treasurer of Budo Response. He was all the more welcome because he had brought with him and steered through the customs procedures and roadblocks a big consignment of sports kits.

> So the school now has 16 pairs of football boots (the things that caused most joy!), 10 footballs, 2 basketballs, 2 netballs, 6 cricket balls, 6 rounders balls, 5 rounders bats, whistles, 20 tape cassettes, typewriter ribbons, and carbon paper, and 3 projector bulbs [all virtually unobtainable in Uganda].[27]

He had arrived during the school holiday but was surprised to find Budo regarding the forthcoming examinations with unusual anxiety. The O level classes had performed so poorly in their "mocks" that they had been required to return for two weeks of the vacation for extra teaching and private study. Transport remained a chronic affliction with the school bus breaking down almost every week. Watson recommended that Budo Response should make a large contribution towards a second-hand, but mechanically sound, estate car which the Uganda Bookshop had offered the school at a generously low price. Car theft was endemic so "a slightly tatty body would be an asset in security terms!"

Watson was also concerned at the effects of the spiralling prices of basic foods, not only on the student diet but on the families of teachers, trying to stretch meagre salaries. Staff were aware that their own untidy appearance in badly worn clothing set a poor example to students.

> Many of them find all their wages taken up in buying food, especially if they have large families. Some have been to Eliezer asking for help, saying that they could not afford to buy trousers, shirts and shoes to teach in. He wondered if there was any way

in which we could help, and thought that second-hand clothing would be very welcome.

By the end of the year Budo Response ensured that several bales of good summer clothing were on the way to the school at the reduced rate of airfreight which had been introduced in recognition of this serious national problem.

While Budo was much engaged by such mundane matters, staff and students knew that throughout Uganda lives were daily at risk. Every Budonian, past or present, with whom I discussed the comparison, felt that the second Obote regime was in many ways even worse than Amin's. This was not only because they considered Amin an uneducated but clever savage, while Obote had received all the advantages of secondary and university education. It was because under Obote violence was indiscriminate and unrelenting. Kasozi had no doubt:

> Violence had been a permanent feature of the Amin regime. Each day, someone in Uganda was at the receiving end of political or other forms of violence. However, violence under Amin was like a tide, peaking and subsiding at certain periods. Whenever there was a political crisis in the ranks of the regime itself, or when an attempt was made to dislodge the dictator, violence intensified. But in the second Obote period violence was always at high tide.

> The greatest disservice Obote did to his country was to return to power undemocratically in 1980... Human error had again changed the course of Uganda's history in a direction that led to more violence... By the time the National Resistance Movement stormed Kampala in 1986, close to half a million people had been killed, the infrastructure destroyed, social services neglected, the economy ruined, the need to preserve the environment forgotten, social discipline abandoned and the quality of life undermined. The Obote terror machine used all methods possible to get victims from the general population.[28]

By the end of 1981 Budonians could have no doubt that these barbaric processes were in full flow. They could counter them only by staying true to their own best values and having faith that in time their tortured country would return to sharing them. Rash attempts by small groups to overthrow the illegal regime had proved suicidal against an iron-fisted government. The news was gradually spreading, however, that Museveni was patiently recruiting and training a guerilla army committed to gaining the confidence of the people by its disciplined defence and support of the innocent. A number of Old Budonians, most notably former head prefect and Makerere graduate Matthew Rukikaire, were committed to supporting him in the bush.

The first term of 1982 hinted at further progress at Budo, with able staff recruited to meet growing student numbers. This was reflected in more good results at O and A levels. Even the difficulty of finding mathematics staff seemed to ease; head of department, Henry Ongicha reassured Davis:

> I am glad to inform you that the department you left ... is now fully staffed and well settled. We now examine the HSC students in March, giving us an extra term which enables us to cover the whole course. Thus you can see the results that our efforts deserved. Another blessing was that the Bazungu group of Old Budonians in Britain sent us some sets of the SMP Advanced Maths - at least one set of books 1-4 between two students.[29]

Yet within six months Ongicha and two other maths teachers had left the country - one to teach in Lesotho and the others to find work outside education. The department was forced to change to an alternative syllabus for S5, pending further appointments. Deputy headmaster, John Mpagi, resigned to take up a post in industry and was succeeded by William Kayondo. Illness and strain took their toll on senior staff. Bawuuba himself had been diagnosed as diabetic but with stable medication soon resumed his strenuous daily routine, which began at 5 am. Robina Mirembe had two periods in hospital with fever and was left with permanent blood pressure problems which limited her activities for several months. But to the surrounding villages the school on the hill must have appeared a haven of calm security; villagers were so fearful of night raids that a number came up every evening to sleep on the compound.

The minister's supportive speech at the 75th anniversary celebration had not translated into much tangible assistance and the third term of

1982 brought a severe shock. The ministry announced that the capitation grant was to be reduced at once to a sixth of the previous year's figure. In effect, the message was that in future they would continue to pay the teachers' inadequate salaries, but all schools must somehow find the rest of their expenses. Budo Parents Association, most of whose members were relatively prosperous by national standards, voted to increase their termly fee payments from 6,000s to 9,000s which was generous but met less than half the deficit. Parents at most other schools could do very little to help. Tom Nabeta wrote to Davis, with baffled concern:

> General education in the country is undergoing some "transformation" - something difficult to understand. Teachers, because of high costs, must supplement their incomes by some other additional jobs. The cost of keeping a child at school has become impossibly high; children in the lower classes have been absorbed into the general money hunt. Teaching materials are inadequate. To run a boarding school is extremely difficult. Morale is generally low.[30]

Budo responded early in 1983, by publishing an impressive edition of *The Budonian*. At a time of intense shortages and low budgets, when hardly any school could produce even a simple broadsheet for local circulation, this 96-page, well printed edition was an outward-looking manifesto to show the country that Budo was growing stronger. The editorial apologised for the long gap since the last edition and thanked all those who had helped the school, and the production of this issue, explaining the wide range of articles, from former staff and from past and present students, young and old:

> To celebrate Budo's 75 years we wanted a kind of "Come together", something that would unite many people in so many different places.[31]

As well as the usual reports from houses, sports teams, societies and clubs, three Old Budonian professors contributed scientifically challenging articles on the prevention of fatal infant diseases in Uganda, important diseases of domestic animals, and the importance of agriculture in schools. Old Budonian lawyer, Eva Mulira, wrote on women and the law; four senior Budo girls wrote two articles "Train a Woman: A Nation Trained," and "Coeduation in Africa Today," concluding confidently that "coeducation is a modern phenomenon and it is here to stay". There was an optimistic report from Manager Azaliya Matembe on the school farm which now had four units - dairy, piggery, poultry and crop. The dairy unit had six cows, three heifers and two bull calves; the poultry unit had over 300 birds and an ambitious target of 1000. The first cassava crop was due in June from 2000 plants, with 80 additional hectares just acquired for the crop unit, a tractor was an urgent need to supplement the usually willing and effective student labour.

The efforts of students and staff on the farm were not, however, entirely altruistic, nor was Budo Response the only overseas body supporting the school - as Samalie Kirya explained to Davis.

> The World Food Programme came to the rescue of the schools in Uganda, by providing milk,beef, tinned fish, rice and cooking oil. The money which would have been used to buy some of the foodstuffs is used for agricultural investment, so that in future we can be self reliant. So every Wednesday afternoon and Saturday morning, selected classes and teachers go down to the farm to work. At the beginning people resented the whole idea, but after the first lot had worked they were each given a tin of fish and the exercise of giving a tin of fish after working continued ... it seems people even beg to go on the farm! On the whole the project seems to have a bright future.[32]

It did. But the school latrines did not. The sealing of old, full latrines and the digging of deep new ones is a skilful and fairly expensive task. It had not been undertaken on the Hill for some years and this year several latrines in the students' Houses collapsed. These occasions created both excitement and initiative. Again Kirya provided wry commentary:

> The latrines at the boys' end are now all down, except for the Australia ones. So there is always a scramble to those - or a quiet visit to the nearest teacher's. The walls of the Nigeria latrine crumbled today. So we all rushed to see what had happened.[33]

Luckily there were no casualties in all this sanitary subsidence and some of the lost latrines could gradually be replaced.

It is salutary to reflect, in view of the erratic water supply which has been a minor theme of this history, what would certainly have been the far worse state of Budo health if Engineer Ian Robinson had not stuck firmly to his unpopular decision that flush sanitation should not be installed. A community of more than 800 students and 200 other residents (including all staff and extensive families) would almost certainly have been frequently afflicted with typhoid fever - as had other communities whose waterborne sanitation had failed. On such apparently minor decisions the survival of even an influential African school can depend.

In mid-year the increasing staff shortage was eased for some weeks by the arrival of Makerere student teachers on final practice. But the school community was dismayed at the loss of a young agriculture teacher, Denis Kabigumira, who died in a motor accident on his way to his home district where he was to be married. Agriculture was slowly growing in popularity with Budo students but good teachers of the subject were still hard to recruit. Staff records and notes suggest that the busy third term went well and that the school stayed fairly healthy in spite of food problems and sanitary shortfalls. At the start of the long December-January holiday, Bawuuba felt able to make a hectic two-week visit to Britain, where he visited many members of the Budo Response team and Old Budonians to offer personal thanks for the help already given and to urge the continuing needs of the school. He was particularly moved by his stay with Ian and Do Robinson in Suffolk:

> On the Sunday I had the opportunity of attending a service in the church of which Ian is Vicar. It gave me a sensational feeling to sit in the pew and see my former headmaster - when I was both pupil and teacher - continuing his leadership role in that different capacity. That afternoon there was a most touching and historic moment when Celia and Timothy Cobb came over to Westleton. It was a most sentimental moment for me to meet again the two senior Headmasters who had contributed so much to Budo, and both been my Headmasters ...Their big shoes into which I stepped are still oversize... but they have done so much to minimise the harsh effects of the prevailing conditions, so that the maintenance of some reasonable standards can still be a reality at Budo.[34]

The year 1984 began well, though first terms were now as intense as others because the large A level classes stayed on for their examinations in March and the top secondary schools depended mainly on A level success and consequent university entrance rates to maintain their reputations. Budo's latest results, from the 1982 entry, had been particularly encouraging. Of 102 candidates 73 gained 3 principal passes - the best results in the country. The growth and popularity of the school meant that the selection processes and other administrative demands were much increased. Bawuuba responded wisely with a restructuring of the senior administration and the appointment of a second deputy head, Robina Mirembe, to share responsibility with William Kayondo. She also shared her apprehensions with Davis:

> I am a lot better healthwise. School has grown larger - 875 students. Real overcrowding. Conditions are rough but we push on somehow and new teachers are added. The Fellowship is at its largest I have ever known. Contact is also large. While all that continued I was promoted Deputy Head... I feel so unworthy and inferior to these experienced people... I still have a full timetable and this makes me totally inefficient on either side. Please ask Mary Kamuhanda to come and pick up my biology! [Mary and Stephen Kamuhanda were teaching in Lesotho.]

In spite of further water problems, when the pump motor at Nansove was again stolen, and a long arid spell affected the crops, the farm boosted the school diet with a regular supply of milk, eggs, maize, potatoes, cassava, groundnuts, green vegetables and - to the delight of Baganda students - the planting of a first large crop of matooke on the newly acquired land. Health continued to be good and the sports programme was well supported. Both football competitions roused great enthusiasm, with Africa House (formerly South Africa) winning the senior cup and Canada the junior.

Late in the year, as violence and lawlessness worsened throughout the country, Budo boys were involved in an incident with villagers. Knives were drawn and one student was killed and four injured. It seemed that the school would be inexorably dragged into the national cycle of slaughter. To those who read the story of Uganda's sufferings twenty years later, it may seem incredible that international outrage was not quickly aroused after Obote's illegal seizure of power and immediate atrocities. It has to be understood, however, that Obote's government quickly suppressed internal criticism, closing down five privately owned newspapers which had tried to report truthfully. Foreign journalists seeking to expose government crimes were promptly deported. Moreover, Obote recruited prominent journalists and African "experts" who were willing to deny reports of massacres by his troops:

> The result was that the groans of Ugandans were inaudible not only within the country but also abroad. The suppression of information was helped by the fact that the international community saw Obote as the only leader who could heal the wounds Amin had inflicted... During the second Obote period, the international community was reluctant to publicise human-rights violations in Uganda. Indeed, various bodies made every effort to strengthen Obote's government.[35]

The first reliable public report of the true scale of the atrocities was made in August 1984 to a committee of Congress, by Elliot Abrams of the US Bureau of Human Rights. He revealed that between 100,000 and 200,000 people had been killed in Uganda since 1981, especially in the infamous "Luwero Triangle". His revelations were not widely reported in the British and European media but, meanwhile, Museveni's trained army, its sphere of operations and its popular support were steadily growing and a notable communication breakthrough resulted:

> That Luwero was indeed the "killing fields" of Uganda is evident from the skeletons, the roofless houses, unkept roads and destroyed schools found in the area from 1986, after the National Resistance Army victory... [This] was revealed to the outside world by William Pike, an independent journalist who spent ten days in the bush with the NRA. Writing in the "Observer" of 19th August 1984, he stated that he had visited the subject areas, seen hundreds of corpses, and interviewed many civilians and several NRA officers. He supported his claims with photographs. This was the first time a credible journalist had given the outside world published reports of the massacres endured by the people of the Luwero Triangle for more than three years.[36]

The school year 1985 opened with the cheering news that the Kamuhanda family were indeed planning to return to Budo. Mary with the children arrived for the last few weeks of the first term and duly relieved Robina Mirembe of much of her biology teaching load. Stephen was to follow in the second term, but they could hardly have chosen a more difficult time to demonstrate their Budo loyalties. Late in March armed men had been seen at Nakibuuka, the coronation site on Budo hill, close to the school boundary. One had questioned a student about the stationing of the school's night watchmen.

On 11 May, about 11pm, a gang of about thirty armed robbers (kondos) arrived on the hill and watchman John Sekimera, who challenged them, was shot dead. They forced entry to the bursar's house and robbed him, two assistants and three other school workers of all their personal belongings. They then ordered the bursar to take them to the headmaster's house. There Bawuuba, his wife and children were threatened at gunpoint and the house was ransacked. Bawuuba was then warned of the watchman's fate and threatened with instant death unless he took the intruders to the bursary. Christine remembered proudly:

> I can never forget the way Eliezer reasoned quietly with them, knowing that they might shoot him at any moment. But they forced him to open the Bursary. They had come for money and they got it.[37]

The timing of the raid was either well-informed or lucky, because there was an unusually large amount of cash in the safe and over 4 million shillings was taken. But no more blood was shed. It was a terrifying ordeal for the Bawuuba family - and was shortly to be repeated.

On 15 July Bawuuba's home was again invaded. This time his hands were tied and he was taken at gunpoint to the houses of the bursar and the purchasing officer. Lessons had been learned from the first robbery and there was little in the safe - which, with hindsight, might well have enraged the kondos and cost Bawuuba his life. All three houses were again plundered, and the stock of essential drugs stolen from the sick bay. The delusion that Budo was a safe haven had been shattered.

Meanwhile, national events were moving rapidly against Obote. The revelations of August 1984 had led to the withdrawal of most of his international support. After the death in action of his chief of staff, Oyite Ojok, wide divisions opened up between his Acholi and Langi supporters in the army and the cabinet. One faction wanted to negotiate with Museveni and his NRA, the other, led by Obote himself, was determined to fight on. By late June, Obote's new chief of staff was being openly disobeyed by General Tito Okello and in the north General Bazilio Okello ignored Obote's personal orders. Obote was unable to resist the mutiny and on 27th July 1985 Radio Uganda announced that he had been deposed and his government replaced by yet another Military Council. Its chairman, Tito Okello, became head of the government and president of Uganda, with Bazilio Okello as chief of staff. Obote had fled. With Museveni's NRA still gaining ground, few believed the new regime could last long.

At Budo, Deputy Head William Kayondo's loyal service had been recognised by his promotion to the headship of Busoga College, Mwiri. Stephen Kamuhanda, experienced and popular former Budo teacher and deputy head, was expected to succeed him. Arriving just after the July attack on the Bawuubas, he had a dramatic reintroduction to Uganda:

> There was great fear all round and parents were doing their best to calm the situation... There were meetings between staff, parents and workers. It appeared there were some informers or collaborators within the system. However there have not been any attacks since I came - we are relatively quieter and calmer. But on Saturday - the Coup!... When the second term ended on July 25th little did anyone know that Obote's second government would be overthrown on the 27th and Kampala looted for the second time!...I was in Kampala that morning. I hid for three days. I found the school very worried that I had "disappeared" - they were very happy to see me back. Our Toyota car was looted and dismantled... but many people have lost immense properties and many lives continue to be lost in the country. Peace is still elusive! We are being hemmed in on many sides, notably the western...
>
> The school is good. I was appointed Deputy Head on August 25th and we opened again on the 26th. Many students returned

- others waited and have been trickling in. The school is very orderly and well run. Students, prefects etc. run everything... The system is, surprisingly, moving smoothly despite the problems. It is a tremendous encouragement - we are trying to do our best. Chapel is attended in full - but very few teachers come! There are many young teachers so the staff is lively. The school is very big, around 1000. Many stand in chapel and in the mess but there are no problems. Still staff are not enough. Sports Day was September 14th but fewer guests than were expected turned up, due to the situation - two days after clashes between the army and the NRA in various parts. Those who turned up were very encouraging.

Peoples' morale is just incredibly high for the school - and their support in kind (bus being repaired by parents! etc). Robina is well - very commanding. The three of us, including Eliezer, work harmoniously. It is a happy atmosphere, if it was not for other factors beyond our control. Budo community welcomed us very warmly and their warmth has kept us going... In Uganda now we don't know what the next hour will bring.[38]

With Museveni's NRA gaining ground from Masaka towards Kampala, and the Okellos' army - still known as the UNLA - trying to create defensive positions along the Masaka road from the city towards Budo hill, it seemed inevitable that the school would again be embroiled in the war. On 19 October it was rumoured that fighting near the hill was imminent and many parents came up to the school asking to be allowed to take their children home. Bawuuba was off the hill and Kamuhanda and Mirembe, sympathising with the parents' anxiety allowed a number of students to leave. When Bawuuba returned, the triumvirate discussed the issue carefully and decided that, since students were likely to be at least as safe at Budo as they would be in homes near Kampala, or travelling home long distances in lawless conditions, no more departures should be supported. They knew that the ministry would not authorise the closure of the school, since that would be to admit that the regime was at risk.

Yet without reasonable numbers in class it would be difficult for the school to function. As rumours grew wilder - with no one able to contradict them confidently - parents grew more insistent. But Bawuuba and colleagues, convinced that school routine could be maintained, required parents to sign a form accepting responsibility:

> After getting a briefing from the Headmaster that the school is still running, and that there was no reason as yet to close it, I still have decided to withdraw my child, on the understanding that the withdrawal is indefinite.[39]

One parent - hedging his bets - signed but added the reservation "To be contested later".

Kamuhanda wrote an impressive account of what followed; the events and motivations warrant substantial quotation from it:

> Withdrawals continued and children were taken home in large numbers. The staff decided to continue teaching - a courageous act... Budo was in the danger zone. If the NRA forces moved from their hideouts in the Western - Mpigi direction fighting was inevitable and Budo would again either be caught in the crossfire or used as a battlefield... By October 30th only 250 students remained. They were mainly O and A level students who had chosen to remain, to "read" on their own. The staff were willing to help them. It was a tremendously challenging experience.
>
> At the short staff meeting on November 1st it was decided that internal school exams would be conducted as scheduled. The staff were determined to make this a success. Learning that both internal and O level exams would be held, some parents then started returning their children. Almost all were returned... on November 10th shooting, at times with heavy weapons, broke out close to Budo - it caused a lot of concern. O level exams started on November 11th. As the candidates were beginning their first paper, the master on duty came running to report that a group of soldiers were advancing towards the school from Kitemu to the west, and the people were already fleeing their homes in the villages. A quick decision was made to ask the two policemen now stationed on the campus, to wear their uniforms and go to meet the soldiers to implore them not to disturb the school.
>
> Meanwhile large crowds of villagers were already pouring onto the campus, some with stories of people who had already been beaten up in the villages. As the policemen moved towards the soldiers we were busy directing the refugees to the lower field,

near the Girls' End. At the same time we were trying to calm down the other students - who had become excited at the whole incident - while hiding the whole scare from the O level students writing their exams in the Main Hall. By noon the soldiers had been persuaded to go back to Kitemu/Nsangi, people were returning to their homes in the villages, and the candidates had completed their papers, ignorant of what had happened.

The examinations and the normal end of term proceeded without serious interruption. On November 25th, Budo's cherished annual end-of-year Prize Giving was held. The Guest of Honour, Mr S. Kiyingi, praised the school's stand and achievements:

Although we are living in an abnormal situation due to the current war, Budo's courage to push on has been noted by all interested in the school.

While that ceremony was going on the Budo choir had been into Kampala in the school lorry to record Christmas carols for Uganda Television. On the way back their lorry had been stopped at the Budo junction on the Masaka road and commandeered by soldiers of the Okello government. The choir were forced to get out and had to walk the two and a half miles up the hill to the school. The driver and his assistant were then ordered to take the soldiers to a battlefield west of Budo, to carry dead and wounded back to Kampala mortuaries and hospitals. Having done so, the drivers were, surprisingly, released with their lorry to return to Budo. The school year ended on November 29th.

On 17th December a peace agreement was signed in Nairobi between the ruling Military Council and the National Resistance Movement and Army. It was soon breached by the Okello army, however, and robbery and killing continued unchecked. Staff and students spent an anxious Christmas on the Hill, with armed soldiers sighted several times - once retreating in the face of shots from the school-based police. The conviction of Bawuuba and his deputies that students would be safer at Budo was sadly confirmed, when S6 student Herbert Miiro was shot dead at his parents' home at Nakasozi, having raised the alarm as UNLA uniformed men forced the doors.

The beginning of 1986 was rather peaceful at Budo... The new term began on January 6th. The school electricity supply was disconnected on the 16th, to allow dangerous trees to be cut down. It was to have been reconnected the following day but this was not in fact to be done for over two weeks, until February 1st.

On 17 January, exactly a month since the Nairobi Agreement was signed, heavy fighting resumed between the Military Council and the NRA. Heavy firing continued in the neighbouring villages, and the Kampala-Budo road was quickly cut off - the very thing everyone had feared all along... There was nothing else to do now, no safe direction to take. We feared the deadly helicopter gunships that were flying from Entebbe close to Budo to bombard the NRA positions in the Buloba area. The drama of the gunships, added to the heavy artillery bombardment and small arms fire, lasted the whole day and successive days.

There was only one short-cut - through Kasenge village to join the Entebbe-Kampala road - to reach the city. Fighting had not yet spread that way, but it was very risky to attempt it. The headmaster risked it in order to reach Kampala, to get the UEB technicians to reconnect the electricity.

Meanwhile, Deputy Head Prefect Edward Lubwama, alerted the deputy heads that the school was becoming very alarmed at the situation. As Bawuuba left the hill, Kamuhanda convened a full assembly in the chapel. With a commendable show of optimism he advised every one that there was no point in panic. Since they were now cut off from parents in almost all directions it was best for all to stay together on the hill. His cheering message was somewhat undermined when the chapel walls were shaken by very heavy artillery fire, just north of the hill. Bawuuba managed to reach the UEB but their promise of reconnection the next day was negated when the fighting spread to the Kamapala- Entebbe road and there was no longer any way through from the city to Budo.

Having no electricity throughout these two violent weeks must have been unnerving, especially at night while the guns continued to pound. But school morale held. An attempt to get the Red Cross to bring food and drugs - and perhaps raise their flag on the hill in the hope of gaining immunity from attack - failed. This was not only because the school was completely cut off; the Red Cross already had more wounded refugees in and around Kampala than it could treat or feed.

Lack of power affected the school greatly. We had no water - students had to carry it from Nansove. The maize mill could not work; posho, the diet we depended on, was running out - and there was no maize grain to mill anyway. Since we could no longer get assistance from anywhere we had to cope as best we could. We worked out a system of security precautions. When going for water students had to wear white school uniform, for identification. They had to move together and not panic on seeing soldiers. In spite of this frightening and hopeless situation, we continued with classes.

On 22nd January a number of pigs had been slaughtered on the farm. This was to "save" them from being eaten by unruly soldiers who were expected to attack at any time. We were all enjoying a rare meal of pork when reports reached us that government UNLA soldiers, having been hit hard by the NRA, were pulling back in panic towards Kampala. Our fear intensified. As a last resort UNLA forces could attack us as they pulled back. "Refugees" were pouring onto the campus from the villages. These were accommodated in the Main Hall and the Music room.

On 24th January we attended classes as usual. Those who still had radio sets were telling us that... NRA forces had reached the outskirts of Kampala, which was experiencing the heaviest artillery bombardment - for the second time in less than ten years. By 2pm the artillery duels were so heavy and demoralising that everybody had to vacate classes and all reading activities stopped.

The students and staff and the entire community gathered in groups on the eastern side of the hill - to watch the city burning. Our morale reached the lowest level ever, as we did not know what would happen to parents, relatives and friends in the besieged city under such intensive fire. As we watched the exchange of artillery and the burning fires in Kampala, we could not contain feeling a sense of security for ourselves. The UNLA soldiers had completely pulled out of the surrounding areas, while the NRA had actually taken over the same areas without a fight.

By 25th January Budo was being used as a place of refuge for our still unfortunate countrymen from the battle areas along the Entebbe-Kampala road and the outskirts of the city. 300 students from St Mary's College, Kisubi, were warmly welcomed from the fierce battle around their school. They were accommodated, and were fed on the last of our posho and beans rations, in a spirit of love and brotherhood.

Preaching in the school chapel in a dramatically changed situation on the morning of January 26th, the Headmaster, Mr Bawuuba, humbly declared that Budo had been saved from catastrophe miraculously. On January 29th as Yoweri Museveni, the leader of the National Resistance Movement and Army, was being sworn in as Uganda's tenth Head of State since Independence in 1962, the Budo staff travelled peacefully by the school bus to Kampala, some to witness the ceremony. The road to Kampala was now open and Budo was able to replenish in time the posho that was almost running out. As far as Budo was concerned, Uganda's second Liberation War was over.[40]

The achievements of Yoweri Museveni and the National Resistance Army had been patient, slow, relentless and unique. Kasozi found the right words with which to salute them:

> The duty of the National Resistance Army was to organize and win the war effort, politicise the army, educate the public and defend the population. Few Ugandans can say that it did not achieve these goals and it did so by strong organisation at the grassroots level, forming resistance councils in villages, parishes and in sub-counties with clarity of aim and dedication. It accomplished its task because its aims and military strategies were clear...

> The NRA victory in Uganda was quite unusual in Africa. It marked the first successful overthrow of an indigenous government by a locally based guerrilla movement. The NRA was the first locally trained army on the continent to defeat a professionally trained army led by majors and captains who had trained in the best military academies of the West and the East. It was the first fighting unit in Africa to depend on internal resources: it captured most of its war materials from the enemy, it was sustained by local resources and it depended on local manpower. What little help it got from abroad (not over five percent of its total needs)

was of supplemental value only. And lastly, as far as Uganda was concerned, the myth of "warrior tribes" was exploded. There was a belief that only Lwo and Sudanese speakers (Northerners) could fight and that Bantu speakers of the South could not... The Bantu speakers can fight, just as the Lwo speakers can, if they are well trained and equipped with a cause.[41]

Museveni's cause was nothing less than the complete freedom, safety and prosperity of his people. It seemed possible that after eighteen years of suffering, Uganda might enter upon a new era.

The physical, economic and spiritual ravages of the now vanquished tyrannies had cut so deep that, even under the most enlightened and successful new government, the recovery of the country and of Budo was bound to be slow and painful. For the school there was poignant irony within days of Museveni's victory. Headmaster Eliezer Bawuuba was taken ill and by March he and Christine knew that he would have to continue his leadership - through the first period of peaceful and consistent government support he had experienced - with a stomach cancer which the doctors considered serious but treatable. Typically he did not allow this to prevent him presiding at the 80th anniversary celebrations on April 20th, near the end of a turbulent but ultimately joyful term which had lasted four months. Government approval was signalled by the presence, as guest of honour, of the new prime minister, Old Budonian, Dr Samson Kisekka. (Museveni himself had not been "Budo and Makerere" but - equally distinguished in quality if not antiquity - "Ntare School and University College, Dar es Salaam". He was to prove a staunch supporter of Ugandan education in general and of Budo.)

In welcoming the many guests - some of whom had just returned from exile, had not seen their school for almost 20 years and found it sadly changed - Bawuuba was both proud and ruefully realistic:

> It is always a moment of great pride and gratification to welcome back such distinguished sons and daughters of King's College, Budo... 80 years should have been marked by a lot of development in many fields... Instead, 80 years have found us almost in the seventh of Shakespeare's "Seven ages of Man" - "sans teeth,

sans eyes , sans taste, sans everything!" Some of our buildings are near collapse from lack of maintenance, teaching is very impoverished for lack of textbooks, scientific equipment and scholastic materials...

However, we are not completely without... We have exerted ourselves to maintain the tradition of excellence, in the academic field, drama, music and sports... In academic performance we rank among the best five schools in the country. Our average admissions to the University stand at about 70% and most of our other A level students gain entry to other higher institutions...[42]

He catalogued the range of school achievements from football and athletics to music, farming and drama, ending with an invitation - laudable considering the events of the term - to a National Theatre performance, the following week, of the school's production of Gogol's *The Government Inspector*.

He ended by listing the fund-raising events planned for the second term - a sponsored walk, a lottery and an auction - appealing for the support of all present, to supplement whatever help a hard-pressed government might be able to give. He thanked his colleagues and appealed on their behalf:

Lastly, we hope that in this ninth decade, the dignity of the teaching profession will be restored, so that the teacher's monthly salary will enable him, or her, to buy more than just two or three bunches of matooke, as is the case at the moment. We also hope that travelling up the Budo road will be made more comfortable.

The government had an overwhelming list of "priorities". Both pleas would eventually be granted, but not until Budo's tenth decade.

Students and staff returned cheerfully for the second term, perhaps expecting that their new freedom from fear and high hopes for the future would be reflected in excellent discipline and mutual support, especially of their ailing and much-loved headmaster. Human communities seldom function so predictably, schools and colleges being no exceptions. Robina Mirembe kept Davis up to date:

We have gone through a very trying time as administrators. With high fees (many schools charge more than us!) and some loopholes, students were itching for a strike. The worst was when breakfast porridge was poor - not too poor to be taken though - and boys poured it all over the Mess, threw dishes in all directions - and then cooled off. We then suspended some and, funnily enough, the Minister didn't like it! There is increasing misconduct... some few parents and students want Eliezer removed. Well, the truth is that with the new Government, this strict fellow with his saved group, should be removed... The Board is with us. So is a number of PTA members and of course a number of parents. Many of those who make noise might have been disappointed at the suspension of their children...

A happier note. Our O and A level results were very good - A level the best we've had for years. Maths was so good, especially Subsidiary Maths which the biologists usually fail - and it's now a necessity at University. Other schools did relatively poorly but when one takes into account the time of war, then they tried! Maths teachers are a problem...Chemistry has only one graduate teacher, going on maternity leave any time now... Inflation is at its worst... [43]

Anxieties about violence gave way to strains of real financial hardship among the staff, who had themselves to try to raise school fees for their own children when their salaries would not stretch even to buying second-hand clothes. Yet they worked loyally through the rest of the year which ended calmly, with discipline improved and the tough response to the Mess demonstrations vindicated. Bawuuba proposed and the governors approved a scheme for reduced fees at Budo Primary and Secondary Schools, for the children of lower paid staff who had served for several years.

Early in 1987 a new edition of *The Budonian* appeared, carrying a good range of articles including Kamuhanda's account, quoted above, of Budo's survival of the war of liberation. It included a tribute to an outstanding Budo student, teacher, parent, governor and friend, Erisa Kironde, who had died of a heart attack in November 1986 aged 60, still with much wisdom and energy to give. Also significant, following the bold lead of Museveni's government, was a frank article by Old Budonian Dr G .M. Jagwe on "Slim or Aids - Acquired Immune

Deficiency Syndrome". The syndrome appeared to have claimed its first Budo victims: Three students had died in three months, one of leukaemia and two of infections possibly not resisted because of AIDS. Any student with signs of serious sickness was now being dispatched to hospital. Dr Jagwe advised:

> By mid-September 1986, the World Health Organisation had received reported cases of AIDS amounting to 31,646 from 100 countries. 26 countries had not reported cases, though we are told that diseases do not respect political boundaries! The Americas accounted for 26,166 cases - mostly from the USA. Europe for 3127 cases and Africa 1008 cases, from 10 countries. These figures are but a small fraction of the disease. Uganda had reported 766 cases to WHO. This was because the Government took an open attitude towards this disease. Hiding a disease or the facts about a disease, is a sign of backwardness.

The school took his advice and later gave a lead to other schools keen to launch programmes of AIDS education.

On Founders Day, 29th March, Bawuuba found a tactful way to express his disappointment that the good intentions expressed by many Old Budonians were not yet being validated by generous gifts. His skilful sermon on "Building and Re-building" drew on The Book of Nehemiah, but the sting was in the introduction:

> "Gakyali Mabaga" is a response from someone who is actively and actually engaged in the task of building. It cannot apply to someone who has only a theory about building, however elaborate that theory might be. It would seem that the assumption behind the school motto is that everyone who goes through this school would be engaged in the act, the task of building or rebuilding. Budonians of all categories: Teachers, Students, Old Boys and Girls, should all be engaged in the task of building, to live up to their motto.[44]

A few weeks later, Bawuuba was again in Mulago Hospital for treatment and then at home for a period of recuperation. Stephen Kamuhanda was acting head and though Robina Mirembe also had a few weeks sick leave, she was able to support him and their colleagues in steering the school through the rest of what she described as "a busy year which had passed quickly".

Stephen Kamuhanda wrote to Davis at the beginning of the new year 1988, with Bawuuba again in Mulago and apparently responding to treatment. It seemed that there had also been some generous responses to his stirring Founders Day sermon:

> We've been very busy... I have been to the Political School in the Luwero Triangle representing the Headmaster who could not go on health grounds. He has severe back pain but is slowly improving... But we are working in a peaceful environment. The only problem is the ever-worsening inflation which the government has not been able to arrest...There have been permanent, frequent power cuts, water shortages, pump breakdowns etc until the pump was completely written off. The new term has started without water and students have again to carry it from Nansove. We are trying to import a new pump but don't know when it will be here. The parents will pay, so fees will go up. Exams were well conducted. Teachers remained fairly stable though a few left. There are also some achievements as well. We got a new tractor, paid for by the World Food Programme. Then we got two new lawn mowers, one donated by an Old Budonian, the other by our Finnish PE teacher, Paula Turpeinen. We got a new Isuzu pick-up from the Ministry of Education. Kenya has now closed the border and there is a shortage of fuel in the country.[45]

The school negotiated hard for foreign exchange to pay for a new diesel engine from Kenya for the water pump. It arrived, but over Easter thieves broke in and stole it. Kamuhanda and colleagues spent hours in the forest down the hill and actually found it, with a number of parts stripped off. The recently recruited new bursar then absconded with a large sum of money; throughout the country crimes of violence had decreased but embezzlement was still rife.

Eliezer and Christine Bawuuba were flown to England where he had the latest cancer treatment at the Royal Marsden Hospital and responded well. The government had not offered any substantial improvement in the pay and conditions of teachers and because, as the national economy began to recover, graduates were in demand by commerce and industry which promised much higher remuneration, significant numbers of teachers left the profession. From Budo, for example, Samalie Kirya joined Uganda Hotels and was sent for training to the University of Leeds in England, while Mary Kamuhanda joined the Bank of Uganda. With class sizes now touching 60, even for O level, teaching seemed a constant struggle. Budo had one interesting advantage, that the police post which had been provided during the year before the NRA victory, had been maintained and provided a considerable sense of security.

Because of Bawuuba's long stay in England, Founders Day celebrations of the 82nd anniversary were postponed until October. Kamuhanda welcomed a large gathering and was happy to report that Bawuuba was back at Budo after successful treatment and would be joining the celebrations. He stressed the urgent needs of the school - new buildings for the increased numbers, repairs to old buildings, a replacement for the unreliable ten-year-old lorry, books, and classroom, laboratory and sports equipment. He announced a positive innovation:

> The Executive of the Old Budonian Club has decided to award a King's College, Budo Order of Merit. It is planned that this Certificate will be awarded to distinguished Old Budonians.

(During sixteen subsequent years of the award the selection process has been austere, and has insisted that recipients shall have made a notable contribution to Uganda as well as to their school.) It was also announced that, to co-ordinate the efforts of all who wished to help the school, it had been agreed to set up a standing committee of representatives from the governors, the Old Budonians and the Parent Teacher Association. This was a self- effacing gesture by all three bodies, particularly the Old Budonians who had in the past often enjoyed influence well beyond their level of support. Bawuuba, warmly welcomed, pursued this theme in his short speech. He struck two warning notes, one of them personal:

> I first of all give thanks to God that I am able to be with you at all ... to welcome you to this lovely hill, King's College, Budo. As I have not completely recovered and am in fact expecting to go back to Britain shortly for further treatment, I will make only a few remarks for your contemplation. If you have read "King's College, Budo: The First Sixty Years", you will have noticed that a lot of the

building of the school was done by the involvement of students and Old Budonians, as well as leading figures of the Buganda government at that time. This spirit of self-help, especially by the Old Boys and Girls of the school, is, unfortunately, not as strong and healthy as one would have desired. I want to appeal to you, Ladies and Gentlemen, that this spirit is revived...

I have noticed that a number of Old Budonians love the school as long as they are parents; once their children leave the school, their love tends to vanish! Secondly, a number of prospective Budo parents show a lot of enthusiasm and love for the school, but if they fail to get admission for their children that tends to be the end of the story... Budonians are now so many that it is impossible to expect that every Budonian will have at least one child here... I therefore appeal to you, not to love the school for what you can get from it, but to love it because it has contributed in making you what you are...

Ladies and Gentlemen, if in the course of my remarks I have offended anybody, I beg your pardon, but my remarks were made in good faith, in the hope of provoking you to action for the betterment of King's College, Budo.[46]

It was a stirring Founders Day summons, which made an impact and probably gave no offence. Those of us who knew Bawuuba, as student, teacher, headmaster and friend, would be confident that he would have made the same gently provocative speech if he had known that it would be his last.

Stephen Kamuhanda could not know this either. In his meticulous handing over notes of 2 December, he expressed his great joy at his close friend's improved health. He paid tribute to the staff, especially deputy head Robina Mirembe and acting deputy Ida Songa, for their energy and loyalty during the head's long absence. He stressed the inadequacy of the government grant of 1500s per student per term, and that Budo's termly charge of 13000s to parents was one of the lowest in the country for comparable schools. In spite of additional PTA help, Budo was running on a bank overdraft. Dscipline had been good overall but there had been some beatings of S1 students and he thought the staff needed "to tighten up even more on acts or threats of bullying next year". The farm continued to contribute well to the school diet but was not, he warned, making any profit. He looked forward greatly to continuing their partnership in 1989.

But it was not to be. The ministry, in confidential consultation with the governors and Mulago Hospital, ruled firmly that the pressures of the headship were too great for Bawuuba's precarious health.

The ministry kept its promise that he could, if he wished, return at any time to his former post of assistant chief inspector of schools; it now asked him to do so. He lodged a courteous written protest, but then settled down to prepare his long handing-over report, which he submitted on 12 January 1989. It included warm tributes to colleagues, students and governors:

> I would like it to go on record that I have enjoyed the highest co-operation possible from the Board. Their sacrifice of time, energy and talent has been commendable and most appreciated.

Characteristically, his final concern was for the future of his colleagues and of the staff assistance packages which he had developed over several years, with governors' support. The aim had been to help staff in a variety of ways, to attract them to stay for many years at Budo. He was sure that they had been a major factor in enabling the school to retain its senior staff. Ten such packages were being offered in 1989. He asked that the scheme not only be retained but expanded.

In assessing Bawuuba's ten years of leadership, it is salutary to remember that though a number of schools in the Luwero Triangle had been destroyed during the second Obote regime (though with nothing approaching the systematic national scale of destruction achieved, for example, in Cambodia / Kampuchea in the 1970s or in the catastrophic floods in Mozambique in 2000) hundreds - primary and secondary–had survived the dictatorships of both Obote and Amin. In his valuable doctoral study, published as *Preserving Order Amid Chaos: The Survival of Schools in Uganda 1971-86*, John R Paige[47] studied four secondary schools in the Kabarole district of Toro: Kyebambe Girls; St Leo's College; Nyakasura and Mpanga. He suggested three possible interpretations of "survival": As disabled war veterans, whose recovery would be slow; as institutions continuing in irreversible decline towards slow death; or as permanently failing institutions.

He stressed the importance of not having been physically embroiled in the wars. Kabarole had been relatively peaceful throughout the Amin and Obote regimes and the schools had never been attacked. Even in 1985, Obote's UNLA had surrendered to Museveni's NRA without a battle, sparing Fort Portal (Kabarole) from damage. [The contrast with schools near Kampala was striking.] Other main features which he believed had enabled the schools to continue had been: Freedom from government interference; support from parents, families and clans; a spirit of acceptance, fostering patience, hope and ingenuity; Uganda's legendary thirst for education; and the influence of religion/ support of the churches. Budo's first three African headmasters had all skilfully either fostered or exploited these advantages. But they had huge added hardships and dangers to negotiate - none more than Bawuuba.

He continued as long as he could with his inspectorate responsibilities, carrying a gradually lightening load until, after more than a year, it was beyond him. He died on 29 June 1990. The ministry's judgement had been both sound and kind. That did not dissuade some excessively loyal colleagues and parents from protesting that "government" had dealt harshly with their lost leader.

Christine would have none of it. She looked back gratefully to the Budo years:

> The Government tried hard to save his life. I shall always feel happy that he was successful at Budo, raising academic standards and improving the discipline, music and games. I shall always be glad that we came back.[48]

They had given all they could to Budo during ten years which, in spite of all the problems and perils, can perhaps best be described as - blessed.

Notes

1 Headmaster's address, Founders' Day, March 1980. KCB archives.
2 Christine Bawuuba in personal conversation with the author, March 2004
3 Samalie Kirya to Colin Davis, 12 November 1979.
4 Kasozi, *op. cit.* pp. 129-131.
5 *Ibid*, p.133.
6 *Ibid*, p.134.
7 Allen, Sir Peter Jermyn, Days of Judgement, London: Kimber, 1987. pp. 179-182.
8 *Ibid*, p. 182.
9 Mutibwa, Phares: *Uganda Since Independence*, Kampala, Fountain, 1992, p. 122
10 E.K. Bawuuba to I.C. Robinson, 21 November 1979.
11 R. Mirembe to C. Davis, 7 April 1980
12 G. Kasozi to C. Davis, 21 March 1980
13 Kasozi, *op. cit.* p. 135.
14 Headmaster's address, Founders' Day 29 March 1980. KCB archives.
15 E.M.K. Mulira to I.C. Robinson, 28 February 1980
16 Kasozi *op. cit.* p. 136.
17 R. Mirembe to C. Davis, 9 September 1980.
18 S. Kirya to C. Davis, 28 September 1980.
19 Kasozi, *op. cit.* p.144.
20 R. Mirembe to C. Davis, 16 April 1981.
21 E.K. Bawuuba: Letter to Old Budonians and Friends, 26 September 1980
22 Museveni, Y.K. *Sowing The Mustard Seed*, London: MacMillan 1997, pp.121-128.
23 E.K.Kironde to Hemingford,Cobb, Robinson, Kyanda and Uyirwoth, 9 April 1981.
24 E.K. Bawuuba to I.C. Robinson, 29 December 1981.
25 R.Mirembe to C. Davis, 16 April 1981.
26 C. Davis, Journal, 20 June to 6 July 1981.

[27] J. Watson to I.C. Robinson, 11 September 1981

[28] Kasozi, *op. cit.* p. 145.

[29] H. Ongicha to C. Davis, 17 June 1982.

[30] T. Nabeta to C. Davis, December 22nd 1982.

[31] *The Budonian* 1983, p. 5.

[32] S. Kirya to C. Davis, November 29th 1982

[33] *Ibid*, April 1983.

[34] E.K. Bawuuba, Report of a Trip to Britain, 23 February 1984.

[35] Kasozi, *op. cit.* p.161.

[36] *Ibid*, p. 185.

[37] Christine Bawuuba, personal conversation with the author, March 2004.

[38] S. Kamuhanda to C. Davis, 18 September 1985.

[39] *The Budonian* 1987, p. 10.

[40] Ibid, pp. 9-15.

[41] Kasozi, *op. cit.* pp. 165 and 175.

[42] Headmaster's address at 80th Anniversary celebrations, 20 April 1986, in KCB archives.

[43] R. Mirembe to C. Davis, 30 September 1986.

[44] Headmaster's sermon, Founders Day, 29 March 1987, in KCB archives.

[45] S. Kamuhanda to C. Davis, 24 January 1988

[46] Headmaster's address at 82nd Anniversary celebrations, 2 October 1988, in KCB archives.

[47] Paige, John R, *Preserving Order Amid Chaos*, New York/Oxford: Berghahn Books, 2000

[48] Christine Bawuuba, personal conversation with the author, March 2004.

12 🦁

Peaceful Expansion: The Challenges of Success 1989-1999

Bawuuba formally handed over on January 27th 1989 to the new headmaster, Samuel Busulwa, who brought to Budo even wider educational experience than his predecessor. He had been a pupil first at Mengo Junior School, then at Bishop's School, Mukono to O level and at Old Kampala School for A levels. At Makerere he had graduated with a BA in Economics and Religious Studies, and then completed the one year post-graduate certificate in Education. After three years as assistant master and hostel master at Bishop's Mukono he was, as Bawuuba had been, awarded a two-year scholarship to the USA. He took a master's degree programme in Religious Studies in Virginia and then courses in Education at Teachers College, Columbia, New York.

Returning to Uganda he taught briefly at Ngora and Masaka secondary schools and was then head of department of RE and history back at Bishop's Mukono. Valuable experience of a crowded "two shift" system, as head of History and director of examinations at Kitante Secondary School was followed by headships at Aggrey Memorial School and then Mengo Senior Secondary School, where he had served since 1985 and also been elected chairman of the Secondary Head Teachers Association. In that capacity his advice on the Budo situation had been sought by both Bishop Kauma and the Minister of Education, distinguished Old Budonian, Mayanja-Nkangi. After a special meeting of the new standing committee of governors, Old Budonians and PTA representatives, Busulwa had accepted the invitation to be interviewed, knowing that some Budo staff resented the ministry pressure on Bawuuba to resign - though the chairman of governors had actually asked him to do so.

Budo was lucky to have such a well-reputed and experienced candidate, but apparently not all members of the panel thought so. Early in the interview a governor asked him how he thought he would cope with the serious disadvantage of not being an Old Budonian:

> I replied that I saw little difficulty in this since most of their previous headmasters had not been Old Budonians.[1]

It was an adroit, irrefutable - and no doubt irritating - response. In the twenty years since Kyanda's appointment a conviction had gained currency among Old Budonians that only one of their number could truly appreciate the complexities and traditions of their unique school. This ignored the inconvenient truth that four of Budo's successful leaders - H.W. Weatherhead, Gaster, Herbert and Cobb - had not even seen the school before joining it. Moreover, Grace, Robinson and Uyirwoth had known little of its intricate history, strengths and weaknesses; each in his own way had demonstrated the value of an outsider's fresh look at procedures and customs. The notion that to have been a student at Budo is a necessary qualification for a successful head of the school is best forgotten.

A tradition should be a means by which the past enriches the present and perhaps the future. If, on careful re-examination, we suspect that a particular tradition does not, then it is probably inhibiting healthy development and should be abandoned. Hundreds of letters, reports, logbook entries and conversations have convinced me that there is another unacknowledged tradition which Budo should shed: All its headmasters except H.T.C. Weatherhead and Eliezer Bawuuba have, in their early years, been frequently and unfairly criticised - simply for not behaving exactly like their predecessors.

Chapter Four has illustrated how unreasonably Grace was undermined for not being Sabaganzi. H.T.C. Weatherhead escaped censure because he was Sabaganzi's brother and deputy. Though not quite matching H.W.'s extraordinary drive and energy, he had continued the established routines and was already well known by present and past Budonians. Gaster and Herbert, though eventually accepted, both initially suffered because they were not Grace. Cobb was at first resented by some Budonians because he was not the now eminent Hemingford, Robinson because he was not Cobb and - most unjust of all - Kyanda because he was not Robinson. Many contemporaries felt that it took Busulwa some time to surmount not being Bawuuba though he himself charitably assured me that he felt quite well received from the outset.

For more than ninety years the infallible remedy has been for a "new" head to stay at least six years. By his seventh there would be no students who remembered the school without him. He was then assured of respect and affection - with reverence imminent. Similar attitudes to new leaders are common in well-established institutions world-wide. But it would be a step forward for Budo if, throughout its second hundred years, Budonians could acknowledge that a healthy school must continually change, that change is better initiated by policy than by accident, and that vigorous heads are likely to offer their most original insights in their first few years of leadership. Long-serving teachers and governors who greet a newcomer with the warning "This is the way we do things here" should expect to be asked "Why?"

From his varied experience, Busulwa had developed a firm philosophy of school education:

> A good school is surely a place where everyone has the maximum choice in developing his or her talents - the opportunity of finding out what he or she is good at, of finding a sphere in which he or she is particularly interested, has a valuable contribution to make, or in which he or she can excel.[2]

Before he took up his headship, he confided to his Makerere contemporary and friend A.B.K. Kasozi that though he knew much work would be needed on the buildings his first priority would be "books" - lifting the school's academic standards and ambitions even higher. When he had assumed the headship of Aggrey Memorial - a day school - the examination results had been poor. By early concentration on academic standards and establishing the school's first proper library he and his colleagues made rapid improvements which resulted in the school being awarded A level status . Interviewed by senior students for the *The Budonian*, he was asked to compare opportunities at boarding and day secondary schools. He shared his convictions about the priveleges enjoyed by Budo and other leading schools, and the urgent need to widen educational opportunity, as the National Education Commission - chaired by Old Budonian Senteza-Kajubi, with Busulwa himself a member - had just recommended:

> First of all I would like to point out the Government policy to encourage the democratisation of education, making it more accessible to all Ugandan children. A boarding school may not be the best institution to achieve that cherished aim. However, boarding schools, in our circumstances, have obvious advantages. A day scholar suffers from lack of adequate contact hours with the teachers. Even the few hours with the teachers are not effectively utilised, for the student and the teacher meet each other when they are both tired. This is the result of walking long distances on the part of most of the students, and of the teachers doing what is commonly known as "Mungo Parking" [ie doing more than one teaching job]. Tired teachers teaching tired and distracted students does not augur well for education...
>
> My call is this: It is our turn, our time to rise up and sacrifice to give education to more people. Let us give them meaningful education. Parents, teachers, students, headmasters and government, be committed to the education of this nation. Give what is due to each equitably.[3]

Asked what plans he had, in view of these new aspirations for all Ugandans, towards diversifying the Budo curriculum, he signalled firm intentions:

> We should move away from examination-centred education. Emphasis should be on integrating knowledge and encouraging creativity - designing, inciting, maintaining and using. Competence-skill-based subjects and courses should be introduced in schools. King's College Budo should always be mindful that education should transcend all times. The solutions and methods of today may be obsolete tomorrow. Academic excellence is very good, but so is the use of our hands.

In spite of the administrative demands of the large, complex school that Budo had become, Busulwa remained convinced that a head teacher's prime responsibility was academic leadership. He was therefore pleased when the ministry proposed that he should attend an international curriculum development course for African educators, in Mauritius in July and August 1989. It was not ideal to be away for several weeks of his first year, but he later felt that he drew on the experience throughout his early years of change and development for Budo. He knew too that he had an able and loyal deputy in Kamuhanda, who - though he would have been well supported by Old Budonians and many current staff - had not been an applicant for the headship.

The unexpected excursion gave Busulwa time to reflect on his early impressions of Budo. He admired Bawuuba's courage, persistence and achievements and at once showed his own strong support for the Christian ethos of the school. Robina Mirembe, one of many staff who at first found it difficult to accept the appointment of a non-Mulokole head, nevertheless reported enthusiastically to Davis her early impressions:

> It has been a fine Easter Day with school in session - a reminder of my own school days, at least in some of the activities. Tonight there is an Easter play by Contact. There has been a dormitory inspection - though the students are not as enthusiastic as we were - good meals and a good Sunday service. Parents flocked to be with their children, having lunch in different groups on the campus... Chapel choir has been revived and we had good singing ... The new Headmaster has settled down. We are trying to get used to him.[4]

Busulwa was, however, uneasy about the financial administration, sensing that Bawuuba, in his later years battling with cancer, may have been too trusting of contractors and finance staff. The ministry had allocated 6m shillings for the renovation of the buildings; there had been some sound repairs, but much of the contracted work had been done badly and some not at all. Budo was not highly reputed for its accounting; investigations revealed that millions of shillings had been misappropriated and there were dismissals and subsequent imprisonment of finance staff. Busulwa determined to give personal attention to future budgetting and contracts and the Board introduced security checks.

He also scrutinised academic achievements and shortcomings. As he had remarked in *The Budonian*, boarding schools had a potential advantage in the formal and informal staff-contact time available to students; he suspected Budo was not making the best use of it. He disapproved too of the practice of withdrawing from examinations, or entirely "discontinuing" - in effect, expelling -, the relatively few students who were not responding adequately to the school curriculum. "We were not there just to teach those who could get Grade Ones."[5] He also suspected that the Budo punishment system, with its Monday morning parade of those who had not turned up for their Saturday tasks, had become counter-productive.

He was therefore neither surprised nor alarmed when, on his return from Mauritius, Kamuhanda presented a frank and severe handing-over report. The main theme was that discipline, of both students and staff, was poor. A new venture had been planned for the August holiday, in line with Busulwa's view that the school had a duty to apathetic or less able students, to provide a remedial course for S4s who were considered to need it, in preparation for O levels. The programme had not gone well. Some of the students had not turned up, some staff had made their disenchantment with the project obvious to the students who did attend, and discipline had been poor. Moreover, the water supply had failed completely from August 26th to September 10th, the pump having yet again been struck by lightning which burnt out the motor. A temporary repair had only postponed the expense of a new motor. There had been other minor irritations and Kamuhanda's final comment struck a note of impatience that was rare from him, but helpful to Busulwa:

> If everyone involved did as they were supposed to do at Budo, and realised that they are here to serve, then administration at Budo would be a lot easier.[6]

Both Kamuhanda and Mirembe wrote frequently to Davis, whose visits during hard times had been much appreciated. Kamuhanda shared Busulwa's concern about the buildings:

Sam is working a lot, trying to learn the system, and seems to have a lot of goodwill. Budo is well but with lots of problems, as expected. The main hall/classroom block roof is badly leaking and in danger of collapse because of unsatisfactory work done on it. The chapel is very badly affected by birds - we are trying to seal it off but it's another expensive undertaking... However, it's not all sad. The farm still gives us plenty of work to do and foodstuffs to eat. The campus is well trimmed due to the tractor and mowers... We are happy with the hopeful, encouraging atmosphere in the country.[7]

The middle term had been long and hot and the vacation project had deprived some staff of half of their holiday. The daily routine care of the campus had been sadly disrupted by the death of the superintendent of the porters and gardening staff:

We are all missing Mr Senkya greatly. He passed away after a short illness. He had served the school for thirty years. He was seventy-five but still so strong! His son died of AIDS the day after we had buried him. It was so sad. His knowledge and experience of the school and his devotion to duty will be hard to replace.[8]

The third term went well and having declared his aspirations Busulwa began to act on them and to respond to Kamuhanda's report. Some staff complained that he was demanding but Samalie Kirya who had rejoined the teaching staff was more tactful, though complaining about basic shortages:

The priorities of the new Headmaster are different from the old Head and it will take us some time to understand him... I am now attached to Canada House and it's fun working with the boys. But cleaning is quite difficult to do with no cleaning materials or very few. It takes quite a long time. One wing of Canada has been in darkness for some time because of no tubes or starters! It's pathetic. We've just had the Founder's Day celebrations. Prince Badru Kakungulu, Ernest Sempebwa and Bishop Shalita were given the Budo Order of Merit. The turn up was very good and Budonians seemed to enjoy themselves.[9]

Though not an Old Budonian, Busulwa seemed to relish Founders Days and PTA and Old Budonian occasions, and he quickly established a reputation for shrewd and friendly public relations. In mid-June he welcomed the Prime Minister on an informal visit to the school and when the news of Bawuuba's death saddened the whole Budo community, he led the school's representatives at the Kawempe funeral on July 1st. Robina Mirembe wrote immediately to Davis to share her grief but ended on a positive note which suggested that Busulwa, if not yet universally popular, was making an impact; she approved of his push for higher academic standards and was keen to raise her own:

> Budo is very hot and dry. The students are working hard for examinations and the teachers are busy.... I wish to do an MEd degree in Administration. I got admitted to Birmingham - but sponsorship is a problem.[10]

In spite of the past dangers and continuing minor difficulties, the Kamuhanda family remained grateful that they had returned to Budo, and that Museveni's NRM government was making conspicuous efforts to restore the country:

> ...Anyway we are all well. We have no complaints. We are used to the situation here - high cost of everything etc - that's normal life. But we are very happy that we are peaceful, not threatened and not living in uncertainty. We are very thankful about Budo - very peaceful, beautiful, a disciplined school, good academic performances ... We have teachers, many of them Christians.[11]

But even some of Uganda's leading schools were badly short-staffed and the Budo governors were apprehensive. Three months later Kamuhanda wrote again with news of a successful celebration - and an improbable request:

> Budo is well. We celebrated the 85th Founders Day on March 24th 1991. Very many dignitaries attended and it was a happy, lovely day. The Budo Order of Merit was presented to five distinguished Old Budonians, including the Hon Abu Mayanja, the Deputy Prime Minister, and Professor Senteza-Kajubi, Vice-chancellor of Makerere. Last year's O level results were very good, but these create more problems for Budo - more pressure for entry.
>
> The Board of Governors has asked me to ask you and Ian to try to persuade and recruit Bazungu teachers for Budo. They will try

to cater for their interests while they are here. You see, people are worried because Ugandans do not want to stay in teaching. They are running off to better paid jobs to escape the ongoing economic squeeze in the country. So please take this appeal seriously when you meet ex-Budo staff or friends ... A son of the Boltons came earlier this term. I took him to the house they occupied at the time he was born. You cannot imagine the pleasure the young man showed at being at Budo. I was amazed. You people love Africa so much! Incredible![12]

He had understated the chronic problem of pressure for places. This was difficult for other leading schools but particularly damaging for Budo - not because it was necessarily better than other schools but because so many Old Budonians believed they had a special right to places for their own children and even the children of their extended families. The ministry had laid on head teachers an obligation to "advise" parents on possible alternative schools for youngsters who had failed to gain entry to their first-choice schools, either at S1 or S5 level. At Budo this resulted, twice a year, in the head's office being beseiged by crowds of parents, ostensibly seeking advice on alternatives but actually putting pressure on the head to "re-consider" the rejection of their offspring and somehow provide a place. Busulwa wrote feelingly in *The Budonian*:

> This is the unpleasant job that headmasters have to do, but more so at Budo. I don't know whether I have managed to cope without injuring parents' and teachers' feelings. I have tried to be available to all parents, listened to their pleas and also tried to explain our situation. I have tried to plead with teachers to agree to teach more students on the one hand, and on the other requested parents to help teachers to do their job. Honestly, it is an almost impossible task, but we trust that people do understand occasionally. I have gone out of my way to look for places in other institutions. The answer really lies in ensuring that the schools we have are comparable.[13]

Chapter 14 notes that the problem was even worse thirteen years later and suggests a constructive way of relieving head teachers of this impossible and destructive requirement.

Meanwhile, the Kajubi Commission's Report had been widely discussed, a White Paper published and, by 1992, the National Resistance Council (parliament) approval given for the broad thrust and much of the detail . The most radical objective was the achievement of Universal Primary Education by the year 2000. The Secondary Heads' Association followed Busulwa's lead in welcoming this, well aware that it would create demands on their own school governors and PTAs to provide even more of their own funds.

Another democratic government initiative had been the involvement of communities and institutions in preparing a draft constitution for Uganda, to be debated, amended and eventually approved by the Constituent Assemby. The secretary to the Constitutional Commission Old Budonian, Professor Phares Mutibwa, lectured to the HSC students, challenging Budo as a leading school to take a leading role in the formulation of the constitution. With guidance from historian Kamuhanda, the HSC students elected a local constitutional committee and over a period of four months, solicited views from the entire student body. Their memorandum addressed issues relating to parliament, the executive, the army and local government:

> Our document was well received by the Commission who not only expressed their gratitude but also furnished us with several books, pamphlets and other documents related to our constitution. The entire exercise deserves credit as it woke up our student body to their national and patriotic spirit.[14]

Budo's growing concern about AIDS was focussed by an official visit by the wife of the president of France, accompanied by Uganda's first lady, Janet Museveni, and Old Budonian Mrs Joyce Mpanga, Minister of State for Education. Welcomed by songs from the Nightingales and traditional Ugandan dances, Madame Mitterrand outlined, to a large open-air gathering of Budonians, local officials and villagers, the work of *France Liberté*, a society of which she was patron, which was producing for schools in Africa materials prepared in consultation with teachers, to combat the menace of AIDS. Urging Budo students to be sensitive to the danger and to strive to keep their generation AIDS-free, she presented books and materials to the school.

Deputy head Robina Mirembe, as senior biologist, had been active on the AIDS issue for some time and hoped to direct her master's degree studies towards it. In 1992, with adequate funding now available, she was seconded to the University of Birmingham, England, to begin what was to become a significant project in the developing maturity of Budo.

Meanwhile, in September 1991, Busulwa's first deputy, Stephen Kamuhanda, who had given outstanding service to many aspects of the school's development since his student days, had been appointed headmaster of another of Uganda's top schools. Ntare School, Mbarara, is in what was then his home district, Mbarara, where he was to serve with distinction for the next twelve years. He had come to Budo as a student in 1961, joining Robina Mirembe in Junior One. They had become a formidable but popular duo of deputy heads nearly twenty years later. The 1992 edition of *The Budonian* paid warm tributes to both, describing Kamuhanda as:

> ... quite a composed man, quite calm - this made it easy for those he led to approach him... Being cautious in decision-making, this quality proved useful when the issues tabled were sensitive. A rather reserved man, Mr Kamuhanda tried to keep peace with everybody, a listening man, to students, staff and parents - which earned him friends.

> Mr Kamuhanda treated staff as colleagues and yet maintained his leadership role. He was quite a programme man, an example of those who kept to the school daily programme , attending most of the school functions. An "agreeable" man.[15]

Budo and Busulwa were fortunate to have two able senior teachers willing to take up the deputy roles. Patrick Bakka Male was a committed Old Budonian who had been head prefect in 1982, took a BSc degree at Makerere, returned to teach at Bawuuba's invitation in 1986 and had since been awarded a Makerere MEd degree. Mrs Ida Songa, a Zambian graduate, had joined Budo in 1982 and proved an outstanding teacher of English with a talent for calm administration.

During his first three years, Busulwa had shown a disarming capacity for inoffensive bluntness. He put it to good use in his contribution to the 1992 edition of *The Budonian*, which he devoted to the abuse of examination systems. In the previous year there had been a massive leakage of examination data from the Kenya Examinations Council which resulted in the cancellation of the entire Primary Leaving Examination. In 1992 more than 5000 Ugandan P7 pupils had had their results cancelled and been required to resit. There had also been irregularities in some O and A level subject examinations and at the Institute of Teacher Education, Kyambogo, the year's examination results had been withdrawn. Busulwa, as spokesman for Ugandan secondary education, believed the integrity of the whole system was threatened:

> The major culprits have been identified as the candidates themselves, teachers, parents, money -hungry people, invigilators, headmasters, setters, moderators, printers, DEOs, police stations, distributors of papers, and to make matters worse, those who work with examination bodies. It has been argued that we experience examination malpractice because of the stiff competition for the few available places at universities and good schools...

> What is however certain is that examination malpractices render the education system impotent... the certificates given become valueless and the products of the system lose respect ... How do we combat this scourge and cleanse our education system? I personally feel we should once again recognise hard work and individual effort. Much attention should be placed in our system on values.

> The time has come to look at our assessment and ask whether we should rely on the cognitive dimension of our learning experiences or should also include the affective domain. Should we also design some ways of assessing the students' manners, behaviour, contribution to the community, to sports, drama etc.? Is it possible to separate achievement from exam selection and placement? The call now is to resolve to go in for the education of the whole person and not merely prepare students for certificates.[16]

Some of Busulwa's thinking may have seemed unacceptably radical to more conservative educators and a hard-pressed ministry. But at least he was thinking and trying to provoke change, however strongly it might be resisted. He had a powerful ally in Professor Senteza-Kajubi. The Education Commission had urged the government to push its 1989 introduction of cost-sharing in education much further. In a trenchant contribution to the 1991 published symposium "Changing Uganda"- to which he gave the title "Tackling the Diploma Disease" - Kajubi shared some facts and figures which his commission had uncovered. Government per capita expenditure on tertiary - ie university level - education was a staggering 300 times that on primary pupils. Yet in 1990 Makerere University had 60 percent of its professorial posts and 40 percent of lectureships unfilled. As already noted, there was a dire shortfall in secondary school staffing, but the commission added the depressing news that 40 percent of those in post were untrained. For primary staff the figure was 56 percent. There was much to deplore but few to blame:

> The civil strife in Uganda over the last two decades; external pressures arising from worsening terms of trade; the back-breaking public debt, resulting in the declining value of the Uganda shilling, have combined to strike a heavy blow to the financing of education and other social services. The proportion of government's recurrent budget devoted to education declined from 21% in 1983/84 to 11% in 1986/87, although in 1987/88 and 1988/89 there was a slight rise to 11.8 and 12.2 respectively.[17]

This was the international economic context in which the slow but perceptible recovery of the country and of Budo has to be understood. Kajubi nevertheless proposed an optimistic agenda for national education, in spite of daunting social and cultural problems which highlight the remarkable multi-tribal, learning community which Budo was founded to be and still strives to become:

> A major problem for educational reform in Uganda is the difficulty of identifying a national ethos that could unite Ugandans into a coherent social order, and whose core values would animate and guide education. Small and compact as it is , Uganda is, as Wrigley rightly observes (1988 p. 28) "culturally a heterogeneous and historically shallow collection of people with none of the attributes of a nation". There are as yet no accepted national, political and cultural norms and values that can be internalised by

individuals, beyond the usual slogans of "fighting disease, poverty and ignorance". There is, for example, no common language, let alone a "we-feeling" of national identity, and ethnic loyalties and religious sectarianism are still much stronger than collective nationalism. Political instability, social and physical insecurity and blatant violation of human rights have been almost permanent features of Uganda life since independence.

Plato suggests in *The Republic* that problems of national unity can be overcome with the right kind of political education. The Education Policy Review Commission accepted this view, and kept Uganda's baffling political and social problems in mind throughout its deliberations. It concluded that national integration is the single greatest challenge and that the type of education provided should have a pivotal role in creating it...

The commission identified five basic national goals and objectives that should guide and animate the education system:

1. The forging of national unity and harmony ...

2. The evolution of grass-roots democratic institutions and practices in all sectors ...

3. A guarantee of fundamental human rights...

4. The creation of national wealth to enhance better quality of life and self-reliance...

5. The promotion of ethical values...[18]

[My own working visits to Makerere and Budo, 1998-2005, encourage me to believe that the Ministry of Education has remained committed to these aspirations.]

The word "self-reliance" in the fourth of them recalls the courageous "Arusha Declaration" proclaimed by President Julius Nyerere of Tanzania in 1967. Dismayed by the failure of the richest nations of the West to offer serious help to the poorest nations of Africa, South America and Asia, he determined that *Education for Self-Reliance* should be the guideline for a country committed to offering all its citizens "a fair share of the little we have." *The Budonian* of 1992 contains an account of a ten-day visit of Budo teachers, led by Busulwa, to Tanzanian schools, now reorganised on a pattern which helped to alleviate the problem of the very successful and therefore heavily oversubscribed school:

> Iroboru Secondary school ... was founded in 1946 by the Lutheran World Foundation. It was nationalised like many others in Tanzania on July 1st 1967 and so became a government secondary school - one of the best in Tanzania, with over 800 students.

> As such it has a problem of numbers due to the fact that many parents would like their children to study in it. The problem is alleviated by the fact that it is a school with an agricultural bias and admission into Form 1 is based on this... As a matter of policy schools in Tanzania are grouped according to subject combinations. The applicants choose combinations but not schools. The school curriculum is centred on the concept of Self-Reliance, which emphasises that the education one gets in a school should be part of one's future. Secondly, that a school should be part and parcel of the community.[19]

The Budo staff were impressed by the range of enterprises which were managed entirely by the Iroboru students. These included a dairy unit, a vegetable garden in which every student had a personal bed, the bakery, the posho mill and a workshop in which students made and repaired school furniture.

> We envied their clean compound, dormitories, and well-equipped science laboratories and we left the school determined to do something back in our motherland, Uganda.

Almost a generation had passed since Nyerere's far-sighted manifesto but it is exhilarating to read the envious accolade of a group of Ugandan teachers for Tanzanian schools which had realised their president's vision, in which

> the most important thing is that the school members should learn that it is their farm and that their living standards depend on it. Pupils should be given the opportunity to make many of the necessary decisions...By this sort of practice and this combination of classroom work and farm work, our educated young people will realise that if they farm well they can eat well and have better facilities in their dormitories and recreation rooms. If they work badly then they themselves will suffer. Government should

avoid laying down detailed and rigid rules; each school must have considerable flexibility. Only then can the potential of that particular area be utilised, and only then can the participants practise - and learn to value - direct democracy.[20]

They found four other schools, in Arusha and Dar-es-Salaam, also impressive for the level of student responsibility. Two of them specialised in commerce and accountancy; in all schools the HSC subject combinations were very limited and students were selected according to their career intentions. In relation to the Uganda Education Commission's concern for greater national identity and unity, the Budo group reflected on the fact that the language of instruction throughout Tanzanian primary schools was Swahili, with English taught as a foreign language at upper-primary level.

There was plenty for Budo and Uganda to think about. In 1994 Busulwa had the Tanzanian experience reinforced when he visited California, where he particularly admired the American "Magnet" schools, which also related their programmes closely to possible career choices by students and had effective links with industry and commerce for the provision of work-experience - for example, in banking. Significantly, from the early 1980s British sixth forms and universities were being encouraged in a similar direction, notably by the Royal Society of Arts project, pointedly titled "Education for Capability".

In spite of the ferment of ideas on education and constitutional patterns of government, the most notable event at Budo in 1993 signalled a remarkable return to tradition. The NRM government, having accepted the restoration of the rulers of the hereditary kingdoms, on the understanding that the posts were to be purely ceremonial and imply no political status or involvement, meticulous preparations were made for the coronation of Crown Prince Ronald Mutebi as Kabaka of Buganda. This was the third twentieth-century coronation on Budo hill and though the ancient rituals that had enthroned Daudi Chwa (see Chapter 3) were somewhat modernised, the reed palaces were built again and much of the ancient pomp was preserved. The event was televised and shown all over the world. Erisam Kanyerezi, who taught history and Luganda at Budo, wrote a full account for the 1995 edition of *The Budonian* - with some shrewd commentary:

> Current Budonians welcomed, accommodated and fed the Bataka (clan heads) on their royal hill ... and many students of King's College streamed towards the site. They were greatly excited when they saw the reed palaces mushrooming... The many cars rolling by and the stalls put up by local people were a spectacle. With unquenchable curiosity they toured Bwanika [Bamunanika] Palace where the Crown Prince would go for a bath ... the Buganda Royal Palace... the Nakibuuka where he sits on the royal stools called Nnamulondo and the Masengerengosaze, the ancient royal crown. All these sounded old-fashioned to the students but they were a great historical and cultural lesson.
>
> Apart from that, the Budo students slashed the grass within and outside the sites and, together with Old Budonians, prepared the main road and the paths leading to them. Those who participated in this ceremony did not however find a smooth road. They encountered opposition from cliques of anti-monarchists questioning the significance of the coronation. They jeered and sneered at those who had love for the institution and vehemently attacked the ceremonies as being divisive....
>
> Then in the early morning hours of 31st July 1993 the Budonians made history. [The Kabaka] was crowned by the Mugema (the traditional grandfather of princes), the Kasujju (traditional keeper of princes) and Old Budonian Mayanja Nkangi who was the Katikiro at the ceremony... All the Old Budonians at the site spontaneously burst into ululations as the Ssaabasajja vowed to defend his people...
>
> It was a moment for the republicans to brush shoulders with monarchists as a gesture of reconciliation in both national and international politics. The President, Lt. General Museveni, honoured the occasion and this helped in leucotomising the anti-monarchists. Most memorable to the students of Budo was the moment when the headmaster Mr Busulwa was leading the clergy to move before the King... they were there to emphasise to the King that the new ideologies that had come to Buganda more than a century ago had come to stay. The new King had therefore to recognise and accept them in this rapidly changing world.

This occasion ended well. It manifested that there can be reconciliation rather than confrontation in politics, as well as unity both locally and nationally. It also showed that people of various religious and cultural biases could still come together, talk, laugh and live together.[21]

Coincidentally, this extraordinary day also appeared to bequeath to King's College a permanent memento. In fact it was a generous grant from the PTA which met the cost of removing for ever one of Budo's most uncomfortable traditions:

Most memorable of all, the occasion acted as a catalyst to the tarmacing of the road to King's College, Budo. The huge potholes which used to hamper movement of people along the road are now things of the past.[22]

In sharp contrast, another important, unifying but sombre gathering at the school was the major event of 1994. By October 1993 Robina Mirembe, had completed her MEd degree in Educational Administration at Birmingham. She had devoted much of it to a study of "Aids Education in Ugandan Schools" and had been recommended to develop it in a doctoral thesis. This would take at least three years and, wishing to apply her study to Uganda's urgent needs, she returned to Budo in November 1993. Having obtained funding support from the World Health Organisation, she played a leading part in the first term of 1994, in the launch at Budo of the first school-based Sex Education Programme in East Africa to incorporate particular attention to AIDS.

It was designed to involve all students from S1 to S6, and divided into four units: Formal teaching; informal teaching; behaviour enhancement and materials production. The Biology staff and other teachers, including Busulwa, volunteered their services and in response to the urgent international challenge, Budo offered a workshop, in April, to enable interested schools to see work in progress and take part in in-service sessions. Fourteen schools responded and, with funding from UNICEF and the Uganda Government Aids Control Programme, a team of doctors, teachers and counsellors came together for a week of intense activity, demonstration and discussion. The programme made heavy demands on students and staff, not least for changed styles of teaching and learning. Joseph Kayaye, who headed the Formal Teaching Unit, gave an early account:

> The Unit presents sex education to students of S1 and S2 on a weekly basis. It is hoped that repeated messages become part of lifestyle and that, since the message includes AIDS prevention the young will learn to avoid it. The child-centred nature of sex education exposes students to negotiation, reasoning and making choices that are crucial in the prevention of HIV infection... The activities of the Unit include role-playing, debates and panel discussions.

> The Informal Unit, headed by Florence Sitenda, is aimed at involving the upper classes, S3 to S6. Students are involved in activities that help them to develop positive attitudes towards their sexuality and enable them to realise their individual responsibilities. The activites require the teacher to be innovative and creative since there is no set syllabus. They include discussions, art work, films, videos, music and drama. They are programmed as extra-curricular activities and carried out during students' free time. Counselling and guidance is also provided in the Informal Unit.[23]

The Behavioural Enhancement Unit, headed by Deborah Ojiambo, reinforced the learning done in the formal sesssions and one of its main activities was instruction of Budo Junior School pupils by older students. There was special enthusiasm for the panel discussions led by visitors, who shared with students their wider experience and specialisms. The project also became a valuable addition to Budo's community work in the local villages. Many children extended their involvement in the AIDS education units, into work on basic literacy. At a more advanced level the Materials Production Unit had completed, by the end of 1994, a book based on the lessons and creative activities of the Formal Unit.

In 1998 Robina Mirembe was awarded her DPhil for her thesis, "Aids Education and Gender in Ugandan Schools". She continued to contribute to Makerere and WHO health education projects into the twenty-first century, while Budo maintained its commitment to sex/

AIDS education and partnered programmes at Comboni College, Lira; St Catherine's College, Lira; Ntare and Gayaza High School.

One of the most creditable aspects of this radical curriculum development was the positive response of the governors, the Old Budonian Association and most of the parents. The content of some of the units may have shocked older Budonians but, in the light of the government's forthright approach to AIDS prevention, there were few protests about the breaking of taboos or cultural traditions. Busulwa and his senior colleagues had given thought and tact to developing good relationships with the PTA; the supportive reception of the AIDS education programme was a well-deserved vote of confidence. Budonains were proud of the example their school was setting.

But it was still by examination success that most governors, parents and Old Budonians judged the progress of their school. Here too they had much to applaud. In Busulwa's first six years, the O and A level results had improved from adequate to very good, occasionally being the best in the country and meriting the overused accolade "excellent". The tables below summarise:

Uganda Certificate of Education (O levels)

Year	1991		1992		1993		1994	
	N	%	N	%	N	%	N	%
Div. 1	106	66	143	73	104	64	139	86
Div. 2	43	26	40	21	50	31	21	14
Div. 3	10	6	10	5	8	5	0	0
Div. 4	1	1	0	0	0	0	0	0

Uganda Advanced Certificate of Education (A levels)

Year	1991		1992		1993		1994		1995	
	N	%	N	%	N	%	N	%	N	%
3PPs	46	60	42	62	84	84	78	82	96	86
2PPs	22	28	21	32	13	13	15	16	14	12

The 1995 A level results were even better than the table shows. The school had encouraged stronger candidates to attempt 4 subjects at Principal level because the universities now looked favourably on all-round performance. Of the 96 candidates with 3 Principal passes 42 obtained a 4th. All these achievements reflected fine efforts by students and staff. Busulwa's exhortations for higher standards seem to have had some effect.

Within these raw statistics was a development that especially pleased him - a big improvement in the girls' performances at both levels. Looking back, four years after his retirement, he confided:

> Co-education was my passion at Budo. I felt that over the years the staff had made too many rules geared to "protecting" the girls. I studied all their exam results back to the 1940s and then held meetings with the senior girls to try to find out what seemed to be hindering their progress. A good point was made by a girl who had come with a Grade 4 - ie top pass. She told me she had chosen Budo because she wanted to study with her friends of both sexes. So I wanted to trust the girls to do their prep up at the boys' end. But many staff were opposed to this so I settled at first for only the HSC girls coming up. But eventually staff wanted all the girls to come up for co-ed prep.[24]

In an interview for the 1995 edition of *The Budonian* he expanded on this theme:

> Often we don't assess the girls' performance correctly. We measure them against boys here or girls in top schools like Gayaza - which is wrong. We should compare their P7 results when they came to us, with their results when they are leaving. There has been a great improvement in their performance. At A level, for example, we have tried to show that girls from Budo can take up engineering. In the past three years, at least two girls per year have joined the Faculty of Engineering at Makerere University. At O level we have not had any girl failing.
>
> We have tried to expand their facilities and started by renovating Gaster House. We are also building a reading shade for Gaster and Grace houses. We have provided furniture and built an extension for Grace House and we are currently extending old Grace House. To solve their water problems a big new tank has been built and

the Sabaganzi tanks have been renovated. One of the things hindering their academic progress is that they are relatively few in number due to accommodation. That is why we are expanding their accommodation. We have increased the intake of girls and they have not let us down in their performance. So I think they are utilising these facilities...

Power is very dim most of the time so although we have reading facilities down at the Girls' End, they cannot read at night. So a generator was bought for them and as soon as its house has been completed it will be installed.[25]

The governors had proposed in 1992 that the school should not grow beyond 1000 students, as there were still great difficulties in providing adequately for such numbers on a campus built for only 450. Yet determination and ingenuity had achieved some expansion of the curriculum, from which the girls had benefitted as much as the boys. Budo had responded to the Education Commission's plea for better teaching of Uganda' indigenous languages.

We have introduced new subjects, such as German at O and A level... and have gone back to teaching one of our local languages, Luganda, to show that it is not only German, French and English that are important... This year we have started teaching Electricity and Electronics to emphasise technical education, but we lack materials.[26]

Other improvements during 1994 and '95, in time for the 90th anniversary celebration, included the refurnishing of the Big School classrooms; re-wiring and re-chairing of the Main Hall; provision of six small flats for single members of staff; and at last providing sufficient stock to reintroduce the Sunday uniform for boys and the wearing of belts, stockings and Budo sweaters. The PTA had provided generous help and the improvements had made an impact; one of the headmaster's student interviewers commented: "Budo seems to have got quite a face-lift of late."

Asked what had been the major challenges of his first six years, he included that perennial problem for all reasonably open-minded leaders - the balance between democracy and decisiveness:

First the old age of the buildings and traditions that are hard to change within a short time. Also preparing a future for those who have served beyond retirement age poses a big challenge. Another is the democratisation of education, where we allow students to give their criticisms, but within limits. It is also challenging to change from one policy to another all the time, for the good of the school and to try to get ideas from the 54 teachers in the staffroom - because some would rather sit on them.[27]

When I first met Sam Busulwa, in 1998, we talked of our different experiences of Budo, thirty years apart, and I said that I had been impressed by Robinson's patience with long democratic debates, because he seemed to me to be temperamentally decisive. Sam nodded slowly and replied "Yes, democracy is good," - long pause and broad grin - "Authority is better!" We both had a good laugh - but he meant it.

The year 1995 had been good for Uganda as well as for Budo, with further economic progress and the Constituent Assembly finally approving a new, patiently elaborated national constitution. The year 1996 would be even better, with Yoweri Museveni becoming the country's first democratically elected president - after 34 years of independence - and Budo exuberantly celebrating its 90th anniversary.

Plans for Founders Day 1996 had been laid well in advance by an organising committee chaired by Dr Suleiman Kiggundu who, after academic distinctions, had become one of Uganda's most successful businessmen, as founder and managing director of the Greenland Bank. In his foreword to the Founders Day souvenir booklet, he turned his business acumen towards the most worthwhile way of celebrating the school's longevity:

Ninety years, even for a human being, is such a long period as to warrant physical fatigue. Likewise, King's College, Budo has suffered its fair share of wear and tear. But we in the committee, by making school improvement the agenda for the 90th Anniversary celebrations, feel that this situation should not be allowed to continue. We therefore call upon Budonians, parents and well-wishers to face up to the challenge of redevelopment of Budo by donating generously to the fund for face-lifting the school and for the construction of a new library ...

We also wish to appeal to all of you to create a permanent endowment for the task of continuously assisting Budo. Great schools the world over have this arrangement. Budo as well should pick it up.[28]

He had set a fine example by donating the funds for a spacious new science laboratory, to be named after Budo's most famous Muslim student, Prince Badru Kakungulu, and to be opened by the Chief Guest, Kabaka Mutebi II.

The day was happy and successful. From before 8am hundreds of guests luxuriated in the drive up the tarmac road and the Kabaka was ceremoniously greeted at 9.15. The service of thanksgiving in an overflowing chapel was followed by an excited, 1956 Cobb-style, march past of Budonians grouped by decades. The headmaster then welcomed the huge gathering and underpinned Kiggundu's message that involvement and giving were the distinguishing marks of Budo's true friends:

Budo has come a long way in fulfilling her mission of providing quality education. Since Budo's inception, the spirit of self-help, self-reliance, has not failed us. We are grateful to the founders, who insisted that the parents, students and the people of Uganda should contribute to the building and developing of their school, or else they would not value their education...

As is well known, Budo has always been a pace-setter. We should now be preparing for the 21st century through reinforcing management, environmental and gender education, and the necessary technology. We appeal to you to join hands with us in providing the infrastructure, tools, equipment and workshops, so that we may provide an all-round education.[29]

Musical interludes followed addresses by the chairman of governors, the minister of education and the Kabaka, who then declared open the Prince Badru Laboratory and, in an act of faith on behalf of the whole assembly, laid on a central site the foundation stone of a three-storey library building which for seven years had been the keystone of Busulwa's vision of even higher academic standards. After lunch the Kabaka departed and the rest of a long day remained for informal socialising, and much hearty reminiscence, as former students of each decade recalled their shared years - which of course were the best years - of the King's College.

A feature of the occasion was a celebratory edition of *The Budonian*. It contained recollections by survivors of every decade from the 1920s - among them outstanding contributions from Ernest Sempebwa, John Nagenda and Stephen Kamuhanda, which have already been quoted in this history. Two other notable articles concerned the Parent Teacher Association and the progress of women's education at Budo.

The PTA chairman, E. T. Kiyimba-Kagwa, noted that - excluding staff salaries - the association was now meeting almost 90 percent of the school's recurrent costs:

> "If you think Education is expensive, try Ignorance" - is an expression kept close in the minds of the PTA of King's College, Budo. The journey of education charges is very long, stretching from pre-school to university and beyond... Education is cheaper than Ignorance when children attain the academic and social values expected. The willingness and enthusiasm of the parents at Budo to do all they can to meet the costs of educating their children is extremely impressive.

Acknowledging the good fortune of Budo and other well-established schools in having many parents who could meet the costs without real hardship, he made a self-denying PTA proposal on behalf of poor parents:

> Government's promise of funding the schools fully, without PTAs participation, is eagerly awaited. Parents hope that it may become a reality soon. Let us call a spade a spade. If this country is to make headway in increasing the number of schools, government should spend less and less money on schools which do not need government's assistance and should start spending more money on establishing new ones.[30]

Mrs Rhoda Kalema was well qualified to write on girls' education at Budo 1933-1996. She had been a student at the Primary and Secondary schools for eleven years, 1937-47, a Budo teacher 1950-53, wife of an Old Budonian, and parent and grandparent of Budo students. As a delegate to the former Constituent Assembly and current representative on the National Resistance Council, she had first-hand experience of the work of Old Budonian women in positions of national responsibility. She had also personally interviewed all the survivors of the first Budo girls' entry of 1933. She had no doubts about the impact of the school's pioneer contribution to co-education and adduced four factors which had been key to success, the most important being the support of the parents:

> It is very fair, while analysing the basis and continuity of co-education at Budo, to praise the vision and optimism of the first parents of the pioneer girls. It was a completely new idea to these men... It was a new idea to Canon Grace too, because Britain's history did not show co-educational boarding schools. We shall never know exactly what advice and consultations went on between headmaster and parents who had such faith in the scheme that they sent their daughters to a boys' school.

> Margaret Mulyanti Mukasa [one of the pioneers] says this: "Our parents, mainly fathers, encouraged the co-education and they tried to see that we did not fail. Many important leaders - and church leaders - wrote to the press to criticise this new practice, but our parents were firm. And therefore more parents were encouraged to try co-education for their daughters.[31]

The other three factors were the care taken by successive headmasters to ensure the safety and security of the girls' accommodation, with staff housing nearby; the recruitment of generous numbers of women teachers and matrons to ensure their physical and intellectual welfare - "They were real mother substitutes"; and the inclusion in the timetable from the outset, of "gender-biased" courses for the girls, e.g. in Domestic Science and Needlework, to supplement what they were being offered in the normal classes with the boys. Mrs Kalema had no doubt about the long-term value:

> To present and future girl -students and to all Budo teachers it is crucial that the foundation which was laid by the determination

and optimism of Canon Grace, a few parents, their daughters and a long line of male and female staff, should be rewarded by even stronger determination "not to fail". As we celebrate 90 years of the school and 63 years of co-education, we are proud that there is evidence that the majority of girls who attended this school, using their co-education and total experience here, are outstanding in their various fields, all over the country and the world. They are independent, confident and courageous women, making an immense contribution to society, as professionals, mothers and grandmothers.[32]

Appendix I provides a sample indication of the prowess of women Budonians in influential positions at home and abroad but can give little sense of the depth of their professional contributions to, for example, education, law, medicine and politics, or - equally important - to family life.

In planning this history I had intended to devote a separate chapter to the problems and successes of co-education - which had for so long been contentious. For my Ugandan visit in 2004, I asked several prominent Old Budonians to organise group meetings of representatives of various decades, to help me complete my research and had forewarned that co-education would be a key topic. To my surprise, although I did my best to incite criticism, I was unable to provoke a single dissenting voice, male or female. All Budonians seem to prize their early experience of mixing and competing equally with the opposite sex. Dr David Matovu, distinguished scientist, Director of Entebbe Research Institute, long-serving MP for Entebbe and chairman successively of Makerere and Nkumba University Councils, had offered me, two years earlier, what proved to be the general view:

> I valued the mix of boys and girls very highly at the time and even more in later life. I found myself very much at ease in mixed company at University [in Germany] and later. Budo girls did very well socially and intellectually, at Makerere and in their careers, while quite a lot of girls and boys from single sex schools lacked social confidence and found mixing quite difficult.[33]

Anyone who knows Budo well will have noticed that wherever a group of its free-thinking products are gathered there are sure to be several points of view on any complex topic. The unanimity of Budonians about co-education is a fine tribute to those who pioneered it and those who have fostered it since. It augurs well for the future - and, I hope, for expanded numbers - of Budo girls, whose predecessors have taken such full advantage of what, for many years, was a unique opportunity in Ugandan secondary schools.

The years 1997 and '98 were of steady progress. The farm was enjoying its longest period of success, without major crises and with beneficial effects on school health. The health centre building had been renovated and expanded, with a small laboratory for simple medical tests and a staff of four. But progress on the library had been sluggish. The contributions, of which there had been high hopes, had been slow to arrive, as in Grace's time, so, to Busulwa's disappointment, work had been temporarily halted. Interviewed for the 1998 edition of *The Budonian*, he nevertheless, replied buoyantly when asked whether the academic trends of the past few years had impressed or disappointed him:

> There is no disappointment at all. For example, at O level over 80% passes in First Grade, given the number of students we have, is no mean feat. Last year 17 students obtained between 8 and 12 aggregates for 8 subjects and we had the best results in the country in English, Maths and Accounts. Our A level results have remained unbeaten for three years running and we have sent more students on to university than any other school, despite not discontinuing or allowing students to repeat - except when changing subject combinations - as is the case in other schools. Even at O level we register all the students... I am pleased with the performance of the previous years and if the past can predict the future then I will say the future is bright.[34]

One reason for Budo's increasing success was that the school had at last achieved the stability of staffing which had eluded Busulwa's predecessors as far back as Robinson thirty years before. The 1998 staff list shows that of 74 teaching and senior non-teaching staff, 40 had served ten years or more and they were supported by well-qualified younger staff. Only three new appointments had been required in the past three years - one teacher in 1996 and two administrators in 1997.

Budo had at last become again what it had been for its first fifty- five years - an institution at which people liked to teach, live and stay. This was fair reward for the leadership, guidance and friendliness of Busulwa and his senior colleagues, and for the improved conditions of service which the governors and the PTA were now providing. Senior teacher Mrs Bessie Sekamwa, looking back 23 years, probably spoke for most staff in praising the responsibility and support of present students.

> Discipline when I came here in 1975 was bad. The whites had just left and students were not sure of the African staff. So many drank a lot and relaxed the rules. But later these rules were put into effect when the teachers became more strict. Now it is only some S4s who become unruly, but otherwise discipline is good... Success in teaching has been the greatest motivation, since students encourage you by doing well.[35]

Timothy Musiime, head prefect in 1998, provided a complementary student view:

> The school system instils in us certain values and disciplines that we often resent at first, but appreciate later in life. That is why, for example, several Old Budonians have confessed that they now value the compulsory chapel they were required to attend every morning - even though they resented it then...
>
> Many students from Budo who leave after O level and join other schools for A level, become prefects and even head prefects in their new schools. Every year we hear of a Budonian as head prefect in his or her new school... I would attribute this to the system at Budo which exposes students to various leadership roles right from their O level year. Being a house official at O level is quite an achievement and this is where the leadership starts.[36]

His deputy, Adam Kawuzi, described another valuable development in Busulwa's time. The growth of the school and the tightness of funding led to the decision that all school cleaning, including classrooms, laboratories and communal buildings, must be done by students - in addition to dormitory cleaning for which they have always been responsible. The 1992 impressions of Tanzanian schools may have gone deep.

The Communal Work Department is directly under the office of the Deputy Head Prefect...every Wednesday afternoon and Saturday morning students participate in the general cleaning of the compounds and the classrooms are cleaned daily. To ensure close supervision the DHP appoints monitors for morning housework and communal work, who are under his direct supervision... For better results we work in close co-operation with the Environmental Club, Flower Club, School Council unit concerned with litter, and the Farm Department.[37]

The curriculum reports of 1998 suggested that though French and German flourished, the recent revival of Luganda was in some difficulty. A major problem was that very few of Budo's feeder primary schools now taught it, so unlike the S1 students of the previous generation who arrived with a solid foundation in the language the new generation prefered to promote more frequent use of English, which they knew was the key to secondary education: So in spite of the aspirations of the Education Commission and Budo's exemplary initiative, fostering Uganda's indigenous languages was proving difficult. Erisam Kanyerezi who was head of the Luganda department and also taught history, wrote a balanced and sometimes moving analysis in *The Budonian*:

For any curriculum project to be successfully implemented those concerned must believe in it. It is very difficult to teach a subject when the students do not believe in some of its aspects, or their parents deliberately discourage them ... and there are other internal forces. For example, the writer vividly remembers a colleague in 1993 arguing relentlessly, "But, Mr Busulwa, Luganda is going to undermine the standards of English Language." ... Such outspoken negative attitudes indirectly affect the timetabling of the subject and the choices made by students at both levels. Currently international institutions of higher learning, such as Makerere University, welcome students whose subject combinations at A level include Luganda.

For schools trying to support local languages, the national examination figures for the UCE and UACE were discouraging. From 1990 to '97 there had been a total entry of only 56 candidates offering Luganda at O level. Four had obtained Distinction grades, 47 had passed with Credit and only one had failed. At A level there had been 30 candidates; none had obtained an A grade but there had been 9 B grades, and 8 C grades. Five students had failed. Kanyerezi was undaunted:

> As long as students and teachers are disciplined and persistently working hard, the chances of scoring distinctions will be maximised. Students need to remember the Luganda proverb "Ky'osimba onaanya - ky'olyako ettooke". (No, pains, no gains.) Who knows? The optional subject may end up as the breadwinner for some students in the near future. Recently the school top administration bought textbooks for the department. It is now up to the teachers and students to use them for the good of the school. It will be encouraging to see students reading Luganda novels and newspapers, listening to Luganda radio programmes openly and with confidence - and practising spoken Luganda regularly. There is no school rule that bars students from speaking Luganda - or German, or French.[38]

Other staff must have been encouraged by the numbers of voluntary clubs which the students had established in relation to their subject studies. These included a Writers' Club, Mathematics Society, Computer Club, Economics Club, German Club, French Society and Music Club. The active religious life of many students was also reflected not only in chapel choirs and functions, in a flourishing Contact group and a new development for young Balokole, Senior One Contact, but also in a 60-strong Roman Catholic group and the Budo Muslim Club, which now had just over 100 members.

It was the effects of peace, gradual economic progress, and a sharp decline in lawlessness which made possible such cultural development in schools. One achievement of the NRM government was prized above all others. When the British journalist Fergal Keane who had visited Uganda in 1994, returned in 1998, he reviewed the country's progress in a frank discussion with a group of businessmen. He was not surprised at their unanimous response to his question "What do you consider the greatest gift of the Museveni government?" It was: "Freedom of speech and freedom from fear."[39]

In 1999, however, the Budo governors were surprised to find that they were not entirely free from interference. The Ministry of

Education announced a major reorganisation of leadership posts in education, which was to include the transfer of Busulwa, who had now completed ten years at Budo, to Ndejje Senior Secondary School, and the appointment of the Ndejje head, Old Budonian George Semivule, to Budo. Busulwa was almost two years from the retirement age of sixty and the governors, well pleased with his achievements - which had deservedly earned him the coveted award of the Budo Order of Merit in 1997 - were unanimously opposed to the ministry's transfer proposal. Professor Apolo Nsibambi, who had recently been appointed Minister of Education, upheld their appeal and - to general acclaim - Busulwa remained in post.

He did not rest on his laurels. An optimistic 1999 edition of *The Budonian* paid tribute to his persistent pressure for computer education. With a grant from the World Bank and technical leadership from senior teacher Lawrence Ssenkubuge, the school's piecemeal provision was expanded and concentrated in historic, central premises. Ivan Kutosi of S3 enthused about the breakthrough:

> The Budo Arch ... one of the oldest structures on the hill, formerly housing the Prefectorial chambers and S4B, now houses the most important and reliable way of getting to know about the world - the computer room - now fully equipped with the information super-highway, the Internet. With this, students now have the chance of downloading thousands of websites which can be educative, leisure-packed and full of ideas. With the thought of receiving e-mail from anywhere in the globe... we hope that the room will grow to become a famous website known internationally by Budonians.[40]

Far from complacent about Budo or Africa, Busulwa devoted his own article to "Some Causes of Indiscipline in Schools and the Way Forward."

> Schools are expected to be places where the growth and development of the individual occurs. They are the major entrusted agents of change for the improvement and progress of the individual and society. Schools are also expected to be places where children examine their prejudices and learn to live in unity and harmony.

Hence schools are agents of liberation and of the conservation of what are considered to be the norms of society.

When therefore indiscipline occurs in school all stakeholders get worried ... throughout the world, educationalists and the public are concerned about inappropriate behaviour and violence in schools. Recently the mass media has been reporting murder cases...

Citing examples in the USA he moved closer to home, recording the recent murder of a student by his classmates at Namilyango College, assaults by students on teachers at Trinity College, Nabbingo, the closure of Ngai School during the examination period and the suspension, for indiscipline, of 80 girls at Namagunga School. There had been occasional indiscipline and bullying at Budo and the message was clear: Discipline had to be worked at continuously, by students and staff, school administrators who planned programmes, parents and the community. He listed causes of indiscipline under each of these four headings, being particularly sympathetic to parents and students, struggling with the pressures of modern society and often spending too little time together for the young to have confidence in sharing their problems:

Parents fail to decide what is appropriate for their children in terms of proper dress, language etc... They may not know what videotapes and TV their children are watching... Whereas in the past a community or village/homestead knew what was acceptable, today we seem not to know. Hence, given influences coming from the global village and the generation gap, many parents are at a loss in the task of parenting... Children are under pressure to be part of their peer-group. When individuals succumb to peer-pressure they lose their self-respect and end up engaging in inappropriate behaviour.

He urged parents to try to participate in school events, follow up their childrens' progress - giving special attention to reports - and to link up with the parents of their childrens' friends. The community too should be made aware by the school of the influence it could have, and where possible be given access to school facilities and occasions.

These were all things at which he and his colleagues had worked hard for a decade.

> At King's College Budo we try to encourage parents and community to be involved in our activities, for we believe that character formation is a great tool in personal fulfilment.[41]

But for discipline perhaps more than any other school aspiration, the Budo motto rings true. Every year, as about 170 students leave and 170 uninitiated S1s arrive, there is always "So much to do".

Laban Bombo, who had now served 20 years as chaplain, knew this as well as any teacher, having for many years been chairman of the school disciplinary committee. *The Budonian* published a warm tribute to him, by Victor Walusimbi. He had been deputy head of Budo Junior School, head of Nsangi Primary and tutor at three teacher-training colleges, before joining Budo from Trinity College, Nabbingo, to teach mathematics, still combined with his chaplaincy - and his famous good humour:

> Reverend Bombo is amused by how times change. He claims that today's students are much younger than in years past. However, the classes are too big, with more than 50 students, compared to those he taught earlier with a maximum of 35. But it is simpler for teachers now because in former days one taught about 27 periods a week –"And the big students would even make one timid!" ... When asked how he had managed to remain popular with both old-timers and current Budonians he says he is proud of Budo and that being chaplain has been a blessing to him. "I am liberal and I move with time. I treat generations differently. I always consider other peoples' opinions because I am aware that I don't know it all."....
> He says he managed [as Chair of the Disciplinary Committee because... "there was always mutual agreement and co-operation when taking decisions. We also bear in mind that we are dealing with humanity - society always has wrong-doers. We punish with love so that the punished don't hate but love us."[42]

Another strong influence towards good discipline and a spirit of co-operation was the School Council, on which the secretary, Caroline Bwango (S6B), reported enthusiastically:

The School Council had always been perceived as a body that advocates students' rights, when violated by prefects. This is a misconception. The Council is more interested in ensuring that the school system is faring well, in as far as it achieves the academic, social and spiritual welfare of the students. Dialogue is a good way of getting things done. The School Council is very interested in positive and amicable inter-action between the student body, the Prefects' Council and the staff...

Most importantly the School Council is used as a channel of students' ideas on the running of the school... [It] acts as a forum on matters of administration, on policies and decisions affecting the students, passing on the students' ideas and getting responses from the authorities. Together we hope to complete these tasks, to make Budo a better, bigger and more comfortable place to live.[43]

The expanded games programme also encouraged teamwork and relations with other schools. Cricket, athletics, soccer, rugby, football, tennis and swimming all continued to a high standard. Girls and boys were chosen for the national table tennis team, the girls' hockey team visited Jersey (UK), basketball and volleyball were popular and Saturday morning "Trot" was revived. Old Budonians Sam Walusimbi, William Kamanyi and John Nagenda maintained their support for Ugandan cricket.

The students' performances at A level were consistently very good throughout the decade, and at O level the progress in the four years 1996 to 1999 was from very good to excellent. In 1996, 151 students (88.3 percent) gained First Class certificates; in 1997, 162 (88 percent); in 1998, 140 (91.5 percent) and in 1999, 164 which was a remarkable 95.9 percent. There had been a total of 60 Second Class passes, but over the four years, out of 679 candidates only 2 had passed in the Third Class and there had been no failures. Busulwa was justifiably pleased that no students had been discontinued on academic grounds, or barred from examinations, and there had been no evidence of any examination malpractice.

It was not necessary for Busulwa to draw attention, as he usually did, to the outstanding performances of the girls; student Ernest Katwesigye did it for him:

It has come to the notice, and interest, of many of us that lately a revolution is taking root... For the last few years girls have been taking up the top positions in Primary, Ordinary level and Advanced level final examinations. For instance, 19 of the best 25 students in the O level examinations of 1998 were girls. This has caused alarm and discomfort among many of the boys and some have actually adopted a theory that girls are favoured...

"You reap what you sow" the old saying goes. I have a strong conviction that in this world ... no God - however feminine - has bestowed undeserved favour on girls... I tend to believe that, of late, girls have been hardworking and so their good results are merely harvesting what they planted... It is common knowledge that academic excellence goes hand in hand with discipline. There is something striking that differentiates [girls] from boys ... they have a greater level of discipline which has facilitated their study and hence excellence... Girls have relatively less distractions from their studies. They usually engage in less - and at the same time less demanding - sports... they are usually less engaged in extra-curriculum activities than boys ... I also believe that cleanliness affects one's academic life. I do not need to convince you that girls are generally cleaner than boys... Girls are also generally neater than boys. Their work is usually smartly presented and their handwriting usually more legible than boys'.

His classmates might have contested some of his tendentious arguments but would probably have conceded his ringing conclusion:

Girls have excelled of late because they have worked for it and surely they deserve it. And boys - pull up your socks.[44]

Sometime in this twenty-first century it will surely occur to a perceptive male student contributor to *The Budonian* that girls just might be doing better than boys because they are cleverer. Meanwhile, Busulwa's consistent support for the education of girls and young women was recognised by the Forum of African Women Educationalists, which awarded him its Certificate of Merit.

In April 1999, in his last full year as headmaster, Busulwa, on behalf of the governors, PTA and staff, invited a number of academics, Budonians and friends of the school to take part in a full-day seminar on the topic: "Possibilities for Budo in the Next Millennium - A Critical

Analysis." Addresses by Professors Timothy Wangusa and Apolo Nsibambi were to be followed by workshops the same day, and then in July, by a public debate on the issues raised. Apolo Nsibambi had been invited as Minister of Education but shortly before the event he was, to the delight of thousands of Budonians, promoted to the office of Prime Minister - the third Budonian to succeed to the position since the liberation of 1986. His new duties prevented him from attending, but his able replacement was yet another Old Budonian professor, Dr Fred Kayanja, vice-chancellor of Mbarara University of Science and Technology.

Professor Wangusa summarised the main events and processes of Budo's development over 93 years, as essential background to the consideration of alternative futures. Among the possibilities suggested in the letter of invitation were that Budo might:

1. Revive its status of the 1940s and '50s, providing commercial as well as academic studies.

2. Continue as a secondary school but with a wider curriculum including more practical subjects.

3. Become a specialist Sixth Form College on the current English model.

4. Be accorded higher education status and offer degree level programmes.

5. Become a non-residential higher education institution on the model of the Open University in UK.

6. Continue with its present structure and curriculum, expanding its intake on a second campus.

Professor Kayanja spoke firmly for Alternative 2 and subsequent wide debate over several months confirmed this as a strong majority view. He urged colleagues to be aware of the great expectations which Universal Primary Education would inspire within a few years.

> King's College Budo is one of the few schools which we can correctly refer to as excellent, popular and providing Quality. The New Millennium could see schools of this type disappear, unless

they are part of the solution to the constraints responsible for the poor quality of life the majority have to live.[45]

He was convinced that Budo should continue to set excellent academic standards but also offer a wider range of practical subjects on which some of its students might base their careers.

The aspirations to university status seemed to some an unworthy echo of the old jealousy of Makerere. Uganda now had seven new universities - perhaps already more than it had excellent secondary schools (out of nearly 2000). The Sixth Form College option was more subtly seductive, exploiting Budo's supremacy in A level studies. But Professor Senteza-Kajubi had powerful reservations:

> Budo has and continues to deserve great prestige as a full-range secondary school. It should not become a Sixth Form College because there is too great a danger that it would become merely an "academic transit lounge". Very bright students would undoubtedly continue to come, but for only two years and only for the academic curriculum. It would all be too specialised. Budo has always been much more than that.[46]

Planning and staging the seminar and the subsequent debates and discussion groups made heavy demands on Busulwa, Robina Mirembe and senior colleagues; but the results - in range and quality of argument, in issues resolved and in policies formulated - had been well worth the effort.

The new millennium ushered in Busulwa's final terms as headmaster and his valedictory contributions to *The Budonian*. He was pleased with the progress of staff as well as students. The governors and PTA had supported a now-established programme of school-based in-service workshops and courses, which had improved the schemes of classroom work, quality of delivery and methods of evaluation. Staff had also attended

> national and international workshops and conferences and they have pursued further studies. So far one of our teachers has obtained a Ph D degree, three have obtained B Eds, two have Masters degrees and five more are completing their Masters.[47]

The school was proud of the hundreds of former students who had obtained good degrees, and it had recently had letters of commendation from the vice-chancellors of the Universities of Dar-es-Salaam, Leeds and Kent (UK) on the outstanding performances of Budonians. Mindful of less fortunate students and of the continuing ravages of AIDS, the PTA generously established a Benevolent Fund to enable students who had lost their parents while still at Budo, to remain at the school and complete their courses.

While the various programmes of campus renovation continued as funds allowed, it was a big disappointment that the library building at the heart of the campus, remained, after four years, only half-finished. The ground floor was furnished and in use, but work was again halted by shortage of funds.

Busulwa had expected to retire at the end of 2000 but shortly before his 60th birthday in September the ministry ungenerously informed him that he would be required to leave immediately on reaching retirement age. In all my discussions with him he never complained about this unnecessary and entirely undeserved snub. Throughout its history the Ministry of Education has not been at its best in arranging the retirements of Budo's African headmasters. A lesson may have now been learned from the ungracious treatment of Busulwa, who was so far from having exhausted his educational skills and ideas that he was promptly invited by Vice-chancellor Senteza-Kajubi to become academic registrar of Nkumba University, a position he has filled with distinction.

His leadership is well remembered by his colleagues and by hundreds of students, many of whom speak warmly of his friendly availability and of the wisdom he imparted at his Monday morning assemblies. At these he spoke forcefully but briefly about the issues of the week - local and national - and also invited students to express their own views to the assembled school. He believed this helped to strengthen Budo's sense of community and shared endeavour.

So did his hospitable home in which he was sensitively supported by his wife Joyce, daughter of an Old Budonian, ex-Gayaza student,

Makerere graduate and mother of five children. In a growing tradition of professionally successful Budo wives, Joyce skilfully combined family loyalties and responsibilities with a fine career in which she became deputy secretary to the Treasury and then permanent secretary at the Ministry of Commerce - a notable example for Budo's aspiring girls.

Four years after his "retirement", I asked Busulwa how he now thought of Budo - and enjoyed his cryptic reply:

> I believe that in my time, and still, Budo is admired, loved - and resented. I was very pleased when David Rubadiri*, accepting his Budo Order of Merit, said to the students "It is not a sin to be proud of your school".[48]

Busulwa can be proud of his school and of the twelve years fine service he gave it.

Notes

[1] S. Busulwa in personal interview with the author, March 2004
[2] *The Budonian* 1996, p.1
[3] *The Budonian* 1991, p.2
[4] R. Mirembe to C. Davis, 26 March 1989
[5] S. Busulwa in personal interview with the author, March 2004
[6] S. Kamuhanda, Handing over report to HM, 14 September 1989
[7] S. Kamuhanda to C. Davis, 10 April 1989
[8] R. Mirembe to C. Davis, 30 June 1989
[9] S. Kirya to C. Davis, 27 March 1990
[10] R. Mirembe to C. Davis, 17 June 1990
[11] S. Kamuhanda to C. Davis, 2 October 1990
[12] *Ibid*, 27 March 1991
[13] *The Budonian* 1991, p.3
[14] Ibid, p.16
[15] *The Budonian* 1992, pp. 28-29
[16] Ibid, pp. 4-5

---

* Accomplished poet, former academic at Makerere University and presently vice-chancellor of the University of Malawi.

[17] Hansen H.B. and Twaddle M. *Changing Uganda*, London: James Currey, 1991, p. 323

[18] *Ibid*, pp. 327-8

[19] *The Budonian* 1992, p.11

[20] Nyerere J.K. *Education for Self- Reliance*, Dar-es-Salaam, Republic of Tanzania, 1967, p.19

[21] *The Budonian* 1995, pp. 38-39

[22] *Ibid*, p.40

[23] *Ibid*, pp. 31-32

[24] S. Busulwa in personal interview with the author, March 2004.

[25] *The Budonian* 1995, pp. 5-7

[26] *Ibid*, p. 6

[27] *Ibid*, p. 8

[28] "Through Ninety Years 1906-1996" The 90th Anniversary Supplement p. 4

[29] *Ibid*. p. 5

[30] *The Budonian - 90 Years*, p. 2

[31] *Ibid*, p. 43

[32] *Ibid*, p. 45

[33] Dr D. Matovu in personal conversation with the author, March 2002

[34] *The Budonian* 1998, p. 4

[35] *Ibid*, p. 7

[36] *Ibid*, p. 17

[37] *Ibid*, p. 31

[38] *Ibid*, pp. 33-35

[39] Keane, Fergal; "Return to Uganda"; BBC Radio 4, March 1998

[40] "*The Budonian* 1999, pp. 16-17

[41] *Ibid*, pp. 3-4

[42] *Ibid*, pp. 8-10

[43] *Ibid*, p. 34

[44] *The Budonian* 2000, pp. 13-14

[45] Kayanja, Dr F. "Possibilities for Budo"; Seminar Address, 10 April 1999

[46] Prof Senteza-Kajubi in conversation with the author, March 2002

[47] *The Budonian* 2000, pp. 7-8

[48] S. Busulwa in conversation with the author, March 2004

13 🦁

Twenty-First Century: Progressive Conservatism? 2000-2005

The Budo governors had successfully resisted the premature removal of Busulwa but were happy to endorse the second phase of the Ministry's proposal for the school. They duly confirmed George William Semivule to be their twelfth headmaster, from October 2000. He was much involved on the Hill in November and December 2000 and came into residence in time for the Christmas Day Carol Service for Budo residents and local villagers, at which he introduced himself, his wife Helen–also a teacher–his daughter and four sons.

He was born in Bulemezi, his father being Deputy Katikiro of Buganda. He was brought up on the Makerere farm at Kabanyoro and was early made aware of university life through his mother's domestic bursarship at Makerere. He spent eleven student years on Budo hill, arriving at Kabinja in 1961 and leaving King's College in 1971 as house prefect of England House and with a good academic record. So his secondary career had been under Ian Robinson, except for his final year, which was Dan Kyanda's first. At Makerere he read Physics and Maths for his BSc degree and Education Diploma and so became the second scientist, after Robinson, to lead Budo in its first 100 years.

After teaching at the Aga Khan School he was appointed early to a lectureship in Physics Education at the National Teachers College, Kyambogo, also teaching Physics part-time at Nabisunsa SS School. In 1983 he was appointed to his first headship at Sir Apolo Kagwa School. This was followed by a nine-year headship at Ndejje S S School and – after the Ministry's attempted coup – eighteen months as head of Busoga College, Mwiri, while Busulwa completed his service to retirement age. Budonians present and past made up handsomely to Busulwa for the Ministry's discourtesy: the staff hosted a farewell celebration in late November with 400 guests invited to the Hill for lunch and tea; in late January the Old Budonians gave a fine Farewell Lunch–and a generous cheque–in his honour, at Lweza Resort on the lake shore. With several other celebrations, a personal message of congratulations and thanks from the Kabaka, and his senior university post to look forward to, he certainly felt well appreciated.[1]

On 3 February 2001, Semivule chaired his first full staff meeting, apparently at a brisk pace; it ran from 10.15 am till 1 pm, which some colleagues thought rather short. He convened his first top administrators' meeting on the 13th and his logbook records that for the next four days the headmaster's office was yet again besieged by earnest parents, ostensibly seeking "advice", but almost all urging reconsideration for offspring who had failed to gain S1 places. On 12th March Budo provided one of the polling stations for the presidential election, which saw Yoweri Museveni re-elected on a strong popular vote for a second 5-year term. Founders Day celebrations on the 25th gave Semivule the chance to introduce himself and his plans to a large congregation of Old Budonians and national and local dignitaries.

He first offered his congratulations and thanks to Sam Busulwa–with whom he had co-operated for many years through the Head-teachers' Association, Old Budonians Association, and as a Budo parent–for his outstanding contributions to Budo's development form 1989 to 2000:

> Mr Busulwa has presided over the unprecedented academic performances by the school. He expanded Budo and made many improvements, particularly in the conditions for the girls.

Having paid tribute to the past he outlined his plans and hopes for the future: The basic aim was to achieve better conditions for living and learning in the school. The major long-term project was to complete the ambitious Library and Learning Centre. Among other priorities were the replacement of all asbestos sheeting in buildings; the completion of the Sabaganzi House improvements; the paving of walkways; improved sanitation and showers–which could be permanently achieved only by the installation of a mains water supply; a major advance in computer studies, to include full instruction programmes for S 1 and S2, with greatly expanded facilities and a specialist computer room for staff. Long-term plans would be laid for a new dining hall and kitchens and a purpose-built office block to replace the present administrative headquarters in the old deputy headmaster's house.

This was a costly programme, and he drew attention to the pledge forms available for contributions from Old Budonians, parents and friends of the school. He also confided some of his own less expensive enthusiasms: to give more support to the Nightingales–he had been a student member–and the school band, "to change the face of the school and to kick out litter and bush."

In my own first conversations with him he stressed the importance of strategic planning, with the 2006 centenary as a target date–"Modernising Budo to 2006". He already felt well supported by the Board of Governors, parents and Old Budonians. During his first year the land in front of the chapel and the administrative offices had been cleared, broken-down vehicles removed and a new garden planned and partly planted, greatly improving first impressions of the Hill. He also emphasised his strong value for the Christian life of the school:

> I believe that Budo has four strong pillars–the Library, the Main Hall, the Mess and the Chapel. We must not neglect or weaken any of them. All are used on a daily basis and continually influence the life of the school community. Compulsory Chapel was much debated and then abandoned in Dan Kyanda's time, but I believe strongly in its value. I agree that the Balokole have sometimes been divisive, but I'm convinced that they are the "salt" of our Christian influence, working very hard to organise much of the life and fellowship of the Chapel.[2]

Only two days after the enthusiastic Founders Day gathering there was some disappointment that Budo was ranked only fifth in the latest Uganda Certificate of Education (O level) result tables. But a comparison of the school's last four years' results was revealing.

	Class	1	2	3	% 1ˢᵗ class
1997		162	21	1	88
1998		140	13	0	91.5
1999		164	7	0	95.9
2000		158	10	1	93.4

The latest results, for 2000, had still been very good and Budo's policy on admitting students to the examination remained more liberal than most schools', with exclusions very rare. Budo's numbers were very large and the simple percentage figure is not always the most accurate indicator of the value of a school's performance. Moreover, other schools were improving, which was good news for the country.

Budo's A level results were even better, but nevertheless Semivule asked the teachers of S4 classes to meet with him early in April to consider strategies for improvement. There were a few staff murmurs that the new administration was "panicking".

In mid-April the Semivule family's first Easter Sunday in residence was celebrated with the traditional hymn singing around the Hill at dawn, organised by Robina Mirembe who also gave the address in Chapel. In the same week the extent of Budo's self-reliance was reflected in the minutes of a meeting of the Parent-Teacher Association's finance committee. Apart from staff salaries, the PTA was now meeting three-quarters of the school's annual recurrent expenditure as well as being a major contributor to many capital projects. In the following week Old Budonians gathered for the funeral of one of their most vigorous chairmen of governors, Professor Herbert Nsubuga, who had consistently urged the need for such self-help rather than dependence on government grants. He had been Uganda's first graduate in Veterinary Science in 1962 and rose to be the first Ugandan Head of Veterinary Services. May 12ᵗʰ brought another national "first" for the school, when re-elected President Museveni was sworn in by Old Budonian Chief Justice Ben Odoki.

Early August saw the launch of enterprising campaigns by some thirty candidates standing for election as school prefects. The 'hustings' lasted three weeks, exercising the debating skills of candidates and of hecklers among their audiences. Many Old Budonians who have risen to high office have paid tribute to the apprenticeship to democratic responsibility which the school gave them. But a wise tradition insisted that there were limits; on this occasion the teaching staff disqualified eight candidates whose own disciplinary records had been poor. To command at Budo you have first to learn how to serve. Amidst all this excitement the Uganda Rugby Football Union announced that five, clearly self-disciplined, Budo seniors had been selected for the National Under 19 XV to meet the Kenya XV. Budo also won the Uganda Schools Cricket Championship for the first time in eight years, beating old rivals Mwiri in the final.

Late in August a special careers exhibition was mounted, available to the whole school but particularly geared to the needs of S2 students who would shortly have to narrow their range of subjects as they entered their third year. The effectiveness of this provision can be gauged from the strong support of export exhibitors: 16 professions provided stalls, staffed by 45 experts, including 8 doctors, representing specialisms which many Budonians had practised over the past 50 years.

At the termly governors' meeting held during this exhibition, concern of a different kind was expressed. There had recently been a number of "strikes" and disturbances in secondary schools and some governors wondered whether Budo–so often a barometer of national unease–could remain immune and what precautions, if any, could be taken. Semivule made little comment, and when a few weeks later windows were broken and furniture damaged in classrooms he did not immediately assume that students were responsible. A low-key investigation probably vindicated him when no useful information was forthcoming and there were no further incidents.

Early in the third term the 2001 edition of *The Budonian* was published. It included tributes to Busulwa from staff and students, some rhapsodic, others lugubrious. The editors invited readers to

> Please share the sentiments of our young people about the retired headmaster, which are a blending of laughter and tears.

They had also interviewed the new headmaster who seemed to have made an impression:

> He is a straightforward man who takes no offence at the truth but tolerates no rumours. He is approachable and makes no promises that he cannot keep. He is a social person who admits his weaknesses...he is a prolific reader who wakes at 4.30, to read and write. He is a principled man, learnt at Budo, and a devoted Christian who had committed much of his time to church work. He is a farmer with cows–and a view to horticulture ...His biggest dream is to see every child in the country educated and he spends much of his money on helping his relatives to acquire quality education...at Budo he learnt to use his private time and became a self-motivating person.

> He is still observing, but intends to maintain Budo as a centre of excellence by setting very high targets and trying to achieve them, which calls for team work. ...Budo has its own strengths which must be kept, to attract the best students in the country. O level performances in the sciences must be improved–there is a method of demystifying sciences and making them popular.

He was known to have striven for high intellectual standards in the schools he had led and there was no doubting his determination to maintain Budo's pre-eminence. But when asked about the greatest difficulties he had faced in previous posts he described a contrasting situation:

> His biggest challenge was going to a very remote school, where he was in the centre of everything dealing with different people, many of whom were not skilled. The school was Ndejje–which was in the Luwero Triangle–with hardly any teachers and indisciplined students. Skulls and bones were still on the rocks on the way; it was not easy to develop that school to such a standard.

The third term of 2001 progressed without disruption and the complex examination arrangements for more than 200 candidates were efficiently completed. In his first year Semivule was supported by an experienced, competent and stable staff, augmented for a year by a young expatriate, Joshua Robinson–grandson of former headmaster, Ian–who was to take up his degree course in English at Cambridge, in October. He spoke glowingly of the warmth of Budo's welcome, settled quickly and made fine contributions to the teaching of English, Drama and Music and to Rugby Football and Chapel activities.

The year ended with a major demonstration/exhibition for International AIDS Day. The Budo school-based Sex Education programme was now in its eighth year and had many co-operating secondary schools. Representatives from fourteen of them joined discussions and workshops based on Dr Mirembe's continuing work, sharing their experiences with each other and with the Budo teaching team. This is a liberal and energetic piece of ongoing outreach.

Late in 2002, Semivule reported for *The Budonian* on a year of good progress towards the targets he had set in his first term:

> Last year we came up with the theme "Modernising Budo towards the Centenary Year 2006", and our short-term objective was to improve on the living, teaching and learning environment by 2003...In the past year parents and the school have rehabilitated Ghana, Canada and Australia Houses. Old Budonians have built an Enviro-Loo to cater for the A level girls and have reroofed and renovated the staffroom. As a major project we have renovated Sabaganzi. Improvements have also been made to several staff houses.
>
> In the same period several teachers have attended sandwich courses within and outside the country. We had a trip by staff and students to South Africa, and 23 members of staff flew to UK for a ten-day education trip in September. The UK Old Budonians have continued to support us in modernising our teaching by donating an overhead projector and accessories, and have given tokens to long-serving teachers to motivate them.
>
> We continue training teachers in the applications of ICT, and the production of reports has now been computerised. For the long-term, the school, with the community around us, has gone a long way in contributing to the NWSC piped water project, expected to start this year, from Nateete...
>
> As we come closer to the Centenary Year there is still a lot to be done in renovating the old infrastructures:

the completion of the New Library and Resources Centre–and stocking it; moderninsing and stocking the Computer Laboratory; improvement of the general school environment.

All these within the next three years. Our humble wish is to see a new and better Budo by 2006.[3]

The South African venture, early in March, had enabled teachers Robina Mirembe and David Ssenkungu, with eleven students, to visit three schools in Gauteng Province and also Benoni and Soweto township and the main Union buildings, monuments, museums and the Legislature of Gauteng Province. This helped them to appreciate how much the South African government still had to do to transform black educational opportunity, and as David wrote:

to appreciate South Africa's past, as well as to understand the new democracy... Schools within towns are dominated by Whites and are better facilitated, like Queenstown High School–a private school–and unlike the township schools for the Blacks. But the South African government gives a lot of support to public schools; even the poorest have basic requirements.[4]

The group returned to Uganda with a keener appreciation of the privileges of Budo and were happy to help entertain the Gauteng party which came to Budo in April, for a reciprocal visit to Ugandan schools and tourist attractions:

Due to the Exchange Programme we made new contacts and friends and some of our Budo students even intend to have their university education in South Africa.

Godfrey Kasamba was co-ordinator of the party of 27 teachers, led by George Semivule, on the intensive week's educational and cultural tour of England. He reflected, in the same edition of *The Budonian*, on one of the highlights:

The trip to Ipswich was organised by another Old Budonian, Dr Tom Boto and the transport provided by Old Budonian Club UK. Ipswich School is the school at which Josh Robinson studied before coming to Budo...Mr Ian Galbraith, the Headmaster, gave us a brief history of the school. A staggering 600-year history. He even showed us a copy of one of its earliest printed books–dating back to the sixteenth century. *Gakyali Mabaga* made a lot more sense then to Budonians.

We were later divided into groups in our respective teaching subjects, moved into classrooms and got first-hand experience of English secondary school classes. We observed the lessons and some of our members actually taught. The students were very disciplined. Everyone was very time–conscious. The school was extremely neat and students smart in their school uniform. Classes were small and the use of computers as teaching and learning tools was clearly evident.

We were later hosted for lunch–in the school cricket house (pavilion)–a magnificent work of architecture![5]

But perhaps the most striking article in this thoughtful edition of the school journal was from a male Old Budonian in praise of the achievements of Budo women since the start of co-education 70 years before. Dr Edward Kayondo, "Mobiliser" of the Old Budonian Club, certainly mobilised readers' thoughts with a startling headline, *Budo now a First Choice for Girls:*

...Twelve girls were admitted to Budo in 1933... by 1958 there were 22, in 1970 there were 100, and today we have 300+. However, for most parents Budo was perceived to be a boys' school which was a second choice for girls who had failed to get into Gayaza, Namagunga or Nabisunsa.

Over the last few years the situation has changed. The gap between the cut-off points has narrowed to 15 for boys and 17 for girls–down from 15 and 20. ...the cut-off for girls at Budo is now the same as that for Gayaza and Namagunga and stiffer than those of almost all other girls' schools. Girls at Budo have now reached a critical mass–about 30% of the population–and they have passed the take-off stage in performances as well, sometimes doing better than the boys at both levels. This new-found interest in Budo is fuelled by our products, who act as role models: Justice Julia Sebutinde, Justice Leticia Kikonyogo, Mrs Gladys Wambuzi, Mrs Male (Headteacher of Gayaza), the Late Hon. Betty Okwir, PS Kisakye, Mrs Joy Maraka (Rector of Greenhill), Hon. Winnie Byanyima and many others...

The stakeholders in the school are baffled by this new phenomenon and have not decided how to proceed. The Headmaster receives up to 2000 applications for 120 places in S1 and 1000 applications for 80 places in S5. 40% of these are from girls. The Board of Governors is of the view that the present 1000 students should be the maximum. Some of the old-timers think that 30% girls population is too high and should be reduced. I am of the opinion that maybe we should expand further, targeting a 50% population of girls, bearing in mind the great contribution the girls have made in moderating the behaviour of the boys, and their superb academic performance.[6]

My own impression from ten days in residence at Budo in March 2004 support Dr Kayondo's final suggestion. I was generously entertained by the Semivule family and though my main preoccupation was final research on records, reports, letters and documents for the last three chapters of this history, I took full advantage of the free access I was allowed to school activities. As on previous visits, in the A level English classes I joined, there was spirited discussion in which the girls were every bit as confident and articulate as the boys. Semivule conducted the Sunday handover meeting of the Houses on duty in a completely democratic and relaxed manner, listening far more than he spoke. The reports by the prefects were clear and responsible, with the girls' contributing sensitively to the discussion of complex problems, and providing many of the agreed solutions. Overall school enrolment is already nearer to 1200 than to the 1000 the governors had proposed; if it can be stabilised at about that number, and the girls maintain their superior performances in the entrance examination, then an actual majority of girl students–around 650–could justly be achieved within a decade.

Such numbers should only be sustained however if accommodation can be improved and expanded in accordance with Semivule's plans, and if a reliable mains water supply can be achieved- and afforded. March 2004 was unusually hot. Water supply was an acute problem and I admired the patience and ingenuity with which students and staff managed. Most days there was a feeble supply from the taps for an hour or less and water had to be collected from the school kitchen. For nine of us in the headmaster's house there were three jerrycans for the day. Students could not shower and I watched a persevering junior boy make a fair job of washing his white Budo sweater in a half bucket of grey-looking soapy water – no chance of a final rinse. Yet the students looked clean and smart in class and in the Mess and–somehow–the packed Sunday chapel congregation displayed a sea of gleaming white shirts. They did not deserve the following week's disaster.

At about 3pm on the very hot afternoon of 16th March 2004, England House was discovered to be on fire. Afternoon school was in progress so there were no students or staff in the building. By the time the alarm was raised the fire had a strong hold and though, in the early stages, a few students risked retrieving personal possessions, the Fire Brigade's strenuous efforts could not prevent the virtual destruction of the whole building and its contents. There were no casualties but England House residents lost a great deal of clothing and personal property, including study notes and books. The cause of the fire has never been confirmed. There were rumours of arson–of which there had recently been cases in other Ugandan schools–but an electrical fault, or the heat of sunrays through glass windows onto paper, were also possible explanations.

Semivule urged calm and took immediate action. England House students were temporarily re-located in other houses and in makeshift dormitory accommodation on one floor of the Library and Resources Centre. The governors, PTA and the Old Budonian Association launched an immediate appeal which precipitated a remarkable response on the Hill on the following Sunday, 21st March.

A special chapel service and award ceremony had been arranged at short notice during my visit, at which I was to be presented with the Budo Order of Merit. As soon as I heard about the England House fire I suggested that the ceremony be postponed and an informal, low-key presentation held later. Semivule a had a bolder and better idea. Service and ceremony went ahead as planned, in a packed chapel with many prominent Old Budonians and friends of the school in the congregation. The speeches were short and to the point, and the hymn singing inspiring. Staff, Old Budonians, friends and senior students then walked down to the scattered remains of England House, where an area had been cleared of debris, and seating provided under awnings against the sun. After brief welcomes and a summary of the surveyor's and architect's preliminary reports, the headmaster announced that rebuilding would begin as soon as possible at a total coast of about 700 million Uganda shillings–£220,000 sterling. Donations and pledges would now be welcome.

We were then "led" or, to be more precise, were wittily harangued, by an ebullient Professor Senteza Kajubi, rejuvenated although still convalescing from severe treatment for cancer. In an astonishing feat of memory, without notes, he enticed or embarrassed most of his audience into offering large donations or pledges, many of them as "recompense" for our now publicly alleged sins of omission or commission during our King's College years. It was a virtuoso performance which, with staff on hand to provide confirmatory forms which had to be signed and witnessed, ensured that by the time we left the site in mid-afternoon and in high good humour, more than a quarter of the required rebuilding costs had been donated or pledged. It was a "special effort" of which Semivule could be proud.

Re-building plans could now proceed confidently, only a week after the inferno. Donations continued steadily–a particularly touching one being presented by prefects of Gayaza, on behalf of their school, to Budo prefects, standing together on the charred site, shortly before it was levelled. On 4 November, a new foundation stone was laid by the British High Commissioner, Adam Wood, and if all goes according to plan, visitors to the Centenary Founders Day celebrations in March 2006 will see a fully functioning new England House.

Ironically, this disaster and the school's admirable response to it, had occurred just after the 2004 edition of *The Budonian* had gone to press, carrying Semivule's report on the governors' priority projects for the Centenary year, on continuing academic success and on a dubious "reward" for it.

> The Centenary Committee and the Board of Governors have identified three projects to be accomplished by the year 2006: The completion of the Library Project; the Building of a Swimming Pool/Sports Complex [on the main school compound]; and a general Face-Lift for the school.

...We thank God for the sustained high academic performance in both O and A level examinations. This comes with a demand to increase intake. There has been an increase in the S1 intake, to cater for the increasing Primary Leaving Examination products. This has put a lot of pressure on the school's limited facilities.

We therefore call for innovative solutions, both medium and long term, to help us cope with these challenges... "The only constant in life is change". We have to keep on changing with the change because if we don't it may change us- with unpleasant consequences.[7]

Along with the many improvements to buildings and equipment Semivule's persistence secured a notable addition to the A level programme. We have recorded the frustrated aspirations of several headmasters towards diversifying the Budo curriculum away from the theoretical and academic; Busulwa's eventual introduction of Electronics and the revival of Woodwork, both at O level, now seemed firmly established. Under the direction of Geoffrey Kizito, an A level course in Technical Drawing was sampled by 30 students, 9 of whom, including 2 girls, chose it as one of their 4 subjects and in December satisfied the examiners. Star performer was Edward Muwagga, who, with an A grade to add to his A's in Physics, Chemistry and Mathematics, was Uganda's top science student of the year. It had taken some nerve for nine students to risk this new discipline and Kizito, in stressing its value to potential engineers and architects, proudly claimed:

After analysing the results I discovered that the performance of each candidate was directly proportional to the degree of tolerance, determination and hard work that each student exhibited.[8]

The year 2004 saw the departure of two of the outstanding women teachers of Budo's first century. Dr Robina Mirembe had served 30 years, including secondments to Birmingham University, had been the school's first female deputy headteacher and its first staff member to be awarded a doctorate. She had made fine contributions to the teaching and development of Biology, to the efficiency and fairness of school administration, to the quality and expansion of co-education, to the Christian life of the school, the organisation of chapel and

Contact, and to the school's leadership of Aids education initiatives and programmes in East African schools. This is one of Budo's truly innovative contributions to African education, which she now continues through her ongoing research and teaching for Makerere and other Aids education sponsoring agencies.

Mrs Ida Songa, a Zambian, had given almost all her teaching career to Uganda, at St Edward's Bukumi, St Mary's Kisubi, Namilyango College, 7 years at Namagunga and 22 at Budo. From shared classroom experience I know her to have been a gifted teacher of A level English, a role model for girls and boys alike. Her scholarship was never paraded but her guidance of students' reading, writing and responses was underpinned by careful reading and listening and keen awareness of the range of students' potential, temperaments and limitations. To her administrative and pastoral work as deputy head-teacher she brought a similar combination of clarity, firmness and kindness, much appreciated by students, parents and colleagues. In her farewell article for *The Budonian* she wrote appreciatively of the many colleagues "who have remained at Budo for many years and have formed a strong family unit":

> What about the students? Teaching at Budo has been a challenge. There have been those moments where one had a class that one got along with and others when going into class required the Grace of God! ...A level literature was particularly satisfying because there one could discuss matters with fairly mature students, whose ideas one could learn a thing or two from![9]

So 2005 saw new senior colleagues in post for the start of the school year. The governors appointed Old Budonian Miss Erina Musoke from Bweranyangi Girls High School to succeed Dr Mirembe as deputy Head-teacher and made two acting appointments to further deputy headships: Sam Buyinza, head of Mathematics, was promoted internally and Old Budonian Rebecca Kiwanuka was appointed from Gayaza. In addition, the school responded to the ministry requirement that all large secondary schools should appoint to a new designated post of Director of Studies. Budo's choice was Erisam Kanyerezi, head of Luganda and teacher of History. His responsibility is "to supervise and monitor the teaching and learning process throughout the school."

But the new top management team would not yet have the advantage of an adequate water supply. The piped mains flow began to come through in August 2004, from a booster pump at the bottom of the hill, close to the main Kampala/Masaka road. But it is pumped only three days a week, leaving the school still heavily dependent on the smaller Nansove pumps and on rainwater tanks. Persistent load-shedding of the electricity supply also affects both water sources; a new distribution (reticulation) system has been planned for the campus but cannot yet be funded. The water charges are also higher than hoped so even when a full weekly supply becomes available the school is unlikely to be able to afford it. This is disappointing after all the efforts and initiatives that Semivule has co-ordinated. But the 2005 supply is the best the school has had in the 35 years since student numbers grew beyond the 450 that can comfortably be accommodated on the Hill. It is also a boon to the local villagers and of course represents unattainable luxury for the overwhelming majority of Ugandans in what remains very largely a rural country.

At the 2004 AGM of the Old Budonian Association UK branch we had a spirited discussion about the proposal for a new swimming pool. Some members thought it wrong to commit hard-won funds to such a peripheral project while the Library and Learning Resources Centre, which is crucial to Budo's continuing academic success, remained little more than half-finished. Prioritising has always been essential for this school, which has often had to wait years for facilities which secondary schools in the rich West would regard as indispensable. It is a theme I return to briefly below, but this particular tension has been happily resolved by the generous commitment of the Budonian Association of North America to fund, in two phases, both the Swimming Pool–which should be open for the 2006 celebrations–and a Sports Hall to stand beside it. Canon Grace would have been astonished and delighted at such munificence–and at least a little envious.

Other developments which continue in the school's 99th year include further computerisation and the expansion of the Budo website; careful monitoring and improvement of the school diet, to accompany the sensible emphasis on sports and exercise (the headmaster leads the revived Saturday Morning Trot); international links including student exchanges with Brookes School, Massachusetts, USA, and visits from teachers from Norway and Japan; gradual renovation and restocking of school furniture, and improved security fencing at the Girls' End.

As in any healthy institution, new challenges arise every year, but the first five years of Semivule's calm and insightful leadership have exemplified Uyirwoth's 1979 plea for "Progressive Conservatism". He has led careful innovation and worked hard to maintain a mutually supportive community of teachers, students, governors, parents–and of generous Old Budonian Associations in Uganda, Britain and the United States. Together they have earned the respect in which the school is held–and a successful and enjoyable year of Centenary celebrations.

Notes

[1] Personal conversation with the author, March 2004
[2] Personal conversation with the author, March 2002
[3] *The Budonian* 2003 , p. 3
[4] *Ibid,* pp. 16-17
[5] *Ibid,* pp. 13-15
[6] *Ibid,* pp. 52-53
[7] *The Budonian* 2004, p. 2
[8] *Ibid,* p. 54.
[9] *Ibid,* p. 4

14🦁
Afterword

During the writing of this book some of my readers and advisors have suggested that I should offer more of my own opinions about Budo controversies and possible developments. I have tried not to yield to their kindly persuasion. I asked for "Ugandan Voices" and have been well provided with them. I hope I have quoted them sufficiently to give a fair impression not just of what has happened at Budo, "but of what people thought about it when it was happening." I have tried to provide the kind of record that may help future Budonians to use the past to enrich, not limit, the future of their school. So I have relegated to an Afterword some thoughts on challenges that probably lie ahead, and possible solutions. They are offered for consideration, in the confidence that they will be rigorously exposed to the wide differences of interpretation and conviction that are voiced whenever Budonians gather.

First the issue of growth and "ideal size". When Lord James, then vice-chancellor of the new University of York, addressed us at the Uganda National Education Conference in 1962, he was asked by Victor Gilbert , Budo's head of History, what he considered the ideal size for a secondary school. He replied without hesitation, "The best school in England has 500 pupils"– and he meant not Manchester Grammar School, where he had been High Master, with about 900 pupils, but Winchester College, where he had taught. His reply has little relevance to Uganda, or anywhere else, forty-four years later. We have all moved on, into greatly diversified curricula and electronic communication. But I had earlier learnt a sharp lesson about the delusions of ideal size in educational institutions.

In 1972 I was principal of Bishop Otter College, in Sussex, England and was involved with several different institutions facing expansion. As a governor of Chichester Theological College I was surprised at the hesitancy with which fellow governors discussed increasing from 45 students, at which the college was financially viable, to 60, at which it might be safer. At Bishop Otter I was trying to persuade the governors to welcome growth from 720 students to 1000. We were an affiliated college of the University of Sussex, which had approved growth from its current 3000 students, but was reluctant to go above 5000.

I then represented the University at an international conference on planned expansion, at Colorado College, USA, where assembled representatives of the former American Land Grant Colleges, most with between 4000 and 8000 students, were considering extending their curricula beyond professional education into the liberal arts. None of them wanted to exceed 15,000 students. In all four locations arguments against "excessive" growth ended with an almost identical assertion: "... because when you get beyond X number of students you lose that sense of community that students and staff value so highly". On the plane back to UK I talked with a student from the University of California at Berkeley. He spoke glowingly, as many Bishop Otter students did, of the "sense of community" on campus and of feeling "at home" there. At the time Berkeley had 35,000 students; Bishop Otter had 760.

These experiences suggested that friendliness and a sense of community in a school or college could not depend on size and prompted me to reflect on my own good years at Bristol University from 1950. Although I suppose I never got to know more than a tenth of the 2500 students and staff, I quickly felt at ease because in every part of the university in which I studied, played or relaxed – from the English Department, the Library and the Debating Society to the Cricket and Rugby clubs and the The Students Union – there were friendly staff and senior students who welcomed me and made me feel valued. Some of them gradually became my close friends. Student numbers increased in each of my three years but seemed to have no impact on that essential quality of caring. That, I later realised, was because the university worked at it, unobtrusively but hard. A few long-serving professors grumbled that the university was "not what it used to be" but most staff realised that carefully planned growth could bring new strengths and need not damage the strong sense of academic community.

Budo, with 1200 students and 90 teaching, administrative and ancillary staff, probably seems at first more formidable to a newcomer than the school of about 300 did to my wife and I in 1959, and is certainly a more complex institution to administer. But as long as it remains determined to nurture friendship, care, high standards and special watchfulness for the needs of the underconfident and less articulate students, it need not fear further growth, as long as the required additional accommodation, equipment, recreational space and able staff can be provided in good time for any expansion.

Staffing is paramount and requires mutual understanding and co-operation between the governors and the Ministry of Education. Uganda is rightly proud of Budo and its other leading secondary schools, most of them long-established and some with religious foundations. Budo should continue to recognise that, in spite of the large financial contributions of its PTA and the Old Budonians, the Ministry's continuing provision of staff salaries and some capitation allowance confers obligations on schools to strive for high standards, use their government funding wisely and take great care in the appointment of staff.

The ministry, in sharing the credit for Budo's achievements, should in turn acknowledge that no school can sustain its particular ethos unless it is allowed to select and retain its own teachers and senior administrators. As Ida Songa observed, loyalty and a sense of "family" in a school takes time to build and requires a stable core of long-serving staff. If the recent policy of arbitrary transfer of teaching staff at short notice into and out of Budo and other top secondary schools is allowed to continue, their standards will quickly decline. This is not to under-estimate the strains on less developed upcountry schools. It is to caution that, if Busulwa was right that Budo is "admired, loved – and resented", the Ministry needs to be aware that the politics of envy will quickly undermine excellence, be resented by teachers, and probably help nobody. This is a crucial issue. If government will not restore the school's right to select and retain its staff, then governors, PTA and Old Budonians should brace themselves to provide the 20 percent of funding that the ministry now offers, to make Budo self-supporting and able to control its admissions and growth. Quality education is costly.

Excellence originally meant "standing out above others; among the very best". It is now more often used to signify "of very high quality".

(In this sense Uganda may eventually have 200 excellent secondary schools, but they could not all "stand out" above all others.) Whichever meaning we prefer cannot be sustained, even by gifted long-serving teachers, unless students have access to good facilities, equipment and accommodation and are not over-crowded. On my visits in 2002 and 2004, I was concerned at the still incomplete Library and Resources Centre. There has been some improvement since but I hope that in spite of the pressure resulting from the success of Universal Primary Education, the ministry, governors, PTA and Old Budonians will agree that there should be minimal increasing in admissions at Budo until its own strains can be eased. They have been negotiated by staff and students with commendable patience but that does not justify them.

The modern demands on the headmasters of Budo have been heavy, complex and incessant. The ministry has wisely allowed large schools to appoint two or even three deputy heads, and the new Director of Studies posts should prove valuable. There is one particular burden of which heads should be relieved. It is the "tradition" by which parents whose children have failed to gain a place at the top school of their choice have the right to meet with the head to seek "advice". Everyone knows that this had become a hypocritical charade; it has little to do with advice. It is about protest, recrimination, and pressure. The heads are urged to "reconsider" and to admit hundreds of excluded boys and girls, for whom secondary places are available elsewhere but some of whose parents behave as if their children have a prescriptive right to enter Budo and other prestigious schools.

I have quoted Busulwa's typically restrained protest but it has been ignored. In 2004 I was in residence at Budo while Semivule was obliged to devote three and a half exhausting and fruitless days to such "interviews" with 180 parents. In Chapter 8 I expressed admiration for Ugandan courtesy to unexpected visitors, but this generous tradition cannot justify pressure on head-teachers to manipulate the award of secondary places. There is a fairer way of offering parents advice.

Shortly after the initial allocations of secondary places, the Ministry could require all government schools, and invite all approved private schools, to notify a central "clearing" office of their vacancies for boys and girls. The schools should be asked to display lists publicly, at their own premises, while the ministry could display them at the clearing office and distribute them to regional offices. The national newspapers might be willing to publish them. Well-informed senior teachers should be available at advertised times to advise parents, but it should be announced that neither the results of the PLE nor pleas of 'reconsideration' would be discussed. This would be an open and fair procedure which would free head-teachers from outrageous pressures, to concentrate on leading their schools in an orderly start to the new year.

I have limited my own comments on the "Christian Witness" of the school, preferring to rely on the judgments of Old Budonians and critics. Laying claim to Christian influence seems to me counter-productive. Governors, staff, students and Old Budonians have to strive to express Christian, or Islamic, values in everything we do in and for the school, and hope that our actions will speak for our faiths. One of the saddest verdicts I have read on institutionlised Christianity–our churches and so-called "Christian countries"– was Mahatma Gandhi's. He admired Jesus and said that he had seriously thought about becoming a Christian; it was the behaviour of so many Christians that put him off. There is a sharp Jewish moral for us here:

Outside the Israeli Knesset (parliament) stands an imposing carved bronze Minora, the gift of the UK Government. One of its oddest carvings is of a tall man standing on one leg. It recalls Rabbi Hillel who lived about the time of Christ and was once asked by a seeker "Tell me about your Faith–while I stand on one leg" - i.e "make it snappy". The Rabbi thought for a moment and replied "Love thy Neighbour–all the rest is commentary".

The word democracy occurs more often in this study of a school than some readers might have expected. This is not only because I believe that it is the most moral and effective form of government for any institution, from a family or a tiny school to the largest country. It is also because it can create community, which is at the heart of the Christian faith, and because it limits individual power–even of well-intentioned head-teachers. This point seems to me to have been put unanswerably by the American theologian Reinhold Niebuhr: "Our capacity for justice makes democracy possible; our inclination to injustice makes democracy essential."

Budonians and indeed all Ugandans may be hard-pressed in the next decade or two to maintain their hard-won democratic processes. they should ponder some wise words of Apolo Nsibambi - when he was still Professor of Political Science at Makerere:

> Uganda's major problem remains obtaining consensus on institutions for resolving political conflict. The elites of Uganda who have historically been poor at making political concessions, must learn to do so.[1]

Two final points – being continually aware of our privileges as Budonians, and being open to sensible change and modernisation–are encapsulated for me in my strangest experience at Budo.

In 1961, during a hot dry spell, I was engrossed in a discussion with one of my A level Literature classes in the old lower school block. About noon we were surprised to be interrupted by a prefect who said quietly that the headmaster would like to see me urgently. Knowing that Ian Robinson would interrupt a lesson only for a very serious reason I asked the class to carry on with the discussion and went to his office. He had just received a message from Kisozi village that there was a body in the swimming pool at Nansove. There were no details, except that it might be a suicide. As I was master in charge of swimming and was at the time coaching four boys for the Royal Life Saving Society's Bronze Medallion tests, Ian asked if I would go down to investigate and do what I could.

It was a sombre walk down through bush and banana groves and as soon as I reached the pool–still silent except for the birds and the cicadas, and shaded by the huge trees which surround it–I could see the top of a graying head at the deep end. I pulled the man out, as gently as I could, and laid him respectfully on the poolside. He had tied large stones to his feet with banana fibres and had died in a standing posture in six feet of water. He was strongly built, aged I guessed about 40, with a broad chest and muscular arms and thighs. My first thought was what a fine swimmer he might have made–given the chance. My second was to call out–for some advice on what to do next. No one came, but there were sounds of movement among the trees and I felt that I was being watched.

I waited for a while and then walked slowly back up the hill, pondering sadly that I was returning to a fulfilling and well–paid job in a centre of learning providing interest and good prospects for hundreds of fortunate boys and girls, while, a mile down the hill, lived hundreds of poor, mostly illiterate, villagers, shut out from any prospect of education or paid employment. We Budonians need to be daily grateful for our many privileges and never proud of them. (Later it emerged that the poor drowned man had been a "loner", ignored and sometimes ridiculed by his neighbours, though a competent small farmer. The previous night he had been heard shouting, had set fire to his hut and *shamba*, and then dropped to his death in the pool which gave my students and me so much fine exercise and pleasure.)

My reverie was suddenly intrrupted. The banana fronds parted on the path back to the school and an enormous Muganda fireman, in traditional British uniform of thick navy serge suit buttoned to the neck, heavy boots, metal helmet and truncheron, stood before me sweating heavily. "Where is the body?" he asked. I told him what I had done and only his obvious disappointment at being too late to help prevented me from laughing aloud at the thought of Uganda's Fire Bridge- called out and immensely resourceful in emergencies of any kind – sending a colleague twelve searingly hot miles in utterly inapproprioate nineteenth-century uniform, to retrieve a body from a swimming pool. Fire Brigades and Budo must move on, in response to changing times and opportunities, watchful for traditions that have become obstructive and absurd.

It has been an honour to write about Budo again. My own loose translation of *Gakyali Mabaga* is "We have a lot more to do and can probably do it better." The first hundred years have been only a beginning–but not a bad one.

Notes

[1] Nsibambi A. *Decentralisation and Civil Society in Uganda: The Quest for Good Government*. Kampala, Fountain 1998.

Bibliography

Books

Allen, Sir P. G. *Days of Judgement.* London: Kimber, 1987.

Alagia, G. *A Passage to Africa.* London: Little Brown, 2001.

Apter, D. E. *The Political Kingdom in Uganda.* London: OUP 1961.

Cook, Sir A. *Uganda Memories.* Kampala: Uganda Society, 1945.

Cox, Richards and Warren, *Gayaza High School 1905-1995.* Kampala 1995.

Gale, H.P. *Uganda and the Mill Hill Fathers.* London: MacMillan, 1959.

Gresford-Jones, H. *Uganda in Transformation.* London: CMS, 1926.

Gunter, J. *Inside Africa.* London: Hamish Hamilton, 1955.

Hills, Denis. *The White Pumpkin.* London: Allen & Unwin, 1975.

Hunter, G. *Education for a Developing Region.* London: Allen & Unwin, 1963.

Huxley, Elspeth. *Forks and Hope.* London: Chatto, 1964.

Huxley, Sir J. *Africa View.* London: Chatto, 1931.

Ingham, K. *The Making of Modern Uganda.* London: Allen & Unwin, 1958

Some Aspects of the History of Buganda. Kampala: Uganda Society 1956.

Ingrams, H. *Uganda: A Crisis of Nationhood.* London: HMSO, 1960.

Kasozi, A. B. K. *The Life of Prince Badru Kakungulu Wasajja.* Kampala: Progressive, 1996.

— *The Social Origins of Violence in Uganda 1964-1985.* McGill-Queen's University Press 1994. Kampala: Fountain Publishers, 1999.

Kyemba, H. *State of Blood.* New York: Ace books, 1977.

Low, D. A. *Political Parties in Uganda 1949-1962.* London: Athlone Press, 1962.

Low, D. A and *Buganda and British Over-rule.* London: OUP, 1960.

Lucas, E. *English Traditions in East African Education.* Nairobi: OUP 1959.

MacMillan, M. *Introducing East Africa*. London: Faber, 1952.

MacPherson, M. *They Built for the Future*. London: CUP, 1964.

Martin, D. *General Amin*. London: Faber, 1974.

Mazrui, A. *The Africans: A Triple Heritage*. London: BBC Publications, 1986.

Mitchell, Sir P. *African Afterthoughts*. London: Hutchinson, 1954.

Mphahlele, E. *Down Second Avenue*. London: Faber, 1959.
The African Image. London: Faber 1962.

Museveni, Y. *Sowing the Mustard Seed*. London: MacMillan, 1997.

Mutibwa, P. *Uganda since Independence*. Kampala: Fountain Publishers, 1992.

Nsibambi, A. ed. *Decentralisation and Civil Society in Uganda*. Kampala: Fountain, 1998.

Nsimbi, M. B. *Ammanya Amaganda N'Enno Zaago*. Nairobi: E.A. Lit. Bureau, 1956.

Paige, J. *Preserving Order Amid Chaos*. New York/Oxford: Berghahn, 2000.

Roscoe, J. *The Baganda*. London: MacMillan, 1911.

Sklar, R. *African Politics in Postimperial Times*. Trenton NJ: Africa World Press, 2002.

Taylor, J. V. *The Growth of the Church in Buganda*. London: SCM Press, 1958.

Thomas H. B. and *Uganda*. London: OUP 1935.
Scott, R.

Tucker, A. R. *Eighteen Years in Uganda and East Africa*. London: Arnold, 1908.

Williams, C. K. *Achimota: The Early Years*. London: Longmans, 1962.

Journals and Reports

Church Missionary Society Proceedings, 1896-1950.

Church Missionary Society: *Uganda Notes* 1904-1922

Church Missionary Society: *Gleaner*, 1912

Church of Uganda: *Uganda News*, 1925-1950

Education in East Africa: Report of Phelps-Stokes Commission 1925.

A Review of African Secondary Education in East Africa: Turner Report 1946.

African Education in Uganda: de Bunsen Report 1952.

Reports of the Uganda Government Department of Education 1925-1963.

Reports of Ministry of Education, Uganda, 1963-2005.

Ebaluwa eri Banabudo abe Kings School: (Letters to Old Budonians) 1911-1927

The Budonian: 1962-2005. (Published intermittently, with gaps of several years 1972-1988)

Unpublished Sources

Letters, Reports, Minutes and Records in King's College, Budo, Archives.

King's College, Budo Logbooks – intermittently 1942-2005. KCB Archives.

Order of Merit

(Please note that the positions of the names have no connection with the quality or importance of the Order of Merit awarded.)

Name	Years at Budo	Distinction
Dr Samson Kisekka	1930-33	Prime Minister, Vice President
Eridadi Mulira	....	Politician, Member of the King's College Budo Board
Hon Paulo Kavuma	....	Prime-Minister (Buganda Kingdom)
David Lubogo	....	Judge
Rt Rev. Kosea Shalita	1921-23	Anglican Bishop
Prince Badru Kakungulu		Patron of Uganda Muslims
Rev. P.K. Kakooza	1929-31	Composer of Buganda Anthem
Ernest Sempebwa	1929-35	Chief Education Officer
Joel Wacha Olwol	1942-44	District Commissioner, Member of The Presidential Policy Commission
Prof. William Senteza-Kajubi	1943-46	Vice Chancellor Makerere & Nkumba Universities
Hon. Abu Mayanja	1945-49	Attorney General, Deputy Prime Minister
Hon. J Mayanja-Nkangi	1947-49	Minister, Prime Minister Buganda Kingdom
Dr Barnabas Kununka	1933-35	Medical Practitioner, Minister
Prof. George Kakoma	1937-42	Composer of the National Anthem
Rev. Canon Binaisa	1913-15	Early Anglican Priest
Rev. Canon Daniel Lubwama	1924-1926	Early Anglican Priest
Rt Rev. Disan Senyonjo	1947-1952	Anglican Bishop
Erivastone W. Kiggundu	1936-1938	Principal Private Secretary to Sir Edward Mutesa
Haji Juma Katende	1927-1929	Magistrate
Mrs Hannah Namuli Lule	1933-1944	Former First Lady
Justice Benjamin Odoki	1960-1965	Chief Justice
Prof. Alexander Odonga	1940-42	Surgeon, Dean Medical School

Hon. John Sebaana Kizito	1952-1954	Minister, Mayor, Presidential Candidate 2006
Charles Kikonyogo	1954-1956	Governor, Bank of Uganda
Dr Sulaiman Kigundu	1961-66	Governor, Bank of Uganda
Mrs Sarah Ntiro	1938-45	1st Woman Graduate in East and Central Africa
Prof. Herbert K. Nsubuga	1936-1947	Distinguished & 1st Vet Doctor, Board Chairman of Budo
Hon. A.P. Waligo	1941-1946	Prime Minister
Hon. Grace Stuart Ibingira	1951-1953	Minister of Justice
James Kahigiriza	1941-1943	Prime Minister (Ankole Kingdom)
Hon. Rhoda Kalema	1937-1947	Member of Parliament, Minister
Dr Jack Jagwe	1954-1956	Senior Consultant and Physician
Henry Barlow	1936-1948	Permanent Secretary
Hon. William Rwetsiba	1939-1941	Permanent Secretart, Ambassador
Albert Kalanzi	1938-1942	
His Royal Highness Wako Muloki	1927-1941	Kyabazinga of Busoga
William Bakibinga	1940-1946	Surveyor, Minister
Dr Martin Aliker	1944-1947	Chancellor Gulu University, Senior Presidential Advisor
Prof. Frederick Kayanja	1946-1956	Vice Chancellor Mbarara University
Mr Fred Semaganda	1956-1958	Mayor of Kampala City
His Majesty Ronald Mutebi	1962	King of Buganda
Dr George Kamya	1943-1945	Senior Consultant Surgeon
Julius Muheru Byagagaire	1945-47	Minister, Development Consultant
Prof. David Rubadiri	1941-1950	Vice Chancellor Malawi University
David Kyagulanyi Ntwatwa	1942-1952	Quantity Surveyor, Board Chairman King's College Budo
Michael Sozzi	1948-1950	Univeristy Secretary Makerere
Gladys Nsibirwa Wambuzi	1939-1950	Senior Educationist, Head mistress Greenhill Academy
Tom Buruku	1959-1964	Commissioner Electoral Commission
Prof. Apolo Nsibambi	1952-1959	Rt Hon. Prime Minister
Hon. James Wapakhabulo	1965-1966	Speaker of Parliament
Hon. Kintu Musoke	1952-1957	Rt Hon. Prime Minister
Dr Rt Rev Michael Senyimba	1962-1963	Bishop, Chancellor Ndejje University

Thomas Makumbi	1932-1939	Education Officer
Eugena Maitum	1960-1961	Insurance Consultant
Prof. Timothy Wangusa	1962-1963	Prof of Literature, Minister, Vice Chancellor
Prof. Bwogi R. Kanyerezi	1952-1954	Senior Consultant, Physician
Catherine Z. Kisumba	1953-1955	Pharmacist
Prof. Phares M. Mutibwa	1951-1956	Prof. of History
Paulo Sebalu	1941-44	Senior Advocate
Dr Jack Luyombya	1956-1963	Senior Consultant Urologist
Apolo Kironde	1927-1929	Teacher, Lawyer, Minister
Eric Kigozi	1952-1958	Secretary Inter University Council of East Africa
Stephen Kamuhanda	1961-1968	Headmaster Ntare School
George William Kabugo	1951-1953	Private Secretary to Kabaka Mutebi
Prof. Edward B. Kakonge	1951-1956	Professor of Biochemistry
Prof. Albert Lutalo Bbossa	1959-1960	Vice Chancellor Kyambogo University
Hon. Alfred Mubanda	1947-1950	Permanent Secretary, Minister
Ibrahim Kabanda	1948-1950	Board Chairman, URA
Hon. Crispus Kiyonga	1971-1972	National Political Commissar, Minister
Prof. Samuel Turyamuhika	1962-1963	International Consultant Prof of Statistics
Hon. Tucker Lwanga	1951-1953	Minister of Information Kabaka's Government
Prof. Julius Z. Kitungulu	1955-1960	Prof. of Agriculture Makerere University
Rev. Canon Paul Luzinda	1945-1947	Senior Anglican Priest
Edward Nsubuga	1954-1960	Entrepreneur, Proprietor of Ranch on the Lake
H.E. Geoffrey Binaisa	1927-1936	President of the Republic of Uganda
Prof Florence M. Mirembe	1966-1967	Senior Consultant Gynaecologist
Lady Justice Leticia Mukasa Kikkonyogo	1959-1960	Deputy Chief Justice
Dr William Kalema	1958-1969	Board Chairman, Uganda Investment Authority
Norman Shalita	1948-1954	Permanent Secretary
George Egaddu	1963-1964	Principal Partner Pricewater house Coopers
Sam Kutesa	1968-1969	Attorney General, Minister
James Isabirye Mugoya	1962-1967	Entrepreneur, Proprietor Mugoya Construction

Justice James Ogola	1964-1965	Principal Judge
Daniel Kyanda	1947-1958	Headmaster Kings College Budo
Ruth Masika	1960-1961	Registrar General

Distinguished Ladies from Budo

Name	Years at Budo	Distinction
Justice Julia Sebutinde	1972-1973	Judge
Justice Alice Mpagi Bahigaine	....	Judge
Christine Guwatudde	....	Secretary Health Service Commission
Rebecca Kiwanuka	1970-1975	Deputy Head-teacher, Kings College, Budo
Erina Musoke	1970-1975	Deputy Head-teacher, King's College, Budo
Jane Kabengwa	1958-1961	Retired Senior Superintendent of Police
Eva Konde	1965-1970	Public Relations Officer Uganda National Examinations Board
Sarah Birungi	1960-1963	Headteacher, Author
Jennifer Semakula Musisi	1980-1982	Legal Advisor Makerere University
Sarah Katale	1967-1971	Mechanical Engineer
Dr Edrone Rwakaikara	1967-1972	Demographer
Hon. Betty Okwir	1964-1967	MP, Minister
Emma Lugujjo	1965-1968	Head-teacher
Hon. Beatrice Lagada	1969-1974	Member of Parliament
Betty Kamya	1973-1974	Political Activist, MP
Veronica Nyakana	1957-1960	Administrative Officer
Agnes Kalibbala	1969-1970	Deputy High Commissioner to Kenya
Hon. Winnie Byanyima	1975-1976	MP, Political Activist
Harriet Migereko	1970-1975	
Dorothy Moeller	1970-1975	Property Manager
Joy Male	....	Head-teacher
Jennina Zaramba	1965-1969	Banker
Gladys Kalema	1984-1986	Veterinary Surgeon

Index

"AIDS Education in Ugandan Schools" *339, 340*

"Antigone of Sophocles" *165*

"Arusha Declaration" 1967 *335*

Abate, Aggrey *208*

Abrams, Elliot *302*

Achimota *82*

Achimota College *4, 28, 44, 53, 73–74, 80, 91, 97*

Achimota TTC *121*

Acholi *116, 202, 256, 304*

African Education Committee 1940 *101*

African Native Medical Corps *39*

Africa Christian Press *183*

Africa House *270, 301*

Aga Khan High School *214, 276, 364*

Aggrey *53, 73–74, 83*

Aggrey, James *44*

Aggrey Memorial School *111, 322, 324*

Agricultural Club, Budo *210*

AIDS Education *314, 331–332, 339–341*

Alcoholics Anonymous *219*

Aliker, Dr Martin *ix, xi, 116, 187*

Allen, Miss Alfreda *6*

Allen, Sir Peter *278*

Alliance High School, Kenya *220*

American Land Grant Colleges *381*

American Magnet Schools *337*

Amin, President Idi *197–202, 216, 242, 252–256, 264, 269, 276*

Amukun, Erasmus *165*

Ankole, Omugabe of *144*

Apter, Dr D.E. *93, 105, 111*

Australia House *270, 299, 370*

Awori, Aggrey *165*

"Balokole" *146, 182, 275, 283, 293, 352, 366*

"Barretts of Wimpole Street, The" *151*

"Budonian, The" *209–211, 298–299, 313*

"Budo Teachers" *37, 39–41, 43*

Baden Powell, Lord *52, 89*

Bakaluba, Erasito *27*

Bakka-Male, Patrick *ix, 332*

Barbour, T. *28*

Bawuuba, Eliezer *203, 214, 223, 271, 275–319, 329*

Bawuuba, Mrs Christine *ix*

Bazongere, Samson *26*

Bell, Dr Andrew *3*

Bell, Sir Hesketh *25*

Bengo, S. *116*

Binaisa, President Godfrey *277–279, 286*

Binns, A.L. *133*

Birmingham University *332, 376*

Bisase, K. *75*

Bishop's School, Mukono *23, 322*

Bishop Otter College, Sussex *380*

Bishop Tucker College, Mukono *16, 41, 65*

Blair, Lieut. General *242*

Bloch, Mrs Dora *253*

Bolton, Mac *152*

Bombo, Revd. Laban *263, 290, 355*

Boston, Patrick 210, 266
Boto, Dr Tom *viii*, 371
Brewer, Revd H.A. 76
Bridges, Dr R. *viii*
Bristol University 381
Britton, Revd J. 36
Brookes School, USA 379
Brown, Bishop Leslie 144, 159
Brown, Mrs Winifred 144
Budo, the man 10
Budo Building Fund 58, 62, 78, 88, 90
Budo Hornbills 165
Budo Muslim Club 352
Budo Primary School 62, 114, 119, 129, 131, 136, 151
Budo Teachers Conference 1918 41
Buganda Constitutional Committee 137
Buganda Road Primary School 276, 294
Bunyoro, Omukama of 143
Burkitt, Dr Denis 192
Bush Schools 3, 23, 36, 48, 91, 96
Busoga College, Mwiri 76, 88, 149, 160, 270, 304, 364, 368
Busulwa, Mrs Joyce 360–361
Busulwa, Sam *ix*, 322, 324–361, 364–366
Buyinza, Sam 377
Bwango, Caroline 355
Bweranyangi Girls High School 377
Byanyima, Hon. Winnie 259, 372

"Changing Uganda" 334
"Contact" 250, 253, 259, 261, 262, 263, 290, 293, 301, 326, 352, 376
"Current News" 134, 137
Callaghan, Rt. Hon James 242
Callwell, Lieut. Commander 43, 48, 58, 64, 66, 76, 88, 101, 121
Cambridge Higher School Certificate 149, 154

Cambridge School Certificate 90, 96, 114, 126, 130, 133, 145, 150, 152, 177
Canada House 43, 261, 268, 328, 370
Carney, Rita 134, 143
Castle, Professor Edgar *viii*
Chapel, New 1964 182
Chapel, Old 1912 25, 30, 31
Chapel Appeal Fund 157
Chichester Theological College 380
Chisholm, Dennis 201, 212–214
Churchill, Winston 108
Church Missionary Society *xii, xv*
Clifton College 26, 32
Co-education, Budo *xii*, 53, 66, 84, 94–95, 107, 124, 135, 142–144, 161–162, 168, 262, 342, 347–349
Cobb, Timothy *xi*, 84, 121, 123–147, 161, 290
Cohen, Lady 144
Cohen, Sir Andrew 136, 138, 144
Collins, Barbara *viii*, 209, 218, 259, 261
Comboni College, Lira 242, 341
Computer Club, Budo 352
Cook, Sir Albert 1, 6, 7, 118, 120
Coombe, Dr Trevor *viii*
Cooper, E. 127
Coryndon, Sir Robert 40
Crawford, Sir Frederick 156
Crawley, Don. 165, 169
Cricket XI 164
Crittendon, Captain F. 96, 100

"Daily Telegraph" *xv*
"Dido and Aeneas" 130
Daniell, Revd. E.S. 16, 37, 41
Davies, C. 22
Davis, Colin *ix*, 178, 209, 214, 245, 250, 251, 253, 255, 258–264, 294
De Bunsen, (Sir) Bernard 133, 146, 161
De La Warr Commission, 1937 101

Dillistone, H.G. *10, 24*
Dodd, Lewis *178, 192*
Dover College, England *146*
Dramatic Society, Budo *146*
Drown, Mrs Gwyneth *169*
Drown, Revd Dick *viii, 141, 145, 169, 182*
Dundas, Sir Charles *115*

"Ebaluwa eri Banabudo" (Letters to Old Budonians) *21*
"Ebifa mu Buganda" *20, 31, 32, 120*
"Education for Capability" *337*
Economics Club, Budo *352*
Edmunds, Revd. K. *120*
Education Department, Uganda *92*
Elizabeth, the Queen Mother *153. See also* Queen Elizabeth II
Emmanuel College, Cambridge *19, 149*
England House *169, 268, 364, 374*
English Public Schools XI *210*
Environmental Club, Budo *351*
Eswau, C. *165*
Evors, Miss J. (Mrs T. Harrison.) *60, 70*

"France Liberté" *331*
F.R.O.N.A.S.A. *265*
Fisher, Archbishop Geoffrey *165*
Flower Club, Budo *351*
Founders' Day *12, 26, 184, 213, 251, 275, 284, 290, 314, 344, 365, 375*
Fraser, A.G. *4, 7, 38, 80, 82, 99*
French Club, Budo *200, 352*

"Gakyali Mabaga" *28, 123, 314, 372, 387*
"Government Inspector, The" *312*
"Guardian, The" U.K. *253*
Galbraith, Ian *371*
Gandhi, Mahatma *384*

Garrett, Revd. G. *32–33, 42, 46–49, 55, 61*
Gaster, Canon L.J. *xi, 82, 87–88, 90, 94–97*
Gaster House *267, 268, 270, 342*
Gayaza High School *xii, 7, 23, 341, 342*
Gayaza Junior School *6–7, 94*
Gayer, Miss D. *95*
Geffrye Museum *134*
George V, King *32*
George VI, portrait of *108, 110, 113*
German Club, Budo *352*
Ghana House *153, 370*
Gilbert, Victor *152, 380*
Governors, Budo Board of *27, 49, 59, 67–68, 73–75, 105, 111, 113, 121, 140, 159, 191, 208, 209, 222, 264, 272, 352*
Gowers, Sir William *62, 64–65*
Grace, Canon H.M. *viii, xi, 20, 42–43, 49, 52–84*
Grace, Michael *viii*
Grace, Mrs Mollie *53, 56–57, 59, 79*
Grace House *95, 270, 283, 342*
Grant, Captain J. *xv*
Guides, Girl *138, 144, 164*
Guild, Uganda Schools *39*
Gunther, John *134*

"Hansel and Gretel" *126*
"Hassan" *130*
Hahn, Kurt *100*
Hall, John *169, 179, 293*
Hall, Lady *117*
Hall, Sir J.H. *128*
Hampton Institute, U.S. *53*
Hannington, Bishop J. *xv*
Harrison, T.W. *60–61, 70, 74, 82, 88*
Hattersley, C.W. *2–6, 23, 91*
Hemingford, First Lord *99*
Hemingford, Lady *140*

Hemingford, Second Lord.*See* Herbert, D.G.
Herbert, D.G. *28, 99–121*
Hillel, Rabbi *384*
Hillier, R.E. *103, 140, 152*
Hills, Denis *241–242*
Hunter, Guy *150*
Huxley, Elspeth *1, 171–172*
Huxley, Julian (Sir) *45, 68*

Id, Festival of *207*
Ingham, Professor K. *93, 138*
Ingrams, H. *13, 64, 105, 171*
Inson, John *213*
Inspectorate of Schools, Uganda *170, 243*
International AIDS Day *370*
Ipswich School *371*
Iroboru Secondary School, Tanzania *336*
Italiaander, Dr *134*

Jackson, Sir Frederick *38*
Jagwe, Dr G.M. *313–314*
James, Lord Eric *380*
Jesse Jones, Thomas *44, 92*
Jewell, Mary *157, 165, 168*
Johnston, Sir Harry *xvi*
Jones, Bishop H. Gresford *46, 52, 172*
Jones, Dr Thomas Jesse *44*
Jubilee, Golden of Budo *143*

"Kabaka Yekka" *166, 181*
"King's Quadrangle" *83*
"Kings College, Budo: The First Sixty Years" *vii, xi*
"Kyama" *66*
Kabaka's Cup *27, 55, 78, 144*
Kabaka Daudi Chwa II *12, 14, 25, 33, 54, 62, 70, 90, 104*
Kabaka Mutesa I *xv*

Kabaka Mutesa II *104, 107, 110, 125, 136–138, 140, 143, 163, 174–177, 181, 198*
Kabaka Mwanga *xv–xvi*
Kabaka Namugala *9–10*
Kabaka Mutebi II *337–338, 345–346, 365*
Kabigumira, Denis *300*
Kaddu, A.W. *viii*
Kagera Salient, Tanzania *264–265*
Kagwa, Sir Apolo *4, 8–9, 13, 14, 49, 53, 58, 90*
Kaima, E. *60, 105*
Kajubi, Prof. W. Senteza *viii, 116, 152, 155, 158, 325, 329, 334, 359, 375*
Kakumba, Maliko *31*
Kakungulu, Prince Badru *viii, 54–55, 78, 198, 328, 345*
Kalanzi, Edward *112, 115*
Kalanzi, Ernest *ix*
Kalanzi, Stephen M. *ix*
Kalema, Mrs Rhoda *ix, 80, 346–347*
Kalimuzo, Frank *207*
Kamanyi, W. *165, 356*
Kampala High School *214, 223, 276, 282*
Kamuhanda, Mrs Mary *301, 303*
Kamuhanda, Stephen *ix, 189, 214, 216, 221, 254, 301, 304, 306, 314–319, 326–329, 331–332*
Kamuli High School *76*
Kangave, E.Z. *170*
Kanyerezi, Erisam *337, 351–352, 377*
Kasamba, Godfrey *371*
Kasirye, M. *143*
Kasozi, Gideon *283, 295*
Kasozi, Prof. A.K. *ix, 54, 155, 211, 324*
Kasubi, Kabakas' Tombs *198*
Katana, S. *123, 130*
Katetemera *120*
Katwesigye, Ernest *356*
Kauma, Bishop M. *275, 322*

Kaunda, President Kenneth *197, 217*
Kavuma, Paulo *138*
Kawalya-Kagwa, M.E. *118*
Kawuzi, Adam *350*
Kayanja, Dr Fred *358*
Kayaye, Joseph *340*
Kayondo, Dr Edward *ix, 372*
Kayondo, William *282, 297, 301, 304*
Kennedy, Presd. J.F. *190*
Kenya Examinations Council *333*
Keyimba-Kagwa, E.T. *346*
Kibuka, E.Z. *107*
Kigezi High School *142*
Kiggundu, Dr S. *ix, 344*
Kikonyogo, Justice Leticia *xii, 372*
Kikoosi Maalum *265, 278*
King George V *32*
Kintu *9*
Kironde, A.K. *111*
Kironde, Erisa *152, 158, 223, 277, 291, 313*
Kirya, Samalie *262, 288, 299, 315, 328*
Kisaka, John *152, 169*
Kisekka, Dr Samson *311*
Kitakule, Revd Henry *11*
Kitante Secondary School *322*
Kiwanuka, Benedicto *166, 197, 207*
Kiwanuka, Rebecca *377*
Kizito, Geoffrey *376*
Knesset (Israel) *384*
Kulubya, Serwano *34, 36, 133*
Kutosi, Ivan *353*
Kyanda, Dan *ix, xi, 191, 196–223, 241, 257, 261, 276*
Kyebambe Girls Secondary School *318*
Kyemba, Henry *201, 214, 256, 257*
Kyeyune, Joel *268*

" L e t t e r s   t o   O l d Budonians".*See* "Ebaluwa eri Banabudo"
Labour Corps, East African *52*
Lango College, Lira *242*
Language Laboratory *185, 188, 192, 281*
Lea-Wilson, R. *77*
Lea-Wilson, Revd. J. *42*
Leeds University *316*
Library and Learning Resources Centre *378*
Lincoln, Abraham *284*
Literary Society, Budo *151*
Lloyd, Revd. A.B. *20*
London Chamber of Commerce Examinations *104, 120*
Low, Dr. D.A. *106, 137–138, 154*
Lubiri S.S. School *191, 196*
Lubwama, Edward *308*
Lucas, Prof. Eric *viii, 173*
Lugalama, Yusufu *31*
Lugard, Lord Frederick *xv*
Lule, Y.K. *111, 133, 265, 269, 271, 277*
Luswata, Dr Chris *ix*
Luwum, Archbishop Janani *255–257, 264*
Lwabi, James *209*
Lwanga, Canon Benoni *145*

"Macbeth" *151*
"Magic Flute, The" *128*
"Magic Horn, The" *130*
"Man with a Lobelia Flute" *241*
"Mau Mau" *132*
"Merchant of Venice, The" *168*
"Midsummer Night's Dream, A" *164*
"Murder in the Cathedral" *292*
MacDonald, Helen *219*
Mackay Memorial Workshop *79*

Madhvani Family 185
Madox, Revd L. 5
Makerere College/University 35, 44, 48–49, 56, 73, 94, 101, 111, 116, 117, 132, 133, 149, 154, 207, 214, 334, 342, 348, 351
Makumbi, Mrs E. 120
Malawi University xi
Male, Mrs Joy xii
Malire Prison 241
Malvern College, England 178
Maraka, Mrs Joy 372
Martin, David 216–217
Masagazi, A. 243
Matembe, Azaliya 285, 299
Mathematics Society, Budo 352
Matovu, Dr David ix, 348
Matovu, Mrs Rita ix
Mayanja, Abu K. xii, 137, 329
Mayanja, Lieut. N. 35
Mayanja-Nkangi, J. 322, 338
Mbarara High School 49, 52–53
Mbogo, Nuhu 54
Mbogo, Prince 6
McCrae (Whitty), Susannah ix
McGregor, Gordon xi, 152
McGregor, Mrs Jean vii, 118, 171
Mengo Central School 4
Mengo High School 5–6, 10, 23, 32, 39, 43, 48, 49, 61, 88
Mengo Hospital, CMS 60
Mengo Senior Secondary School 322
Miiro, Herbert 307
Millar, Revd. E. 26, 32, 40
Mill Hill Fathers 4–5, 40
Mirembe, Dr Robina ix, 214, 263, 264, 266, 282, 290, 293, 297, 301, 303, 312, 314, 317, 326, 329, 332, 339, 340, 367, 371, 376
Mitchell, Lady 95
Mitchell, Sir Philip 94, 101, 103, 129–130, 136
Mitterrand, Madame 331

Moore, Wendy 212
Mothers' Union, Uganda Branch 27
Mpagi, John 214, 252, 270–272, 275, 297
Mpanga, Mrs Joyce 331
Mpanga S.S. School 318
Mt St Mary's College, Namagunga 221, 354, 377
Mukasa, Lieut. A. 35
Mukasa, Margaret Mulyanti 347
Mukasa, Sir Ham 9, 14, 56, 112
Mulira, Dr Ham Mukasa ix
Mulira, Enoch 170
Mulira, Eridadi M.K. viii, 82, 107, 111, 137, 155, 208, 244–245, 260, 275, 286
Mulira, Eva 298
Mulira, Nathaniel 244–245
Musazi, Ignatius 75, 137, 154
Museveni, Mrs Janet 331
Museveni, President Yoweri 181, 265, 278, 288, 297, 304, 310–311, 338, 344, 365
Music Club, Budo 352
Musiime, Timothy 350
Musoke, Erina 377
Mutibwa, Prof. Phares 199, 213, 279, 331
Mutyaaba, Godfrey 268
Muwagga, Edward 376
Muwanga, Paulo 280, 287, 289

Nabeta, Revd. Tom 263, 298
Nabisunsa SS School 364
Nabumali High School 117, 169, 270
Nagalabi 9–10
Nagenda, John ix, 141, 346, 356
Naguru Remand Home 180
Nakasongola 267
Nakasozi 307
Nakawuka 267–268
Nakibuka, Buganda Royal Palace 9, 303, 338

Namasole, The of Buganda *106, 144*
Namilyango College *5, 270, 354, 377*
Namirembe *3, 8*
Namirembe, Bishop of *263–264*
Namirembe Cathedral *118, 145, 295*
Namirembe Music Festival *145*
Namukwaya, Elvaniya *153, 163*
Namutamba *58, 77*
Namutamba Farm School *82, 89, 101, 103*
Nansove *80, 116, 119, 259, 301, 309, 315, 378, 385*
National Constitution 1995 *331, 344*
National Consultative Council *277–278*
National Resistance Army (NRA) *302, 304–310, 307, 319*
National Resistance Council (NRC) *331, 347*
National Resistance Movement (NRM) *296, 307, 310, 329, 337, 352*
National Teachers College, Kyambogo *276, 333, 364*
National Theatre, Kampala *168, 292, 294, 312*
Ndagire, Nalinya *197*
Ndejje S.S. School *353, 364, 369*
Neogy, Rajat *242*
Ngai School *354*
Ngogwe Primary School *275*
Ngora *322*
Niebuhr, Dr Reinhold *385*
Nigeria House *167, 266, 299*
Nightingales Club, Budo *xiii, 118, 130, 153, 164, 165, 200, 283, 331, 366*
Nkata, L. *60, 72*
Nkumba University *116, 348, 360*
Normal School, Mengo *36*
Norwich, Bishop of *292*
Nsalambwa, Gideon *27*
Nsereko, Marjorie *ix*
Nsibambi, Mrs Rhoda *ix*

Nsibambi, Professor Apolo *153, 160–161, 353, 358, 385*
Nsibirwa, Martin Luther *118*
Nsubuga, James *158*
Nsubuga, John *174, 175*
Nsubuga, Prof. Herbert *367*
Nsubuga, S. *163*
Ntare School, Mbarara *189, 270, 311, 332, 341*
Ntiro, Mrs Sarah *xii, 188*
Nyakana Kiddu, Veronica *ix*
Nyakasura School *43, 58, 93, 121, 127, 318*
Nyangabyaki, Pesuery *141*
Nyerere, President Julius *197, 217, 265, 289, 335*

"Omuwalajjana Kintu" *130*
Obote, President Apolo Milton *155, 166–167, 174, 184, 187, 191, 197, 202, 265, 278, 287, 296, 302, 304*
Oboth-Fumbi, Charles *256*
Ocheng, Daudi *108, 116*
Odoki, Chief Justice, Benjamin *367*
Oguli, J. *244*
Ohio University *276*
Ojok, Isaac Newton *294*
Ojok, Oyite *286*
Okello, General Bazilio *304*
Okello, General Tito *304*
Okot, Chief Inspector Y.Y. *243*
Okwir, Hon. Betty *xii, 372*
Old Budonian Association *23–26, 34–35, 43, 61, 117, 316, 365, 374, 378–379*
Old Kampala School *322*
Oommen, E.S. *viii, 169*
Order of Merit, Budo *316*
Oryema, Erinayo *256, 279*
Oundle School, U.K. *99, 203–204*
Oxford University *xii, 99*

"Papageno" 128
"Perspective" 205, 241
"Punch", U.K. 241
Pain, A.C. 100
Pan-African Fellowship of Evangelical Christian Students 191, 196
Parent Teacher Association (PTA), Budo 260, 316, 317, 322, 339, 343, 346, 359, 367, 374, 382
Parma, Jimmy 253
Parry, Prof. Kate ix
Phelps-Stokes Commission 1924 21, 44–48
Pike, William 302
Political School, Luwero 315
Political Society, Budo 163
Ponting, David viii
Portal, Sir Charles xvi
Posnansky, Prof. M. viii
Pratt, R.C. 106
Public Safety Unit (PSU) 248–249, 262

Queens' College, Cambridge 52
Queenstown High School, RSA 371
Queen Elizabeth II 153, 242, 292
Queen Elizabeth National Park 151
Queen Mary 32

Radio Uganda 198–199, 207, 287, 289, 304
Rayden, Alan ix, 203, 210, 220
Rayden, Mrs Eleanor ix, 220
Red Cross, Uganda 151, 171, 308–309
Repton School, U.K. 74, 149
Republic Day, Uganda 218, 221
Rhodes, Cecil 28
Robinson, Fred 60–61, 81, 89–90, 132, 133
Robinson, Ian Cameron viii, xi, 149, 169, 187, 189, 196, 280, 300
Robinson, Joshua 369

Robinson, Mary 183, 193
Robinson, Mrs Dorothy 149, 158, 169, 175, 300
Robinson, Mrs Elsie ("Nakabugo") 81, 133
Robinson, Nicholas 183
Roscoe, J. 12
Royal College, Nairobi 150
Royal Marsden Hospital, U.K. 315
Royal Society of Arts 337
Rukikaire, Matthew 163–164, 297

"Sabaganzi" 22–23, 94, 143, 144, 323
"Saint Joan" 168
"Sister Gold" 78
"Sphere, The" 22
"Sunday Night at Eight" 183
"Sunday Times, The" U.K. 258
Sabaganzi House 22, 38, 117–118, 214, 244, 263, 270, 283, 290, 343, 365, 370
Sajabi, Yacobo 32
Salvation Army hostel 180
Sanderson, F.W. (of Oundle) 99, 100
Sanyu Babies Home 180
Save the Children Fund home 180
Savile, H.O. 35, 42
Saxton, Dr G. 180
Saxton, Mrs 180
Schools Mathematics Project (SMP) 178
School Council, Budo 192, 204, 207, 211, 213, 244, 351, 355–356
Scouts, Boy 53, 81, 89, 95, 144, 164, 250, 261
Sebutinde, Justice Julia xii, 372
Secondary Headteachers' Association 322, 365
Sekamwa, Mrs Bessie 350
Self-Governing Schools, Uganda 112–115, 119, 125, 129, 145
Selly Oak College 75
Semivule, George xi, 364–379, 383

Semivule, Mrs Helen *ix*
Sempa, A.K. *75, 82, 111*
Sempebwa, E.K.K. *ix, 84, 103, 138, 163, 169, 175–176, 188, 189, 292, 328, 346*
Senkatuka, Catherine *117*
Senkya, J. *328*
Serwanga, Nuwa *31*
Sex Education, Budo *370*
Shalita, Revd Kosia (Bishop) *44, 146, 251, 328*
Shonubi, Dr Alan *ix*
Sir Samuel Baker School, Gulu *169*
Sitenda, Florence *340*
Songa, Mrs Ida *ix, 317, 332, 377, 382*
Songa, Peter *ix*
South Africa House *81, 301*
Sozi, Michael *128, 130*
Speke, Capt. J.H. *xv*
Spring Protection Project *181*
Ssenkubuge, Lawrence *353*
Ssenkungu, David *371*
Standing Committee, Budo *316, 322*
Stanley, H.M. *xv, 20*
State Research Bureau *248, 256*
Strathmore College, Kenya *150*
Stuart, Bishop C.E. *82, 112, 132*
Stuart, Mrs Mary *132*
Stubbings, Dorothy *78, 81*
St Andrew's Preparatory School, Turi *169, 261*
St Augustine's College *75*
St Catherine's College, Lira *341*
St Edward's School, Bukumi *377*
St Leo's College *318*
St Mary's College, Kisubi *68, 154, 310, 377*
Sudanese Mutiny, *xvi*, 1897 *7*
Sussex University *381*
Sylvester, Revd Hugh *182, 293*

"Times, The" U.K. *161, 241*
"Tobias and the Angel" *146*

"Transition" *242*
"Twelfth Night" *57*
Tabula, A. *120*
Taylor, Revd. John *2*
Teachers College, Columbia *322*
Temple, Archbishop William *74–75*
Thomas Committee *119*
Tibasuboke, S. *77*
Tomblings, Douglas *ix, 35, 38–39, 66, 101, 132–133, 167*
Tomusange, Bishop *145*
Toro, Omukama of *143*
Towelli, Ali *248, 279*
Trinity College, Cambridge *7, 10*
Trinity College, Kandy *4, 38, 82, 87*
Trinity College, Nabbingo *354, 355*
Tucker, Bishop A.R. *xvi, 1–14, 24*
Turner, George *119*
Turner Report *125*
Turpeinen, Paula *315*
Tuskegee Institute, U.S. *53*

"Uganda Church Review" *53, 66, 75, 88*
"Uganda Notes" *6, 22, 24*
"Uganda Post" *135*
Ugandan Asians *201–202, 214–217*
Uganda AIDS Control Programme *339*
Uganda Cranes *210*
Uganda Development Corporation *151*
Uganda Education Commission, 1952 *133*
Uganda Education Commission, 1988 *325, 334, 337, 343, 351*
Uganda Hotels *315*
Uganda Hotels Swimming Championship *210*
Uganda House, Kampala *292*
Uganda National Congress *137*
Uganda National Education Conference 1962 *380*

Uganda National Liberation Army (UNLA) *288–289, 305–309, 319*
Uganda National Liberation Front (UNLF) *265, 268–269, 280, 287*
Uganda National Movement *111, 154*
Uganda Progressive Party *137*
Uganda Railways *18*
Uganda Rugby Football Union *368*
Uganda Schools Cricket Championship *368*
UNICEF *171, 339*
United Budonian Association *62, 94*
Universal Primary Education *2, 331, 358, 383*
University College, Dar es Salaam *311*
University of California, Berkeley *381*
University of Nairobi *196*
University of Science and Technology, Mbarara *358*
USAID *201*
Usher-Wilson, Revd Lucian "Ginger" *60, 81, 95, 251*
US Bureau of Human Rights *302*
Uyirwoth, Ishmael *ix, 242–259, 268–271, 379*

"Voice of Uganda" *217*
Verona Fathers *101*
Vincent, Revd.T.C. *65*

"White Pumpkin, The" *242*
Walker, Alan *128, 130, 165*
Walker, Colin *80*
Wallis, H.R. *40*
Walusimbi, Victor *355*
Wamala, Henry *ix*
Wambuzi, Gladys *xii, 372*
Wangusa, Prof. Timothy *358*
Wareham, R.W. *169*
Warship Fund *108*

Watson, Jonathon *201, 295*
Weatherhead, H.T.C. *xi, 8, 19, 24, 30, 33, 38, 46–47, 52, 72, 78, 146, 183*
Weatherhead, H.W. *xi, 7, 19–20, 22, 24, 27, 28, 117, 285*
Weatherhead, Mrs A. *16*
Weatherhead Memorial Library *83, 90*
Westleton, U.K. *280, 300*
Weston, David *191–192*
White Fathers *xv, 4, 40, 68*
Wildlife Society, Budo *210*
Wilkinson, Bishop *24*
Williams, Dr G. *44*
Williams, Revd. C.K. *45*
Williams, Vaughan *145*
Willis, Bishop J. *31, 41, 48, 54, 71, 73–74, 83*
Wilson, Bryan *ix, 152, 169, 178*
Wilson, George *5, 12, 18*
Winchester College *380*
Wood, Adam *375*
Wood, John *292, 294*
World Bank *353*
World Food Programme *299, 315*
World Health Organisation *314, 339, 340*
Wright, Stephen *ix, 60–61, 79, 83–84, 87, 96–97, 103*
Writers' Club, Budo *352*

Yawe, Augustine *203*
York University *380*
Young, G.M. *x*

Zake, Hon J.L. *111*
Zerubaberi, Y.L. *16–18, 21*
Zoo, Budo *168, 262*